BOB DYLAN
THE MAN IN HIM

KEN BROOKS

AGENDA

Agenda Ltd
Units 1 & 2, Ludgershall Business Park
New Drove, Ludgershall, Andover, Hampshire, U.K., SP11 9RN

Bob Dylan, The Man in Him

First Published August 1999

For Lara Brooks-Lynch

British Library cataloguing in publication data
A catalogue record for this book is available from the British Library

ISBN 1 899882 01 4

CONTENTS

INTRODUCTION

Talent is an adornment; an adornment is also a concealment.

Friedrich Nietzsche 1844-1900

When Agenda Publishing presented The Blotting Paper Man and The Man in the Long Black Coat to the public at large in 1993 they were as far as they could ascertain the first track-by-track books available. Now the bookshops are full of them, previously it was only fanzines that examined each track and found unexplained origins in the lyrics. The two Bob Dylan books mentioned earlier were the brain-child of eminent Dylanologist Dave Thomas who at this time of writing is languishing with his wife Dina and family in Israel, and apparently enjoying life to the full.

Of course within these pages it will be necessary to comment on songs and lyrics, that is the only way to learn what it is that makes Bob Dylan tick. Van Morrison was investigated fully in another Agenda book, (In Search of Van Morrison) and it became apparent that Van was an under-achiever at school who gained a thirst for knowledge and the desire to be perceived as an intellectual as he grew older. Van also delved into religious theosophy to learn alternative reasonings concerning the after-life and also to explore the origins of The Celts and their affiliation to the World as a whole, and their religious relationship with nature. Van Morrison is perceived as an Irish Singer when in fact he is a British Singer from Northern Ireland, in recent years he has spent most of his life living as an exile, like so many other writers and poets from the Irish Island through the years.

Bob Dylan is American, his exile periods are his touring days. Like Van Morrison Bob is a multi-millionaire who continues to work, when Van is asked why he continues he answers 'I have to do it, it is my job'. In the pages of this book Van Morrison's name will invade the prose many times, there are so many parallels between the two men, although Bob is four years older than Van, life for all of us war babies started with radio and then of course rock 'n' roll. Anyone born between 1939 and 1945 would have to wait for rock 'n' roll in 1955, the best possible year in my opinion to be born would have been 1941, Robert Zimmerman-Dylan was born in 1941.

In the following pages we will examine Bob's response to questions in interviews, a situation that he has often used to his advantage. Both he and Van have difficulty in suffering fools gladly, the stupid question is often answered with and equally stupid answer. For example when Van Morrison was asked by an interviewer why he called himself Ivan on one album he answered "Because it is my name!". I must add here that Captain Beefheart made a superb response once within my hearing. The Captain was asked by the interviewer why there were no coloured musicians in his group? He smiled

7

seeing his chance and replied "All my musicians are coloured or you wouldn't be able to see them!" If the interviewer had selected his words more accurately and said 'Black' rather than 'coloured' then The Captain would have needed to answer in a more serious manner.

Bob Dylan is considered to be the spokesman for his generation, there can surely be no argument against that profound statement, it is a powerful aphorism. An aphorism 'must convince every reader that it is either universally true, or true of every member of the class to which it refers, irrespective of that reader's convictions', it is not an epigram. An epigram need only to be true of a single case. I will present to you a few pertinent aphorisms, (pertinent of course to the life and times of Bob Dylan), as we progress through this analysis. Oscar Wilde wrote 'Experience is the name everyone gives to his mistakes', M.M.E. Necker wrote 'Fortune does not change men; it unmasks them'.

The Late Show on BBC-2 a few years ago had a complete programme titled 'Keats versus Dylan'. A succession of luminaries from the world of arts and literature expounded their thoughts on the matter. Top presenter at the time Humphrey Burton was convinced that Keats was a thousand times better than Bob Dylan, his reason was 'Because Keats had stood the test of time'. Have you ever heard anything so ridiculous. Has Albert Camus stood the test of time, has Pablo Picasso, Jackson Pollock, James Joyce all modern aesthetes that I suspect Burton would applaud with extended eulogies. True John Keats covered many subjects such as melancholy, the human seasons, nightingales and Grecian Urns, but he didn't have to put them to music? At the end of the programme they imitated Bob's film for Subterranean Homesick Blues by reading Keats and throwing down the cue cards. Of course Bob will agree with John Keats' view of women, Keats wrote 'Woman, when I behold thee, flippant, vain, inconstant, childish, proud and full of fancies'. As a concern for the time when the lyric muse dries-up Keats wrote 'If poetry comes not as naturally as the leaves to a tree then it had better not come at all'. I prefer Bob Dylan for the ambiguities, I would not be able to bear it if Bob wrote and sung an ode to a Grecian urn.

I was sitting in a restaurant with three other music fanatics. One of them was looking past me and over my shoulder, it was obvious that he thought he recognised somebody sitting behind me. We all moved our head to the centre of the table like drooping tulips to hear what my friend had to say. "I think the bloke sitting behind you is A.J.Weberman". My two friends could turn their heads easily in the direction of the person and one agreed, the other wasn't so sure. I never turned to look, if I had one would have said "Don't look now". There was little point in my looking because I had no idea what he looked like. The discussion continued, was it or wasn't it A.J. Weberman? Now Alan Jules Weberman was known to be a thorn in the side of Bob Dylan, he was the ultimate crazed investigative fan, allegedly renown as the first jewish drug dealer ever arrested in Michigan, hardly something of which to be proud. As we left the restaurant I took a long look in the direction but as there were at least ten men in the area rearward of my seated position I had no idea which would be Weberman.

I had heard of him before and I had read some of his articles on Bob. Rolling Stone Magazine had reviewed a single made by David Peel concerning Weberman, my copy had a great cartoon cover, the music was in a word repetitive. On returning home I found my copy of the famous telephone call between Bob and A.J.Weberman when they discussed an article that A.J. had written, it is one of the greatest Dylan conversations and says so much about Bob in such a short time.

But first I have another encounter to mention. I was sitting in the bar at The Kuramo Lodge Hotel which is annexed to The Echo Hotel in Lagos, Nigeria. I was the only white man in the bar which was full. Suddenly a white man dressed in a lumberjack shirt entered and purchased a bottle of Gulder, the local strong lager. Looking around the bar he became aware that I was the only other white man present, so in typical Livingstone and Stanley fashion made his way towards me. He introduced himself as Don Meanz (this could have been Means, Meins or any permutation of many), he was a mining engineer working in Kaduna in the North of Nigeria visiting his head office in Lagos. I soon learned the reason for his wanting to meet me, all the hotels were full and he had nowhere to sleep. Anyway we got chatting and he said he came from North America, from a town called Hibbing. As the one-sided conversation continued I kept drifting off, thinking why I should know 'Hibbing', was Frank Sinatra born there, no that was 'Hoboken', I knew that it was somewhere in my subconscious. At a break in the conversation I asked Don what Hibbing was recognised for. His response was to inform me in great detail that it was the site of the largest open cast iron ore mine in the world, The Iron Range, discovered by Frank Hibbing in 1893. No, that couldn't be it, I pressed him for more information. Roger Maris the baseball player came from Hibbing, never heard of him. How about Gary Puckett and The Union Gap, the pop group.

"Vachel Lindsay?" he added. I knew that he did not come from Hibbing but of course Don Meanz was being deliberately obfuscating, he knew who was the main man. I pretended to give up and Don then threw in the line "Of course Bob Dylan came from Hibbing". That was it, Bob Dylan, but Don placed him below Roger Maris and Gary Puckett in the line of famous citizens, in fact as Don was a mining engineer to him Frank Hibbing would be the most famous man. Don then added for a reason known only to himself "Bob Dylan's a jew you know". So here I was sitting in Nigeria with a man who thought that Bob's basic religion was more important that his music,

9

there remains the need to categorise people. I also realised that he would not have even mentioned Bob if I hadn't still pressed him about Hibbing's famous names.

"They stick together you know". I felt like saying "What stick together magnets", but I didn't. I also thought no wonder they stick together if this is the type of christian that abounds in Hibbing. Anyway Don now was off, full steam, I couldn't stop his conversation, it was self lubricating. Perhaps talking about Bob's jewish ancestors made him feel less homesick and lonely, I did ascertain that it was twelve months since he had been home. All Don's information would be hearsay, he was just 30 (it was 1984), Bob had his bar-mitzvah in 1954, the year when Don was born. What it brought home to me was that Bob was living in an area where there were only a few jews and as they (as usual) were out numbered they had to make every effort to be even nicer to others than the majority populations which were gentiles. I was aware that Bob's father and brothers ran a furniture and electrical goods business, and that Bob's mother worked for 'Feldman's' another jewish business. Toby Thompson had published articles concerning his visit to Hibbing in The Village Voice Magazine many years earlier, suddenly talking to Don Meanz it was all coming back, but surely Meanz is a jewish name. I obviously had imagined the spelling wrong because he was indignant that it definitely wasn't, my subsequent spelling of his name is just guess work.

By the time he got round to asking if he could sleep on my hotel room floor I already had the excuse to refuse, thankfully I never saw him again. I just hoped that he wasn't the standard imprint of the population of Hibbing. If we assume it was then it would certainly be character building for young Bobby Zimmerman who never went to jewish schools. We will return to A.J. Weberman later, but this seems the best place to commence our investigation into Bob Dylan, the question is can we find out from his words and lyrics 'The Man in Him'?

HI I'M BOB DYLAN

The telephone has too many shortcomings to be seriously
considered as a means of communication.
The device is inherently of no value to us.
Western Union Memorandum 1876

I am writing this book years after my meeting with Don Meanz in Nigeria. I did check out one of the names he threw at me, Vachel Lindsay. He was a writer not too well known outside the confines of American literature. He may have been an influence on Bob Dylan but I could not trace any references by Bob connecting himself to him, that doesn't mean he hasn't read the works of the man. There are similarities between Bob and Vachel Lindsay. Lindsay has always been considered to be a poet, yet the man wrote a large number of prose pieces. He wasn't a musician but he was a troubadour and raconteur, he used his poetry usually recited at shows and meetings to jolt the awareness of people to the problems of the day. He was born in Springfeld, Illinois (500 miles south of Hibbing) and walked from his home town to New Mexico (1500 miles) preaching his gospel in a crusade of religion, equality and beauty, three subjects consistent to the career of Bob Dylan and of course the British singer song-writer Van Morrison. Lindsay created chants for audience participation which assisted in imbedding his ideas into the brains of his audience. His style was personal, his attitude taken from Walt Whitman, and his reading included the complete works of the mentally erratic Edgar Allan Poe and the English lyric romantic poet Algernon Charles Swinburne. His work 'The Congo' made Lindsay the leader of the new poetry movement in 1914, and 'Johnny Appleseed'(1923), a poetry collection, is his most well known work. Vachel Lindsay's story does not have a happy ending he became psychotic and died by suicide drinking poison in 1931 at the age of 52. I had heard of Vachel Lindsay before meeting Don Meanz but I was not aware that he was in real terms a poetic troubadour just like Bob Dylan, perhaps Meanz was inferring that Bob had copied Lindsay, I that it is unlikely, Bob was influenced by another, Woody Guthrie.

Sense of humour is a strange thing and of course being able to control one's temper in a fraught situation is a gift, Bob has proved that he has both of these attributes, in many cases he has resisted the urge to lose his 'cool' especially with interviewers, choosing a powerful sarcastic phrase in lieu of a fit of rage. Bob Dylan's manners are impeccable.

"Hi I'm Bob Dylan" are the introductory words on Bob's answerphone, he continues "I'm in the studio right now, but leave a message". In the infamous conversation A.J. Weberman is calling to discuss an article he has written on Bob. Bob of course is not happy with Weberman's intrusion into

11

his private life. He had been filmed searching through Bob's waste bins searching for syringes and other signs of drug use. All this seems strange for an intelligent writer, but the telephone conversation says so much about both men. It was January 1971, the 'New Morning' album had been released and Bob was contemplating his film part in the film 'Pat Garrett and Billy the Kid' which was to be filmed in Mexico. Of course Weberman was publicising himself as the man with more knowledge of Bob Dylan than most others. I still have that song recorded about A.J. Weberman where the lyrics are self promotional but by David Peel and The Lower East Side, 'The Ballad of A.J.Weberman' which appears on the 'Bob Dylan Vs A.J.,Weberman' release from 1977.

It may seem a curious place to open this analysis but extended telephone calls can say so much that words can't portray about the psyche of people. Weberman's fan worship gradually turned around full circle to become a vendetta. How many times have you been interrupted by a telephone call that goes on for so long that you end up, because you don't wish to appear rude or discourteous, by agreeing to the comments made in the hope that the other person will hopefully end the call. I don't intend to write a typescript of the call but to take relevant remarks, the audacity of Weberman and the responses of Bob Dylan are a joy to behold.

A.J. had discussions with Bob after an interview, Bob telephoned A.J. Bob starts in an aggressive manner stating that he never realised it was an interview, and what is worse never realised it was taped on a secret tape machine. Bob wants interviews to be 'above the table', not secret recordings. They agree that A.J. should deliver the interview to Bob's house, but the problem is that Bob is making and fitting some tables and shelves in his house. A millionaire working fitting shelves, a great remark, and certainly true.

Then Bob rings Weberman again after reading the interview. Bob says that he objects to the vagueness of some of the remarks to Bob liking of Johnny Cash in the past, and that a certain lyric was not written about A.J. Bob Dylan said that there were lies in the article, A.J. does not flinch from the verbal assault in fact he gives as good as he gets. A.J. actually re-reads the article over the telephone and Bob suddenly becomes agitated when there is a mention of Bob's family. It was apparent that A.J. had upset his children when he was searching around Bob's property. In the interview Bob had mentioned his children but wanted the remarks he made at the time removed, A.J. has it all on tape and doesn't want to change the article but he ultimately agrees. Bob is even saying 'please' remove sections of the article, he realises that he has said things that he wished he hadn't.

A.J. has a dig at 'Nashville Skyline' and 'Self Portrait', Bob doesn't really defend them but stated that without those albums there could have been no 'New Morning'. A.J. mentions that Bob eyes looked alright and that he wasn't on drugs, Bob thanks A.J. for helping him sell plenty of albums. Bob is also very quiet for long segments of the discourse, Bob doesn't know if Johnny Cash is his friend or not, but he loves him.

Suddenly in the middle of the conversation A.J. says "Hang on for a second Bob I want to turn the tape over". Bob can't believe it and is now very unhappy. He asks how much of this conversation is on tape. A.J. mumbles that he can't use the tape because his machine is playing up, but when pressed by Bob on just how much of the telephone conversation has been recorded A.J. phlegmatically answers "All of it". Now any self respecting person could be forgiven for an out burst full of expletives or for slamming the receiver down, but what does Bob Dylan do? Firstly A.J. continues as if nothing has happened, we can hear that Bob is seething at the other end, his tone has changed, he adds a few "fucks" and offers a few more to be included in the next article. Bob actually threatened A.J. in the so called interview but now wants the threats removed because it doesn't sound like him, he is not like that. Bob Dylan says he has written song called 'Pig' for A.J. but Weberman responds by calling Bob a pig, his reason was because Bob has a million dollars which A.J. calls surplus wealth. To make matters worse A.J. then states that the tape recorded is a good one and is still running. They end up laughing, the phone goes dead.

Soon they are talking on the phone again. A.J. Weberman was also certain that he was being taped when he later telephoned Bob's office. Bob is now calm again and it is obvious he is enjoying the repartee, it may well be because there is no sycophancy in A.J. voice. A.J. states that all his articles are written and published free, he just interprets Bob's words. Bob suggests that Weberman should buy a guitar and write his own songs. A.J. is soon to be off to New Haven to discuss Dylanology and when Bob is asked for a message for the students, he has none. He returns to calling A.J. a pig, it seems to be the only word that phases A.J., but he starts laughing and Bob keeps on mentioning that A.J. is a pig. A.J. says that he can name people that write better songs than Bob. A.J. mentions Creedence Clearwater Revival, Bob's says their music is faggot bullshit. Gordon Lightfoot, he's alright says Bob. Barbara Keefe-no, Ken Lauder,-who?, John Lennon-no, George Harrison-maybe, Jim McGuinn-no, Keith Reid-alright, Grace Slick ..."does she write stuff?" says Bob. Country Joe-too political. A.J. tells Bob that the interview is going to every underground newspaper in the USA, Bob now wants to see the final typescript and will make time to read it. Bob again reverts to the 'pig' routine, Bob then states that A.J. doesn't have permission to use his words, A.J. feigns worry and concern, and is really hurt by the 'pig' remarks.

One assumes that the Weberman interview was finally published but Bob argued his case particularly well against Weberman, once he realised that he never liked being called a pig Bob never gave up, he was like a terrier dog gripping your trouser turn-up, however much A.J. twisted and turned the conversation, the word 'pig' really set him back. Bob was intending to make a 'pig badge' for A.J. to wear. The conversations last over 30 minutes but it is so interesting and amusing it seems half as long. In fact my copy which I have just replayed for this chapter has 'The Ballad of A.J. Weberman' at each end and a Grace Slick song as an interlude section where Bob is discussing song writers and their song quality.

It proved that Bob although tired of Weberman's incessant intrusion into his life, could still discuss with him serious subjects, and only loses his cool when he learns that the telephone conversation in which Bob is discussing a previous interview that was recorded surreptitiously is again being recorded. It was true that in 1971 Bob was emerging from one of his poorest composing periods, 'New Morning' had been hailed as a masterpiece but the accolades evaporated after the album had become part of the furniture of Bob's career. It is now recognised as better than 'Self Portrait' and 'Nashville Skyline', but not much better. It was a stop-gap album, CBS would release the infamous 'Dylan' album of out-takes and 'Planet Waves' would not be released until January 1974.

What we learn from the tape is that Bob can certainly argue his corner adequately, but woe betide any person that reveals their achilles heel to him, he will play on it until you lose your temper and ultimately the argument.

AMBITION

Vain the ambition of Kings,
Who seek by trophies and dead things,
To leave a living name behind,
And weave but nets to catch the wind.

John Webster 1580-1625

Bob Dylan was always ambitious, well he knew from the age of ten what he intended to do with his life and achieved it. As I am a person who has never had any ambition whatsoever the early centralising of any of life's targets by a young man is to be admired. The problem as I see it would be that if a ten year old boy has such a tight perspective on his future life he has to decide what he would wish to learn at school, he only needs the basics plus what would help him in his future career? Does the individual forget mathematics and science and concentrate on music and literature? In Bob Dylan's situation it is evident that he just concentrated on reading books, listening to music and playing his guitar, he learned some music notation predominantly the chords?

Robert Allan Zimmerman was born May 24th 1941, at St Mary's Hospital, Duluth, Minnesota. The town was just 200 miles south of the most northern part of the USA, excluding Alaska of course. Bob attended Hibbing High School which was situated 50 miles north of Duluth. It seems that Bob read books and wrote poetry, one wonders just what the other boys in his class thought of him, it doesn't seem to have been recorded. I went to a UK grammar school none of my class mates would have admitted to writing poetry. Of course there have been films made which include discussions with people that knew Bob, but the consensus seems to be that he was a nice quiet young man that had a special way with young girls, he could become a little boy lost and consequently the type of boy that girls like to mother. As Bob is reported to have run away to Chicago at the age of ten and joined a travelling circus at 13 this vision of the studious gentle quiet lad seems bizarre. Chicago is 500 miles away from Duluth, it was the centre of the Muddy Waters blues, a town of black migrant workers who couldn't find work in the South.

At home Bob had been growing up in an area which didn't have many jews. Bob's grandfather, a cobbler, had travelled to the new-world from Russia during the hardship of the 1920s. Bob's father contracted polio, strangely called 'infantile paralysis' at the time, it ruined his father's active life completely. In 1946 the family moved to Hibbing, Minnesota, where they lived with Bob's grandparents. Bob's father and his brothers ran an electrical business and shop together. When the Biograph boxed set was released in 1991 it included a photograph of Beatty (Bob's mother) and Abraham taken in 1939, they are immaculately dressed, Bob's father has the same curly hair and looks very much like Bob, it may be one of Bob's aunties that is standing in the rear of the picture.

Bob got his Silvertone guitar on hire purchase ($5 down $35 to pay) from Sears and Roebuck when he was 12 years old, but he was probably aged 15, (biographers differ on that fact) he sat most of the time playing it. Bob was trying to learn the chords from a Nick Manoloff guitar tutor, the American version of Bert Weedon. Bob later traded-in the electric guitar for a Martin (or Gibson) acoustic guitar, he had heard an Odetta record and wanted to create her sound. In interviews Bob often mentions Harry Belafonte at the same time as Odetta. Belafonte had introduced the mainstream public to Odetta when she appeared as part of his Carnegie Hall Concert in 1959. This is one of the greatest live shows of the 1950s, and of course Odetta is best known for duet with Harry Belafonte on 'Hole in the Bucket' which was light years away from her usual style. It is probably the recording where Bob first heard her, Odetta of course returned to Carnegie Hall as a solo artist shortly after for one of her greatest recordings. She returned the favour to Bob by releasing an album titled 'Odetta Sings Bob Dylan' which is over-due for a re-release on CD. Odetta's own songs and the folk songs she sang have regularly appeared on Bob's records, the early days bootlegs are full of them.

Bob was writing short poems for friends and relations for their birthdays. It was soon recognised that Bob could hear a song once and then sing it, he could also find most of the correct guitar chords. It was Echo Helstrom who said that he could 'soak up songs' which eventually gave Bob the subtitle of 'The Blotting Paper Man'. Bob's predominant musical influences were Woody Guthrie, Cisco Houston (he recorded with Woody), Hank Williams (Bob ordered all his available 78s) and Little Richard. The first two were recording from 1950 when Bob was nine, Little Richard arrived on the scene in 1956, so really he would be a much later inspiration. Bob also acknowledged that he listened to Hank Snow and Hank Payne. Snow was influenced by Jimmie Rodgers, Payne was probably Leo Payne who sang and wrote 'I Love You Because' and 'Lost Highway' which was recorded by Hank Williams, he gave the song immortality. Bob's friend at the time John Bucklen confirmed in an interview that Bob did travel to Fargo, North Dakota, to play with a band called The Shadows, it is assumed that this band included Bobby Vee. Bob and his friends in Hibbing played rock 'n' roll, yet they called themselves The Satin Tones.

Of course when Bob finally got a recording contract the management decided to create an image for him. They stated that he had run away to Chicago when he was 10, and joined a travelling Texas Circus Carnival at the age of 13, both disproven. Toby Thompson's interviews with Bob's mother Beatty and other members of his family explained that Bob was just an ordinary home loving boy that got into the occasional scrape from time to time. In fact Bob became angry when it was reported that he returned home for his father's funeral, he considered it an invasion of his privacy, yet it would have seemed so much worse if it was reported that he had never bothered. Abraham Zimmerman was a man loved by everyone, it seems that no one ever had a bad word for him. Another of the Hibbing population had to make the statement at the time that Abraham was buried in a jewish cemetery in Duluth, not Hibbing, inferring yet again that jews stick together. Bob would later remember his father when he named his third child Seth Abraham Isaac Dylan, the name Isaac added to change the initials from 'SAD' to 'SAID'.

Of course Toby Thompson's visit explained many other anomalies. Although Bob's uncle owned two theatres in Hibbing the film 'Don't Look Back' wasn't shown there and Bob never appeared there either. Apparently the reasons were the bad language, the drug references and they didn't want to upset the few intolerant people of Hibbing. Echo Helstrom also said that Bob called himself 'Dylan' after Dylan Thomas and not after frontiersman 'Matt Dillon' as mentioned in many books.

Bob's best friend was John Bucklen and of course Echo Helstrom was Bob's first love; the girl from the north country. John Bucklen said that Bob went with other girls at the same time as he was with Echo, Barbara Hewitt and Betty Anderson were two that he named. Bob had a preference for big breasted girls, he didn't mind if the girl was fat. Bob had met Echo in 1957 when they were both ice skating. I remember when I read Toby Thompson's articles I expected the relationship between Echo and Toby to grow, but it didn't get past holding hands, at least in the articles it didn't. They actually recorded together, Echo wrote a song 'Boy from the North Country' for Bob, she also wrote a loving poem to Toby. It was mooted by Echo that the song 'Motorpsycho Nightmare' is for John Bucklen and Bob who were once running down the street to evade Echo Helstrom's father. The scene created in the 'nightmare' is what Bob considers would have occurred if they had been caught. Bob also had another motor-cycle accident many years before his 'infamous' accident. Bob hit a child and although the child wasn't injured he had to file a police report, Bob sold the bike the following day. Probably a good omen because. Echo Helstrom had tried to ride the bike before learning how she could stop it, she couldn't and crashed into a tree leaving Bob horrified. In the later highly publicised accident Bob fell off the bike whilst riding around his garden, cracking his vertebrae and incapacitating himself for some considerable time.

What one has to realise is that at the time of Bob's youth living in Hibbing, there was little television and few people could afford a TV-set anyway. If it was anything like the UK at the time then one had to live in

London to be able to receive the broadcasts, in the 1950s the shows started at 20.00 hours and ended at 22.30 hours and for much of that time we were sitting watching a card which stated 'Normal service will be resumed as soon as possible'. In fact I can remember the whole evening being given over to the wonderful technical achievement of receiving pictures from France, Calais to be exact, less than 150 miles from London. In those days only few people ever travelled by air it was always coach train or ship. Bob's family were lucky enough to have a telephone but they were on a party line with six other subscribers so usage was limited and privacy impossible. I read once that Bob Dylan never took a plane trip until 1964 when he was already 23 years old.

Hibbing was a town that could come straight from a John Steinbeck novel, if a person didn't work at The Iron Range then they would be working in a shop or supply company all reliant on the money earned from The Iron Range. Of course eventually it became too expensive to extract the ore and the company moved elsewhere, the larger countries exploiting other less powerful and needy countries. In an interview in 1985 Bob stated that Hibbing had such a small jewish population that they had to go to Duluth for a rabbi. A rabbi did arrive (all the way from Brooklyn apparently) in Hibbing and remained long enough to teach Bob for an hour each day the rudiments of Judaism and what was expected of him. After Bob's bar-mitzvah the rabbi left town. Barmitzvah means 'son of the law', after the ceremony and celebration that ensues the 13 year old boy is then expected to assume his full religious obligations. Bob of course was a free-thinker and would investigate other religions later in his life.

Bob knew that he wanted to be a 'folk' singer which was the title for the genre at the time, he has avidly throughout his career endeavoured to avoid categorisation. He has changed direction many times to make it even more difficult to place him in any particular pigeon-hole. Bob did not seem to be arrogant in his ambition, in fact when Toby Thompson returned to Hibbing to write a series of follow-up articles for US Magazine the inhabitants were as kind about Bob as the first visit. The Hibbing inhabitants didn't really follow his music, perhaps they were unaware of his enormous growing fame in 1969. Bob was known to dislike Toby Thompson's remarks made concerning his father, although Toby never denigrated the memory. Although Bob's mother was also angered by Thompson she granted him a second interview and was as kind and helpful as she was at the first encounter. Bob had (has) impeccable manners, his mother was constantly proud of her son and I would expect like all mothers would criticise Bob herself but go for the jugula of anyone else that dared criticise him.

THE BIG APPLE

The skyline of New York is a monument of a splendour
that no pyramids or palaces will ever equal or approach.
Ayn Rand 1905-1982

So the ambitious young poet and guitarist left Hibbing and made his way to New York in search of fame and fortune, a young man leaving the family for the first time, unless you believe in his later disproven press releases concerning Chicago and the Texas Circus. He was entering one of the most cut-throat industries, full of cheshire-cat smiles and half baked promises. Woody Guthrie's advice was ringing in his ears, 'Some people will rob you with a six gun, others will rob you with a fountain pen!' It was a journey down Highway 61. Bob was leaving his unfinished course at The University of Minnesota, Minneapolis, behind, also in his past were The Golden Chords, Elston Gunn and The Rock Boppers with their high volume shows. Bob's short time at University introduced him through books to the bohemian lifestyles of Allen Ginsberg, Gregory Corso, Lawrence Ferlinghetti, Jack Kerouac and other Beat Generation writers. Bob was singing 'Ruby Lee' by The Sunny Mountain Boys and Jack O'Diamonds, Bob had heard Odetta's version of the latter, so had Lonnie Donegan in the UK.

Bob spent time in 'Dinkytown' the cafe district, and of course sung 'Dink's Song' which appeared on some of the early bootlegs. 'Dink's Song' was in fact registered by Alan Lomax. In 1963 it appeared on an album by The Big Three. The song was then titled 'Nora's Dove'. The Big Three were Mama Cass, Jim Hendricks and Tim Rose who had already written 'Come Away Melinda'. John Bauldie researched 'Dink's Song' for his 'Telegraph Magazine'. He located the song in the Alan Lomax song book 'Adventures of a Ballad Hunter' which was published in 1947. The song was titled 'Fare You Well, Oh Honey' which of course is Bob's chorus line. Dink is a woman and the song is sung from her point of view. Alan Lomax re-arranged the stanzas from the original 1917 song for some unknown reason. W.H.Auden also used some of Dink's song in The Oxford Book of Light Verse, published in 1938. Bob's version has extra verses which he probably wrote himself, but he says on the bootleg that he was taught the song by Dink. Dave Van Ronk, Barbara Dane, Pete Seeger, Josh White, Ramblin' Jack Elliott and Cisco Houston all recorded versions with the verses in no particular order. The original Lomax song didn't have a tune just the lyrics, so the conundrum of whom recorded the first version with the melody continues.

Bob was also a good pianist and although it seems that no-one can actually remember seeing him play, he joined The Bobby Vee and The Shadows on piano for a short while in North Dakota. Reading between the lines the truth seems to be that Bob saw Bobby Vee play and then tried to convince Echo and John Bucklen that 'he' had recorded 'Suzy Baby' under the name Bobby Vee. When the single came out everyone was amazed, but it was all a scam. It was just a part of the scene which continued with the Oklahoma accent that he used when he was with Bonnie Beecher. It was as if he was intent on pretending to be someone else, Bob Dylan and not Bob Zimmerman. Bob was on The Highway he was hoping to meet his surrogate mentor Woody Guthrie. Woody was incapacitated by the gradual debilitating potency of Huntington's Chorea, it had now paralysed him after eight years of attacks. Woody was soon to die of the illness it meant that most of Bob's heroes had died young, Arthur Rimbaud, James Dean, Hank Williams. Bob did get to see him in the later stages of Woody's paralysis. Highway 61 had other famous connections in Elvis Presley who was born close to it, Martin Luther King who died on it and Bessie Smith who died lying on it injured waiting for an ambulance.

John Bucklen and Bob had recorded 'Blue Moon', The Hollywood Flames' song 'Buzz Buzz Buzz' and 'Jenny Jenny' alongside the first self composed song that Bob recorded 'Hey Little Richard'. Bob stated in an interview that the first rock 'n' roll song he ever heard was 'Henrietta', I could only locate one version still available and that was by Doug Sahm, another of Bob's favourites; another 'Henrietta' by The Trashmen wasn't recorded until 1964. The first song composed by Bob varies from who one reads or to whom one listens. 'Brigitte Bardot' a song that may have finally received an alternative title was mooted as the first, although 'Hey Little Richard' is the first for which a recording that can be located. I wondered if 'Blue Moon' was a family favourite as Bob regurgitated it for the 'Self Portrait' album many years later. The first version was Bob singing in the style of Johnny Ray, Bob had been impressed in the manner that Johnny sang the first lines of 'Cry'. Bob would later meet Johnny Ray in a lift in Sydney, Australia. Bob told Johnny that he enjoyed his music, Johnny's response was not recorded, in fact he may not have heard, Johnny Ray was almost deaf, he had worn a hearing aid from the age of 14.

Bob hitchhiked from Minnesota to Wisconsin and then on to Chicago, Illinois, for a couple of months. Finally sharing driving duties he travelled with some college students to New York. It was the coldest winter in New York for sixty years, but Bob was hardened to bad weather, Hibbing had more than its fair share. Bob would have thought that Hibbing was big, then Duluth was larger, Minneapolis and Chicago even larger, New York must have seemed immense for a lad on his first journey away from the home-nest.

Bob met Woody Guthrie at Greystone Hospital in New Jersey. The reports of the meeting have been re-used many times. Bob informed Woody that he had written a tribute song to him, his response was not recorded. The inference that Bob walked arrogantly into the hospital shouting out 'Hey Woody, I wrote a song for you!" would be absolutely nonsense. A well mannered God fearing lad from Hibbing would arrive quietly and in due deference, he already was aware that Woody would die of the disease.

Bob needed to get himself known in New York. It is likely that the entertainment industry's jewish hierarchy would have at least given Bob a few contacts in New York, although these helpers seem to have been transparent. Bob was just another troubadour singing from club to club, or even on a street corner. Dave Van Ronk, John Lee Hooker, Carolyn Hester, Rambling Jack Elliott, Spider Koerner, Mark Spoelstra, Jim Kweskin and John Glover were all working the clubs. John Koerner taught Bob 'John Hardy' and 'Golden Vanity'. Bob was attending parties where as he had his guitar he could give impromptu performances. Many were recorded and would later be made available on bootleg recordings. Many of these performances could be cleaned up and given releases as archive material. It is likely that all Bob's fans would already own copies but if Frank Zappa could recover his illicit recordings and release them then why not Bob Dylan, at least the correct royalty payments could be made. The most famous tapes were The Bonnie Beecher Apartment-Minnesota, Minnesota Hotel, McKenzie, Gaslight Club and Oscar Brand Folk Song Festival, all recorded between December 1961 and October 1962

'San Francisco Bay Blues' the Jesse Fuller classic, was also recorded earlier in February 1961 and was made available on a bootleg release, but of course not until Bob has achieved some fame. It has been inferred that Bob played strip clubs in Colorado, which of course may be true, it may be just another myth as it was detailed in the first album's sleeve notes. Bob's first acknowledged gig in New York was at Gerde's Folk City Club, April 11th 1961, where he opened for John Lee Hooker who had been recording since 1952 but was becoming popular for his 'Boom Boom' and 'Dimples' which were released in 1963 and 1964 respectively. It was during this performance that Bob's harmonica playing was heard. Bob's style (and so many others) was based on Walter Jacobs who was just emerging from his time playing with The Muddy Waters Band in Chicago. Bob was singing 'V.D. Blues', 'V. D. Waltz' and 'V.D. City' (all on Minnesota Hotel tape), he was a walking public service announcement. He was also singing his version of songs he heard from Dave Van Ronk, namely 'Long John' and 'Cocaine'. The Lord Buckley influence manifested itself in Bob's performance of Buckley's 'stream of verbal' 'Black Cross'.

Bob was asked to play harmonica on a Harry Belafonte album titled 'Midnight Special', Bob was paid $50 and he can be heard on just one track on the album. Robert Shelton reported on Bob's performance at Gerde's Folk City for The New York Times, mentioning Bob's brakeman cap, it was an early trademark for Bob, also a lifetime's trade mark for yodelling brakeman

Jimmie Rodgers. Bob was the supporting act for The Green Briar Boys which included Eric Weissburg on banjo, Eric thought that Robert Shelton was mistaken in his view of Bob's high calibre. (Eric Weissburg's 'Deliverance Band' later played on Bob's 'Blood on the Tracks' album, and Bob discarded most of the 'Deliverance' tracks). John Hammond at Columbia/CBS Records saw the Robert Shelton review and asked Bob to play on Carolyn Hester's album. Bob played on four tracks the traditional 'Swing and Turn Jubilee', 'I'll Fly Away', 'Los Bibilicos' and Albert Brumley's 'Come Back Baby'; Carolyn would later release Bob's 'Playboys and Playgirls' as a single. John Hammond suitably impressed then offered Bob a solo recording contract. It is again questionable that John Hammond would contract Bob without hearing him sing or play guitar. Bob probably carried with him his tape recordings from the various parties that he had attended to display to John Hammond the variety of his performances.

There was now a woman in Bob's life Suze Rotolo, her sister Carla worked for Alan Lomax the folk music historian and archivist. This was fortunate because this gave Bob access to rare and unusual folk performances, it can't be verified if he actually used any of the songs, but the tunes could be recycled as traditional. Suze Rotolo was an activist for civil rights and she naturally influenced Bob. Bob was already singing 'Emmett Till', 'Poor Lazarus', 'Gospel Plow', 'See That My Grave is Kept Clean', 'Ain't Got No Home', 'Rocks and Gravel' and 'The Ballad of Hollis Brown' amongst others. Bob was now listening to Odetta, Robert Johnson and Jimmie Rodgers in addition to his beloved Hank Williams and Woody Guthrie. Bob had read 'Catcher in the Rye' and 'On the Road' and they had fuelled his itinerant thoughts.

AN ALBUM FOR WOODY GUTHRIE

For most singers the first half of the career involves
extending one's repertoire, the second half trimming it.
Ethan Mordden

Bonnie Beecher's Minneapolis Hotel suite recordings were recorded on a primitive tape machine, Bob sounds to have a deep voice. It emerged that the recordings were made by Tony Glover. Bonnie Beecher was a blonde haired actress and girlfriend of Bob who seems to have just been on the art-scene when Bob was in Minneapolis. Bonnie considers that she is 'The Girl From the North Country'. (Bonnie married Hugh Wavy-Gravy Romney, and moved to California). Bonnie and her friend Barry Hansen had a large collection of blues records which attracted Bob. (Barry Hansen was later to become the 'weird music' disc jockey Dr Demento). It may have been wishful thinking but in a break between songs Bob infers that his photographs make him look like James Dean. Bob makes a joke of being paid in chess pieces in lieu of money and getting three pawns and a bishop in change for a queen when buying a beer. Bob was also recorded at The Oscar Brand Folksong Festival on 29th October 1961 where he sang 'Sally Gal' (similar to Woody Guthrie's 'Sally Don't You Grieve') and 'The Girl I Left Behind'. It was at The Oscar Brand Festival that Bob said that he came from South Dakota and had travelled with a Carnival for six years from the age of 13, thus inaugurating the myth that is still presented as fact in The Guinness Book of Rock Stars.

The Mac and Evie McKenzie Tape from a New York party a month later in November 1961 was recorded on another reel-to-reel tape recorder running at the wrong speed, replaying on modern cassette players gives Bob a high squeaky vocal sound, the lyrics are almost inaudible. Mac and Evie McKenzie had befriended Bob on his arrival in New York. These two archive recordings of the embryonic Bob Dylan were recorded before Christmas 1961. There is second Bonnie Beecher tape in circulation dated 22nd December but there are over-laps with material on the first tape, research does not confirm that Bob returned to Minneapolis in December 1961. Bob has said that he was living the life of a down-and-out whilst in New York, the truth was that he was mothered by a succession of people, the McKenzies, the Van Ronks, Sid Gleason, Suze Rotolo and others. It was stated later that Bob's first meeting with Woody Guthrie was not in fact at a hospital but at the home of Sidsel and Bob Gleason, Woody spent time there when he was in remission and if possible most weekends.

On the 20th November 1961 Bob Dylan went into the studio with John Hammond and recorded twenty songs. Bob sang what he knew through once and John would say yes or no, he never enquired the names of the composers. The recording took two days and the album was in the shops within four months. The album was destined to be a minor hit but at a recording cost of just $400 it was ideal for Columbia. This was their first attempt at the youth market, or even the folk market. They were best known at the time for Original Broadway Cast albums and Soundtracks with Barbra Streisand and Mitch Miller in the vanguard of their solo artist roster. John Hammond did have Bessie Smith, Billie Holiday and Aretha Franklin on his list of singers that he found as a 'talent-scout'. .

Bob wanted to break away from the various folk categories and play in any style and any song, Bob seemed to be the only one moving in this direction, he was creating a sound of his own. The **'BOB DYLAN'** album had just two self composed songs 'Song to Woody' and 'Talking New York Blues'. The sleeve notes were by journalist and critic Robert Shelton who must be acknowledged as the first person to recognise that Bob Dylan had a special talent. Shelton compared Bob to Charlie Chaplin, this may have evolved from Bob's statement in 1962 when he said "My biggest idol on stage, even off stage, running through my head all the time was Charlie Chaplin". Many of the songs on the eponymous first album had been heard in the clubs and parties that Bob had attended. He was continuing to adapt traditional songs to his own style with lyric modifications, there were just a few self composed songs.

The album cover has a reversed photograph taken by Don Hunstein who worked for Columbia. It is obviously reversed because the guitar is strung wrong and unless Bob is wearing a woman's sheepskin coat the button holes are on the wrong side. He is also wearing a 'Huckleberry Finn' hat, he mentions it in an out-take of 'I Shall Be Free' recorded in 1962. The sleeve notes are by Stacey Williams which was a pseudonym for Robert Shelton, he assisted with the Sioux Falls and Gallup New Mexico myth, but that, one assumes, is what Bob and Columbia had told him. The CD cover is slightly different, compare the fingers, apparently Columbia had lost the original negative and used the next picture on Hunstein's film roll and of course reversed it, again.

The incorrect title **'She's No Good'**, is correctly titled 'You're No Good' in the liner notes and the recording tape identification sheet, even the CD re-release still titles the song 'She's No Good'. To make matters more confusing the Jesse Fuller song on his own album was actually titled 'Crazy About a Woman' so we had Bob's first ever song on record and it was our first puzzle. Jesse Fuller was a one man band and by using his feet his hands and his mouth could play six instruments simultaneously, the cover of his album 'The Lone Cat' shows Fuller with an arrangement of instruments and devices. The song gets the album off at a reasonable tempo and the reason that this track was probably sequenced first is because it is quite simple. 'Talkin' New York' is a diary commentary song, New York was experiencing its coldest winter for 17 years, really 28 years, although the press releases stated 60 years, hyperbole had arrived in statistics. Bob stated at the beginning of his 'Writings and Drawings' book, 'If I can't please everybody, I might as well not please nobody at all, but there's so many people and I just can't please them all'. This was Bob writing in 1972 but it does make the lyrics a series of 'please yourself' declarations, but by 1972 Bob would realise that most intellectuals loved his work. This talking song is our official introduction to the lyrics of Bob Dylan. Here he mentions robbing with a fountain pen which was taken from Woody Guthrie's 'Pretty Boy Floyd'. The whole track is almost a tribute to Woody's 'Talkin' Hard Luck Blues', which Woody still managed to make sound optimistic. This track set out Bob's direction in the footsteps of Guthrie with hints of his 'Talking Subway Blues' which told of Woody's first thoughts of New York, which were continued in his 'New York Town'. I have always wondered just how much of this song was already written and prepared by Bob before he even arrived in New York. Bob had also joined the musician's union, they were extremely powerful and could stop unattached singers working, they could also close clubs down with boycotts, but they did work tirelessly on behalf of their members. Bob adds a drawing in his book for this song which depicts two lonely or perhaps unemployed people sitting in a park or a bus station. If Bob felt cold in New York it must have been cold, a young boy from North Minnesota would experience much colder conditions at home. **'In My Time of Dying'**: Bob plays guitar using Suze Rotolo's lipstick holder as a slide. There is an extended version of this song by Led Zeppelin on their 'Physical Graffiti' album. Probably Bob heard Josh White's version of 'In My Dying Room' which was available through Elektra in the 1960s. The song comes from 1927 as Blind Willie Johnson's 'Make Up My Dying Bed'. Bob's performance seems to be under-rated by many a critic, he shows a distinct maturity and an early recognition of life as being finite, sadly I don't think Bob ever bothered to sing this song live, although I may be wrong. **'Man of Constant Sorrow'** (is also on Minnesota Tape & Bonnie Beecher's) was previously Judy Collins' Maid of Constant Sorrow'. The sorrowful cry of a lonesome man, (or a maid, girl, woman), it is only the first line that needs a gender alteration; Joan Baez would also sing her version as 'Man'. **'Fixin' to Die Blues'**: This was an impromptu composition from Booker 'Bukka' White released on a 10" shellac 78, in 1940. This is yet another track with the theme of death. Bob has again increased the tempo, Bukka's version was closer to a dirge. This of course can be transferred to a theme for The Vietnam War but of course Country Joe wrote his own song with that theme adding 'I-Feel-Like-I'm' to his title, '1-2-3 what are we fighting for?' **'Pretty Peggy-O'** also recorded by Simon &

Garfunkel and many others including Joan Baez. A Scottish song with Bob amused at something going on in the recording studio in his version. When Bob visited England to act in the BBC 'Madhouse' play he sang this on stage with an extra verse, but it never appeared in the show. The song progresses down the army ranks, Bob sang 'The sergeant he is gone long gone, he's fighting the wild man down in Borneo'. The BBC audience found it very humorous, it may have been because with Bob's accent they thought he was singing 'farting' not 'fighting'. This pearl of comic wisdom was presented in a Matthew Zuckerman interview for Isis Magazine by Martin Carthy. Bob still manages to rhyme 'rodeo' with 'areo', for 'area' I presume.

'Highway 51 Blues' (C.Jones): In the UK the composers rarely write of motorways yet in the USA many of the main Highways and Routes have songs. I contended many years ago that the Texan bluesman Curtis Jones credit was incorrect, it is not the same as his song from the 1962 Delmark Label album. Gorgen Antonnson solved the puzzle when he located two verses that were extracted from 'New Highway No 51' by Tommy McClennan, one wonders how we all missed it for so many years. Bob does add a second verse of his own creation, and the spectre of death invades once more. It opens like a hybrid of 'Wake Up little Suzie' and 'C'mon Everybody' or even 'Bye Bye Love'. Although Bob changes the lyrics he didn't claim the registration that it was 'arranged by Bob Dylan'. 'Gospel Plow' (Minnesota tape): Keeping one's hand on the plow was the same as keeping one's nose to the grindstone, one needs to keep working. Odetta and Mahalia Jackson often sang this, Bob heard it on Odetta's 'Live at Carnegie Hall' album. It has also been recorded as 'Hold On', 'Hold on to The Plow' and 'Keep Your Hand on the Plow'. There is also a Len Chandler version as 'Keep Your Eyes on the Prize', 'the prize' in question being the ever elusive equal rights. 'Baby, Let Me Follow You Down' (Minnesota). This is a song for 'Suze', she always agreed that it was for her. The Animals 'Baby Let Me Walk You Home' was based on the song. Ric rather than Eric Von Schmidt is credited as the composer. It was Bob himself that indicated that he thought Schmidt had got his song from that of Horace Sprott, who had recorded for Folkways. To my ears Eric Von Schmidt had the best voice of all the folk singers, if he only could have written songs as good as Bob Dylan.

'House of The Risin' Sun': Another song which was a hit for the Newcastle group The Animals. Dave Van Ronk was not happy that Bob stole his arrangement, evidently Bob recorded it before asking if he could use it. When asked, Ronk said "No", but it was already recorded and ready for release. Dave Ronk did release his version under the title 'Gambler's Blues' on the album 'Black Mountain Blues'. In the UK the song (and 'Midnight Special') is registered to H.Phlange and J.Home, now there's a mystery, no not really, the song was also a big hit in the USA for 'Frijid Pink' in 1970 when

26

it reached No 7, it was their one and only hit. **'Freight Train Blues'**: The Roy Acuff version seems to be Bob's inspiration here, but Ramblin' Jack Elliott was also singing it at the time. Chas McDevitt and Nancy Whiskey's version was a different song which was taken from Elizabeth Cotton's 'Freight Train' which she composed when she was just nine years old. Her style of finger-picking guitar is very similar to that used by Bob on his 'Worried Blues'. Bob's version is not registered to John Lair who also has a music registration for the title, Columbia have designated it as traditional, but the original recording sheets state by 'Lair'. We were probably lucky that Bob didn't add a 'Boxcar Willie' train engine vocal on this, but he does attempt the train whistle on harmonica.

'Song to Woody': This song uses Woody Guthrie's '1913 Massacre' as basic tune and includes a line from Woody's 'Pastures of Plenty' which is 'come with the dust and (are gone) we go with the wind', the parenthesis indicate Bob's slight modification. As a digression I must add that Loudon Wainwright in his 'Talkin' New Bob Dylan' on his 'History' album says "Hey, Bob Dylan, I wrote you a song". David Bowie did similar on his 'Song For Bob Dylan' on his 'Hunky Dory' album when he sang "Hear this Robert Zimmerman, I wrote you a song!". Ultimately a tribute to Woody, Bob does mention Sonny Terry, Leadbelly and Cisco Houston within the lyric. Bob also betrays that he wants to make it as singer taking an easier route than Woody had to take. It is only in the second and last verses that Bob rhymes both sets of twin stanzas. **'See That My Grave is Kept Clean'** (Minnesota, Beecher's & Gaslight): A Blind Lemon Jefferson song from 1928. His version included the line 'Dig my grave with a silver spade' which was also used by Buddy Knox for his 'I Think I'm Gonna Kill Myself', however Bob's spade might be silver but it is also 'bloody'. Yet another song pertaining to death in which Bob takes Lemon Jefferson's almost happy and optimistic rendition and transforms it to a hymn.

There were a number of remaindered tracks and some were detailed in The Writings and Drawings book. **'He Was a Friend of Mine'** was included in The Bootleg Series release in 1991. It was a Leadbelly song titled 'Shorty George' from 1935. It concerns a man that Leadbelly met in a penitentiary, he later died on the road poor and destitute. It has been adapted by Bob, apparently it was discovered for Bob by Carla Rotolo. Bob later stated that the version he heard was by Blind Arvella Gray but Eric Von Schmidt claims that he sang the song to Bob first. Eric's album which includes his version can be seen on the cover of Bob's album 'Bringing it All back Home'. Dave Van Ronk's version is on his 1963 'Folksinger' album. Leadbelly's 'Shorty George' can be found on his 'Early Morning Blues' album. I could only locate one album by Arvella Gray 'The Singing Drifter', it was a white cover and label edition but I couldn't hear 'He was a Friend of Mine' on it, perhaps Bob (or I) was mistaken. **'Man on the Street'**: Another Bootleg Series release, it is Bob's modern Samaritan and Pharisee song, it utilises Pete Seeger's 'The Young Man Who Wouldn't Hoe Corn'. Bob had observed a policeman poking a man lying in the street to see if he was asleep or dead, thus establishing inquisitiveness rather than compassion. Suze Rotolo was working on the production of 'Brecht on Brecht' at the time and the late John Bauldie wrote that he considered this lyric to be influenced by Brecht's 'Litany of Breath'. It was in fact Brecht's 'A Liturgy of Breath' that had a similar section. In Brecht's poem an old lady dies in the gutter and is buried. A man stands up against the police and is struck down by a rubber truncheon. A third bearded man was shot as were a group of people. It was a big bear that came by and ate the birds. These birds were silent after each attack in Brecht's poem. The only similarity is the gutter and the policemen but Bob could have heard Brecht's poem before writing his song. **'As I Go Ramblin' Round'** (Guthrie): This Woody Guthrie song was also titled 'Ramblin' Blues'. **'House Carpenter'** tells of the situation of a woman leaving her husband and three children to sail to Italy, it has been mooted that she may have left with another woman, the ship was holed and sank. The narrator returns from the sea to marry her after avoiding marriage to another. She is already married to a house carpenter, but leaves him. F.J.Childs collected this into an anthology as 'A Warning for a Married Woman' and dated it 1685. The thought of leaving a husband 'for' another woman is unlikely to be the truth of the song, 'with' another woman is more suitable word for 1685.

With the album selling slowly Bob decided to appear on The Broadside Radio Show on New York's WBIA-FM in March 1962. Just before he was due in the studio to record tracks for the second album in April, Bob had been practising at the room at the rear of Israel (Izzy) Young's 'Folklore Centre', Izzy was championing Broadside Magazine at the time. Izzy Young, Pete Seeger and Sis Carmichael appeared on the show with Bob. Pete Seeger had been part of The Almanac Singers with Lee Hayes, Millard Lampell and Woody Guthrie. The Broadside Magazine was available for 35 cents and printed the lyrics and music of new and adapted folk songs, some of Bob's had appeared in he magazine. In the radio interview Bob exaggerated by saying that he wrote 5 songs last night on scraps of paper an gave them all away, hardly the ideal of 'waste not want not'. Bob also adds to the myth by stating that he was raised in Dakota, a place where you can go farther and see less. On the programme Bob sang 'The Death of Emmett Till' and 'The Ballad of Donald White', the first was available on Bonnie Beecher's Hotel tape, the latter a song using Bonnie Dobson's 'Peter Amberley' tune is superb, for some unknown reason, not recorded for the forthcoming new album. The Broadside Show introduced the radio listeners to 'Blowin' in The Wind' on which Bob was please to announce that he was using minor chords for the

first time, the lyric was to be featured on the cover of the new Broadsi
Magazine. There was another magazine called 'Sing Out' which had similar
aspirations to Broadside, but Bob went to their offices for help and advice and
was shown the door. Bob was perplexed by their attitude as they promoted
themselves as 'being helpful to up-and-coming writers'. As Bob had taken his
guitar and tapes to folk record labels such as Elektra, Vanguard and Folkways
and not been heard, one can forgive him for feeling that there may be some
anti-Dylan feeling circulating.

The rockabilly influenced **'Mixed Up Confusion'** was released as a
single, Bob told Izzy Young that he had written it in the taxi on the way to the
studio. It is a song where Bob is flexing his muscles. Certainly autobiographical he is writing songs for people that are too hard to please. It
comprises just eight two line stanzas and presents the emotions of ambivalence
a young man is feeling. Many writers have discarded this lyric as easy and
superfluous probably due to Bob mentioning how and when he wrote it. What
it shows is that the often wordy Dylan lyrics could be short sharp and precise.
An alternative version of the single finally got an album release when it was
included in The Biograph Boxed Set in 1985.

Bob continued to visit Woody Guthrie but he was destroying his own
dreams of the man, familiarity bred uncertainty in Bob's illusions of meeting
his mentor. It would be 1967 before the crippling Huntington's disease finally
killed Woody at the age of 55. Woody thought that Bob had talent, he often
would say that he was convinced that Bob would make it big. Bob was even
considered for the part of Woody in the biopic 'Bound For Glory' which told
the tale of Woody's travels, but the part would eventually go to David 'Kung
Fu' Carradine. Woody was also a mentor for Lonnie Donegan who recorded
many of his songs. 'Have a Drink on Me' was an adaption of 'Take A Whiff
On Me' and 'Grand Coulee Dam' was a big hit in Britain. Woody really lived
the life of a troubadour within the confines of John Steinbeck's 'Grapes of
Wrath', The Dust Bowl ballads were perfect reflections of those days. Woody
also sang cowboy songs, children's songs and lullabies. He is best known for
'This Land is Your Land' and 'So Long It's Been Good top Know Ya', as
with most of songs they are optimistic, of course his son Arlo Guthrie
continued by having great success with his 'Alice's Restaurant' a song first
then a film. At the time of meeting Woody Bob also met Cisco Houston one
of the great unsung heroes of American folk. Bob said that he looked like
Clark Gable, Houston died on April 29th, 1961 so he never saw Bob Dylan
achieve his ambition to be a star. Bob went into the studio in March 1962 with
Victoria Spivey and Big Joe Williams and added harmonica to the albums
'Three Kings and a Queen Vol 1 and Vol 2'. Although Vol 1 was released in
1964, Vol 2 was only released in 1972. A photograph of Bob holding Big
Joe's nine string guitar at the session would later be included on the rear of

, album. Bob returned to the studio in April 1962 to put
his second album. He was still recording tracks at the end of
album 'THE FREEWHEELIN' BOB DYLAN' was to be
1963. This was no mean achievement when one considers that
tracks used were taken from the recording session on April 23rd,

o legally changed his name to Dylan in August 1962 and appointed
Albe. Grossman as his manager. Grossman was also the manager of Peter
Paul and Mary who recorded Bob's songs. Bob wrote the cover notes for Peter
Paul and Mary's album. These notes which started with **'Snow was piled up'**
were Bob's observations of New York in that cold winter. He discusses the
Gaslight Club, buried beneath the middle of Macdougal Street. Bob also
details the problems the club experienced with the police and the bullies, the
protection racketeers.

Bob had appeared at The Gaslight Club in October 1962 and premiered
a couple of tracks from the second album and one from the third in 'Hollis
Brown'. The bootleg recording from The Gaslight was almost professional and
one track **'No More Auction Block'** was cleaned up and used on the official
'Bootleg Series' set in 1991. Bob had met Spider John Koerner and Tony
Glover, learned from Ramblin' Jack Elliott and Dave Van Ronk and had also
played on sets with Fred Neil. Fred had already written a minor hit in 'Modern
Don Juan' for Buddy Holly and now had a contract with Elektra where he
recorded the 'Tear Down the Walls' (with Vince Martin) and 'Bleecker and
Macdougal' albums.

In January 1963, Bob took his first trip to England, (it is reported that
The BBC sent Bob a free plane ticket out, but he had to pay for the plane
home) as it is noted that Bob never flew until 1963 it is assumed that he
travelled the Atlantic by ship, but the dates can be incorrect. Bob was given
the part of a folk singer in the BBC radio play 'The Madhouse on Castle
Street' and he sang the yet un-released 'Blowin' in the Wind' and the never
released 'Swan on the River'. It was also known as 'The Ballad of the Gliding
Swan' and was the first Bob Dylan collaboration, Evan Jones wrote the lyrics
Bob added the tune. Bob said that all he had to do was look at the camera. A
girl says "The old man tells me your the only person in the house that tells the
truth", and then hits him on the shoulder. This was followed by a close-up of
them looking at each other, and that was all. Bob had met Evan Jones the
playwright and Philip Saville the Director at the reading stage, Bob just
couldn't manage to read the lines convincingly. Evan Jones re-wrote the part
splitting it into two with David Warner playing 'Bobby' and Bob playing
'Lennie' the singer, for which he received $2000 and a room at The Savoy
Hotel, totalling a fortune in 1963 especially for an almost unknown performer.
The play was broadcast on January 13th, 1963.

Suze Rotolo was spending some time in Italy with her mother, Bob remained in England for a few months meeting the top folk singers. He became friendly with Martin Carthy and made an enemy of Nigel Denver by disrupting one of his shows. On his return to the USA Bob sang his first large solo concert at New York's Town Hall on April 12th 1963. He had missed Suze's return from Italy and they had spent longer apart than was necessary, but they now set up home together on New York's West 4th Street. The concert was recorded for release as a live album but it was shelved. With a new album released Bob had to do some promotion to sell more copies than the first album. As this album included some major self composed songs, it set Bob up as the leader of the new 'folk' scene. An appearance was arranged for Ed Sullivan's CBS coast-to-coast television show. Bob rehearsed 'Talkin' John Birch Society Blues' but was asked to substitute it with an alternative, Bob's refusal meant that he was deleted from the show and action which gave Bob more publicity than if he had actually appeared. Bob was seen by the populous as a rebel. Elvis Presley had also achieved notoriety on that show when his swivelling hips were not shown, the cameramen were told to keep their sights above his waist. During the same month Bob met Joan Baez for the first time at The Montery Folk Festival in California; Joan introduced Bob's performance.

Peter (Yarrow) Paul (Stookey) and Mary (Travers) recorded 'Blowin' in the Wind' and it became a million seller, it achieved No 1 in the USA and No 13 in the UK. Their follow-up record was 'Don't Think Twice It's Alright' which reached No 9 in the USA, they also recorded 'The Times They Are A-Changin'' which crept into the UK top 30 stalling at No 44. Peter Paul and Mary had two other No 1 hits with 'Puff The Magic Dragon' and John Denver's 'Leaving on a Jet Plane'. It would be 1965 before Bob Dylan dented the Top 40 singles charts, but the success of Peter Paul and Mary sent Bob's album up to No 22 in the Billboard album charts achieving a gold record. The cover of 'Freewheelin'' was another photograph by Don Hunstein of Bob and Suze walking down a snow covered Fourth Street in New York. James Dean must have been in Bob's mind when the cover photograph was taken, there exists an almost identical picture of James Dean walking down the centre of a street with his hand thrust into his pockets. Dean had a cigarette in his mouth but so do some of Bob's other photographs taken at the time by Hunstein in the street.

'Blowin' in the Wind': Bob said the biggest criminals are those that turn their heads away when they see wrong doing, when they know it's wrong. The only way to face-up to these questions is by first asking them. The song was written with David Cohen, (later David Blue) in a cafe and played for the first time within minutes of completing the lyrics. Bob used the tune of 'No More Auction Block'. If Bob and so many others confirmed that they had been influenced by Sam Cooke it was not a surprise that Sam wrote and recorded 'A Change is Gonna Come' in 1965, although this may of course been influenced by Bob's 'The Times They are A-Changin''. 'Blowin' in the Wind' includes nine 'how many's' followed with such superb imagery that it beggars's belief that it could have been written so swiftly. As a poem it is a remarkable achievement as a song it is absolutely sublime. When The Freewheelin' album was released this song was already in the system as a massive hit for Peter Paul and Mary, whereas their version seemed to be just a nice song when one listens to Bob sing it we become aware of the questions that need answering, we are still waiting for all the answers 35 years later. **'Girl From the North Country'**: A song directed towards Echo Helstrom or Bonnie Beecher, sung to the tune of 'Scarborough Fair' which Bob learned from Martin Carthy; Scarborough is in the North West of England. In the 'Writings and Drawings' book issued in 1973 the title word 'from' has become 'of', as it has in various songbooks over the years. It is just a song as Bob would say, but it is surprising that she would forget him so soon, especially if it was once 'true love'. People involved in 'true love' never forget, ever.

'Masters of War': This song presents the insignificance and the feelings of impotence of the masses in their efforts to affect the warmonger's brain, especially those living within a civilization that juggles its own means of oblivion. The USA budget for war also covered self-interest and self-protectionism. The song was inspired by UK folk singer Bob Davenport's version of 'Nottamun Town', which was known as Jean Ritchie's song in the USA. Although the tune is apparently extracted from 'Nottamun Town' Bob's lawyers managed to convince Geordie Music that he had created a different song entirely. Bob had also listened to the Jackie Washington version of 'Nottamun Town' which was released by Vanguard Records. In Eric Von Schmidt's book 'Baby, Let me Follow You Down' it mentions that fact and adds that Bob went to Vanguard Records and got a promotional copy from label owner Maynard Washington. It is pertinent to mention that the song 'Moonshiner' was also on that Vanguard album. Although Bob's version of 'Masters' wasn't recorded until 1963 he was singing this during his first visit to London. Ewan McColl and Peggy Seeger both commented on the song at the time, they thought that Bob should have named the culprits within the lyric and thus confronted the situation. I disagree very strongly, if Bob had done as they had proposed then the song would have soon been out of date and irrelevant, as it is it will last forever and always be applicable to a war-monger situation. In Bob's drawings book the song has a collection of seven and a half faces, six men, one boy and half a woman. The men that send in the troops are always well out of the line of fire. Surely the line 'Set back and watch' should have been 'sit back and watch'. Bob includes Jesus and Judas within this lyric, he is preaching his fire and brimstone lecture advising the leaders that Jesus will not forgive them, so it is christians at whom this song is targeted. The last verse would have the C.I.A. investigating any upstart revolutionary with these views, hoping that 'he' will die and watching the burial to ensure that 'he' is dead. Subsequently politically incorrect when one investigates the percentage of female leaders that have been involved with wars and conflicts, Golda Meir (Israel), Margaret Thatcher (Britain), Mary Robinson (Ireland) Benazir Bhutto (Pakistan). There are a few more that you can add, the question is how many female world leaders have **not** been involved in a serious conflict or war? This is a masterful anti-war song, so much said with such obvious feeling for the subject, but did Bob already know that he would not be sent to Vietnam. If he had not already been discarded due to poor eyesight then it makes this song brave as well as brilliant. If Bob was influenced by any poet in creating the song then 'Minister of War' which was translated from The Chinese text by Arthur Waley could be a candidate. It was a favourite of Joan Baez and was included on her spoken word album 'Baptism' released in 1968. The 'Baptism' album also throws up another thought. Joan included French poet Jacques Prevert's 'Song in the Blood' which although also influenced by The Book of Revelation might well have influenced Pete Seeger for his 'Turn Turn Turn'. Prevert's poem is full of 'turns' as it asks where all the blood goes that is spilt in wars and accidents. It is a known fact that matter can not be created or destroyed just changed from one form to another. **'Down the Highway'**: This, according to Bob, was based on a Big Joe Williams blues. The song was written by a love-sick Dylan, Suze was away in Italy, the country gets a mention. A 12-bar blues, he is love lorn and depressed on the highway to nowhere. Bob lost some body-weight whilst Suze was away, this happens for so many people in love. This song portrays the weakness of many men under the power of a woman's love, the one that loves least always has the upper hand. It was Suze's mother that took her to Italy, it was thought that she was attempting to drive a wedge into the relationship; it ultimately worked. I have always felt that this was two sets of lyrics combined. The five verses are a simple travelling-gambling on the road blues, it is the penultimate verse that indicates Bob's personal involvement. The ocean, she packed her suitcase with his heart, she went to Italy. This song is ordinary when it is considered that it follows a sublime lyric that is 'Masters of War'.

    'Bob Dylan's Blues' deemed an off the cuff song, this is far too clever to have been created solely in that manner. I have always contended that this was created in the William Burroughs style cut-up method. It makes the verses seem like a stream of consciousness composition. This is a song which possibly influenced the later 'It Ain't Me Babe' especially for the similar line of 'Go away from my door and window'. The first verse with The Lone

Ranger and Tonto follows on to the last verse as the six shooter is pulled out to rob a bank, or two. If you read the lyrics like a poem then you will notice that the 'dream' becomes less fractured if the order is changed, try it. **'A Hard Rain's A-Gonna Fall'**: This has the same fears as presented in 'Let Me Die in My footsteps'. 'Hard Rain' was written during time of the Cuban Missile crisis during October 1962. Presumed to be influenced by Arthur Rimbaud, Andy Gill called it 'a French-Symbolist extension of the Lord Randall theme', to encompass both conjectures. The pellets of poison, Bob explained, were the lies that we were being given to us by the masters of war. An explanation of the horror, the horror that ends T.S.Eliot's poem 'The Hollow Men' perhaps. The first three verses of Bob's song are as visual as any video, as we hear the lyrics we can imagine this apocalyptic landscape where everything is in decay. Bob expertly adds two lines of hope within this desecration when a young girl gives the narrator a rainbow and another man is only wounded by love. The title is a warning that the apocalypse is going come, it is inevitable, the song is past tense but prophetic. One line with particular personal relevance is 'I saw guns and sharp swords in the hands of young children'. I saw this first hand in Africa in 1980 and I lived to tell the tale. If ever a song was written with so much to say to people that still don't listen then this is it. A clarion call to persons that add more importance to greed and personal welfare than to that of the masses. It is this song that made Bob Dylan a sage, perhaps he was just parroting what others were saying but he certainly knew how to say it, and still the moral falls on 'deaf ears'.

 'Don't Think Twice It's Alright', ('All Right' on cover): This is not a ballad, it is a song for singing to oneself, a song to ameliorate your problems. A new form of love song for Suze, it brought their relationship out into the open and Suze was not amused. Bob is accusing her of immaturity wanting his soul when he only offered his heart. Bob had become enraptured by Suze I have always considered this song Bob's reaction to that invisible control. Bob mentions that she had never called him back and so he pretends to be deaf to her silent calls. It was her that had given him up, she was made aware that Bob and Joan Baez were an item. Here in this lyric Bob is taking the machismo stance that so many men take, the inference that he 'gave her up', at least it may make him feel better, when ultimately it just proves his own immaturity and becomes gross self pity. The inference that she had wasted his 'precious' time is the word that shows the hurt he feels, he is asking her to call him back to waste more of that time. He is really saying that it is only his time that is valuable and thus the remark becomes sexist, it should have read 'our' precious time and I suspect that if Bob was writing the lyric now in the 1990s that is the word he would have used. Dave Van Ronk stated that this song was so similar to Paul Clayton's 'Who's Gonna Buy Your Ribbons' which was itself an adaptation of an earlier song 'Scarlet Ribbons', that perhaps Paul Clayton should have been given a dual publishing acknowledgement. Bob took the composing registration himself although it may have been a management decision. Bob has taken the Paul Clayton song and created a wonderful new song of his own. The similarities in the sentiments run parallel line-for-line, one can imagine Bob creating his own version with his 'mental thesaurus', in fact Clayton's lyrics almost fit Bob's song. Julie Felix sang her version in 1964 and changed the lyrics to make it pertinent from the female stand-point. Bob is accompanied by Bruce Langhorne guitar, George Barnes on bass, Dick Wellstood on piano, Gene Ramey on bass, Herb Lovelle on drums.

'Bob Dylan's Dream': Bob confirmed that this was created after a conversation with Oscar Brown Jr. When Bob was in England he heard Martin Carthy sing 'Lord Franklin' and adapted the tune to suit this song. This is Joycian, James Joyce had written the influential, 'A 'Portrait of an Artist as A Young Man', and used a dream scenario to present the almost impossible to read novel 'Finnegan's Wake', and additionally the thought sequences for Leopold and Molly Bloom in his 'Ulysses'. In Bob's dream we are reflecting on his life as a young man growing up, an observation from someone floating above the ever changing scenes from his early life. There is almost an arrogance in the lyric which seems to pronounce that 'what Bob is doing is what everyone should be doing'. He advocates leaving the insularity of small town life and getting away, the need to stretch one's parameters. What Bob forgets is that not everyone wants to be an achiever, not everyone wants fame and fortune, what the majority want is health and happiness, money can't buy that, and the joke of being unhappy in opulent comfort becomes superfluous to those who reach that situation. A song of immense maturity for such a young man which may also have been influenced by the work of arguably the greatest ever librettist W.S.Gilbert. I can only assume that North American schools and amateur dramatic companies would perform Gilbert and Sullivan operettas but The Lord Chancellor in 'Iolanthe' also has a dream, a nightmare. In W.S. Gilbert's dream one of the scenes is in a railway carriage. Both Bob and Gilbert's dream are relevant to wishes and decisions. Bob is already thinking of his friends and wishing it could be as it was, though not with much sincerity, I am also not sure how long his 'wooden stove' would last, of course it could burn 'wood'. The Lord Chancellor's dream is caused by his wish to be someone that he is not so that he could avoid deciding if Phyllis a Ward of Court should marry Strephon who is 'half fairy'. The Chancellor's dream dissolves into the wonderful song 'Faint heart never won fair lady' which I also consider an influence on another of Bob's songs. Most people realise eventually that all the friends of their youth eventually drift away, especially if you yourself move away to pastures new, they rarely follow.

'Oxford Town': A song for the ordeal of James Meredith the first black man to be registered at 'Old Miss', The University of Mississippi. The initial refusal to accept the student concluded with riots where 300 people were injured and two died. Sung to an old banjo tune that Bob plays on guitar. The lyrics do not require any investigation, it was a statement of fact, one hopes that the perpetrators 'had their heads bowed down'. Bob has given us an extremely serious song with a happy melody, one wonders if it just happened by chance or Bob conceived it to be that way. **'Talking World War III Blues'** is a polemic song for bellicose world leaders. At the time Bob was speaking to the male leaders, this is the science-fiction dream of being the only survivor of the apocalypse, later Bob would go on record as saying that women run the world, no man has ever done anything that a woman hasn't allowed him to do, or encouraged him to do. The song opens as another 'dream', Bob is searching for an explanation on a psychiatrist's couch. A war that lasts for just fifteen minutes is over, he is saved because he was underground in the sewer with a woman at the time. The surrealism arrives when the survivor is so desperate to hear another voice that he telephones the talking clock, which surprisingly is still operational, as is the electrical power to the record player. The Jungian influence of dreams emerges when the psychiatrist states that he has the identical dream and that it would be a good idea if they both appeared in each others dreams, to be companions. I would want a woman in my dreams not a male psychiatrist.

'Corrina, Corrina' (traditional): Different to the original, nearly unrecognisable because evidently Bob had never heard the original. The musicians are as for 'Don't Think Twice' except for the addition of Howie Collins on guitar, Leonard Gaskin bass; George Barnes and Gene Ramey didn't play on this track. Bob accredited the inspiration for this song to Lonnie Johnson's version. Bo Chatman was one of the original writers of the song, Bob would return to Chatman's work with The Mississippi Sheiks in the 1990s. We have to bear in mind that Bob's version does take a few lines from Mississippi John Hurt's version. Bob recorded an alternative version with a better harmonica break which was released as the b-side of the 'Mixed Up Confusion' single. **'Honey, Just Allow Me One More Chance'** (H Thomas/Bob Dylan) Bob had heard Henry Thomas' version but couldn't recall his name at the time. The lyrics again could be for Suze, just like the previous track 'Corrina Corrina' this is more self-pity. The protagonist is asking for another chance, a favour, yet he freely admits that he has been searching for someone else that needs the company of a worried man. The man sounds so weak and pitiful that she would be better off forgetting him. **'I Shall Be Free'** is another supposedly 'off the cuff' song. Bob sang this on the early 'Beecher' and 'McKenzie' tapes and would have used his improvisory method of composition with Richard Rabbit Brown's, 'James Alley Blues' in the back of his mind. A flippant dream of a would-be womaniser. Brigitte Bardot is mentioned which makes us wonder if this was part of the lyric from Bob's first ever song. One must speculate how 'off the cuff' it really was, it is too clever by half. To me this is the song of a drunk. The verses are a jumble of revelation and intuition. It is an amusing song, the woman takes off her wig and he's gone, quick. He covers himself with black paint, advises Jack Kennedy, lives on a woman's earnings and stands for election. These are all the discussions pouring from the drunk at the bar that has an audience ready and willing to listen to his, as Bob puts it, 'bullshit'. Bob also introduces us to characters from his memory such as Sophia Loren, Elizabeth Taylor, Richard Burton, Mr Clean, Robert Louis Stevenson, Yul Brynner and more. I suspect that actor Ernest Borgnine was flattered to be selected to 'make the country grow' by being put into one room with Sophia Loren, Brigitte Bardot and Anita Ekberg. There are also two other traditional songs 'You Shall Be Free' for the solo singer and 'We Shall Be Free' for a group performance. These titles must have influenced 'I Shall Be Released' written many years later, although I have never heard that song sung with 'We', not even at the end of all star spectaculars.

'My Life in a Stolen Moment': This was first written to be included as notes in the programme for Bob's New York Town Hall Concert performed on April 12, 1963. This writing, which Bob tried to disclaim, gave us more insight to the real Bob Dylan at the time that any of his other prose. Bob claimed that it was just written for publicity and wasn't really pertinent, we all suspected that much of it was autobiographical. Some of the remarks included were ill considered, he must have realised that his family back home in Hibbing would read it, it left Bob trying to inform everyone that it was all hyperbole, well most of it was. Bob gives us details of The Iron Range and the life in a mining town. The mention that he kept running away from home would have his mother wondering 'what would the neighbours think', especially as it was proven to be untrue. Beatty Zimmerman informed Toby Thompson when he interviewed her that she had been told by Bob that most of the writing was created just to add charisma to the character that Columbia records wished to manufacture. Beatty would be aware but it meant that she would need to explain it to all her friends. But as few people in Hibbing paid much attention to Bob's career I suspect that few realised the story that Bob was weaving down south in New York. The long tale would suggest that Bob had paid his dues, lived some life, understood the rough and the smooth and had lived Woody Guthrie's life already, thus making him perfectly positioned to carry on Woody's work.

'Last Thoughts on Woody Guthrie': This is extraordinary because its title suggests that it is either an eulogy or an obituary. Woody didn't die until October 1967, this was certainly written in 1963 and registered in 1973, it was recorded live at New York's Town Hall in December 1963 and was released officially on the Bootleg Series. It is believed to be the only time that Bob has ever returned to the stage after a show to read a poem. This is considered by many to be Bob's masterpiece of writing, to be honest it is near perfect, no wonder Allen Ginsberg was so impressed. The sound that Bob created with the words is similar to the chant that is created by Ginsberg's 'Howl' and 'Kaddish', both of which hark-back to Walt Whitman. When Bob stated that he was writing three novels simultaneously these 'thoughts' might well have been his point of reference. There had been intimations that Bob's written work was influenced by Jack Kerouac, Arthur Rimbaud and even James Joyce but these were tenuous assumptions in 1963. The first 80 lines are descriptive of someone loosing their faculties, the observations that follow add impetus to that loss, it is not until the end that we are informed that Woody Guthrie is in Brooklyn State Hospital and God is in the church of your own choice. The remarkable idea that we can see them both at sundown in The Grand Canyon is sublime Dylan. Bob was writing from his heart, his muse was creating some superb ambivalent poetic lyrics which would later be described by Allen Ginsberg as the greatest by any American poet.

It was certainly true Woody Guthrie and the English folk scene had offered new horizons to Bob, and additionally a quantity of melody lines perfect for the acceptance of his new lyrics. What Bob had already achieved with a pretty average singing voice was immense, his true influences were his upbringing and the people with whom he came into contact in New York. It is no wonder that he was difficult to categorise even at this early stage in his career, as far as we were concerned at the time all the itinerant lifestyle hyperbole was true, the image makers had done a wonderful job in building two separate Bob Dylan's, the one his mother knew and our Bob Dylan.

Two versions of the album became available, Bob's late rush to the studio to record 'Girl From The North Country', 'Masters of War', 'Talking World War III Blues' and 'Bob Dylan's Dream' (all included on Freewheelin') meant that the albums that had already been pressed had to be destroyed, inevitably some copies escaped and now tremendous prices are paid for them at auctions.

The fifth track recorded in this session was **'Walls of Red Wing'**, it was not released until 1991 it tells the tale of life in a reform school for wayward children. It was based on the 'Road and the Miles to Dundee' and is as close as Bob had got to a Dickensian scenario. The school institutionalised many of the children into the ways of prison life, but there is a chink of optimism with the thought that some of the inmates may eventually become lawyers.

The tracks taken off the album at the last moment were 'Rocks and Gravel'(released in 1991 on The Official Bootleg Series), 'Let Me Die in My Footsteps' (1991), 'Talkin' John Birch (Paranoid) Blues' and 'Ramblin'

Gamblin Willie'(1991). The exaggerations on the album notes stated that Bob was now writing three novels, not just one, three, the subjects were also detailed but they seemed to be auto-biographical, Nat Hentoff was responsible for the liner notes. The idea that Bob was writing three books would catch him out eventually when his management signed a book deal on his behalf.

What the 'Freewheelin'' album did for Bob was that it created him as his own man, something that Woody Guthrie had insisted that he attempted to achieve. Bob realised that he wasn't a tall good looking film star type so his best chance was to be first, the prototype, not a second edition of anybody else. In fact he could be two people the hyped up version or the real version that his mother recognised.

As an aside it is pertinent to mention that Bob considers that he is 5'-10" tall, (5'-11" on his passport on the Bootleg Series Book), in photographs with Jack Nicholson and Robert De Niro, Bob appears shorter than either. My guess is that Bob is closer to 5'-8" in his stockinged feet. So many short men feel insignificant due to their lack of stature, rich short men can wear specially designed shoes and boots to add inches, Bob rarely appears without 2" heels on his boots. I once met a man who was so concerned about his height he kept trying to convince me that I was 6'-4" because he had written in his passport that he was 6'- 0", I am just 6'- 2" he was 5'- 9", one wonders why they bother.

Bob's lyrics were improving from song to song, the spirit of the zeitgeist was to be with him for many years to come. Bob used the pseudonym of Blind Boy Grunt to appear on an album of 'Broadside Ballads' harmonizing 'Let Me Die in My Footsteps' to Happy Traum's vocal, the false name was necessary due to Bob's exclusively to CBS Records.

Bob was composing and recording as if there was no tomorrow, many of the tracks and songs continue to become even more dusty in the vaults, many would eventually be released. **'Going To New Orleans'** is possibly based on Muddy Waters' 'Louisiana Blues', where he is going to get a mojo hand, whatever that is. It was also mooted that the song also uses a section from Muddy's, 'Gypsy Woman', but of course Bob adds lyrics of his own creating a new song. It would be possible to extract separate individual words and say that they were taken from many songs, I would suggest that these lyrics were always traditional but perhaps Muddy should have been given some acknowledgement for the early verses. It is evident that Muddy wasn't too unhappy, perhaps he remembered where he had obtained the verses in the first place. **'Sally Gal'** as mentioned earlier is similar to 'Sally Don't You Grieve', which was also a big hit for Lonnie Donegan in the UK. Bob also wrote the Guthrie influenced **'Ain't Gonna Grieve'** which is nine verses of self pity, a man trying to convince himself that he ain't gonna grieve no more. **'Ramblin' Gamblin' Willie'** was included on The Bootleg Series. It follows on from other characters such as Stack-O-Lee, Will O'Conley and Jesse James. I thought this might be 'Rattlin' Roarin' Willie' created by Robert Burns, but all Burns' Willie seemed to do was to consider selling his violin to get money to buy drink. Bob's song presented a 'Robin Hood' character that always paid his way and helped the sick and the poor. As he was a gambler the lyric states that the wives kept their husbands at home when Willie was in town. As Willie had 27 children and no wife it should have been husbands that needed to keep their wives at home. Willie supported all his children and all their mothers, not bad for a drifter, perhaps he did it through a direct debit account. Bob said in 1984 that Willie Brennan an Irishman hanged in 1804 who was celebrated in the song 'Brennan of the Moor' was in fact the protagonist in mind at the time of writing this song, he had heard Brennan's song sung by The Clancy Brothers. The Clancy Brothers have always been a favourite of Bob's. Tom Clancy died in 1990, Paddy Clancy died in 1998. Liam Clancy the last surviving brother intended to record some of Bob's songs in 1996. This excellent track was removed from original 'Freewheelin'' album.

'Death of Emmett Till': He was killed for wolf-whistling a white woman, although that fact is not mentioned in the lyric. The murderer was found not guilty by a jury of whites, some were assumed to have taken part in the murder. This powerful song was denigrated by Bob himself in 1964 when he said "In all honesty it is a bullshit song-I realise now that my reasons and motives behind it were phoney-I didn't have to write it". The song is extremely visual and strongly presents the case for the black man, especially as the allegedly murdering brothers were smiling when they were acquitted. As an aside a Dylan fan once played me a song with the same title over the telephone, it was a different song altogether sung by a group called The Ramparts, he had a 78, 10" shellac copy of the song which he had put on cassette, I never did receive the promised copy. Bob's song appeared in The Broadside Magazine with the tune assigned to black blues singer Leonard Chandler.

'Talking John Birch Paranoid Blues': This was only available as a bootleg recording and was not registered until 1970. The John Birch Society was an extreme right wing organization, a motto of 'rather dead than red' was becoming part of the American psyche during the McCarthy purge. Many of the top folk singers found it impossible to get work, Pete Seeger was one selected as a 'red'. This track was removed from the 'Freewheelin'' album to avoid litigation. In the 'Writings and Drawings' book this lyric is presented in grey type which signifies that it is a 'writing' rather than a 'song'. The narrator suggests the best way to avoid being considered a communist is to become a 'John Bircher'. Hitler is mentioned as acceptable because he was a fascist and not a communist. The John Bircher's might have been deemed extreme fascists. Of course the narrator becomes paranoid looking for reds under his bed, in the toilet bowl, up the chimney. The moral of the song is that once the investigations start they never stop, he concludes the song actually investigating himself. Emmett Grogan a friend to Bob some years later took up the same stance against fascists, he addressed a rally in the UK and gave one of the great speeches which was received with an extended standing ovation. When the applause died down he announced that he didn't know who wrote the speech but Hitler had used it first, Grogan then left the stage to absolute silence. The Bootleg Series included a live version of the 'Birch' blues taken from New York's Carnegie Hall at the end of October 1963. Bob changed some of the words in the live performance to get a few extra laughs. It was so deeply serious it was amusing, just like sniggering in church. The lyric has so much more power when read from the printed page.

'Lonesome Whistle' is the Hank Williams, Jimmie Davis song which has subsequently been recorded by Hank Snow, George Jones and Boxcar Willie complete with his vocal train noises. In the studio this followed the recording of 'John Birch' so perhaps the studio needed some light relief. 'Rocks and Gravel' is not an adaptation of Brownie McGhee's 'Solid Road', which was in turn similar to the lyrics of Leroy Carr's 'Alabama Woman's Blues' from where two verses were taken. Bob heard Big Joe Williams version before creating his own. Dave Van Ronk also recorded his version (which Bob may have heard), but the only song on the lists which is similar is 'Take Rocks and Gravel to Make a Solid Road' recorded by Horace Sprott in 1954. This was another of the songs on 'Freewheelin' which was removed. 'Let Me Die in My Footsteps' released on the Bootleg Series. The inspiration was that Bob had seen a bomb shelter in construction. The inference that the narrator does not wish to go underground to die but would prefer to remain on the surface to be killed is bizarre. The lyric presents a search for a personal Utopia where all the guns and tanks are destroyed, later in his career Bob would realise that religious intolerance has as much influence on wars as the weapons. The masters of war are controlled by the God of their doctrine.

'Baby, Please Don't Go' (Joe Williams), has been recorded by the world and its wife over the years, and not always credited to Big Joe Williams. Mose Allison's version inspired the British versions from Georgie Fame, Van Morrison and Them, Thin Lizzy and Budgie. In the USA Billy Lee Riley, Muddy Waters, Tom Rush, Bukka White, Willie Mae Thornton, Al Kooper and John Hammond all released versions. 'Talkin' Havah Negeilah Blues' was released on The Bootleg Series. It consists of just the repeated title, it is a jewish joke. At least the 'Writings and Drawings' book didn't waste a page on it. 'Milk Cow Calf's Blues' (Robert Johnson) This should have been a shared credit with Kokomo Arnold as some of his 'Milk Cow Blues' lyrics are included. This is also listed as a risque blues... as the inference is that when he awoke he wanted his milk-cow but as she wasn't there he got butter instead. What does he mean..., does he?,....nurse the screens please, quick.

'Wichita (Going to Louisiana)': A Sleepy John Estes song 'Special Agent Blues' or is it 'I'm going down in Louisiana' which is the Muddy Waters song. There are 'Going to' songs for Boston, Brazil, California, Chicago, Georgia, Hollywood, Kansas City, Los Angeles, Little Creek, Louisiana, Memphis, Mexico, Miami, New Orleans, New York, Santa Fe and even Shangri La. Bluesman Noah Lewis recorded 'Going to Germany' back in 1930. Sadly 'Wichita' is one of the few recordings by Bob that I have not heard. 'Talking Bear Mountain Picnic Massacre Blues': Another Bootleg Series release. Inspired by a newspaper report of the Hudson Belle boat excursion. The promoters took the money for extra counterfeit tickets, the river took the lives. Written in the first person, the narrator does not lose his family in the disaster, he lived to tell the tale. Another of Bob's extremely visual lyrics, no ambiguities here. Bob's idea of revenge is to put the promoters on a boat and then sink it. 'Baby, I'm in The Mood for You' is a song for a man that needs some loving. Bob has used some of the ideas that he has gleaned from playing folk blues. The 'milk cow' euphemism, the 'lonesome home', he has his 'overlovin' fill'. This chap doesn't know if he wants to live or die, 'sleep with his pony' or 'do nothing at all'. The written lyrics only state 'Babe', only in the title does it become 'Baby', but by the end of the song we are aware that he is 'in the mood for her', he says it 24 times in 30 lines of verse. Bob said that he was thinking of Jesse Fuller's 'San Francisco Bay Blues' when he wrote this song. The song was released on Biograph.

'Quit Your Low Down Ways': A Bootleg Series release. A couple of the stanzas are taken from Kokomo Arnold's '(Good Morning) Milk Cow Blues', but the song is basically taken from Sleepy John Estes song 'Milk Cow Blues'. Sleepy got his name from his habit of suddenly dozing off due to his low blood pressure. With 'Milk Cow Calf's Blues' and the 'milk cow' also used in 'Baby, I'm in the Mood for You', Bob was immersing himself in 'milk', not literally of course. Bob's lyrics are of a man so much in love with a woman that he has to accept her philandering, but he keeps pleading for her to behave. I still don't know the difference between her 'sinning' and her 'low down ways', but the narrator requires her to quit both. She sounds like a free spirit, one wonders why the narrator doesn't take her as she is. Bob sings the song in a cowboy style and almost yodels. Peter Paul and Mary recorded this song for their 'In the Wind' album and the Hollies added it to their 'Hollies Sing Dylan' album. 'That's Alright Mama'(Arthur Crudup): The Elvis Presley rocker which Paul McCartney added to his Russian album 'Choba B CCCP' (Back in the USSR), the song made Arthur Big Boy Crudup famous but not rich. 'Kingsport Town'(Trad), another track included in The Bootleg

Series release. It is a country waltz with Guthrie's 'Who is Gonna Shoe Your Pretty Little Feet' as its basic idea. Bob sings many 'Who is' questions of his own. Bob was supposed to have sung this with a country yokel accent (called an 'okie' in the USA), sounds like the usual accent to these ears. **'Worried Blues'** was added to The Bootleg Series. This song almost uses a line taken from the Fred Neil song 'Everybody's Talkin''. Fred Neil sings 'Going where the weather suits my clothes', which in turn comes from 'Southern Woman's Blues' from 1925, Bob sings 'climate' in lieu of 'weather'. The song is sung gently, more like the early pre-Columbia recordings. **'Hard Times in New York Town'** The Bootleg Series recording is taken directly from The Minnesota Hotel Tape dated 22/12/61. Bob's lyrics which stated that by the time he leaves New York he will be standing on his own feet came true even before he left New York. An adaptation of The Bentley Boys 1929 song 'Down on Penny's Farm', which was also adapted by others to be 'Tanner's Farm' or 'Robert's Farm'. There are no new revelations in the song, it could have been written by anyone who had never been there. The song opens in the manner of the town crier or the troubadour singing the news. Bob never had any hard times there, he leap-frogged all the other folkies once he had that recording contract. He was looked after by Suze and other friends in considerable comfort, but the song helped create the myth of his 'hard times'. **'No More Auction Block'**: Included on The Bootleg Series is a track taken from Gaslight Club Bootleg Tape from October 1962. Alan Lomax wrote that this was taken from the negro migratory song 'Many Thousands Gone'. Odetta recorded the song in 1960 at The Carnegie Hall, it has the tune used for 'Blowin'' in the Wind'. A song of slavery which has little power when sung by Bob but Odetta's emotional version is sublime and definitive. **'Whatcha Gonna Do'** (when the grim reaper calls): Mance Lipscomb sang 'whatcha gonna do when death comes creepin' into your room', as did Josh White. There are other songs with the same title, even The Drifters recorded one. There is a simple answer to the title, 'not much', when your time has come you will just accept it and drift away. This song is macabre, the shadow is coming to get you. It reminds me of my mother scaring me into going to sleep because the 'sackman' is coming to take me away if I remained awake. Bob turns the Mance Lipscomb theme on its head by changing the grim reaper into the devil. The grim reaper is just the collection-agent I am not sure that he ultimately decides whether you go up-or-down. The last thing that anyone should do is worry about the inevitable, concentrate on the probable and the possible.

'Tomorrow is a Long Time': This is the song that Bob said Elvis Presley recorded, it is true he did. A song for missing Suze, an empty bed blues. The song was originally titled 'Lonesome Would Be Nothing at All' on Bob's own the recording sheets. Bob's version was not recorded until June

1974 at the 'New Morning' sessions. Some of the lyrics such as 'then I'd lie in my bed once again' of 'Tomorrow' are similar to 'Western Wind' a traditional song that I first heard in 1961 when it was recorded by folk trio The Limeliters. Elvis' own version appeared as a bonus track on the soundtrack album to 'Californian Holiday' in 1966. **'Who Killed Davey Moore?'**: This is an anti-boxing song, Sugar Ramos killed Davey Moore in a fight in March 1963, all the entrepreneurs and promoters got their money. The Bootleg Series track is taken from The Carnegie Hall Show in October 1963 recorded by Columbia for a live album that was never released. Bob creates a Pontius Pilate scenario with the fight referee, the gamblers, the sport--writer, the crowd and the manager all washing their hands of all the blame. Sugar Ramos (although not named in the song) excuses himself because he is paid to hit the other man, and of course defend himself at all times. The point that Bob makes with this excellent lyric is that 'boxing' is to blame. Boxing would answer that if the sport was banned then it would continue illicitly without the protection that officialdom can give. I am not sure that Mrs Moore and her children would be really comforted to hear that answer. This is based on 'Who Killed Cock Robin', "I" said the sparrow "With my bow and arrow!". In that fable they all took the blame in Bob's song it wasn't anyone's fault, except of course Davey Moore.

'I'd Hate to Be You on That Dreadful Day': This is the advice to a sinner to repent before it is too late. The pain, the fire and brimstone of Dante's Inferno awaits so behave yourself on Earth or for you it's hellfire. Walking naked, we are all the same, so how can we separate the rich from the poor? **'Walkin' Down the Line'** was recorded as a registration record for musicians that didn't write down their music for their publishers. This was included on The Bootleg Series and was recorded sometime during 1963. The tune is 'My Buckets Got a Hole in It', as sung by Ricky Nelson, Hank Williams (he wrote it) and Lefty Frizzell; not the Odetta, Harry Belafonte duet. Bob's song is a tale of the drifter who follows the railway line. There is a Bob Dylan joke-sketch in the 'Writings' book. The drawing shows a 'Tom Thumb' walking on top of the telephone, so I suspect Bob was thinking of walking down a telephone line. Although it was not recorded for official release by Bob there were versions recorded by Odetta, Jackie DeShannon and Glen Campbell. **'Standing on the Highway'** continues the railway theme of the previous track. He is hitchhiking to see his girl. He has to decide on going to the city or to his grave, which sounds like no choice at all. The city is represented by the ace of diamonds and death by the ace of spades. He is lost lonely and desperate wondering if his girl back home is saying a prayer for him. A great lyric for yet another 'highway' blues.

Poor Boy Blues: Is Bob's amended version of Howlin' Wolf's 'Smokestack Lightning'. He is desperate and on the run from the law.

Strangely this desperado spends a great deal of time crying. This could be Billy the Kid as he tells the bartender that he is not too young for a drink. If the order of the verses was amended then this lyric would have more form, the last verse of the Mississippi running too fast should have been swapped with the conversation with the Judge and Jury. **'Ballad for a Friend'** but I don't know who. This song again mentions the railway as do many of Bob's Guthrie influenced songs. This is for someone run down and killed by a diesel truck on The Utah Road. This was a friend from The North Country who spent time just watching the trains go by. **'John Brown'** is a powerful anti-war song. Tom Paxton almost achieved the same power with his song 'Jimmy Newman', on his album titled 'Six'. John Brown is off to war, he looks wonderful in his uniform when he leaves, everyone is so proud. He returns home so disfigured and crippled that his mother doesn't recognized him, but he does have some medals. Bob touches a nerve with one remark he writes 'when my enemy came close, I saw that his face was just like mine'. In business I have always found that I enjoyed the company of persons from countries that I had been trained to dislike or at least be wary of by my parents and teachers. We tend to dislike people as nations but in a one to one situation they turn the antipathy on its head.

'All Over You': Although this opens with the joke statement 'If I could do it all over again I'd do it all over you', (used in song by Caravan and The Four Preps), this lyric becomes quite exceptional. The tale of a lover's vengeance. Rarely has so much hurt been felt in a song. How many situations of love that turn to hate really get as bad as this. The narrator is even stalking his prey and waiting for his chance to inflict pain. If she has dispensed with his services then it will not be mental torment she will suffer which makes this lyric so close to 'obsessive hate syndrome'. I would have preferred Bob to have found an alternative word to 'thunk' as the past tense of 'think', otherwise it is a majestic poem. **'Long Ago and Far Away'**: A satirical view of history; Slavery, wars, lynching, gladiators are all things of the past, but are they? This song presents the case that nothing changes, it just secures new titles. A song of brotherhood, a christian message, they hanged (not hung) the man of peace on a cross. This song has Bob mentioning the crucifixion years before his religious experience and conversion. **'Gypsy Lou'**: Is the tale of a woman followed from town to town by the same admirers. Bob is redressing the balance because most of the Gypsy folk songs are for girls that run away from home. Here Gypsy Lou has something more than your fortune on offer.

'Long Time Gone': A song to assist with Bob's myth. Leaving home at the age of 12 to join the carnival. At 12 he also suffered in love, a broken heart. There is more self pity as he has to tell her the obvious that her beauty will not last. **'Train-a-Travelin''**: The steam-train represents the spreading of fear and misinformation, as Bob writes 'you just might be misled'. These are the politicians preaching fear, so that we must add the insurance companies that prey on all our fears of what can happen for the worse. What Bob fails to offer is an alternative, nearly all politicians come to power with the best intentions only to learn just how difficult it is. Comedienne Joyce Grenfell had her finger on the pulse when she said "Why is it the revolutionary leaders never mention the drains in their manifesto, you can't run big cities without adequate drains!" **'Ballad of Donald White'**: This song was featured on The Broadside Show when Bob appeared with Pete Seeger, Sis Cunningham and Israel 'Izzy' Young. This song is for Donald White's address to the Court after he has been condemned to death for murder. He tells his story which is of an uneducated man who was orphaned as a child who is aware that he has a problem yet is sent away from an institution due to over-crowding and commits murder. The moral is that these people that know that they have a mental problem might be victims of the society of which they belong. The social services send persons that are aware of their problem out onto the streets. They commit a terrible crime and are then imprisoned at a greater cost for life. This powerful song uses the tune and almost a verse of the traditional folk song 'Peter Amberly'.

'Bob Dylan's New Orleans Rag': Is a great comedy routine and ideal for a video. A man is feeling depressed until another man explains that he knows a woman that can solve his problem. They travel to the opposite side of the river and stop at house No 103. At the door the man sees three men emerging hardly able to walk. He sees another worn out man in the hallway, decides against going in and runs away. The moral of the song is it better to stay miserable than visit the woman at No 103. A great lyric that deserves to · be recorded and released.

To tidy up this period of Bob's career it is necessary to mention the impressive cover liner notes written by Bob for the album **'Joan Baez In Concert Volume II'**. This covers seven pages in the 'Writings' book. Bob encompasses various facets of his life, from watching the iron ore railway, early idealism coupled with the realisation that his idols were in fact human. He travelled and sang although few were listening until he embraced New York City like a long lost lover. It is the fifth section before Bob mentions the girl with the beautiful voice that he met on common ground. In the early part of the piece Bob mentions that if he can't touch it with his hand then he wouldn't understand it, this idea returns when discussing her voice. Is it wondrous, a thing of beauty or just ugly? Only ugly is understood. Bob realises that he didn't begin to touch until he felt what wasn't there, it can't be understood or solved by hands feet or fingertips. He thinks that he is a laughing stock for taking so much time to come to his senses, it was a shame it took so much time. In the final section when he is back watching the ore-train go past he stands up and shouts to the train's engineer "Joanie says hello!" I always wondered if this is what Vanguard Records expected when they asked Bob to write some album notes. They usually comprised of a few flattering remarks and general hyperbole, this was this first time that I can remember such a long poem being included on any album. This wasn't as good as the '11 Epitaphs' but it was certainly interesting.

I once met British writer Anthony Burgess, I was introduced by my friend Brian King who had once tried to sell him a prestige limousine. Anthony Burgess never seemed to listen much, he wanted to talk, I found him extremely opinionated and I was only in his company for ten minutes. When he touched on poetry I mentioned how sublime Bob Dylan's lyrics were in my opinion, especially '11 Epitaphs' and 'The Joan Baez album notes'. His response was that he had only heard some of the songs but had not seen them written down. When I explained that the lyrics were available in book form this rich man suggested that if I sent him a copy he would read them; needlessly to say I never sent him a copy.

Bob was already head and shoulders above folk-singers that had been on the circuit for years, in both celebrity and achievement, it is no wonder that many were laying in wait to denounce him. He had decided that the 'Freewheelin' album did not include enough 'finger pointing' songs and he intended to remedy that with some new compositions. Bob was making many enemies, they were claiming that Bob hadn't paid his dues to the system, I have never understood why it was necessary to be in the industry for years before reaching celebrity. Not unexpectedly it is only those that make it after many years of trying that deem it necessary to struggle for one's career. Bob was on his way, he was his own man, he already had copyists, he still has, but the times were changing.

ONLY LOOKING FORWARD

I am afraid I shall not find him,
but I shall still look for him.
If he exists, he may be appreciative of my efforts.
Jules Renard 1864-1910

The **'THE TIMES THEY ARE A-CHANGIN''** album was released and promoted as an album with a protest theme, it followed the assassination of John F.Kennedy. In April 1964 it achieved No 20 in the USA charts. The Beatles championed Bob wherever they went, as everything that they said was being reported in all the daily newspapers Bob's albums started to sell. 'Freewheelin' reached No 16 in May and 'Times They Are' reached No 20 in July, even the first album's sales doubled. It was at this time that I first became aware of Bob Dylan; the albums were up and own like a yo-yo for a year. 'Freewheelin' went to No 1 in May 1965, knocking The Beatles' 'For Sale' off the top, and 'Times They Are' reached No 4 in April 1965, after a year on the charts. Bob made a statement concerning his new fame, he said 'Jesus got himself crucified for being a leader', the remark never received much publicity, John Lennon would find himself immersed in a christian dilemma when he said The Beatles were more well known than Jesus, truth hurts sometimes.

A friend named Roy Kew brought to my house three albums, 'Dust Bowl Ballads' by Woody Guthrie, Thelonious Monk's 'Quartet and Big band in Concert' and Bob Dylan's first album. He played them to me and our mates, all except Roy thought that Bob Dylan and Woody were awful, but I liked the Monk album. Thirty five years later all three albums are personal favourites, I often play 'Darkness on the Delta' from the Monk album to visitors to show just what a great pianist the man was, it remains, one of the greatest solo jazz piano pieces ever created, in my opinion of course. Roy left the house suitably admonished but said, "You lot just wait in six months you will all be singing his songs!". Of course Roy was correct, in fact I was listening again in a matter of weeks.

Before the album could be made Bob and Albert Grossman had to accept a new producer in Tom Wilson. After a meeting with Tom and John Hammond who continued to press CBS to keep faith with the new singer, Wilson was accepted. It was later reported that for some of the session Elektra's in house producer Paul Rothchild was in the studio with Tom Wilson, but only Wilson was given producer credits. Although Bob had been so prolific he had used up all his early 'poems' and for these new sessions less tracks were to be remaindered, only 'Hollis Brown' played as The Gaslight Club in October 1962 was taken from his earlier songs. Bob was continuing to write long prose pieces and '11 Outlined Epitaphs' (only 'Four' in UK) was written out in full on the cover, and the CD booklet. The USA issue had an insert which continued the Epitaphs onward from No 3, the UK edition selected just four, Nos 1, 2, 7 and 8. No 9 was Bob's response to Andrea Svedburg of Newsweek for her version of her interview with Bob. From the interview Bob created the 'dust of rumours' which he also added to 'Restless Farewell'. No 5 was inspired by a conversation in car after a show. There are references to his upbringing and to the friends and associates he had met in New York. More on the Epitaphs later.

The cover was another masterpiece, designed by Jerold Smokler, it shows a gaunt faced Bob in a black and white photograph taken by Barry Feinstein the husband of Mary Travers during the weekend of the 1963 Newport Folk Festival. The album of the evening concerts of the Newport Folk Festival 1963 (Vol 1) includes Bob singing 'Blowin' in The Wind' and joining in with 'The Freedom Singers' (all the participants) for the grand finale. The album also included Mississippi John Hurt, Ramblin' Jack Elliott, Joan Baez, Ian & Sylvia, The Rooftop Singers and Sam Hinton. A youthful Woody Guthrie is the image presented on 'The Times They Are' cover, a long way from the smiling cherub on Bob's first album. We must assume that Woody is the inspiration of the album, although Bob was now trying to distance himself from Woody's style and be his own man.

Bob was recognised as the leader of the new protest singer brigade, a position that he never wanted, he has always hated categorisation. Of course Woody Guthrie was still alive but incapacitated, although he never seemed to bother to write more songs or even sing them into a tape recorder. David Cohen had become David Blue, Phil Ochs was protesting, Tom Paxton was mixing protest with children's songs, Tim Rose had left The Big Three and Mama Cass; Cass who was also one of the 'Big Three', joined The Mama's and Papa's. Tom Rush was moving from blues to pop, Paul Simon had been to the UK and was gaining popularity. Bonnie Dobson, Joan Baez and Judy Collins were in the vanguard of the female singers, Joni Mitchell was still in Canada, and at last Odetta was gaining fame predominantly due to Bob and Harry Belafonte's influence.

Bob continued to create the myth and soon became unhappy with the chorus line of persons expecting him to support their individual causes. The sudden celebrity did not allow Bob to adjust appropriately, nowadays he would be surrounded by spin-doctor advisers, in the early sixties most artists had to fend for themselves. There had been no claims that Bob was an intellectual, his modified history presented a man that had run away from home at the age of ten, and then joined the travelling circus at thirteen. Schooling was not part of the itinerant history that was being maintained for public consumption. One can imagine the surprise when Bob was honoured with The Tom Paine Award usually given to great peace philosophers of our time, both Bob and the ECLE delegates were amazed. To make matters worse Bob accepted the award in a drunken state and angered the affluent businessmen and their wives by seeming to take the side of Lee Harvey Oswald in the Kennedy assassination. Albert Grossman managed to take some of the abhorrence they felt out of the predicament by arranging for Bob to submit a letter of apology. In a time when careers could suddenly cease, (Jerry Lee Lewis, P.J.Proby and Bill Haley to name just three), Bob surged on as if there was no problem whatsoever, which says a great deal for Albert Grossman's management and tact.

'The Times They are A-Changin'' is the anthem for the young. If Biblical references are to be included then Revelations 1:3 states that 'the time is at hand'. Mark 10:31 says 'first will be last and last first' which is almost used in the final verse. There are many more, one of Bob's favourite prophets Jeremiah wrote 'why gaddest thou about so much to change your way'. The most apt line from the Bible comes from Matthew 'O ye hypocrites, ye can discern the face of the sky but can ye not discern the signs of the times?'. This is Bob's 'Come all ye Faithful', although Bob decided it was to be similar to 'Come All Ye Fair and Tender Maidens' which Joan Baez sang on her 'Love Songs' album. Bob had to sing this song the night President Kennedy was assassinated, so he always remembers the occasion. **'Ballad of Hollis Brown'**: The tune has been the subject of many discussions. Alan Lomax found 'The Gosport Tragedy' an English ballad from the late 18th Century to be the most probable contender, but 'Pretty Polly' and 'Mary Calvin' are two others that are similar in some patterns. Bob saw a pessimistic newspaper item, 7 shots, 7 dead, 7 new people born, in the dust bowl of South Dakota, it makes one wonder if this was a continuation of the thought processes of 7 curses. No matter how poor people are all over the world, the men still make the women pregnant, history has shown in every famine there are so many young babies born into a situation that the parents have no means to support. Hollis Brown had five children, one new born baby?! Bob sang the song for Live Aid in July 1985 yet the excess number of children in the song and in Kenya at the time was never mentioned. Hollis achieved an escape from the responsibility in death he found his true freedom from strife. The Jewish 'special' number of 7 is invoked throughout the song. As 7 die, 7 are born, and for every 7 that die, 7 more will rise up to take their place. Brown decides the only way to stop the suffering of his family is the kill them and then himself, just like Jean Paul Sartre expounded at the end of 'Les Chemins de la Liberte', the only place to find real freedom is in death. Hollis Brown with all his insurmountable problems never resorted to crime. The song has always reminded me of Bobby Darin's version of 'Everything's O.K.' from his folk album 'Earthy'. In that song the water-well has run dry, the crops have failed,

50

the family has Asian flu, but they are still living so everything's OK. In fact, he said, "If things were any better he might just lay himself down and die". Joan O'Bryant also sang of a similar situation of strife in her song 'Life is A Toil'.

'With God on Our Side': Robert Southey wrote 'laws are with us, God is on our side'. The history of an irresponsible America, The Old Testament, The God of Judaism combined with a tune taken from 'The Patriot Game' by Dominic Behan which Bob heard The Clancy Brothers and Tommy Makem singing. Behan had used the traditional song 'The Merry Month of May' as the basis for his composition. 'Patriotism is the last refuge of the Scoundrel', is used, a phrase from Dr Johnson to which Bob would return on 'Sweetheart' on the 'Infidels' album. Germans now have God on their side, but did Judas really have God on his side? All religions have their God but of course there can only be one supreme being. In an interview Bob stated that he wanted firm proof (don't we all) that there was a God, a religious experience. Of course Bob's God must have been his jewish God, the pretence that he had studied many religions at the time and was ambivalent was just part of the fantasy that was being weaved. He of course wanted to appeal to all religions so it was advantageous to be equivocal. God was on the side of the cavalry against the Red Indians, The Inquisition, The Spanish Civil War and the Allies versus the Germans yet Bob doesn't mention the Japanese that attacked Pearl Harbour bringing the USA into the Second World War. The American Civil War was fought by two sides with the same God and although the Russian Communists had no God on their side, they still became powerful. The last lines which state that if God's on our side he will stop the next war is more than a little naive, he has never bothered to stop any others or deal with any of the suffering throughout the world, why should he start now? A song full of good intentions which is qualified by Bob's realisation in the first verse that his name it means nothing, his age it means less. A powerful song nevertheless.

'One Too Many Mornings': The first lines are similar to 'Stagger Lee' with the dogs barking in the dark. A song for the end of a love affair, a final goodbye to Suze. The arguments the differences of opinion the gradual change from love to a fragile friendship. Like people in a water bed, they just drifted apart. Bob had spent some time living with Suze and her sister Carla and later with their mother making it a domestic quartet. Bob was emotionally immature but he realized that the relationship had run its course. The lyric says so much in three verses, read without the music it is one of Bob's great love poems.

'North Country Blues': The closing of the mine, the strife of the unemployed. Bob opens the blues with the troubadour's call of 'gather around and pay attention'. The song is created from the female view of the situation. The undercutting of prices by the low paid Southern labour. The miners would suffer great hardship, Bob's song sounds like a traditional song in the Guthrie style. A.L. Lloyd collected a song titled 'Minstrels of the Mine Patch' and there exists an Australian song titled 'The Miner', which I have never heard which is purported to be similar. Bob's song really does sound reminiscent of another song and I suspect the search will continue.

'Only a Pawn in Their Game' was inspired by Bob reading a newspaper article concerning racism and Medgar Evers. Bob mentions that white-trash are victims as much as are the blacks. There exists a photograph of Medgar Evers protesting for an end to the brutality in Jackson, Mississippi. In the picture not only are there two policemen in hard-hats close to Evers, but two more are lurking in the background whilst a radio station microphone is operated by an engineer attempting to eavesdrop. Evers was the chief organizer for the Mississippi area for The National Association for The Advancement of Coloured People, the word 'coloured' itself became a racist term yet it continues to be used as a gentler euphemism for 'black'. In my own African travels all the persons I met preferred to be called 'black', many detested being called 'coloured' with its South African connotation. Evers was shot dead, John F.Kennedy sent brother Bobby to the funeral and subsequently invited the remainder of the Evers family to The White House, but the racist problems only exacerbated in the southern states. Phil Ochs also wrote a song for Evers which was totally eclipsed by Bob's song, the title of Bob's song refers to the position Evers achieved with his death. The song caused a furore in the southern states, this was the civil rights song that went straight to the jugula. The premeditation of the killing is presented in the first verse, has the soldier that fired the shot ever owned up, it is irrelevant as he was only acting on the command to fire, one suspects that the sentiments of 'Who Killed Davey Moore' reverberate once more.

'Boots of Spanish Leather' is biographical. Arguably Bob's first perfect ballad and should have been sequenced after 'Restless Farewell' and 'Down the Highway' they are all relevant. The last song mentions taking her love away to Italy. On 'Boots', Suze goes to Italy but Bob changes the destination to Spain. Bob doesn't want anything brought back by Suze from Italy he just wants her home. As he realised that her love.is cooling he decides that he would like a pair of boots. Suze wore boots many years before they became fashionable. So if Bob wasn't going to get her love he might as well have something tangible as a memory, a pair of boots. Two of the verses are written from Suze's point of view, a song ideal for a Baez/Dylan duet. One wonders if Suze did bring the Spanish leather boots for him. The folk songs 'Lord Randall' and 'Scarborough Fair' provide the tune. 'When The Ship Comes In': This could be the opening lines of Revelations Chapter 7. Joan Baez said it was written in a state of pique when a hotel check-in clerk never recognised Bob but recognised her. Brecht's 'The Black Freighter' is the basic theme according to John Bauldie, the pirate Jenny's fantasy of revenge. With all the rhetoric Bob might just mean the old adage of the 'ship coming in' when good fortune strikes, as simple as that. John Bauldie also thought that Bob's 'chains of the sea' might have been taken from Dylan Thomas' poem 'Fern Hill'. To me it is possible that the complete song is Bob's interpretation of the sea-faring conceptions of the pastoral 'Fern Hill'. Your days are numbered could be Psalm 90, and Shakespeare wrote in 'Cymbeline', 'fortune brings in some boats that are not steered'. The modern day metaphors for 'Pharaoh's tribe' and 'Goliath' getting their come-up-ance is left until the end, there were plenty of travellers on Bob's ship waiting for it to come in.

'The Lonesome Death of Hattie Carroll': Bob names the guilty man, a real life murder by William Zanzinger. He was convicted and was sentenced to 6 months for manslaughter not murder. Of course eyebrows were raised, but it is unlikely that Zanzinger intended her to die. That is what the jury decided, 12 people honest and true. The situation was heightened by the racist problems of the day. Hattie Carroll was 51, it should be noted that Bob's lyric does not mention that she was black. Hattie was a barmaid who was hit by Zanzinger when she was slow in getting him a drink. Strangely he was the first white man ever charged with murdering a black woman in Maryland. The lyric is excellent and it only contains a couple of rhyming couplets. The intention was to spread the issue wider to present the different levels of life from which the protagonists had been born. Hattie had eleven children but Bob discarded one in the song. This was a very brave song, Zanzinger could have sued Bob for the inferences contained. He was charged with murder which was reduced to manslaughter due to the lack of intent to kill. The Judge set the sentence not Zanzinger, true the punishment doesn't seem to fit the crime but one needed to be present and hear all the evidence before writing of 'rich' men obtaining a lower sentence due to his position within the community. A very brave but dangerous song, Columbia remaindered the 'John Birch' song but thought that this was not likely to receive litigation, their legal department were correct in their conclusions.

'Restless Farewell': Bob claimed this was just a filler track, but with so many wonderful remaindered tracks it seems implausible. Seems like the goodbye from someone with imminent death in mind. The narrator is atoning for the mistakes that he has made and hoping that he will be thought of fondly. The Clancy Brothers with Tommy Makem sang the traditionally Irish 'The Parting Glass' and this song uses both tune and some of the lyrics. Noel Murphy sang a version and The Pogues included it on their 'Dirty Old Town' album.

Bob had written and recorded more songs which were remaindered. **'Eternal Circle'** is a clever song, a girl listening to a long song and the singer thinks that she is infatuated by him, but it is the song, when he finishes

53

singing she is gone. A singer's fantasy, but because she had gone the singer just carries on regardless. **'Paths of Victory'** uses a melody not unlike Johnny Horton's 'North to Alaska' or Billy Grammer's 'Gotta Travel On'. Jean Paul Sartre wrote 'Le Chemins de la Liberte', (Paths to Freedom), where victory in death is freedom, of course 'chemins' is almost an anagram of 'chimes'. I have never really understood this song. Bob uses 'of' rather than 'to' Victory, so Bob creates the scenario that the so called victory has already been won and that he (we) 'shall' walk it, rather than 'will walk it', however bumpy it is. The Bootleg Series out-take with Bob's pounding piano and harmonica changes a few words but the gist remains the same. **'Only a Hobo'** is a rework of Bob's 'Man in the Street' although the former mentioned an affluent man this song is for a tramp. Bob uses 'Poor Miner's Farewell' by Aunt Molly Jackson which was also plundered by Molly herself. Woody used the same tune for 'The Great Divide', this was also used for 'Let Me Die in My Footsteps' included on 'Broadside Ballads' with Bob as Blind Boy Grunt; he was told if you can't sing on the record then just 'grunt' hence the name. The version used on Bootleg Series was recorded for Columbia and is not the track recorded at The Broadside Office. The uncaring society looks at the situation for a dead hobo as one less on the streets. Cisco Houston's 'Hobo's Lullaby' mentions the trouble caused by the police and the uncaring society, if the hobo's mother was still alive she would still love him.

    'Lay Down Your Weary Tune': The song of a composer preferring to compose a melody than write a lyric. Bob has created a superb lyric which can be read as putting a problem to rest. Percy Bysshe Shelley wrote 'The world is weary of the past, oh, might it die and rest at last'. The song was released on Biograph in 1985. A well known folk melody with Bob singing solo with his guitar. **'Percy's Song'** also released on Biograph is the tale of a Judge. In this song the Judge gives a 99 year sentence for manslaughter caused by a car accident. The Judge refused to accept character witnesses. Don't blame the judge blame the law. Bob probably wrote this to makes William Zanzinger's sentence appear inadequate. Bob has used an idea from a civil war song called 'Hyram Hubbard', a song that he had learned from folk singer Paul Clayton. The song is written from Percy's point of view. 'Hyram' was also used for the traditional song 'The Wind and The Rain' which Bob sang in his early days as 'Two Sisters'. **'Guess I'm Doing Fine'** is another hardship song, 'we are still living so everything's alright'. Bob presented a similar scenario with 'Hollis Brown'. This is the song of a troubadour reflecting that although he has no friends he still has his voice and his wanderlust.

    'Seven Curses' is a crooked Judge song, for the pardon of the man the judge desires his daughter's body, she agrees the judge uses her, he then hangs the father and the girl curses the judge seven times. It was pointed out to me that the song is similar to Shakespeare's 'Measure for Measure' and of course

I kicked myself for not realising it earlier. John Bauldie also points out the fact in his Bootleg Series notes. The song is almost exactly the Shakespeare play; let me explain. In Measure for Measure, The Duke of Vienna takes a holiday leaving the righteous Angelo in control. Angelo is expected to bring in laws that The Duke's lenient rule has failed to address. The tale has already shown how easy it is the evade responsibility in political life. Angelo imprisons a man (Claudio) for getting a young woman pregnant and then sentences him to death. Claudio's sister Isabella implores Angelo for mercy, she is soon to take holy orders. Angelo refuses but then becomes aroused with lust after her offers to do anything to get Claudio free. Angelo offers to pardon Claudio if she will give him her body. The Duke returns pretending to be a friar to observe Angelo. Claudio asks Isabella to sleep with Angelo to save his life. Isabella arranges for Angelo's previous lover Mariana to disguise herself and take Isabella's place, which she does willingly. After the liaison has been achieved and thinking that he has been with Isabella Angelo callously orders to execution to continue. Unlike Bob's song 'Measure for Measure' does have a happy ending, believe it or not it is known as a comedy, which you will have to see for yourself, but the resemblance is close enough to be one and the same idea. Shakespeare's play was written between 1604 and 1623. The late John Bauldie discovered (confirmed by Judy Collins) that the song was also based on Neil Roth and Lydia Wood's 'Anathea', which in turn harks back to Shakespeare. Matthew Zuckermann took the idea one step further (in Isis), finding 'Anna Feher' an old Hungarian song which was translated by folk historian Bert (A.L) Lloyd. As Hungarian is one of the most difficult languages on Earth to learn this was some achievement.

'Hero Blues': Bob stated that women ruled the world, women who are a power at home yearn for strong powerful men, like film stars and story book heroes. Most men just want a quiet life leaving the film stars to pretend that they are bold and brave, most of them are wimps in real life.

'Moonshine Blues' is a traditional song which became known as 'Moonshiner'. This wonderful track that was ultimately released on The Bootleg Series was recorded as a traditional song filler at the end of a CBS session, then given to Bob's publishers as a registration tape. Bob rarely sang like he does on this song, it beggars belief that it took almost 30 years to obtain an official release. For many this was the highlight of The Bootleg Series release. A modern ballet company choreographed the song for a dance sequence on a BBC-2 show in 1992, sadly I don't have any further information on that performance. Bessie Smith included a version of 'Moonshine Blues' on her Complete Collection Volume 2.

'East Laredo Blues' was recorded in Columbia Studios in October 1963 as the track following ' The Times They Are A-Changin', it seems that 'East Laredo Blues' is a Bob Dylan composition still awaiting a release. 'Suze (The

Cough) Song', how can this be deemed an instrumental when a cough is created vocally, it is mooted that this is the first Bob Dylan instrumental, preceding 'Nashville Skyline Rag' released in 1969 and 'Wigwam' and 'Woogie Boogie' on 'Self Portrait'. **'Farewell'** the tale of a man off to Mexico or California alone. Based on Bob hearing Louis Killen's version of 'The Leaving of Liverpool', although Martin Carthy also played it for Bob, and Nigel Denver was regularly singing it at the time. Of course with the benefit of hindsight, Bob did eventually go to Mexico where he started the 'leaving and the grieving' when wife Sara missed and yearned for the city life.

'Advice For Geraldine on her Miscellaneous Birthday': This short prose piece was included in the 'Writings and Drawings' book. This is Bob's 'Desiderata', go placidly and take notice of my teachings. Written in low case letters it is a series of short statements, I expected one to say 'keep a good head and always carry a light bulb' which he said in 1965, yes he was carrying a light bulb. Geraldine is not mentioned in the piece and it could be anyone. The thought that this was based on 'Christabel' by Samuel Taylor Coleridge which includes a Geraldine is nonsense. True Geraldine appears as a weary lady taking advice from Christabel but that is where the similarity ends. Comparing the two is as incongruous as comparing 'When The Ship Comes In' with Coleridge's 'The Ancient Mariner'.

I have kept this long vituperation for last because it is more important than it seems at any first reading. **'11 Outlined Epitaphs'** tells us a great deal about the state of Bob's mind at the time. The Epitaphs are not numbered but have a segregating line drawn under each. The narrator lives within his own head with his eyes shut. It is evident that something spectacular brought him to his senses. A 'shot' is mentioned which may be the bullet that killed John F. Kennedy. The ideology has become clear, just like all men that refuse to enter into conversation, he will be considered crazy, but he will not notice if he keeps his eyes closed, head buried in the sand, 'eyes wide shut'. Epitaph **No 2** is more biographical and clear. Bob mentions his parents and the Iron mine. I don't understand how 'North' Hibbing can be in such disrepair when it is such a small town, perhaps that is where most of the miners lived. Hibbing left Bob with his legacy of memories. **No 3** has Bob wishing that he was around in the 1930s, when everything was cheaper. Bob is only interested with the romanticised version of those terrible hard times. Bob uses Francois Villon's 'but where are the snows of yester-year?' and changes the snow to 'forces'. Bob also paraphrases Psalm 23 at the conclusion, making him drink muddy waters. The bells of Rhymney are transported to New York, San Juan, Los Angeles and Toronto. Bob also presents us with his realisation that dreaming of the past is just procrastination, he can no longer walk with ghosts, he has to grit his teeth and move on. **No 4** has Bob turning his pen towards politics. James Forman or Jim Crow is the Jim mentioned. The narrator is reneging against learning what 'they' want him to learn. He also has damaged feelings and is searching for the politics of the escape from the 'fiery cross burners'; the rusty nails of crucifixion and hope end the piece. No 5: The 'Al' mentioned is Al Aronowitz although one would suspect that dear old Alan J. Weberman would naturally assume it was him. Al Aronowitz was an agent a go-between he introduced people to each other for their mutual advantage, I am not sure if he was paid for it or if it was altruism on his behalf. Al's wife Anne seems to have interviewed Bob at her home. She questions Bob about his depressing songs. Lenny Bruce's statement that 'there are no dirty words just dirty minds', was nonsense when he said it and it still is. Bob re-using it doesn't make it true. No 6: Is for Woody Guthrie and Bob's realisation that he is just a man like all other men. At least Bob wasn't too disappointed by his meeting with Woody Guthrie, Bob was soon to suffer from fan idolatry which continues to the present day. No 7: This is a cry from the heart for America to take care of their own rather than worry about the Russians. The Hitler and Robert E.Lee comparison would not be for all Americans. The 'birch coloured knights' is possibly for John Birch, the lower case 'b' makes it confusing. Rats and vermin are prevalent in this epitaph, perhaps they needed a pied piper with a guitar rather than a flute. No 8: Bob is answering the plagiarism lobby. If it rhymes it rhymes if it don't it don't. Bob is like all other composers they take a little section, then change it make it their own. Bob writes 'All songs lead back to the sea'. When Frank Zappa was interviewed he was asked how did he think that one country's songs were suddenly found in another. Frank smiled and whispered "sailors". Bob may have been anticipating the necessity to defend his use of traditional themes in Court as he mentions 'prosecuting attorneys'. No 9: This had much wider implications. It was true that Toby Thompson had travelled to Hibbing for Village Voice and US Magazine but earlier Andrea Svedburg had caused problems from which all writers have suffered the subsequent shock waves. Working for Newsweek she had located Bob's parents and disclosed that Bob's secondary character was in fact a myth and that Bob was a home loving son who only left the jewish home a few years earlier. Bob was so angry that his parents had been drawn into the plot that he has been difficult in magazine interviews ever since. Bob pours his scorn on magazines and journalists alike, all due to the one interference, the pot was blackened forever by the one indiscretion. When Bob sang at The Carnegie Hall in October 1963 his proud parents were in the audience where any loving parents would wish to be, to see their successful son. One wonders why Svedburg thought that this was a matter so important that it was necessary to embarrass Bob and his parents with the disclosure, surely she realised the hurt she would cause. Bob's proclamation, his commandment was, "I shall not co-operate!'. (If Andrea is in fact a man then reverse the gender of the above passage). No 10: A strange turn-a-bout after the bile of the previous piece. One assumes that Sue is Suze and Eric, Eric Von Schmidt. I am reliably informed that Geno is Geno Foreman and of course Dave and Terri would be the Van Ronks. No 11: The times they change and he is being guided. We are then given a list of influences including Villon, Bertold Brecht, Brendan Behan, A.L.Lloyd and Paul Clayton. There are many others and Johnny Cash is sandwiched between William Blake and Pete Seeger. People laugh and cry in the same tongue, songs are all on loan. In the UK the film that included Charles Aznavour was 'Shoot the Pianist' (France/1960), a name on Bobs list within this epitaph. The film was written and Directed by Francois Truffaut, and concerned a bar-room pianist that became involved with gangsters and sees his girl friend killed. Later Elton John would plead 'Don't Shoot the Piano Player', the Truffaut film might have been called 'Shoot the Piano Player' in the USA.

When I was reading Oliver Goldsmith's 'The Deserted Village' I was reminded of '11 Outlined Epitaphs by his lines...

> While the words of learned strength, and thund'ring sound
> Amazed the gazing rustics ranged around,
> And still they gazed, and their wonder grew,
> That one small head could carry all he knew.

It explains exactly how I felt after reading Bob's Epitaphs. Bob's throw-away style appears casual but the Epitaphs are so much more than that, they are the work of genius.

BOB GOES SOFT

God is always on the side of big squadrons
and against little ones.
Comte de Bussy Rabutin 1618-1693

Bob decided that his previous album was designed and created to be seen and heard, to be noticed. It was true that there was no other singer songwriter capable of writing such wonderful lyrics, it seems that Bob was surprised as anyone by his own ability. He was making statements such as 'going back within myself to write songs as if I was ten years old', of course absolute balderdash but it kept the newspaper journalists happy. Bob continued, "The way I like to write is for it to come out the way I walk and talk, I write poetry, poetry can make its own form". All excellent rhetoric but so who creates the poetry in the first place, it seems that Bob thought that the words were floating around in the atmosphere awaiting to be caught in a butterfly net and placed on the page. Whatever the truth Bob decided to dispense with his finger-pointing and present to us another side of his abilities.

Tom Wilson remained in the producer's seat for the next recording and in June 1964 Bob was back in the studio. Bob was now writing precisely for the album and only Mr Tambourine Man' was held over, and then re-recorded, whilst 'Denise', 'If You Gotta Go' 'Mama You Been on My Mind' and 'Playboys and Playgirls were registered with demonstration recordings but not recorded in the studio.

Bob was now wanted for his celebrity, people were making extra demands on his time. He was already tired of supporting so many causes and he was becoming disenchanted with New York. Albert Grossman lived in Woodstock a quiet area within easy reach on the city and Bob spent an increasing amount of time living there. Bob was also feeling that he had lost touch with the ordinary person, sadly this is inevitable for all famous persons. The old friends do not have the financial power to pay their way and thus feel as though they are sponging and ultimately move away. However the affluence does attract professional spongers who have no scruples; God bless the child that's got his own, Billie Holiday knew the truth.

Bob was friendly with Ramblin' Jack Elliott and went into the studio and added harmonica to his version of 'Will The Circle Be Unbroken' for his eponymously titled album, Bob used the pseudonym of Tedham Porterhouse. Bob also added harmonica and backing vocals on the album for (and titled) 'Dick Farina and Eric Von Schmidt' as Blind Boy Grunt.

Albert Grossman had appointed Bob his own personal road manager in Victor Maimudes, with a couple of friends in tow Bob completed the quartet and took a few days off travelling around, getting drunk most of the time.

According to Andy Gill they carried some used clothing to give to the needy striking miners in Kentucky. They arrived in New Orleans and naively tried to mix with black community but of course the police would move them on to avoid trouble with other whites. The segregationalism was a thing to be changed, but it needed to be done gradually. Many of the black clubs did not want white people in them, it is naive to assume that the black people just wanted to be welcomed into the white areas. When out-of-towners and their entourage in their road travels decided that they would make a stand for civil rights in a black area they just made problems for the indigenous population, it is easy for the itinerant inter-lopers they can just move on after they have caused the problems. So after mixing with black performers at the Mardi Gras, sharing bottles with black men and being thrown out of an blacks-only club the quartet moved on to (according to Andy Gill) Dallas and Colorado.

Bob was performing at some of the stops along the way, the whole trip was part of a promotion tour for the new album. One of the quartet dropped out because he couldn't keep up with his crazy cohorts and he was replaced by Bob Neuwirth; Edie Sedgwick always referred to him as Neuwirther. When Bob returned to New York after visiting Joan Baez, Suze Rotolo had moved out. Bob was still writing his new songs, Albert Grossman got Bob a gig at The Royal Festival Hall in London and then went on holiday in Europe.

So the new songs were to be written from 'within him, from the inside', there is no doubt that there was no drop in quality, Bob's muse was again on great form. If the recording details are to be believed then Bob recorded 14 different songs, 47 takes in total, between 7pm and 10pm on June 9th 1964, he was certainly learning his craft.

The 'ANOTHER SIDE OF BOB DYLAN' album was released in the autumn of 1964 and reached No 43 in the USA and No 8 in the UK. The cover was a Sandy Speiser black and white photograph, Bob with his arm resting on his raised left leg, he is now presenting a street-wise image. It was taken at the entrance to The Columbia Offices, 7th Avenue, New York. The photograph was originally in colour proven by the picture in the Bootleg Series booklet. Bob wasn't happy with the album title, but it was Tom Wilson's idea and he was in control, 'Another two sides' would have been more accurate. Bob agreed years later that the title never did the album any harm, he just thought at the time it was over stating the obvious.

'All I Really Want To Do': Influenced by Jimmie 'brakeman' Rodgers' yodelling songs. It seemed as though the previously protesting and finger-pointing Bob, now just wants to be friends with us. The song was assumed to be another written for Suze but it could be for Joan Baez. A naive lover trying to make sense of a complicated woman. If this song was written as a poem and sent to a lover nowadays then it would be taken immediately to the police. Although the writer is saying that he doesn't want to do the things mentioned it would certainly be deemed the words of an unstable individual. He doesn't want to 'beat or mistreat, knock her or lock her up', he sounds damaged but many love affairs end with neither participant speaking to the other, love turns to hate so often. Of course this was recorded by The Byrds as their follow-up to their 'Mr Tambourine Man' No 1 hit. It seems that in retrospect that 'All I Really Want to Do' by The Byrds was a smash hit it wasn't it only achieved No 40 in the USA and lasted just one week on the Top 50 charts, in less inconsistent Britain it reached No 4. **'Black Crow Blues'**: Bob played piano on one of the out-takes of 'The Times They are A-Changin', but this is probably the first time on a released official record. Song to a long lost lover might be Echo but could be for anyone. Bob is playing competent stride piano, there were photographs of Bob playing piano with his harmonica frame around his neck so he probably played both here rather than any over-dubbing. There are similarities to 'James Alley Blues', but the 'sometimes I'm thinking' line could be extracted from many other blues songs.

'Spanish Harlem Incident': The penultimate lines of 'I got to know babe' are sung different to the music books, changed after the song was registered, so the original performance would have been different. Bob sings 'I'm nearly drowning, where you surround me'. Bob sings of Ben E.King's 'Rose' perhaps a gypsy Rose down in 'Spanish Harlem'. Who is the intellectual woman of the song, was she just a ship that passed in the night, or one who never docked at all? There is so much sexual innuendo in the lyric that I agree with Dylanologist Dave Thomas that various sexual acts could be indicated. She may have started by reading his palm but he seems to move on from there to be engulfed by her charms. I don't think that the modified lyric adds anything to the original but the Gypsy Gal is certainly hot stuff. **'Chimes of Freedom'** is supposed to be influenced by Arthur Rimbaud's 'Sonnet of the Vowels'. To that I answer, where? Of course there can be many variations in translation from the French, even Rimbaud's 'Vowels' closes with 'rayon violet de Ses Yeux' which is usually translated to 'the violet ray of her eyes' but 'Ses Yeux' is so ambiguous they could be the eyes of a man or woman, a human being or God, so the translator can select his own ideal. 'Chimes' was undoubtedly the greatest 'poem' that Bob had written to date. One could take each verse and dissect the brilliance of his eloquent rhetoric. This is Bob in his hectoring mood, one just has to listen and try to make sense of his proclamations. I was totally lost in admiration, I still am. This was apparently written on the road trip that also produced 'Mr Tambourine Man'. Bob may of course have read and been influenced by 'Freedom Road' a book by Howard Fast. Fast had written 'Citizen Tom Paine' about the revolutionary pamphleteer, a man that Bob mentions in another song. John Addington Symonds (1840-1893) wrote 'With the flame of freedom in their souls, and the light of knowledge in their eyes'. William Wordsworth wrote in 'The Prelude',

61

'they present themselves as objects recognised, in flashes, and with glory not their own'. The debate continues and probably will never cease.

'**I Shall Be Free No 10**': Failed Presidential candidate Barry Goldwater and champion boxer Cassius Clay are the two named characters in this song. Bob uses mockery contempt and disdain plus a little derision to present his case. Bob enjoys playing with numbers and rhymes, Cassius did likewise to forecast the endings of his fights. The narrator insists that he is liberal and thus favours reform and individual freedom, yet Barry Goldwater was far too liberal for his tastes. The narrator knows someone that wants to kill him, was not allowed to play tennis due to his apparel, set his monkey on the dog and he killed the cat. The whole lyric is an anachronism created to obfuscate and confuse. In the last verse Bob address us, he is aware that we are now totally perplexed, he has something that he learned in England. There is one good point 'he was knocked down and wound-up with the Dean of Women', indeed!

'**To Ramona**': The realisation that love has died. The acknowledgement that the narrator is the partner that has suffered the hurt, although we only learn that with the last line. This is lyric for a lover that is not showing the self-pity prevalent in Bob's earlier songs. The basic theme reminds me of novelist D. H. Lawrence's 'To Women' where he writes as his last lines ' If you want either of us to feel anything at all, you'd better abandon all idea of feelings altogether'. 'To Ramona' was recorded by Alan Price for his 'Price on His Head' album, it is possibly the definitive recording of the song. '**Motorpsycho Nitemare**': This returns us to W.S.Gilbert and his 'Lord Chancellor's Nightmare' taken from the operetta 'Iolanthe'. Bob's song is a reworking of the old joke about the farmer and his daughter named Rita, not forgetting the travelling salesman. Although many writers insisted on delving into the deep lyrics it is just Bob having a good laugh, probably heard the joke for the first time on his road trip. Bob has changed it so that the narrator is chased off for being a communist, I wonder what Rita can do with her fingers and lips, if you don't know the joke then you will never know. Echo Helstrom told Toby Thompson that she thought that this song was based on an incident in Hibbing. Bob and his friend had to jump out of a window at Echo's house because her father came home unexpectedly. The scene portrayed in the lyric is what might have happened if Bob had been caught by Mr Helstrom.

'**My Back Pages**': This is the track where the man-in-him realises who the other Bob Dylan was, he was older then he is much younger now. He is coming to terms with himself, it happens to most of us, we are all older when we think we know it all, the earlier that the realisation arrives, the better for that person and for all those that act as pinball buffers for the polished ego of the man in control of the ball-return flippers. Bob even went on to claim that he had written the earlier songs in the knowledge that they would sell, he knew what people wanted, 'his ideas'. This claim actually reverts Bob back down the 'snake' to an earlier square. He had only released three albums surely he didn't expect us to think that it was planned so precisely, if so then why was the first album predominantly covers of old material? He would later claim having a lack of ambition and just a desire to write. The ambivalences created by these two or now three Bob Dylans seems to have clouded Bob's knowledge of what is the truth and what is mythological hyperbole. Of course we all know the liars who repeat their tales so often eventually believe them to be fact, it is not just restricted to celebrities it happens in all walks of life. John Lennon was once asked why he thought the Beatles were so incredibly popular his answer was that if he knew that he would give up singing and become a manager. Bob by his remarks also presents the circumstance that he had done it all alone, the massive promotional and distribution team at Columbia Records might just have done a little to help, they put up all the finance remember. Bob Dylan was an investment like all other investments. Robert Shelton and John Hammond may have been altruistic in their approach, but they were both employees expected to provide a profit by their work, so now that also applied to Bob Dylan. But back to the song. Bob's realisation that he was so shrewd may mean that he was brazen in his strategy towards other people, or is he aware that he was once impudent and rude. We remember Bob throwing Phil Ochs out of his car for having the temerity to criticise. Bob indicates that he thought it was 'All for one, one for all' and 'equality' as were the romantic ideals of Three Musketeers, yet he proceeded towards confusion and mutiny. The narrative of the song can be argued ad infinitum but Bob was seemingly so honest in his so called 'protestation finger pointing songs' one wonders why he should create vacillations by now saying that they were not from the heart but created to sell albums and gain celebrity. Bob confronts his many ghosts in this song and emerges unscathed at the end, perhaps that was also part of his great master plan. With all this said the lyric remains superb with that celebrated line completing every verse.

   'I Don't Believe You'(She Acts Like We Never Have Met): The inability to understand the short memory of lovers the day after a close liaison, the one-night-stand. Excess inebriation can be blamed or of course the reason is often embarrassment coupled with self-preservation. I was in a situation once where we had picked-up amongst other women for a party, a mother and daughter on holiday. Both mother and daughter slept in separate rooms with a man they had only met at the party. In the morning they met in the hallway and I observed them both pretending that they couldn't remember the happenings of the previous night and hoping that the other would believe their individual smoke-screens. I knew that one was lying as the mother had spent the night with me and very nice she was too. In Bob's song this of course could be Suze or Joan or another, or just plain imagination, the point comes across to anyone who has experienced a one-night-stand and hoped that it would grow into a more fulfilling arrangement.

'Ballad in Plain D': Suze would later state that this song concerned the final act in the relationship between her and Bob. It does seem that Bob was subject to sulking and non-talking sessions an occurrence that ruins so many relationships. Bob also had many arguments with Carla Rotolo, Suze's sister, it seems that she always stood up to Bob especially on behalf of Suze. At a time when Bob would be meeting so many sycophants who agreed with almost everything he said, and laughed at his every joke, Carla would debate on behalf of her sister and good sense. This song arose out of the ashes of the relationship, perhaps it was Bob's attempt to redress the balance in his favour yet it presents cynicism and sarcasm probably the two attributes that Bob most detests in himself. I am assured that Bob regretted writing the song, an imbroglio of feelings. I could not locate a recording date either so it is probable that this was another Witmark registration recording which was included at the last moment. If the album had been delayed then it seems likely that Bob would have remaindered the track. The euphemisms are hardly obscuring. Carla's concern was misconstrued as interference, 'strings of guilt', an age old problem known to all worrying parents. Carla is called a parasite, but didn't Bob rely on her to get unusual songs from Alan Lomax, didn't she introduce him to the work of Bertold Brecht? The lyric is so personal one feels like an eavesdropper. The last four verses which show Bob as a man unable to apologise, a man in tears, a man in love, a man alone, are inspired by his dislike of Carla's intrusion, these verses are as powerful as Paul Verlaine's 'Colloque Sentimental' (Sentimental Dialogue). Verlaine was weeping, trying to forget, he continues until he realises (like Bob) that 'grief without betrayal is grief without cause'. In an interview for Isis Magazine Martin Carthy said that this was Bob's one 'truly rotten song', Bob Dylan agrees, many people agree. I do agree strongly with Bob's last thought that it is pointless being free if you would prefer to be in prison.

'It Ain't Me Babe': Recorded by The Turtles for The White Whale Label and taken up the charts to No 8 in August 1965 at the same time that Bob's 'Like A Rolling Stone' was creeping towards No 2. It has always been a popular song but the lyrics say so much more than are apparent from a cursory listen. A natural sequence from the previous track, more cynicism, more misanthropy, this is the hurt lover trying to pretend that he is fire-proof, and is not his fault. The opening lines of each verse are extremely clever. What is it that goes from the window at its chosen speed, lands on the ledge, floats to the ground and disappears into the night. It might be a love letter discarded into the breeze to float away and melt into the night. It could be anything light that would catch the wind. I would suspect that Bob created the song in six line sets and split them in pairs, two for each verse in order, of course the last two lines of each verse are identical. The lyric is also worth reading as a reverse statement, if what had gone before in Bob's lyrics was true then he was really saying 'It is me, babe'. Sadly she didn't want him back, Suze had finally had enough. Of course it is much more difficult for the macho-man to accept that she doesn't want him, but in Bob's situation he had run, on the rebound, to the welcoming arms of Joan Baez.

'**Some Other Kinds of Things**': Poems by Bob Dylan the 'Writings' book announced, these poems were featured on the rear of the 'Another Side Of' album cover. Although only five appeared on the cover a further six were added to 'Writings and Drawings' in 1973. Perhaps Bob liked writing poems in elevens? The first 'Other Kind' is for 'Baby Black' and her lifestyle, she would do anything for $1, her father a drunk, sells her body. No 2, is for French singer Francoise Hardy and the scenes of Paris the city for young lovers. No 3: This is sectioned into four sub-sections. The first is for a game of chess where one participant is endeavouring to put some 'edge' into the game by inciting the other player to win or be termed the worst player around. The second part is for Juno who takes pills to help his art and the housewife who takes pills from the drugstore. Senator Goldwater returns, Adolf Eichmann dies, Bob compares the morals of Israel, East Germany, all are just observations. The final section is a table tennis match with Henry Miller followed by an interview with a woman that asks questions that Bob has no intention of answering. The final section concerns 'crawling'. The entrepreneurs need to make a profit at any cost, christianity has become a money making industry, it is poles apart from what Jesus intended. No 4: In 1965, Ben Carruthers and The Deep released a single of 'Jack O'Diamonds (b-side 'Right Behind You'), featuring the guitaring of Jimmy Page. Ben Carruthers had been in France and East Germany with Bob and that visit is mentioned in the poems. The Fairport Convention also recorded 'Jack O'Diamonds. A Jack Of Diamonds on the playing card has just one arm and one eye, he is a one eyed knave. Bob also mentions that Dean Martin should apologise to The Rolling Stones, if you saw Dean's introduction for the band when they were on his show then you will know why. The folk song 'Jack O'Diamonds' (Registered to Alan and John Lomax) was recorded by Odetta and Lonnie Donegan, we learned in that song that the 'Jack' is a hard card to fight. Bob agrees that it is a hard card to play. No 5: Joshua has gone to fight his battle without the narrator. A song 'Go Joshua Go', which uses this poem was recorded by Fairport Convention. A man is threatening to jump from The Brooklyn Bridge and although the police and the people are urging him not to jump the narrator realises that he really wants to see him jump. He leaves the scene but wants to know if he jumped, that thought percolates through the remaining poems. The couple who concentrate on changes to their home to keep them together remind me of Mickey Newbury's great song 'Lovers', where he writes that 'they tore down a wall for a door, but now they don't speak any more'. There was a thought that the 'doors' that required enlarging in the poem allude to Aldous Huxley's 'Doors of Perception' which of course could be correct. A group is mentioned that are searching for something to keep them as friends. Fault and blame, answers and truth segue into a scene where he plays his guitar to get a little Greek lady to dance. Finally Joshua is urged to fight his battle alone this time. Odetta's version of the traditional 'Jack O'Diamonds' and 'Joshua' both appear on her 'Ballads and Blues' album. **No 6:** It was revealed, but not proven, that Enzo the subject of this poem met Suze in Italy, so this short poem is Bob's way of dealing with his feelings of jealousy. **No 7:** Charlie slept on a cherub's face. **No 8 :** A tall girl hitchhiker and some spontaneous prose conversation on a trip to Amarillo. **No 9:** The story of a vicious and nasty little lad called Johnny. His parents dote on him and forgive him all his delinquency. He failed school, couldn't get into college. As a prize his parents gave him a car which he crashed. It seems that he is fitted with metal prongs to hold him together and they pierce the pillows, poor Johnny. Of course the parents suffer as much if not more than their errant children, it is so difficult to switch off parental love. **No 10:** Just like Graham Greene's, 'Monsignor Quixote', this poem is a discourse between a pessimist and an idealist. The idealist is one of the 'Hollow Men' straight from the poem of the same name by T.S.Eliot. Bob writes that there is 'blood on the steps'. The resulting moral is that nothing is perfect and there are no politics, confused, so am I. **No 11:** This is a message for Andy Warhol, fair Blondy, Cinderella. The starving actresses would be the ever thin Edie Sedgwick and possibly Nico, two more blondes. A blonde on each arm, blonde on blonde, all is lost. T.S. Eliot's 'The Waste Land' has been compared to these eleven poems. 'The Waste Land' itself has been subjected to line by line analysis over the years and there are slight similarities. Both have a chess game and also mention death by water, which would end the life of the man on Brooklyn Bridge. Eliot mentions playing cards from the Tarot Pack and he mentions crowds of people on London Bridge. A full and thorough investigation should be undertaken by a caring Dylanologist.

'Denise': A song with the same title had been a No 10 hit for New York group Randy and the Rainbows in July 1963, it also starts with the name mentioned twice. Bob's song is for a woman that doesn't respond to his advances. The last line is Bob up to his new tricks. By now he had realised that everything that he wrote would be analyzed. The last line turns the rest of the lyric on its head, is he Denise, is he a transvestite. He looks in her eyes and all he can see is himself, perhaps he has his eyes closed, perhaps he is talking to himself trying to deal with this quirk in his nature, perhaps this, perhaps that. **'If You Gotta Go, Go Now':** This is such a great song, one wonders why Bob discarded it. The album would have been improved by its inclusion. The Fairport Convention did their version as 'Si Tu Dois Partir' and just missed the top 20 in 1969. Manfred Mann took the song to No 2 in the UK in September 1965. The song presents the nature of a man who would like a girl to stay the might but would not stop her if she wanted to leave, we never learn if she stayed or went. **'Mama, You Been On My Mind'**: This was recorded with slightly different lyrics than on the original registration sheet, the song was purported to have changed in the studio yet only one take was made in June 1964 and that track was released on The Bootleg Series. The sentiments and the overall feelings of the song resemble Joe Callicott's Blues, 'You Don't Know My Mind' where he is laughing just to keep from crying, he sings, 'I don't want to hang around the house no more, Babe you don't know my mind'. The tune is as for 'Don't Think Twice'. **'Playboys and Playgirls'** is another song for the rich and powerful people that play with the lives of the less fortunate. Racism, war mongers and lynch mobs are mentioned as are the people that sell 'fallout shelters'.

At this time Bob was introduced to the lovely Sara Lowndes (Lownes) a friend of Sally Grossman, Albert's wife. Bob was living with Joan Baez, and was also friendly with sister Mimi and her husband Richard Farina, a good songwriter himself. Bob continued to spend hours at his typewriter writing down ideas for songs. The pages inside the front and rear covers of the 1973 book 'Writings and Drawings of Bob Dylan' show his typing and the many alterations. Bob also played on a The Blues Project album, not the Al Kooper -Steve Katz group but an album with other folkie friends such as Dave Van Ronk and Eric Von Schmidt. This time to avoid problems with CBS Bob made an anagram of his surname to 'Landy'. The backing group used for the recordings did include Al Kooper, Steve Katz and Danny Kalb who would eventually use the album's title for the name of their own group.

Bob was now infatuated by the beautiful ex-Playboy Bunny Sara Lowndes and didn't want Joan Baez to travel to Europe for the 'Don't Talk Back' tour, but he didn't know how to tell her so she went with him. Sara was a divorcee and had a daughter Maria from her marriage to Playboy Club Director Victor Lowndes. It was alleged whilst in England on this tour that Bob also had a short liaison with British raunchy singing star Dana Gillespie. Joan Baez eventually realised that the relationship with Bob was cooling and it was soon over. Bob Neuwirth and Bob made fun of Joan in scenes in the final version of the film 'Don't Look Back', for a man who couldn't tell her it was over the scenes were extremely unconsidered and hurtful. Joan didn't seem to notice, no wonder they say love is blind. She would speak to Bob for many years in her songs, she continued with her obsession with the man, she considered that many of Bob's songs were for her when they were more suitable for Sara or other women. On the subject of Bob Neuwirth, there was an early photograph showing him in a patterned suit (pyjamas?) holding a child's cycle. The picture shows four of his paintings. Although he was probably influenced by Picasso the paintings are excellent, I have always wondered why Bob has never included any of Neuwirth's work on his album sleeves, they were close friends for years, and some of Bob's album covers needed some good artwork. Bob was expecting the 'Another Side' album to be panned by the critics they were of course lying in wait to knock him down, but the album grew in stature with repeated plays and remains a marvellous album. Bob went on tour in the UK during April 1965 and the tour was documented on film by D.A Pennebaker for the film 'Don't Look Back' but the editing would be a source of continual changes before a final film was available for release. D.A.Pennebaker wanted the film to be comparable in style to Robert Flaherty's great eskimo adventure 'Nanook of The North'. Flaherty never bothered with much narration he allowed the film to tell the story of the tough life of an Eskimo. Pennebaker wanted a warts 'n' all depiction of the life of a pop star, to be fair it does achieve that in some sequences. Watching the film recently one notices that Bob only looks into the camera once, that is when they throw the hotel man out of the room. Bob had little to do with the film after the release because he never got paid, he said he would have liked the film a whole lot more if he had been paid for it. D.A.Pennebaker financed the film to the sum of $100,000, Albert Grossman never invested. Although Bob was already extremely popular in the UK 'The Times They Are A-Changin' was released in the UK as his first single. The tour played to sold-out concerts everywhere culminating with a superb show at London's Royal Albert Hall in May 1965. The tour had opened in Sheffield in April with The Band. The single moved to No 7 in the singles charts and the album reached to No 4. The 'Freewheelin' album had made No 1, 'Times they are A-Changin' No 4 and 'Another Side of' No 8, the first album then moved up to No 13 at the time of the tour, all the above happened within 12 months. In the USA 'Subterranean Homesick Blues' was released as a single and got to No 39, it meant that he was on the singles charts when he returned home and would maintain the career impetus. Bob's new album was also ready for release and it raced to No 1 in the UK still within the 12 month period of all the other successful chart placings. 'Bringing It All Back Home' was No 1 in May 1965, it would be June 1985 before an official sanctioned Bob Dylan new album didn't make it into the top ten album charts, with 'Empire Burlesque'.

Tom Wilson had spent some time adding different backing tracks to some of Bob's earlier recordings, Wilson added folk-rock backing tracks. There was some misunderstanding when many years later as part of a CD-ROM release 'House of the Rising Sun' suddenly appeared with an electric backing dated at 1962, it was one of the tracks that Tom Wilson had enhanced. 'Rocks and Gravel', 'Mixed Up Confusion' and the Lonnie Johnson influenced 'Corrina Corrina' were the other changed tracks. **'Mixed-Up Confusion'** was released on Biograph, mentioned earlier. The song is a hectic cowboy-rocker where Bob realises it is difficult to please all the people. His head is mixed up, he is full of questions awaiting answers. It is believed to be Dick Wellstood on piano and Herb Lovelle on drums.

An album 'Bob Dylan in Concert' was prepared but not released. The Carnegie Hall and New York Town Hall concerts were to be spliced together to form one show. The cover was created showing Bob on stage alone with his high stool behind with some notes on it. The title of the album was written in a crescent above Bob with the Columbia box and number CL2302, at the top left; 'stereo' was written at the top centre.

The tracks for the **'BRINGING IT ALL BACK HOME'** album were recorded over two days, January 14 and 15th 1965. Bob said that his old songs were one dimensional but these songs were more three dimensional, more symbolistic, written on more than one level. The band went un-credited and John Hammond Jr actually claimed belatedly that he never played on the three sessions recorded over the two days. His pay chit was later found to jog his memory but none of the six tracks on which he played guitar found their way to the finished product; John Sebastian was also on those sessions with Hammond. The musicians were Robert Gregg-drums, Joseph Macho-bass, William E.Lee-bass, Bruce Langhorne-guitar, Al Gorgoni-guitar, Kenny Rankin-guitar and Paul Griffin-piano on first session, Frank Owens on third. Five tracks were taken from session one, and six from session three. 'If You Gotta Go' was later over-dubbed by Tom Wilson in May but was only released on The Bootleg Sessions in 1991.

The 'Bringing It All' cover came in for an in-depth study and a search for positive influences. Bob had placed ephemera in strategic positions to create that exact response from critics and fans. Sally Grossman cigarette in hand is reclining on a sofa in the background. The Lyndon Johnson issue of 'Time Magazine', albums by Ravi Shankar (India's Master Musician), Lotte Lenya (In Berlin), Robert Johnson (King of Delta Blues Singers), The Impressions (Keep on Pushing) and Eric Von Schmidt (The Folk Blues Of) are on the table, on the mantlepiece is the album by raconteur (The Best of) Lord Buckley and the Bob Dylan 'clown portrait' made for Bernard Paturel. There is a fallout shelter sign and Bob is reading a magazine that has a Jean Harlow film or show advert on the rear page, visible behind Sally is Bob's previous album sleeve. The other black and white covered magazine is a rare copy of Gnaoua Magazine, rare because only one issue was printed. This becomes more confusing to any person that owns the first edition. It is dark pink with black printing, the cover has symbols of a serpent, two scorpions and a horse shoe which contains a cucaracha, a cockroach; 'gantho' is latin for parasite. The cockroach (or is it a gnaoua) also appears on the rear of the cover, it is not the black and white magazine on the desk in the photograph. Bob's cuff-links were a gift from Joan Baez, they are mentioned in her song 'Diamonds and Rust' which is a song from 1975 showing how much hurt she continued to carry. That just leaves a well dressed and coiffured Bob holding his cat named 'Rolling Stone', not the greatest pet name to stand in one's garden shouting out in the early evening. A series of photographs adorned the rear (and the CD booklet). Ginsberg in a grey W.C.Fields stove-pipe hat and another picture with Bob wearing it. Bob receiving a head massage, Bob at the piano, Bob and Joan Baez together, Peter Yarrow scratching his head as Bob moves through a police cordon. There were also more of Bob's 'notes', written in the stream of consciousness style which Jack Kerouac had taken from James Joyce, he retitled the method as spontaneous-prose, Bob now inherited it on behalf of the youth of the world. These notes would eventually become instrumental in the creation of Bob's book 'Tarantula' which had been sold as 'already in proof form' to a publisher before Bob had commenced writing the book.

The **'Jacket Notes'** for the album were detailed in the 'Writings and Drawings' book. These notes in the book are accompanied by a drawing of a man (probably a roadie) buckling under the immense weight of a vertical pillar of crated musical instruments. The first section is another un-numbered surrealistic 'Bob Dylan Dream'. The mid-section has statements of which many are aphorisms which betray an inferiority complex. There are so many different thoughts that they may have been written to stave off any criticism that might be aimed at the new album. Gertrude Stein and James Dean are mentioned again this time with Bach, Mozart and Tolstoy because they are all dead.

'Subterranean Homesick Blues': The rhythm is based on 'Too Much Monkey Business' by Chuck Berry and uses some of the same ideas, also there are hints of Bob's 'Motorpsycho Nitemare'. Bob confirmed the 'Monkey Business' fact in the Biograph album notes, it was later used at a slower pace by Springsteen for his Blinded By The Light. The short sharp speech pattern was not new, Paul Campbell had done the same for his 'Taking It Easy' only in his song 'Ma was in the pantry with yeast', Bob's Johnny was 'in the basement mixing medicine'. Both songs include the police, but Bob's police are in plain clothes; Paul Campbell was a pseudonym used by Pete Seeger. Bob's song was his first ever single released with a promotional video, although home video recorders were still a thing of the future in 1965. Bob appeared in the discarding-lyric-card routine with Allen Ginsberg talking to Bob Neuwirth in the background, it was an excerpt from the film 'Don't Look Back'. In the lyrics as Johnny is mixing drugs is he a chemist? Bob had already tried Marijuana and LSD. The infamous agitators, The Weathermen, took their name from the song. It is a warning song with anti establishment overtones, there is no optimism in the song, he accepts that the changes are impossible. An acoustic version was recorded a day earlier and appeared on the Bootleg Series it pales in comparison with the electric version. In the 'Writings' book we are shown a page typed by Bob when he created this lyric. It is full of 'xxxx' obliterations, the white plastic paper paint had not yet been invented by Monkee, Mike Nesmith's mother. The page also has two coffee cup stains. We learn that 'users and cheaters' were originally 'teachers and preachers', and 'big pen' was originally 'pig pen' (Grateful Dead?), but that may just be an error in the book. **'She Belongs to Me'** is a song for a self sufficient woman. Joan Baez received a gift of an Egyptian ring from Bob which is mentioned in the song. Is Bob reneging against Joan's wish to keep him working as a protest singer. Bob is using humour to lampoon Joan, she wants to maintain her morals and her religious beliefs. The problem is that the song doesn't give out much of the humour, it reads more like cynicism. One wonders why she would paint the daytime black, unless she sleeps all day, most entertainers become nocturnal as they work at night.

 'Maggie's Farm': Maggie appeared in the opening track, but this 'Maggie' is more aggressive. The lyric is for working on a farm run by a tyrant, like on 'George Penny's Farm' by Pete Seeger. This could be construed as Bob's clairvoyance when so-called right-wing tyrant Maggie Thatcher would eventually put three million people out of work in Britain in the name of progress. It was the rousing version of this song that started the problems at The Newport Folk Festival. It rages at assembly lines, the boredom of the workers and the lack of imagination of those workers. Bob once sang 'Hard Times in the Country' which has a similar theme of exploitation, at least Bob was aware that it was not only the musical industry that was exploitative. The first verse indicates that the brain is not utilised to its full worth, dulled by repetition and drudgery. The whole family in the song sound pretty unpleasant, but of course all employees are working on someone's 'farm', and they will pay you as little as possible for their own benefit in the name of competition. At least the narrator in the song has made a decision to stop working for Maggie. The song is up-tempo and lively and the gaiety in the performance is an ideal backdrop for the seriousness of the words.

 'Love Minus Zero/No Limit'. Originally conceived as a title set like a fraction (not an equation as many writers have written) with 'No limit' under 'Love Minus Zero'. Apparently written for Sara, she gradually invades his thoughts in the song, he considers her as susceptible and unprotected as a bird with a broken wing. This bird is a raven and Bob has often mentioned actor Peter Lorre who appeared with Vincent Price and Boris Karloff in the 1963 re-make of The Raven; a film that included Jack Nicholson in a minor role. I would have been easier to confirm that fact if the film was a 'Hammer-Horror' film as Bob mentions 'hammer' and 'cloak and dagger' in the last two verses, but it was made by Alta Vista. Bob was hoping in the lyrics for a woman with whom he could instigate a faithful relationship. There is nothing like success and 'failure is no success at all'. If Bob's fast talking patter rap songs could be based on Gilbert and Sullivan then these lines recall the 'Faint heart never won fair lady' song from Iolanthe; 'in for a penny in for a pound'. A beautiful song, the pawn and the ceremonies of the horsemen are from a chess set no doubt, this woman has everything a man desires including the need to be comforted. **'Outlaw Blues'** was also recorded earlier as **'California'** and rewritten during the evening and re-recorded with a new title. A 12 bar blues, is it Charlie McCoy on harmonica or John Sebastian, there was an over-dub on this released version but no harmonica player was noted, it might be Bob but it doesn't have his recognisable tone. The song details an outlaw on the run wearing his sunglasses. Bob is having a dig at writers that disseminate his lyrics saying that he might just tell us the truth, but how would we know? Bob sneaked in that line to show his feelings concerning interviews. One thing that Bob didn't seem to realise that the lagoon wouldn't be muddy if the temperature was nine below zero, it would be solid ice. The temperature at 'nine below zero' is identical to that on Sonny Boy Williamson's song of the same name; recorded by Williamson for Chess Records with Willie Dixon and Otis Spann in the band. The original song namely 'California' used the images of the outlaw wearing the sunglasses and having a black tooth but the other verses were more innocuous, Bob just sang of going down south to meet a big fat mama.

'On the Road Again': A American dust-bowl type song for a slovenly woman in a dirty house, in turn the relationship suffers. The first verse indicates that the house is full of lunatics that dress up as Bonaparte or Santa Claus. This seems just like a journey across a surrealistic painting, that's how weird are the characters. Almost a nightmare scenario, the final question as to the reason why she, who is sane, continues to live there remains unanswered.

'Bob Dylan's 115th Dream': There are two attempts at starting the song, first one Bob laughs, the second he misses the first beat. Bob enjoyed the fact that the band failed to play on cue that he asked Tom Wilson to ensure that this laughter appeared on the album, he said he was willing to pay for it to stay on the album. Another song similar to The Lord Chancellor's Dream from Iolanthe. Places and faces come and go as the dream continues. Herman Melville's, Captain Arab and his obsessive desire to kill Moby Dick. Ahab also becomes the leader of the American settlers exchanging beads with the Indians and later has to be bailed out by sailor Bob. The dream starts and ends on board Columbus' ship The Mayflower which gets a parking ticket. In Bob's dreams he his running hectically from place to place, in my dreams I run backwards it is faster. Did I miss something where are Bob's 113 missing dreams?

'Mr Tambourine Man' is one of the very few Bob Dylan songs that opens with the refrain and then proceeds to the verse, 'Spanish Leather' and 'Paths to Victory' are two others. Bob creates ambivalence with the double meanings of 'trip' and 'smoke rings', remember Bob was a cigarette smoker. It was also mooted that Bruce Langhorne was in fact the tambourine man because he brought a massive tambourine into the studio to record a track for the previous album. Bob wrote the song in the early hours of the morning at Al Aronowitz' house. The song may concern looking for inspiration, the tambourine man might be Bob's muse. Bob claimed that he never understood how he created these esoteric lyrics. There have been various opinions on the jingle jangle morning mentioned in the song. It is probably Bob referring to metal wind chimes that tinkle with the breeze in the early morning, perhaps they are chimes of freedom flashing. The Irish writer and poet known more for his regular inebriation, Brendan Behan, wrote of an old triangle jingle jangling. Of course the pioneers and cowboys were often called to their meals by striking a metal bar around a triangle, it is also well known early morning call for many boy scouts out camping. Of course Brendan Behan was referring to the warders in a prison in a scene from his play 'The Quare Fellow'. Bob and The Band are alleged to have recorded Brendan Behan's 'The Old Triangle' as one of their Basement Tapes. There are mentions of tambourines in the Bible called 'timbrels or tarbrets' in the King James edition. Judges Chapter 11:34, 'his daughter came out to meet him with timbrels and dances'. The Psalms, Isaiah, Job and Samuel also mention the tambourine but with the harp or the flute. A favourite of Bob's Jeremiah states in Chapter 31:4 'thy shall again be adorned with thy tambourines and shall go forth in the dances of them that make merry'. It was once suggested to me in conversation that it might be Christopher Marlowe's, Mr 'Tamburlaine' Man, his Empire turned to sand, he took trips on ships and spent time escaping on the run from Bajazeth. Of course Mr Tambourine is whoever you wish him to be, religious salvationist, drug dealer, you, me, or even just a man playing a tambourine, that is what makes the song so special.

'Gates of Eden': This is descriptive of different people, it leaves us guessing what each means. Are the couplets aphorisms, there is no paradise to be found behind these gates of eden, just promises of paradise which are unlikely to be fulfilled. This could be Bob's 116th dream, copious sermonizing and rhetoric. He might be referring to Milton's 'Paradise Lost' and its constant reminders of Eden. It seems that Bob's 'Eden' is the place of silence bliss and sleep, the place of rest after the turmoils of living, there are no Kings in Eden. He may be referring to everyone being the same undressed in the sight of God. Although Bob mentions 'War and Peace' in the first line the lyric-poem as a whole is decidedly Blakean. William Blake wrote 'The Garden of Love' in which, like Bob, he sees what he has never seen. The 'Gates' are shut and this Eden is filled with graves. Bob also mentions the kingdoms of experience, Blake wrote of Innocence and Experience and was also influenced by Milton. Bob may have written his song with Blake's 'Keys to the Gates' and its 16 sections providing ideas for his own lyric. For me Bob's song has all the feelings and imagery presented in William Blake's 'Night' from The Songs of Innocence', 'The Gates of Eden' is as close as Bob ever got to eclipsing William Blake and as any scholar will tell you that is no mean achievement.

'It's Alright Ma I'm Only Bleeding': A President standing naked, perfect for Richard Tricky Dicky Nixon. If this was written without the name of the writer one would be excused for thinking that this was written by Allen Ginsberg. The song title is just a play on words from Arthur Big Boy Crudup's 'That's Alright Mama' and that is where the similarity ends. Bob seems to have read 'Howl' and decided it was his turn to write a similar lyric. There is no plagiarism the ideas of mendacity, duplicity and deception were common themes for most of The Beat Generation writers. 'Howl' continually asks questions, in Bob's song he selects ideas from the stand-point of 'don't do as I do, do as I say!' In 'Howl' Ginsberg's naked persons are 'hysterical naked', which is possible for women but men cannot become hysterical because 'hyster' is Latin for womb and men are not given one. Bob again attacks the profiteering fire and brimstone evangelists, but they can't exist without the money from the masses. The 'masters' and their fake morals, false Gods, and the poor bored workers from Maggie's Farm poke their heads above the parapet to be shot at. One thing that Bob proves with the song is that although he was now important and protected he continued to be aware of what makes the populous tick. I was confused by the 'old lady Judges' and their morals but it seems that this covers all the 'old spinster brigade' with their strange attitudes to sex. 'Disillusioned words like bullets bark' has always been a favourite line, a line that only a great poet could write.

'It's All Over Now, Baby Blue' sounds like one long song yet the transposer in 'Writings' separated it to five verses. Goodbye to the old welcome to the new, or goodbye to Joan Baez. In 1993, Gary Clark took the title of this song and made a wonderful emotional song included on his brilliant 'Ten Short Songs About Love' album, for a while it makes the listener think if he is singing Bob's song, but he isn't, it is sublime try to hear it. Bob mentioned a girl who he called 'Baby Blue' back in high school in The Biograph booklet. Bob used the name then and for this song from a term used by Gene Vincent in his song 'Baby Blue'. Bob added that he was singing to a different Baby Blue, but was that back then or now? Gene Vincent's 'Baby Blue' single was released as a follow-up to 'Walking Home From School', now there's a 'school' coincidence, perhaps not. The most obvious scenario for this song is that Bob himself is 'Baby Blue'. He is talking to himself about his new maturity, his coming of age. The lover has just walked out of his door, forget the past, go start anew. Two other songs were recorded but not released at the time. **'Farewell Angelina'** was recorded by Joan Baez as the title track for an album, she sang the original written version. Strangely Bob's own version was not included on any album before The Bootleg Series in 1991. That version also included a verse not included in the songbooks. It contained references to 'camouflaged parrots'. Bob claimed that the song was 'a chain of flashing images'. This may have been inspired by Rimbaud's 'Illuminations'. The tune used is 'The Wagoner's Lad' a song from Joan Baez' catalogue of folk songs, which in turn came from George Scroggie's 'Farewell to Tarwathie' which is dated as 1850. It is also similar to 'There's A Hole in The Bucket'. Bob mentions 'the triangle' which may hark back to my idea of the Tambourine Man's 'jingle jangle morning' alarm sound. Although this is the only official release the lyrics are slightly modified to the words in the 'Writings' book, the 'sky' presents different ideas and scenes to those in the written lyrics. The flashing images as Bob calls them pass by creating yet another 'Bob Dylan Dream'. **'Love is Just a Four Letter Word':** This is a narrative in which 'love' is deemed unique to each person. A friend has given birth and is alone but she seemed to be happy. He is watching whilst she speaks to the child's father. The narrator considers himself as not being competent to advise her on her situation. The Holy Kiss is the marriage vow whose flame has been snuffed out. One can only guess at the reason behind the song. It is almost as if the writer is considering making the enormous step into marriage and requires re-assurance that love is 'more' than 'just' a four letter word.

The Byrds had recorded their definitive version of 'Mr Tambourine Man' which raced to the charts in the UK and the USA. Bob was such a hot property that other singer songwriters rushed to record his songs. The Turtles had a hit with 'It Ain't Me Babe', Cher with 'All I Really Want to Do' and Joan Baez with 'It's All Over Now Baby Blue' and 'Farewell Angelina'. The infamous well documented Newport Folk Festival performance with Al Kooper and Mike Bloomfield with The Paul Butterfield Blues Band followed on May 25th 1965. Pete Seeger was infuriated by these 'youths' usurping the folk tradition with electric noise, folk historian Alan Lomax came to blows with Albert Grossman, the plug was pulled on Al Kooper's organ and then replaced when Bob said that he wouldn't play without the organ. After the booing and cheering that caused a furore Bob returned to the stage encouraged by Eric Von Schmidt and played 'Tambourine Man' and 'It's All Over Now Baby Blue', accompanied just by his own acoustic guitar. The interviews with Bob make the whole thing seem an accident. Bob was becoming tired of sitting centre stage with just an acoustic guitar. He quite rightly decided that if he was bored with this presentation it would not be long before the audience tired of the repetition. Daniel Kramer wrote in his book of rare photographs

(Bob Dylan by Daniel Kramer/Plexus Books) that the same thing occurred at a show a month later at Forest Hills Stadium, New York. The first half of the show was acoustic the second half electric. Again the crowd booed, at the end of the show Bob just put his guitar down and walked off, the audience expected an encore. Daniel Kramer had been asked by Bob Neuwirth to set the back seats up in their station wagon, it took him some time to work out how the seats worked. Just as he finished he saw the two Bob's running hell-for-leather towards the station wagon. They jumped in and Neuwirth drove out into the street and raced towards Manhattan with Bob Dylan lying low in the front seat.

The 'Bringing It All Back Home' album used electric instruments and rocketed to No 1 in the charts, the disaffected purist folkies were suddenly in a minority, Bob had timed his transformation to electric rock perfectly, all the promotional department need do was advertise. Bob was now so popular he was his own promotional machine. The 'Bringing It All Back Home' album also made it increasing difficult for the music journalists to categorise Bob. He wasn't singing protest songs these were songs with a message. The first signs of the new deep and involved lyrics emerged. Immediately there were English university lecturers making judgements of where Bob's influences were. It is more likely at the time that he had none, he was so busy finding time to read and study must have been almost impossible. His short spells of isolation would be filled with writing his 'poetry' ready for integrating to a melody. Jack Kerouac and Allen Ginsberg would be amongst the writers that Bob would be aware, at the time they were in most of the 'New Generation' magazines that were sprouting in every small town. As for Arthur Rimbaud, Charles Baudelaire, William Blake and Andy Gill (in his book, My Back Pages/Carlton Books) added Francois Villon to the list. Villon is not as well known outside France as the others, but there are certainly similarities between his titles and Bob's work, I doubt if Bob had read Villon in 1965. Villon was sentenced to death twice in his life time, his birth and death dates are not known though guessed at 1432-1464, living just 32 years. He was the greatest French poet of the 15 Century an educated vagabond. He killed a priest, was sentenced to death, pardoned but exiled from Paris. When sentenced for a second time in 1463 he wrote 'Ballad of a Hanged Man' which has graphic surrealistic scenes of corpses pleading to curious onlookers for divine mercy. His poems are collected into two volumes, 'The Small Testament' and 'The Grand Testament', poems such as 'The Ballad of Women of Yore' and 'Regrets of Youthful Folly' would have been ideal for tunes to be added, like James Joyce and W.B.Yeats, Francois Villon wrote poems that should have been sung, many had repeated refrains. As Bob was interested in Bertolt Brecht it may have been through reading Brecht that he found Villon. Brecht wrote a poem titled 'Of Francois Villon'. Brecht writes that Villon was a poor man's son, heaven was denied to him because he stabbed men with his knife, he was never caught but died hiding in some bushes. Another misunderstood bad man, the type of character to whom Bob has always been attracted.

Bob thought that his new writings were more explicit, easier to understand, he even disliked the term 'poet', he preferred 'trapeze artist'. We must take all these remarks as superfluous I am sure that he was delighted to be compared with great writers, it is probable that he was genuinely embarrassed and flattered by the comparisons.

Bob moved into The Chelsea Hotel in New York, the same hotel where Sara and her daughter lived. It seems that Sara's indifference to the advances of Bob made him more determined to be with her. At the time Bob was reading the 'I Ching' which may have been due to Sara who searched out Zen Buddhism, or of course it might well have been Allen Ginsberg who was already a Zen follower and regular meditator. Strangely when I read it years ago it was titled 'Yi Ching', The Book of Change. It comprises separate chapters by different authors, written 1500 B.C. Yi means change in any form, the predominant characteristic of all activities, caused by interaction between Yin (woman) and Yang (male). All change arises from motion which is produced by pushing against that which is passive. Activity is recognised as 'the easy' and passivity as 'the Simple'. It is from the 'simple' and the 'easy' that all complexity and multiplicity of life and change have arisen. In all conduct and affairs the most perilous is always known from that which is easy. In all conduct and affairs, that which is confronted with the greatest obstacle is always known from the simplest. Confused, then read Confucius yourself. Bob may of course just been scoring intellectual points by mentioning the I Ching. He would have gained more cerebral stimulation by reading the 'Shih Ching' a selection of 311 songs, Chinese folk songs of government officials, rulers, songs of metaphor, description, inspiration and allusion. One in particular is aptly pertinent. It discusses, lust, hunting, music, spirits and concludes with...'The existence of any of these things has never been but the prelude of ruin'. Bob Dylan might well be the reincarnation of Confucius who spent his life in the informal teaching of many subjects. Men are by nature good, evil is the result of ignorance. If a ruler does not prove worthy then it is the right of the people to revolt. The Five 'Wu Ching' classics prove that nothing much has changed since 1500 B.C. Bob Dylan was just another in a long line of philosophers, but at least he changed his own situation from poor to rich.

The year 1965 must have seemed to be never ending for Bob Dylan. He recorded 'Like a Rolling Stone' which was released as a single and it zoomed' to No 2 in the USA and No 4 in the UK. The sound was again different with Al Kooper's organ playing making him instantly infamous. The record became Bob's first million selling single. Bob had been back in the studio during mid-

June recording enough songs for the next album whilst the present album was still high in the charts. In October 1965 **'HIGHWAY 61 REVISITED'** was released and it reached No 3 in the USA charts and No 4 in the UK. The musicians were Al Kooper (organ), Robert Gregg (Drums), Joseph Macho (bass), Al Gorgoni (guitar), Frank Owens (piano) and Michael Bloomfield (guitar). Bloomfield was becoming very unreliable, he suffered from acute stage-fright. Bob had telephoned him and asked him to play on the album, he said that he didn't want any B.B.King shit, he just wanted some great blues licks. The truth was the Michael Bloomfield was a left handed man playing guitar right handed and could play guitar like anyone. In fact later in his career he recorded albums with each track impersonating the style of a different guitarist. The actuality that Michael was present at the session in June, July and August 1965 was probably a first and last time in his career that he was ever-present for an appointment. Of course Al Kooper was intending to play guitar but when he saw Mike wipe the rain of his battered guitar and play like an angel he quickly made his way to the organ, an instrument that he had never played previously, he was lucky that it was already switched on, he would not have known how to switch it on. The story of Bob asking for the engineer to turn up the organ sound has passed into pop history.

Russ Savakas played bass on the later sessions and Paul Griffin was on piano, Mike Bloomfield also met bassist Harvey Goldstein at the later sessions, he changed his name to Harvey Brooks played on Supersession and then joined The Electric Flag with Mike Bloomfield, Buddy Miles and Nick 'the Greek' Gravenites.

The Album cover shows Bob wearing a silk shirt over a Triumph motor cycle advertising T-shirt. The legs and camera of Bob Neuwirth are behind Bob. It was this head and shoulders picture of Bob that Peter Blake used for his collage for The Beatles' 'Sgt Pepper' album. **'Notes by Bob Dylan'**, the jacket notes on the sleeve were re-printed in the 'Writings' book. It is the story of 'Autumn' a very aggressive season according to this short article. It is written in a style that was probably influenced by Jack Kerouac's 'spontaneous prose', but it is closer to Kathy Acker. She also used '&' in lieu of the word 'and', used dashes and dots for her continuation-punctuation. The tale includes a newspaper man 'White Heap', Paul Sargent, Nietzsche, Savage Rose and Fixable. I thought (and I still do) that this was Bob just playing games with us. The novella, if that is what it was intended to be, becomes so tiresome to read that one becomes disinterested. Bob uses 'eye' for 'I' occasionally and intersperse those 'eyes' with real 'eyes'. We needed to know more about the 'Insanity Factory', but agreeing that John Cohen, Mozart and Quazimodo were right is impossible without the facts. Obfuscating for the sake of it, file this under 'inconsequential'.

'Like a Rolling Stone': The story starts with 'once upon a time', and then Bob tells us the story. This is arguably the greatest rock song of all time. Genesis Chapter 29:3 & 8 states 'and they rolled the stone'. Exodus 15:16 states 'they shall be as still ('motionless' in N.E.B.) as a stone'. Bob would have read the book of Proverbs and 26:27 'whoso diggeth a pit shall fall therein, and he that rolleth ('rolling', N.E.B.) a stone, it will return upon him'. The Hank Williams song 'Lost Highway' (written by Leon Payne) uses the term of description of a rolling stone, Bob sang it in the film 'Don't Look Back', in fact Bob Neuwirth and Bob can be observed singing 'Lost Highway'. Robert W.Service the poet (although he always insisted he wrote verse) wrote 'The Ballad of a Rolling Stone'. Muddy Waters also recorded a song called 'Rolling Stone' from which Brian Jones chose the title of his group. Bob said that it was originally conceived as a waltz using the 'La Bamba' riff from the Richie Valens song, it only changed with repeated plays in the studio. It is one of Bob's greatest ever compositions, it might not be as catchy as 'Blowin in the Wind' or 'Tambourine Man' but it is all encompassing and contains some astounding lyrics. This was Bob's coming of age, he was at last overtly confident, the derision and the sneer in his voice made the vocal sound as if it was from one who understands, one whose brain is years older than his body. Bruce Springsteen said of his first ever hearing of the song that it sounded both 'young and adult simultaneously'. This song reads like another of W.S. Gilbert's patter songs. That dream (mentioned earlier) was so popular with Todd Rundgren that he recorded it for his eponymously titled double album in 1974. The itinerant is a rolling stone, a lonesome hobo perhaps, one who keeps moving, stands up for himself and faces the world alone. Bob's song is addressed to a woman, a doll, Miss Lonely. The woman has given up all the finery to live rough, she wouldn't compromise. Edie Sedgwick gained celebrity and then lost it, Napoleon in rags might be Andy Warhol. Of course when you have nothing any offer is an improvement, surprisingly she still has her diamond ring to pawn. From celebrity to obscurity, we can guess how it feels. At the recording session Al Kooper had evaded Tom Wilson's eye to play organ whilst Wilson was on the telephone. This was the only track included on the album that was produced by Tom Wilson, the others recorded six weeks later were by Bob Johnston.

'Tombstone Blues': Many celebrities pass before our ears in this song. A good joke from Bob, Mike Bloomfield's brilliant guitaring sets the track aside from the ordinary. This track could have been included on any Chuck Berry album. The Philistine King is probably Lyndon Johnson, sending his soldiers to the jungle. Belle Starr, Delilah, Jezebel, John The Baptist, many are dreamlike in new occupations. Slaves into the jungle may be for the numbers of black soldiers going to Vietnam. The napalm is the blowtorch, the politics of Uncle Sam trying to win friends was actually happening simultaneously.

The song sounds amusing, the lyrics when read are not. Bob also made a version of this with The Chambers Brothers singing back-up vocals, an outtake we are yet to hear. On 'Biograph' Bob released **'Jet Pilot'** which he stated was the original title of 'Tombstone Blues'. The musicians were not credited on the Biograph release of this track. In this version which lasts under a minute we learn that she has all the town boys under her command, yet she is a MAN!

    'It Takes A Lot to Laugh It Takes A Train to Cry': The original title was 'Phantom Engineer'. This song became an Al Kooper favourite, he intended to get Mike Bloomfield to play it, albeit faster, on 'Supersession' but Mike went absent. Mike when interviewed later said he hated the song so much he wouldn't have played it anyway. It was ultimately recorded on that 'Supersession' album by Al and Stephen Stills. Bob recorded this again later at George Harrison's Concert for Bangladesh in August 1971. Many writers have alluded to Bob being influenced by William Burroughs and his cut-up method of mixing texts out of sequence. The actual creator of cut-up was the lesser renown Brion Gysin, he worked it out with Burroughs. But whoever is the prime influence this song does read like a cut-up lyric in lines of four cut and moved. Try switching the last four lines of verse one with the last four lines of verse three. Allen Ginsberg was also helping Bob with his improvised poetry style, in fact he stated that Bob's lyric didn't really need to say anything it just presented his mood or his thought form at the time. Bob said that Charlie Patton was one of his favourites and he may have subconsciously used Patton's 'Poor Me' for parts of this arrangement. The line 'Can't Buy a Thrill' gave Steely Dan the title for their first official album. 'Solid Road cum Rocks and Gravel' was re-used as a basis for some of the lyrics. The song is played to a shuffle beat, listen for Bob exclaiming 'aaa-h' in appreciation after one of Mike Bloomfield's guitar breaks.

    'From A Buick 6': Many of Bob's women since Echo Helstrom have said that he could act the little boy lost and thus they would wish to mother him, on this song he gives the game away. He wants a soulful mama who 'don't make him nervous and keeps quiet'. She also has to listen to him when he needs to share a problem. Whoever this woman is in the song walks like Bo Diddley which sounds unflattering, but she is lucky that Bob didn't write 'Chuck Berry' now that was a strange 'duck walk'. **'Ballad of a Thin Man'**: This song includes the line 'there is something happening here' which was used by Buffalo Springfield in 1967. Mr Jones comes in for some repellent treatment. A Mr Jones was subjected to derision by Neuwirth and Dylan and thus Brian Jones thought the song was lampooning in his direction. My friend and dylanologist Dave Thomas once wrote an article on the sex in Bob's lyrics, intended as a bit of fun it ended up in a top Dylan magazine and on the internet. It was his idea that almost every unexplained innuendo was in fact sexual. This song was for fellatio and Andy Gill followed the idea though in his book on Bob's songs. Meanwhile I suspect that Dave Thomas and Bob Dylan were undoubtedly convulsed with uproarious laughter. The truth was it was Jeff Jones a young reporter on Village Voice Magazine and Time Magazine. He had asked some naive questions of Bob and was then haplessly and spectacularly pilloried by Bob and his entourage, in hindsight unfairly, but Bob was older then he's younger than that now. Journalists have always been good sport for those that think they know better. But it might be 'Brutus Jones' from Eugene O'Neill's 'The Emperor Jones', Fielding's 'Tom Jones', Orwell's 'Mr Jones' from 'Animal Farm', in fact by selecting such a common name Bob has made this Mr Jones universal. With Bob's Guthrie connotations it might have been a slight text change from Mr Joad, straight out of John Steinbeck's 'Grapes of Wrath', the discussion continues unabated and Bob isn't telling. The fact that it is a journalist is presented with the first line, and bearing that in mind the lyric becomes quite uncomplicated. Bob widens his parameters to get his feelings across but admits that the journalist is intelligent enough to have read F.Scott Fitzgerald. We were made aware that Bob had read Jack Kerouac's 'Mexico City Blues', that book does include Jack's piece titled 'I'd rather be **thin** than famous'. The 'Writings' book has a drawing for the song which is a Daliesque surreal drawing of a thin man walking whilst a another man on a hill who is kneeling swallows his sword. The two lines of the song concerning the 'one eyed midget' are an anachronism, out of place and time. Bob is on piano according to the recording notes.

'Queen Jane Approximately': According to Bob in an interview 'Jane' is a man, when we would all think that it is a modification of Queen Joan. This becomes more apparent as we realise that the synthetic surroundings of the attitudes of a cosmetic lifestyle are under investigation here. Joan Baez called Bob The Dada King in her autobiography perhaps that was her way of answering back to Bob's reference to her. I was once approached in Soho by a scruffy man asking me if I wanted any 'Jane'. I declined because I thought he was offering me a woman but I subsequently learned that 'jane' was in fact 'marijuana'. So the idea that the Jane in the song might be the weed maybe true, but the lyric makes no sense using this premise.

'Highway 61 Revisited': Highway 61 runs from Duluth due south to New Orleans. This is the story of Isaac, Abraham's son, God asked him to sacrifice his son to prove his love. Bob's stance on religion was fluctuating, he proved that he had few fears of the wrath of God with this frivolous 'putting me on' attitude to God. We must bear in mind that Bob's father was indeed named Abraham, and this is shortened to 'Abe' in the song. Poor Howard in the text was a Leadbelly folk song. Bob creates a list of weird characters again, Louis the King is possibly Louis Armstrong, Mack the finger might be Lonnie Mack. Bob might have intended this as his own biblical story, with himself as Isaac. Leonard Cohen would write his own version of this Biblical story, it appeared on his 'Songs From a Room' album in 1967. The recording sheets for Bob's track state that 'Samuel' played drums on this track. The Samuel was Sam Lay from the Butterfield Blues Band and previously Howlin' Wolf's Band. Bob plays a whistle on this track a few times, both Al Kooper and Sam Lay claim that the siren whizzer-whistle belonged to them. The BBC-2 television programme Arena had a great scene where the researcher had managed to locate James Son Thomas a black bluesman who had written the original 'Highway 61 Blues'. We are assured that the scene was not staged but it was priceless. The interviewer asks Son Thomas if he had ever heard of Bob Dylan. He looked up extremely puzzled and says extremely ponderously "Bo Dylanny, no I never heard of him". The drawing representing this song is a gasoline truck, and it is a good drawing with some expert perspective.

'Just Like Tom Thumb's Blues': The drug inferences are there for the analyzers to seize upon. Cant get up in the morning, another shot, looking like a ghost, from red wine to hard drugs or hard stuff meaning spirits. The line that he is on drugs because they are prescribed by his doctor makes the drug idea superfluous. The experts wrote of J. Alfred Prufrock by T.S.Eliot, they continued that it was also similar to 'Ma Boheme', My Bohemian Life by Arthur Rimbaud; the latter does mention a dreaming Tom Thumb. Tom Thumb is more likely to being Mister Insignificant, the general population rather than the nursery rhyme character. It is also nearer to 'Tom Thorne' in Robert W.Service's poem 'The Atavist', the poem appears in Service's book 'The Rhymes of A Rolling Stone', now there is a coincidence. J. Prufrock is a timid and aging and alienated sentimentalist, and try as I have the connections with this song are flimsy to say the least. Bob has placed obstacles in his lyrics to make it difficult to evaluate. There are two keyboards Al Kooper on ondioline and Paul Griffin on honky tonk tack piano.

'Desolation Row': This has more excellent Bloomfield guitar. Apocalypse then not now, after the hard rain has fallen the grotesque inherit the world. Ezra Pound and T.S. Eliot are mentioned in the lyric. Now 'The Love song of J.Alfred Prufrock' by T.S.Eliot may have been more pertinent for the inspiration of this song. Prufrock an alterego for Thomas Sterns Eliot has a problem concentrating on a single train of thought, there are abrupt changes of direction within the poem. Mermaids, windows, letters, the sea and flowers are all crossover thought ideas between that of Eliot and Dylan. We get the surrealistic disembodied Mr Apollinax, the twisted faces at the window. Prufrock seems to be addressing us from his own personal hell, not Dante's version of hades and beyond. The likelihood that Bob decided to write 'Desolation Row' after reading T.S.Eliot gains impetus when one considers another of Eliot's poems 'The Hollow Men'. Eliot had written this for Joseph

Conrad's book 'Heart of Darkness' which later became the film 'Apocalypse Now'. This is as desolate a poem that has ever been written. The hollow men are idealists with no substance, in the film Marlon Brando as Kurtz reads the poem. At the end of the film when 'the horror' is repeated against The Doors playing 'The End' is to my mind one of the great moments on film. Bob writes of lame men with rearranged faces, sexless patients, a nurse who is a local loser, all of them are hollow people. A jealous monk, Dr Filth, Casanova and Einstein all pass across the panorama of curiosity, even the good Samaritan is going to a carnival. T.S. Eliot died in 1965 before he could read Bob's lyrics but in Eliot's 'Four Quartets' he wrote concerning the end of the search, the exploration, 'we will arrive where we started, and know the place for the first time'. He continues with 'you see behind every face the mental emptiness deepen, leaving only the growing terror of nothing to think about'. In Eliot's 'East Coker' they wait without hope, and in Part IV the Nurse appears alongside dripping blood, purgatorial fires and sickness, 'through the dark cold and the empty desolation'. T.S.Eliot's 'The Waste Land' may also have been in Bob's mind when he created the title. The poem itself speaks of city life, chess, sermonising, death and burial, all subjects which Bob has used over the years. Bob must have felt that he was safe using Eliot's work as an inspiration. Eliot affirmed in 'Sacred Wood' that 'immature poets imitate; mature poets steal'. Eliot also thought and wrote 'poetry is a mug's game', he would probably approved of Bob sitting with his Eliot poetry book in one hand as he created new lines for his own songs. If Bob has the fear of being alone, lonely rather than a loner, the he would have been aware that Eliot understood precisely. In 'The Cocktail Party' Eliot wrote 'What is Hell?, Hell is oneself, Hell is alone, the other figures in it merely projections-there is nothing to escape from and nothing to escape to-one is always alone'. I must also add that when writing 'The Family Reunion' he could have been observed as clairvoyant of Bob's personal life when Eliot wrote 'Success is relative, it is what we make of the mess we have made of things'.

Jack Kerouac wrote 'Desolation Angels'. Jack worked as a fire-watcher on Desolation Hill, one of the most remote hill top out-posts where he watched for forest fires. The cabin on concrete stilts took three days to reach when Jack was there. He went there to meditate, he had completed the unpublished 'On The Road' and was studying Buddhism. He was searching for a vision of the proof of God in the manner of William Blake. To take this thought a step further when Jack came down from Desolation Hill he was more insecure than ever. He became a member of the aesthetic subterranean low-life with Burroughs, Ginsberg and Huncke and became an alcoholic finding his own personal desolation row. In 'Desolation Row' Bob employs a selection of oddities in absurdity, Bob name-drops historical fictional and biblical characters in this 11 minute epic. Who is Dr Filth? Bob says that he rearranged their faces and gave them different names, Jack Kerouac had his own Dr Sax and gave his friends different names in his books. In fact it is quite a game finding who-is-who in Kerouac's novels, Bill Burroughs was Old Bull Lee in one book and Frank Carmody in another, of course Neal Cassidy was Dean Moriarty and Jack himself was Sal Paradise. The tape recording session notes for the song were either vague or lost, it was reported that it was just Charlie McCoy and Bob playing guitars and harmonicas, it sounds as if that is a correct assumption, it is sparse and beautiful.

Of the album Bob said "I'm not going to be able to make a better album than that one, it is too good, there is a lot of stuff on there that I would listen to". That was reassuring Bob, but he would make a better album. The album and of course Bob's interviews led us to believe that Bob was interested in the work of Charles Baudelaire, Francois Villon, Arthur Rimbaud and by natural association Paul Verlaine. Scholars investigated the lyrics and compared Bob's with the works of these famous French poets. Of course Tom Thumb was mentioned in Rimbaud's 'My Bohemian Life', and Tom Thumb was a person with problems with being short. Bob and Rimbaud would both have wished to be taller. It is my contention that Bob was more interested in the philosophies of these three poets than the poems. Baudelaire was important not only in France, his influence on American and British verse was immense. He managed to present to an unsuspecting public an entire moral, emotional experience in his 'Les Fleurs du Mal'. Baudelaire was expelled from school for homosexuality and by the age of eighteen had already been infected by a venereal disease that would ultimately kill him. He lived a bohemian life style with Jeanne Duval his mistress. He experimented with opium and lived an indulgent hedonistic nocturnal existence with a succession of ladies. 'Les Fleurs du Mal' was prosecuted and banned as being 'an offence to public morality'. Baudelaire's poetry was not an expression of feelings but an experience in itself, just like most of Bob Dylan's work. The subjects of Baudelaire's work are similar to Bob's, in fact Baudelaire's work is full of duality, every existence creates an awareness of the opposite. His ideas would trigger-off others which would move from one poem to another. He also had 'impair' lines where one line does not scan because there are more syllables than the previous line, this was also used by Verlaine in his work. One can imagine Bob Dylan writing long 'talking blues' songs and not bothering to make the lines equal, he would then just sing-speak the words faster to get them out before the verse line ends. Baudelaire died in 1867 at the age of 46, Arthur Rimbaud was 13 years old at the time.

Rimbaud was another man living a bohemian lifestyle, in fact he rarely washed and was known to be flea-infested when he first met Paul Verlaine. Rimbaud is commonly known as an uncompromising, anti-social, adolescent genius, now there is a title that would fit Bob Dylan nicely. If singers can imitate other singers, painters paint perfect forgeries, then at a young age Rimbaud could imitate any writer's style and fool his peers. Rimbaud actually wrote his farewell to poetry in 1873 at the age of 19, which has subsequently made it almost impossible to date his great work 'Les Illuminations'. Rimbaud loved his bohemian life went to Cyprus, Aden and Abyssinia where he was a gun-runner. He never returned to France until 1891, He returned when he had a gangrenous tumour, he died shortly after. His work had been collected by Paul Verlaine and published (assuming Rimbaud to be dead) in 1886 to critical acclaim. I think Bob Dylan was attracted to Rimbaud first because of his bohemian adventurous spirit, and second because their philosophies and ambivalences were almost identical. Rimbaud believed that the genius of poetry was an accidental and unconscious gift. This genius has conscious control over the creative powers and ultimately produces work of great quality that even surprises the writer. Rimbaud also felt that if knowledge other than self-knowledge was pursued with any vigour then the original gift would be damaged or destroyed, in his words 'the process would be impaired'. Rimbaud continued 'long immense and reasoned disordering of the senses in which the writer becomes the great sick man, the great criminal the great outcast, but most importantly the great sage, for he arrives at the unknown, his language will be new it will be of the soul for the soul, encompassing everything'. Rimbaud's ideas were used by composer, writer, mystic Cyril Scott, who wrote in 1933, 'Music, Its Secret Influences Through The Ages', unconvincingly in my opinion. He thought that great music and mysticism might be closely connected. In his book Scott made aphoristic pronouncements that he certainly couldn't prove and probably didn't believe.

Of course if one doesn't understand French then one has to rely on the translator, but Arthur Rimbaud was undoubtedly the Bob Dylan of his day, Rimbaud's poetry cries out for melody as does Paul Verlaine's. Verlaine was the homosexual lover of Rimbaud for many years, he introduced Rimbaud to his Paris clique.

If life repeated itself then Allen Ginsberg and Bob Dylan would be ideal stablemates, although Bob thankfully preferred females. Verlaine shot Rimbaud in the hand after a lovers-tiff, he had left his wife to live with Rimbaud. Verlaine was not a bohemian and helped Corbiere, Mallarme, Cros and of course Rimbaud to become recognised as great poets. The scruffy appearance of Rimbaud was always excused by his genius, he seemed to go out of his way to appear unkempt. Verlaine later became a carbon copy of Rimbaud, succumbing to alcohol and drugs which culminated with illness and degradation. Verlaine's poems are designed to be incantatory tone poems, the first ever 'talking blues'. There is no social reality very few ideas and it is deceptively naive. The dominance of rhyme is weakened, he uses the earlier explained 'impair' line. Verlaine was paramount in the presentation of relaxing the restraint on assonance thus increasing the poetic vocabulary. So with these short explanations one can realise the similarities with Bob Dylan, up until his motor-cycle accident he said that had no idea where his poetics emanated, Rimbaud may have been correct in his assumptions, Verlaine ideal with his incantatory style and Baudelaire used experience for the lyrical content. No wonder Allen Ginsberg considered Bob Dylan the greatest American poet, Bob Dylan has all these attributes.

'Positively 4th Street': This was originally titled 'Black Dalli Rue' and released as a follow-up single to 'Like A Rolling Stone'. It Reached No 7 in the USA and No 8 in the UK. (b-side 'From a Buick 6'). Bob once lived for a while in flat on 4th Street, Greenwich Village, with his girlfriend Avril, a dancer. The object of the song is a person from his folkie days, one perhaps that would not change and is viewed by Bob as one that has lost out due to their intractability, this is Bob's retirement speech. Israel Young thought it was aimed at him. It could have been Phil Ochs who at the time was part of the Dylan clan but struggling mentally and financially. Alan Lomax, Pete Seeger and the rest of the 'don't rock the folk boat' brigade must have felt the breeze of criticism. In a total evaluation of the song it becomes evident that it is the whole conservative archive-folkies that Bob has left behind in his wake, that are now considered by Bob to be a 'drag'. Ewan McColl wrote in the 'Sing Out Magazine' after the furore created by The Newport Festival, 'Bob Dylan is a youth of mediocre talent, writing fourth grade schoolboy verse'. I wonder if McColl changed his opinion after hearing 'Desolation Row'? McColl was a part of the group of singers that remained traditional and outside of the folk fraternity he is relatively unknown, he does have a famous daughter in Kirsty McColl.

'Can You Please Crawl Out of Your Window ?': This was released as a follow-up single to 'Positively 4th Street' in January 1966, (b-side 'Highway 61 Revisited'). The single did not do as well as the previous releases, it reaches No 58 in the USA and No 17 in the UK. It was Phil Ochs criticism of this song that ended the relationship with Bob. It was all captured on film, Bob was now only interested in accolades, he was lucky that he could still tell good from bad himself; although later in his career he couldn't. With Bob moving in a 'don't criticise me' stage in his life he would be likely to surround himself with 'yes men', just like Elvis Presley did. These people laugh at every hint of a joke, congratulate the poorest performance and the artist glows in the warmth of his own personal bloated ego. Bob considered Phil Ochs 'a journalist not a folk singer', it was as if the lowest of the low were writers and journalists, and the highest achievers in the world were singer composers. In this particular case Phil Ochs was on target with his remarks, was Bob losing his Midas-touch? When Phil was proved correct Bob didn't seem to be able to apologise, saying sorry is very difficult for persons who are surrounded by people telling them that they are always right. Phil Ochs would also suffer problems with rejection and eventually took his own life. Phil Ochs left a legacy of good songs 'Flower Lady', 'There But for Fortune', 'Chords of Fame' to name just three. 'Can You Crawl' sounds as though Bob was so convinced that he could contrive the same with other songs like 'Rolling Stone' so he had written another in a similar vein. The single may have also died because the record label got the name wrong calling it 'Positively 4th Street' on some releases. The truth is that the public didn't like it, they were buying anything that Bob released at the time, but not this single, they had 21 attempts in the studio at getting it right and released the very last take on the July studio sheet. In fact it ended up with 33 takes Bob's most recorded song, it was still being recorded in November. There was some confusion later concerning the actual take used for the single it may have come from the November session. Many years later when Michael Bloomfield was struggling with drug and alcohol dependency Bob visited Mike's house at the request of Mike's wife. Bob arrived and knocked at the door but couldn't wake Mike up. As he was concerned for Mike's well-being Bob found an unlatched window and crawled in, one assumes he came out through the front door or the song's title would have been considered clairvoyance. Bob of course may have remembered crawling out of Echo Helstrom's window as mentioned earlier. Released on Biograph, the backing band are The Band plus Al Kooper, Bruce Langhorne on guitar and Paul Griffin on piano. This doesn't have much tune and Bob's voice although perfectly audible is fighting the volume throughout, drummer Robert Gregg is leading The Band along on cymbals, Levon Helm of The Band was not in the studio.

'Sitting on a Barbed Wire Fence': This sounds uncomfortable to say the least. Bob sings "she's making me into an old man and man I'm not even 25". The guitar riff that carries the song seems to amuse Bob at the end? This song was only registered in 1970, yet was first recorded in January 1965. The riff used is the same as for 'Alley Oop' a No 1 hit for The Hollywood Argyles in 1960. 'I Wanna Be Your Lover': This is possible Bob having a joke with 'The Rolling Stones' and 'The Beatles' who recorded 'I Wanna Be Your Man', a line and a tune that Bob re-uses in his lyric. It was intended to be a noisy rocking single and recorded with The Hawks, who were originally The Crackers. It was finally released on The Biograph Collection, it certainly is raucous. Again Bob mentions a few characters such as Phaedra ('Phedre' written by Jean Racine) who fell in love her husband's grown-up son. 'The Masked Man' of which there were many, maybe The Lone Ranger. Rasputin the mad monk, Judy might be Garland or Collins and Mona appeared in a few songs from the 1940s, or of course Mona Lisa. A whimsical song written so that all three leading lights in the music industry at the time could be encompassed in a scenario of wanting to be your lover. For anyone who would wish for an idea how Bob Dylan and the Beatles might have sounded together then you will need to buy an album titled 'Greetings From Planet Love', by the group 'The Fraternal Order of the All'. In fact it was a spoof album by Andrew Gold, it contains many different styles of music, the Bob Dylan track is titled 'Mr Plastic Business Man'.

The Number of remaindered tracks had now dropped, three of those were intended to be singles, two where used the other was not released until 1985. The 'Highway 61 Revisited' album was even lauded by Bob himself, he felt that he would be unable to improve on it. The magazines all discussed the album the predominantly folk 'Sing Out' had pages dedicated to the Newport electrification and the 'Highway 61 Revisited' album. The Dylan, Butterfield performance at Newport was larger than life, now 35 years later the rest of the bill is forgotten, only Bob Dylan and the problems with the acoustic folk brigade remain in our collective consciousness. Pete Seeger so vehemently anti-electric even made an electric album, ask any non-musical person in the UK about Pete Seeger and they will only remember 'Little Boxes' made out of ticky-tacky and he always sounded just the same.

Bob returned to the studio in October 1965 and commenced work on tracks for 'Blonde on Blonde'. A combination of The Hawks with Al Kooper, Bruce Langhorne and session musicians were used, Paul Griffin and Joseph Souter did a five hour session each. By the end of March 1966 the Blonde on Blonde album was completed except for some Bob Johnston overdubbing performed in June by Charlie McCoy and drummer Kenny Buttery. The extraordinary album was recorded on a 4-track machine, it would be 1967 before Bob moved onto an 8-track machine. It was the first ever pop music double album, Frank Zappa's 'Freak Out' was released two months later, Frank was not happy, one wonders why, Frank's album was the first double album by a group, 'The Mothers of Invention'.

Bob had been seen around town with Edie Sedgwick, she was a starlet used by Andy Warhol in his films. (There is a short biography of her interesting and difficult life at the end of this book). The two Bob's (Dylan and Neuwirth) would be seen in the company of Nico (another of Warhol's women), Andy and Edie. Andy and Edie would dress alike and go out on the town as 'twins'. But Bob was in love with another. Nico went on the find fame an fortune with The Velvet Underground, a group championed by Andy Warhol. Nico a beautiful teutonic blonde also recorded a vocal version of Bob's originally instrumental 'I'll Keep it With Mine'. On the 22nd (some listings state 25th) of November 1965 Bob Dylan married Sara Lowndes, completing a wonderful year for Bob Dylan. D.A Pennebaker had made throwaway remark that I thought extremely pertinent at the time. When he made his film of Bob he said that he just wanted to film him with people. He then continued his conversation with "You can't point a camera and know what's in a man head, but it does allow you to speculate". This of course is true of Bob Dylan's lyrics and prose it allows us to speculate on the meanings and influences, albeit with our own personal interpretations. In Harry Nilsson's film and soundtrack for 'The Point' he had a character full of knowledge who pointed out 'You see what you want to see, and you hear what you want to hear', hardly new but so appropriate for Bob Dylan's fans and admirers. So why did Bob carry that large light bulb into the arrivals hall at Heathrow, saying "keep a good head and always carry a light bulb". The May 1966 tour concluded with a great performance at London's Royal Albert Hall accompanied by Ronnie Hawkins' band The Hawks. The show was recorded for a live album that was not officially released, but bootlegs were available within weeks with the famous 'Judas' audience call, Bob responded with 'I Don't Believe You, you're a liar'. There were writers convinced that the 'Judas' remark came from the audience at the Manchester Free Trade Hall Show, but it was at The Albert Hall according to the bootleg album. The audiences continued to show their disapproval, critics and advisers thought The Hawks (soon to be called Levon and The Hawks) were terrible, Bob never wavered from his course. During the tour Bob and Robbie Robertson visited John Lennon where he observed the two leading musical phenomenons at the time compose a song together which was recorded into a portable tape recorder and subsequently lost. Bob was happier playing with a band than alone on the stage with just guitar, he probably felt that the audience got their money's-worth with The Band. The people who saw Bob off duty during the tour realised that he was much happier with a group of friends with whom he could share some of his spare time. He continued to write songs, some with Robbie Robertson, 'Tarantula' was still in progress and a second film 'Eat The Document' was awaiting editing.

May 1966 also saw the released of 'Rainy day Women Nos 12 & 35, it went to No 2 in the USA in May 1966 and No 7 in the UK in June, another million selling single. Albert Grossman wanted To make his new signing Carly Simon into the female version of Bob Dylan, she was already a singer songwriter, and had recorded with her sister as the Simon Sisters. Bob rewrote some of the lyrics of 'Baby, Let Me Follow You Down' for her. She recorded some tracks with The Band; Al Kooper and Mike Bloomfield were present on some tracks. The four tracks produced by Bob Johnston and Albert Grossman and recorded for Columbia Records still await a release. Shortly after the completion of the successful tour Bob became a father, in June 1966 Jesse Byron Dylan was born. There exists an Elliot Landy taken photograph of Bob with a 3 year old Jesse on his lap. In my opinion Bob's best ever picture, two expressionless faces staring at the camera, full of care and love, hard to describe, try to find it. At one of the happiest times in his life the worst was waiting around the corner.

FROM AN ACCIDENT TO RECOVERY

A poem is never finished;
it's always an accident that puts a stop to it-
that is to say, gives it to the public.
Paul Valery 1871-1945

Bob was injured in a motor cycle accident at his home, he was riding a British Triumph 500cc, as advertised on his 'Highway 61 Revisited' album cover t-shirt. He suffered from a broken neck vertebrae. It paralysed the man for a short time. It may have been a blessing in disguise because it allowed him to stop working and re-charge his batteries. He also got valuable time with his wife and son. Bob was living at Woodstock near New York, at that time a place where aesthetes from all facets of the arts lived. It was reported that Bob went to Cape Cod, Massachusetts to recuperate. Bob's friend Richard Farina was not so lucky he died in his motor-cycle accident in 1966.

The music industry was full of innuendo, it was alleged that Bob was an alcoholic and a junkie a broken man. We didn't know at the time if this was just bluster intended to keep an injured man in the public eye so that he could eventually resume his career at the top of his profession. Of course a month after the accident in August 1966 **'BLONDE ON BLONDE'** was released, the greatest album (double album) ever made, this is my opinion and the opinion of many others of my generation. The album went to No 9 in the USA and No 3 in the UK, yet another gold album, it is still selling well in 1999. CBS decided to release another single, 'I Want You' was taken from the album but it only reached No 20 in the USA and 16 in the UK, understandable because everyone already had the album.

The accident also allowed Bob the time to put together his novel 'Tarantula'. The music industry machine must have been considerably concerned, not only for Bob but for the profits they had allowed in their respective budgets for the years ahead.

I was reminded of an extract from Harry Graham's, 'Ruthless Rhymes and Heartless Homes', where he wrote the following and I quote...

"There's been an accident", they said,
"Your servant's cut in half he's dead!"
"Indeed!" said Mr Jones
"Please send me the half that's got my keys."

To That I have to add the anonymous remark attributed to a car insurance company...'After you have heard two eye witness accounts of an auto accident, it makes one wonder about the truth of all history'.

With all the claims and counter claims concerning Bob's health he remained out of sight which made people even more inquisitive. It was John Hammond that decided Bob should record 'Blonde on Blonde' in Nashville with musicians that were competent, just like the musicians that Johnny Cash used on his albums. The head of Columbia, Nashville, at the time was Don Lyle. John Hammond invited Don to a session, unfortunately Bob was recording 'Oxford Town' at the time. This was Oxford, Mississippi, where a lynching had occurred. Don Lyle listened and then said to John Hammond... "My God, if he comes to Nashville we will all be run out of town, no John I couldn't take the chance". He did take the chance and they loved Bob in Nashville. The tracks used on the album were recorded in Columbia's Nashville Studio, with Jaime 'Robbie' Robertson and Al Kooper with country music stars such as Charlie McCoy, Wayne Moss, Jerry Kennedy, Joe South, Kenny Buttrey, Bill Aikins, Henry Strzelecki and Hargus Robbins. In 1969 most of these session musicians released an inspired album titled 'Area Code 615'. Joe South released a superb album titled 'Introspect' in 1969 and had a worldwide hit with 'Games People Play'(1969), and 'Walk A Mile in My Shoes' in 1970. At the time of Bob's sessions these men were just session musicians paid by the hour, but they were experts on their instruments. They were relaxed and versatile and could play anything in any style. Al Kooper took over the job of rehearsing them to a conception created by Bob who then arrived at the studio and sang.

A new word emerged in the critics' vocabulary to describe Bob's work on this album, sophisticated. The cover photograph by Jerry Schatzenberg is slightly out of focus. Bob is wearing a suede jacket on the cover there were other photographs on the inner sleeve not all repeated for the later CD releases on which the songs didn't quite fit, the single CD time maximum was too short.

'Rainy Day Women Nos 12 and 35': It would have been more aptly titled 'Every one must get stoned', but that may have confused the song with the Ray Charles song 'Let's Go Get Stoned'; also recorded by Ashford and Simpson. Bob's song was assumed to be pertaining to drugs, Ray Charles' was for alcohol, a fact confirmed by Valerie Simpson who said the song concerned drinking gin. Although it was refused air-play in the USA and UK it was still a hit. In the film 'High Society' Frank Sinatra and Bing Crosby in their famous duet 'Well Did You Ever' stated that 'stoned' meant drunk, it still didn't convince the radio stations. Bob endeavoured to redress the balance by saying that it was a song concerning alcohol a permitted 'drug' in most non-Islamic countries. It was known that Bob did not consider marijuana or opium to be harmful and LSD was in fact a medicine. Bob had made contradictory statements, he claimed that Sex, heroin and pot were 'groovy', well one out of three is a poor score Bob. It was Bob's opinion that everyone had smoked pot. So we have this, so-called, sophisticated intellectual advocating drugs in one interview and then possibly after management advice turning his remarks on their heads. These remarks were made in 1965 and 1966, by 1969 he would be saying of drugs "I don't have any views at all-I sure wish I did-I sure would like to share them with you all". It was this song and these remarks that started A.J.Weberman on his one man crusade to prove that Bob was a junkie, of course the motor-cycle accident came at a perfect time for those wishing infer that Bob was in fact drying-out and having treatment for drug withdrawal. The recording was something special. Charlie McCoy is playing bass and trumpet simultaneously, Wayne Butler was on trombone, Kenny Buttery on modified drums. The recording sheet actually states that McCoy played the same two instruments on the track 'Most Likely You Go Your Way' but eye witness reports beg to differ. The Salvation Army sound that Bob heard in his head for this track was thus created in the studio and not the parking lot, a song recorded in the early hours of the morning. I think that Bob is using 'stoned' as a metaphor for pilloried and criticised, neither drugs nor alcohol. This makes the song innocuous and ordinary, he is inferring that these journalists will not give up, 'they criticise all the time and whatever I do'; of course the ambiguity in the word 'stoned' is what gave the song the extra news coverage.

'Pledging My Time': This is most often regarded as an existential Chicago blues. The pianist Hargus Robbins carries this track although he has rarely received any appreciation for his efforts. One assumes that the person that got lucky in the song was in fact Bob, but it would have taken some forecasting to predict a verse that would mention an accident and an ambulance, Bob got lucky, he lived. Another song titled 'Pledging My Love' was a posthumous hit for Johnny Ace in February 1955. Johnny Ace was killed in an accident when he was playing Russian Roulette backstage at the Houston Auditorium on Christmas Eve 1954. In Bob's song the 'poison headache' was considered to be a hangover when it was really just 'love'. This is a love song, no more no less.

'Visions of Johanna': I think someone should ask The Rolling Stones if this song inspired their dancing mule on the 'Get Your Ya-Yas Out' cover, anyone with knowledge of both will understand the significance. This song was originally titled 'Seems Like A Freeze-Out'. For me the impact of the song would have been lessened considerably without that superb Joe South bass line, listen to the song and concentrate on that alone and you will see what I mean. The song is filled with visions, if Bob ever purposely created a cut-up-method song then this would be it. The song is really of Louise who is considered to be a inadequate replacement for Johanna his Mona Lisa, his Madonna. Joan Baez thought that she was the target of the song, she felt that there was a separate conspiracy to make her think it concerned someone else, these feelings are the ingredients of paranoia. Bob is singing of visions of flawlessness, a superiority gained by excellence. Al Kooper plays ghost themes after the line in the lyric which mentions a ghost. It probably has no connection but Bob's reference to 'skeleton keys' I always assumed were either piano 'keys' or the 'keys' in which harmonica's are set. Eminent conductor Sir Thomas Beecham once described the sound of a harpsichord as 'two skeletons copulating on a corrugated tin roof'. We must also remember the lines of Geofrey Madan (1895-1947) who wrote 'the cat that isn't let out of the bag often becomes a skeleton in the cupboard'. This song is another of Bob's 'skeleton's in the cupboard'. Dylan has rarely sung, played or confused us with such superb lyrics before or since, sublime Dylan, no question!

'One of Us Must Know (Sooner or Later)': This song was released as a single following on quickly from the poor reception afforded to 'Can You Please Crawl Out'. It missed completely in the USA but reached No 33 in the less fickle UK. This is another song in which Joan Baez considered that Bob was talking to her, Bob never realised when she left him it was for ever. Strange that Bob was doing everything to shake Joan out of his life without hurting her and then decides to twist the knife in a song. Perhaps this was not for her at all, the cliche of 'if the cap fits wear it' may be more pertinent here. The first verse presents a man confused, the chorus is almost an apology. The second verse is the choice he had to make. The last verse is bizarre, ambivalence and apology, almost a reconciliation, then she turns on him as if to get her vengeance, she clawed his eyes out. Again the 4/4 bounce beat of the song conceals the power of the lyrics. Bob said it wasn't about anybody it was just a song. Paul Griffin's piano is excellent on this track, he taught girlfriend (the earlier mentioned) Valerie Simpson to play piano, she had chart success with Nicholas Ashford, as Ashford and Simpson with 'Solid (as A Rock)'.

'I Want You': Another song with a cast of characters more appropriate for The Basement Tapes cover photograph. The arrangement was created by Al Kooper except for the guitar solo from Wayne Moss. As the lyric is evasive the hacks had to infer that what the narrator in the song wanted was drugs, when it was more likely Sara. The guilt ridden undertaker and the inebriated politician could be a scene from a film. 'Born to Lose' is mentioned which was another Ray Charles hit. The narrator is taking advice on his next step with the object of his affections. As in most situations he makes up his own mind that he wants her. Bob mentions The Queen of Spades. If this is his first Tarot reference then 'Spades' are in fact 'Swords'. The Queen of Swords represents 'loss, absence, privation, separation' exactly the premise of Bob's lyrics. The narrator has the desire but is yet to achieve his goal. This could be a reference to Robert Johnson's 'Little Queen of Spades', in his song he wants her, in fact men will not leave her alone. This was the final song completed for Bob's album, it was a surefire hit single reaching No 20 in the USA and 16 in the UK. **'Stuck Inside Mobile With The Memphis Blues Again'**: We get Shakespeare, the pointy-toed shoes of the British pop stars and Mona. She returns to a Dylan lyric is it Bo Diddley's or even Mona from Ambrose and Jack Jackson's Band's song from the 1940s? Joe South is playing the punch-beat guitar. The critical comparing of the lyrics of this song with the traditional 'I Wish I Was A Mole in the Ground' are tenuous. It is true both songs mention that railroad men will kill you or drink your blood like wine, but that is where the similarity stops. Nine long verses of imagery. This could be 'Desperation Row Revisited' or another of Bob's dream-nightmares. It is deliberately complicated, there is just no way into this lyric, but a 'Ruthie' did come back to haunt Bob in the 1990s, claiming to be his lover since 1970.

'Leopard-Skin Pill-box Hat': One take has a Lowery organ door bell effect sounding and the musicians shouting 'Who's there', which was part of the original version of 'Open the Door, Richard', a hit for Ted Heath and The Stargazers in the UK and The Pied Pipers in the USA. It is relevant because Bob would use the song in his Basement Tapes sessions. 'Pill-Box' is a 12-bar-blues in which Bob considered himself to be a just a craze, a fad, just like the ever changing fashion accessory detailed in the song. Robbie Robertson on guitar although Bob can be heard playing at the opening of the song. Bob finds the 'hat' amusing, wants to jump on it. He suggests that he might wear a belt around his head to create a fashion. We are not informed if she removed her hat when the narrator saw her making love in the garage. Released as a single in June 1967 during Bob's recuperation it only reached No 83 in the USA. Of course Edie Sedgwick was photographed wearing a pill-box hat.

'Just Like A Woman': This song which was considered to be politically and socially incorrect was released as a single which reached No 33 in USA, not released in the UK because Manfred Mann recorded it and took it to No 10 in the UK charts. As a statement the title can be read in a derogatory manner or as Bob uses it the song as descriptions of the lady. The New York Times writer Marion Meade thought that the song was full of sexist slurs, what nonsense, still it made a good headline. It reads just like a song for a woman with the appearance of a little girl, why search for deviations, 'evil is who evil thinks'. This is another track believed to be for Edie Sedgwick who had a meeting with Bob at The Kettle of Fish Cafe in 1965. Bob mentions her amphetamines and her pearls. The album title could have been for Edie, but the initials of the album are BOB so many ideas have been presented over the years. Edie was actually being escorted by Bob a few weeks before he married Sara. As Edie had deserted Andy Warhol's clique for that of Neuwirth and Dylan it gave Warhol immense pleasure to upset her with the news of Bob's wedding. Edie would eventually die of accidental barbiturate over-dose in bed with her new man Mike Post. Her friend Robert

Margouleff half of the synthesizer group 'Tonto's Expanding Headband' had taken care of her for some time. Robert Margouleff made a film titled 'Ciao Manhattan' about Edie's life and used 'Just Like a Woman' in the soundtrack. Did this immature man in the song really think that 'all' women were as described, perhaps he just wanted to annoy 50% of the population. The song became one of Bob's most recorded songs there are versions available by The Byrds, Joe Cocker, The Hollies, B.B.King, Nina Simone and Rod Stewart. It is Roberta Flack's version that is the most interesting, she almost creates an answer-back song indicating how women are exploited and deceived. Bob wrote this with Otis Redding in mind, he hoped for a soulful version. He sent a demonstration disc to Otis but he never recorded the song.

'Most Likely You Go Your Way (and I'll Go Mine)': A straightforward blues stomper for the realisation that parting is inevitable.
'Temporary Like Achilles': 'Medicine Sunday' was recorded as a warm up number, 2 takes, in New York in October 1965, just a few minor lyric changes and 'Achilles' was born. Bob wanted to create the 'Mercury' sound so it was no surprise to find 'Achilles' used, only his heel could be attacked, his weak spot. In the song he has to find her achilles heel so that he can break down her indifference. Achilles is also the name of her bodyguard. It was mooted that this might be for the gay community, it certainly could be read that way, it changes all the connotations of the song, but of course it is unlikely, Bob had little time for homosexuals. The song does have the superb line 'I'm helpless like a rich man's child'. I have seen (and employed) so many individuals that came into business life highly educated but so totally unworldly that they rarely lasted more than a month in the job. The 'Writings' book has a drawing of bearded horseman with a shoulder yolk and two small buckets attached. He is holding what appears to be a fly-whisk in his right hand, does this bear any relevance to the song, apparently not.

'Absolutely Sweet Marie': Sexual connotations in 'beating on my trumpet' and 'it gets so hard'. Song created in the studio, Al Kooper did not prepare the musicians for this track. More sexual inferences surface with, train, gate, tunnel, six white horses is a sexual metaphor which was used on 'See My Grave Is Kept Clean' on Bob's first album. Ry Cooder converted the horses to six white boomers for his christmas song. She'll be riding six white horses when she is comes, she'll be coming around the mountain. The narrator has been in the penitentiary, he is out and being stalked by a Persian drunkard. Maria made promises to him but where is she when he wants her? **'Fourth Time Around'**: I always thought that Bob was trying to make this up as he went along in the style of Bukka White, he does get stuck a few times. The basic theme is The Beatles song 'Norwegian Wood' with extra harmonised country guitars. In fact the sound is closer to a mariachi band, Bob was passing through a Mexican music stage. It was also reported that Bob played this song to John Lennon when they were both in London, I am not convinced that these lyrics could be identical, it sounds to be predominantly improvisation to these ears. They would be interested in each others 'crutch' of course but he gave her his last piece of chewing gum and she wouldn't give him any Jamaican rum in return. A throw-away track and although the tune is good the lyrics are only average.

'Obviously Five Believers': A rocking rhythm and blues which uses the 'Willie the Pimp' riff used by Frank Zappa and Captain Beefheart. It is derivative of Sonny Boy Williamson's 'Good Morning Little Schoolgirl' and Memphis Minnie's 'Me and My Chauffeur'. Charlie McCoy is on harmonica and there are some inspired guitar breaks from Robbie Robertson. **'Sad Eyed Lady of The Lowlands'**: A reverential love song which had a side of the album to itself. Bob later admitted in song that he wrote this in the Chelsea Hotel (in 'Sara' on the Desire album) for Sara. Bob told Robert Shelton that he considered this the best song that he ever wrote. Sara's previous husband Victor Lowndes is mentioned as the 'magazine husband' in the song. (I must write that I am confused over his name, on television the subtitles write 'Lownes' as do some of the writers). It is my contention that the inspiration for this song was Lord Byron, we know that Bob had read his poetry, he had named his son Byron. I would think that Bob had read Byron's 'She Walks in Beauty' just before he wrote 'Sad Eyed Lady', the verses of Byron's poem could fit the melody. I am not saying that there is any plagiarism, but Byron's poem perfectly captures the mood of Bob's love for Sara at the time. We had 'Achilles' earlier, now we have 'Mercury' in reference to her mouth. She is his Queen, he is her King, his pack of cards has no Jack or ace. The last verse is Bob's no holds barred 'love verse', if they were not madly in love then this verse would be so embarrassing, as it is it works beautifully. Bob has stolen her, he is her thief and she is on parole. A line that could only be created by 1960s Bob Dylan. The track is very long, one can imagine the tired amusement of the musicians. It was in the early hours of the morning when they were called to the studio to record this track. As it progresses one can feel the musicians building the song to a resounding climax and then pulling back and starting to build again. Just imagine this marathon of a song, these brilliant musicians looking at each other wondering if it is going to finish, mock yawns, looking at their watches, pretending to drop off, but then realising if they made a mistake it would have to start all over again, which brought them back to their senses. Only one take was made and it was definitive even though these musicians must have been terribly tired. Bob was still re-writing the lyrics whilst they kicked-their-heels and waited, perhaps it wasn't written at the Chelsea Hotel after all. The song is shorter than 'Desolation Row' so why didn't CBS add another couple of tracks to the album, side two of 'Another Side Of Bob Dylan' included three more tracks alongside 'Desolation Row'. **'I'll Keep It With Mine'**: When this was originally recorded it was laid down by the band as an instrumental. It was mentioned earlier with reference to Nico. Nico recorded this on her 'Chelsea Girls' album, Bob's piano solo version was released on Biograph, (the rehearsal was included on The Bootleg Series). Both John Sebastian and John Boone played bass, with John Hammond Jr and Bruce Langhorne on guitars in the session details. A harmonica introduction and honky-tonk saloon bar piano accompany, although the piano (probably Bob himself) was not noted on the session details; the other instruments can't be heard on the recording. In the Biograph notes it states that it was originally composed for Judy Collins. On Judy's album 'Judy Collins Sings Dylan' she had written an open letter to Bob. The letter was very personal, she said that Bob spoke to her when she was at the 'edge of the precipice'. She continues to inform us that Bob is always a gentleman, always kind. Once when Judy was staying at Albert Grossman's house she heard Bob singing quietly in the basement, he didn't want to disturb anyone else. Judy sat outside the door and heard him sing 'Mr Tambourine Man' for the very first time. Judy also wrote in the letter of Cisco Houston, Joan Baez, Peter Le Farge, Peter Yarrow, Jack Elliott, Dave Van Ronk and Paul Butterfield, this was their clique. Bob told Judy that 'I'll Keep It With Mine' was written for her. Judy writes with so much love and gratitude for Bob and she closes her letter beautifully when she writes 'As I sang these songs I looked for you, I found you, and I found me'. The Bootleg series recording is of special importance because the dylanophile can hear just how Bob creates a song with the assistance of competent musicians. The song improves as it progresses.

'Tell Me Momma': Something wrong with her, again. The first verse has sexual connotations with Momma wanting a young kid to get it to work like a nine pound hammer, sounds painful. The rest is impenetrable, pun intended. **'She's Your Lover Now'**: The eternal triangle, there is ambivalence here. The narrator is part of the triangle, he is making sense of his ex-lover and her new boyfriend. The narrator is speaking to both of them. He is also not asking for the responsibility, she is his now. The new man is madly in love with her but she wants to re-kindle the flame in the narrator. When this version was released on The Bootleg Series, John Bauldie kindly added the lost lyrics at the end of the song to the album booklet. In this verse he continues to wash his hands of the affair, he is not going to get into another situation, she is his lover now.

Jerrold Schatzenberg was included on the original 'Blonde' cover (not in CD release) sweating heavily. He became a film director and filmed 'The Seduction of Joe Tynan', 'Scarecrow' and others. The original 'Blonde' cover was changed when actress Claudia Cardinale objected to her photograph being included, Edie Sedgwick also disappeared from the subsequent CD release.

Apparently the Columbia design team were not aware that the picture was of Claudia, they thought it was a friend of Bob's. The title might just be a reference to Andy Warhol and Edie Sedgwick who each wore a blonde wig so that she and Andy could pretend to be twins; it was more probable that Bob had seen the show 'Brecht on Brecht' with Suze Rotolo.

Due to Bob's incapacity CBS released a greatest hits compilation in the UK which reached No 6, spending in total 82 weeks in the charts. This collection included 'Positively 4th Street' on an album for the first time. The USA version of the album was different and that too went gold reaching No 10. The USA cover photography won a Grammy Award in February 1968 for Roland (it should have been spelled as Rowland) Scherman and art directors John Berg and Bob Cato. The UK issue had a Jerrold Schatzenberg photograph. Rowland told Rod McBeath that his Grammy Award arrived in the post broken so he returned it and never heard from them again. The USA issue also included a poster insert designed by Milton Glaser. The best album cover of that year went to Peter Blake and his wife Jan Howarth for their 'Sgt Pepper's Lonely Hearts Club Band' collage, Bob's album was in good company.

Earlier I discussed the French poets Baudelaire, Rimbaud and Verlaine, Lord Byron was dead in 1824 at the age of 36, before Rimbaud and Verlaine were born and as Baudelaire was born in 1821 all three could have been influenced by him. Bob Dylan's style of writing is arguably closer to that of Byron than any other poet. His poetry is masculine (read 'Sestos to Abydos'), packed full of satire, 'Don Juan Canto III', at times passionate 'When we Two Parted'. Byron disliked the poems of William Wordsworth and Samuel Taylor Coleridge but enjoyed Alexander Pope and John Dryden, they are all mentioned in Don Juan, one can not mistake Byron's derision for those he doesn't like. When John Ruskin wrote 'Byron wrote of only of what he had seen and known, and spoke without exaggeration' he might have also been describing Bob Dylan or Van Morrison. Byron was a friend of Percy Bysshe Shelley, his wife Mary and Leigh Hunt, they visited him at his home in Italy. Byron joined the Greek revolt against the Turks in 1823, he formed his own regiment with his own money and was eventually made Commander-in-Chief of the armed forces. He caught rheumatic fever and died, his heart was retained in Greece his body sent home to be buried in England.

Bob was getting around again and it was an informed guess that he was recording in the basement studio of The Band's 'Big Pink' studio, a large house in Woodstock painted pink, well what did you expect. A bootleg album became available titled 'Great White Wonder' probably the largest selling bootleg recording ever. The new Dylan tracks that emerged were recorded by a host of top groups. Manfred Mann did 'The Mighty Quinn', Julie Driscoll and Brian Auger, 'This Wheel's on Fire', Peter Paul and Mary 'Too Much of

Nothing'. In 1972 'Coulson, Dean, McGuinness and Flint' recorded a full album of these songs on their 'Lo and Behold'. The CD issue of 'Lo and Behold' included two extra tracks, they managed to make 'Eternal Circle' sound like 'Honky Tonk Woman'. These artists would have been approached by Bob's publishers with Bob and The Band's performances of the songs in the hopes that they might record them. It was Albert Grossman's way of keeping Bob in the public eye whilst he was incapacitated, it was part of the manager's job. The songs were assigned to Dwarf Music rather than Witmark, Dwarf had been formed by Bob and Albert Grossman, and Bob had also opened 'Big Sky Music' for more publishing rights.

Bob's album was not released until 1975 after 'Blood on the Tracks' but for the sake of continuity, and as 'The Great White Wonder' was even available in some official record shops, we will place the album here at the time it was recorded.

THE BASEMENT TAPES cover appears to be in the Big Pink basement but it was reported later that the photograph actually came from a band session in the basement of The Los Angeles Y.M.C.A. David Blue sitting on the floor praying wears the greatcoat. Neil Young, Al Kooper (dressed as a woman) and Ringo Starr (the clown with the red nose) are also supposed to be in the picture, but I doubt it, the belly dancer does looks familiar. The Band are there of course and the rest are just friends dressed as persons mentioned in the songs; the dog's name was Hamlet.

Robbie Robertson re-mixed the tracks and Bob finally sanctioned the release of the double album for July 1975; it reached No 8 in UK and No 7 in the USA. Whilst Bob was incapacitated Woody Guthrie died aged 55 on September 1967. On the 20th January 1968, Bob was seen on the stage for the first time since the accident, he joined the band at a tribute concert for Woody at The Carnegie Hall, New York.

What we have to bear in mind is that Bob could have died in the accident. We have seen over the years what has happened to the work of Marc Bolan, Jim Morrison, Janis Joplin, Buddy Holly, John Lennon, Nick Drake, Tim Buckley, Hank Williams and of course Jimi Hendrix. All these persons that died young have been lauded for their work, they will be remembered though history. It is not just the music industry that pours accolades on the persons that die young there are comparable celebrities in actors James Dean, Marilyn Monroe and Montgomery Clift, comedian Lenny Bruce, writers Arthur Rimbaud, Thomas Chatterton, Thomas Tyler Bootman, Jack Kerouac, Hart Crane, Sylvia Plath, Edgar Allan Poe, Dylan Thomas, Anne Sexton, F.Scott Fitzgerald, Jack London, painters Vincent Van Gogh, Jackson Pollock and Amando Modigliani, dancer Vaslav Nijinsky, the list could go on and on. The point I wish to make is that sad though their deaths were none lived long enough to ruin what they had already created. If Bob Dylan had died in his accident then his name would have been added to the list above, if Allen Ginsberg was correct then Bob's name would have been the most eminent name. So many of the emerging singer songwriters of the day that lived on never created work to compare to their first three albums or five years of writing. Joni Mitchell, Kris Kristofferson (studio janitor in Nashville at time of Blonde on Blonde), James Taylor, Country Joe McDonald, The Rolling Stones, Neil Young, Harold Pinter, John Osborne, Paul McCartney and so many others all reached plateaus in their respective careers spoiled by the new found affluence. They need to be aspiring and needy to perform and write, but of course celebrity takes its toll on the reclusive time needed to create. I realise that many of the dedicated fans of artists that have continued into their dotage would argue against some of the names that I place on this plateau of the 'now ordinary'-'once brilliant' category, but they must be honest with themselves when evaluating. The nearest poetic singers to Bob at the time were Van Morrison and Leonard Cohen, they still are the nearest. Bob Dylan and the others had to continue, they survived but could they maintain the quality of their work, the critics would still be laying in ambush for any drop in excellence.

With Bob at last back performing at The Woody Guthrie Tribute show at least there was hope, but of course the recording at the Big Pink were not officially released. As there were some wonderful songs within the recordings I have always maintained that it was a career error, the songs sit perfectly in the gradual growth of Bob's compositions between 'Blonde on Blonde' and 'John Wesley Harding'.

If the accident happened at the end of July 1966, it would be October 1967 before Bob entered a studio to record tracks for a new album. The basement on the cover shows a concrete wall, the house furnace heating system and pipes hanging from the ceiling, not the best design for a recording studio, the 'big pink' basement must have been similar. One can only imagine the reverberation from those walls as they played, especially from the drums. The characters that pass before our ears on these recordings are as unusual as we would expect from any William Burroughs novel. Apparently some of the songs were so risque that they were either destroyed or secreted away for later use. Where are 'Wildwood Flower', 'The Old Triangle', 'I'm Not There', 'Stones You Throw', 'Dear John' and 'I Won't Be Home No More', that is if they were recorded.

'Odds and Ends' includes Richard Manuel on drums. A song of time lost which is lost forever. On Donovan's 'HMS Donovan' album there was a children's song with the same theme, created from a poem by Ffrida Wolfe, but that is where the similarities end. This was probably remaindered due to the overt sexuality. Columbia would be aware that the dylanologists would examine the lyrics. We get 'spilled juice', 'box' and 'head'. We could easily substitute 'semen', 'scrotum' and 'fellatio'. There is also 'get on someone else' and the premise that this is all very 'nudge nudge' humour with 'you know what I mean'. **'Million Dollar Bash'** was another song recorded by Fairport Convention. The song has a rural barnyard setting, are silly Nelly and Turtle in fact hillbilly's or yokels. The Coasters song 'Along Came Jones' gets a mention as does The Beatles 'Hello Goodbye' and De Dee Sharp's 'Mashed Potato'. This is in fact the story of the musicians creating the basement tapes. Procrastination and working only when the fancy strikes them. A reflection of the quiet mundane life of Woodstock. The Turtle was an expression used to describe Bob when he was wearing his neck brace. Benjamin Turtle appeared in Tarantula. This will be some extravagant show, orgy, party, but at that cost, a million dollars of course. The inference by one writer that 'The Sad Turtle' in Jack Kerouac's 'Mexico City Blues' might be the influence is tenuous, but we do know that Bob has read that book of poems.

'Goin' To Acapulco' was not in the songbooks as it was not registered until 1975. One wonders why Bob always thinks that the only place to have some fun is in Mexico; Tom Thumb's Blues said the same. Rose Marie is a hooker in Mexico giving her services cheap. 'Pump' and 'come' are possible sexual metaphors sung to a slow rhythm of a tune that would become 'I Pity the Poor Immigrant'. Not sure what Bob means when he writes that he liked the Taj Mahal. The later songbook lyrics only vary in three lines of the eight lines in the second verse. **'Lo and Behold'**: The narrator is escaping to Pittsburg to meet his woman. Flights of fancy, another dream, travelling to town on a Ferris Wheel. Why is there a problem revealing his identity to the ticket inspector and coachman on the train? In the recording Robbie was preoccupied which meant that he missed his cue and has to catch up on the second chorus. What terrible deed has the narrator done that when he gives his name, he hangs his head in shame. This line is paraphrased in 'St Augustine' where Bob writes 'I bowed my head and cried'. **'Clothes Line Saga'** was originally just 'Clothes Line' (or 'Answer to Ode') in the 'writings' book. Apparently a response song to Bobby Gentry's 'Ode to Billie Joe' a hit in the summer of 1967. Bob has created a gossip calypso, a scene of persons chatting across the garden fence, it is mostly a conversational lyric. Bob decided to write a song without any deep inner meaning. One can imagine him saying as soon as the recording was complete "Let's see what the analysts make of that lyric!"

'Apple Sucking Tree': Sung to the melody of 'Froggy Went A-Courting'. Bob liked it so much that 'Froggy' was included on the 'Good As I Been to You' album in 1992. Robbie Robertson is on drums, this was one of the instrument-musical-chairs games that they played, all swapping instruments, Bob is on piano. They didn't have a drummer at the time as Levon Helm had left the band in 1966. It is evident that some of the percussion on the basement tapes is someone tapping the 'basement-boiler' in lieu of drums. The lyrics are quite innocuous, you and me under the tree. The last line of 'the 49 of you go burn in hell' is more than a little strange. Is this just the thoughts of being buried together under the tree, or 'making love underneath the apple tree', just like Larry Williams did with his 'Bony Maronie'. **'Please, Mrs Henry'**: Is an enjoyable romp of a song, could be Charles Bukowski influenced reminds me of the late Oliver Reed the well known inebriate. The song for a professional drinker. Chatting up the barmaid, asking her to pump him few more beers, all The Band are falling about laughing at the end. If Mrs Henry is a substitute for a real woman she is certainly wearing her man out in some way or the other. I would suspect that the reason for the sudden fade-out was because the following verses were not considered suitable for young ears, or any ears. **'Tears of Rage'** has music composed with Richard Manuel, (sung by Richard and played by The Band on the 'Music From Big Pink' album). Andy Gill thought that this was Bob's version of King Lear moved to America. Broken promises, regret and bitterness, problems with his children, possibly just for any parent with ungrateful children. It was also supposed by some critics to be aimed at Vietnam, a war of which Americans gradually became tired. The tears for the young men that died for nothing. I can't find anything in the lyric to prove that point. Children always consider that parental advice is interference rather than concern, every generation is the same. The last lines of 'we're so low and life is brief' might just be a call for the discarded child to return home to make their peace before the parent dies.

   'Too Much of Nothing' became a hit for Peter Paul and Mary. One wonders if this was Bob's first overtly Biblical song? 'Isaiah 49:4 states 'Is it for nothing I have toiled'. The Book of Job is full of 'nothings' in the text, also Corinthians 2-6:10 states 'having nothing yet possessing'. Waters of oblivion are mentioned, in the King James Bible, Psalm 88 mentions 'land of forgetfulness' and this was subsequently changed in the New English Bible to 'land of oblivion', are they the same, I think not. Bob's lyric states one can't have too much of nothing, so no-one has control. What is there for a man to lose when he has nothing, a man can try anything and not end up with less. When politicians offer their new ideals to the poor and hungry they will win votes for change, they had nothing under the old system they can't possibly have less with the new. **'Yea! Heavy and a Bottle of Bread'**: This song almost makes better sense if one reads all the all first lines in turn then the second and third. Might be the cut-up method, lines with no connection. This is a comedy song for a drunk drummer. **'Ain't No More Cane'** is a traditional song, Alan Lomax included it on his 'Texas Folk Songs' and Bert Jansch included a version on his 'Leather Launderette'. Rick Danko is on mandolin, Richard Manuel drums, Garth Hudson accordion and Robbie Robertson on acoustic guitar. The Band are so competent that they can switch to any instrument and still produce the same tight sound. **'Crash on the Levee'** is also known as 'Down in the Flood'. The Basement Tapes title was different to the 'Writings' book. The lines 'sugar for sugar salt for salt' are taken from Richard Rabbit Brown's 'James Alley Blues' from 1927. It was included in Harry Smith's Anthology of American Folk Music it was also recorded by Sandy Denny. Richard Brown's song has always been a favourite of Bob's one wonders why he never recorded a full version. Richard Brown died in 1937 in New Orleans, at the age of 57. He was also known as the singing boatman of Lake Pontchartrain were he earned his living. He recorded very few songs (five for RCA Victor) and sadly is only remembered for 'James Alley Blues'; James Alley was the roughest and toughest street in New Orleans, Louis Armstrong was born there. Bob's song may be advice not to get too deep in one's problems, eventually you will lose all your friends. Blood Sweat and Tears also recorded a rousing version of 'Down in the Flood' for their 'New Blood' album.

'Tiny Montgomery' : One writer thought that this for a prisoner saying goodbye to his old cell mates. The return of the prodigal who is a vertically challenged person. Has Bob had a drink or two he sounds just a little slurred. I suspect that they all had considerable fun with this song, it is just a stream, of nonsense, at least by the end we know that Monty says hello. **'You Ain't Goin' Nowhere'**: Sung by The Byrds for their 'Sweethearts of the Rodeo' album where they made it into a country song. The song changes, the serious early verses gradually descend into surrealism. It truly is a great song, one of the few that non-Dylan fans will recognise. The Nitty Gritty Dirt Band and Joan Baez also recorded excellent versions. **'Don't Ya Tell Henry'**: Levon Helm had returned and was again singing vocals. I have always wondered if Bob Dylan is on this track anywhere. Using the traditional calypso theme from Harry Belafonte's show stopper 'Mathilda' this is another song with sexual connotations. If 'Chicken' means 'chick' means 'woman' then the whole song becomes overtly unsavoury. The powerhouse could be the local brothel, but Henry has been caught by the river with a 'chick' down on her knees, and it is the 'chick' that will be in trouble if Henry finds out. Is the girl at his 'fly' named 'Apple', is Henry the pimp? The answers may never be revealed.

'Nothing Was Delivered' is another song recorded by The Byrds. It is similar to Fats Domino's 'Blueberry Hill'. There are no drums on this track. Who is it that didn't deliver what was promised, is it Bob talking to himself? **'Open the Door Homer'**: This is open the door Richard, we must bear in mind that Homer was Richard Manuel's nickname. The original song was always on the radio in the years after the Second War sung by The Pied Pipers and Louis Jordan, the original was by Jack McVea and really should receive some royalties for this song. The 'Writings' book has the sketch of a man knocking on the door of a cubicle or kiosk. The cubicle might be a portable toilet as the line 'round housing flushes' is included. Three friends Jim, Mouse and Mick have all taught the narrator something, wasn't 'Mouse' a flower-power poster artist? **'Long Distance Operator'**: Chuck Berry's 'Memphis' must have been influential on the title. Richard Manuel is on lead vocal. There is another song with the same title and theme written by Gamble and Huff. Bob has drawn a couple of telephone kiosks to accompany the lyrics. The narrator needs to make his call urgently. **'This Wheel's on Fire'** was co-written with Rick Danko, he wrote the tune. The Byrds, Julie Driscoll and The Brian Auger Trinity, and The Band recorded this song. Wheel of fire comes from Ezekiel 'then I looked and behold, the cherubim's stretched their hands into the fire but the four wheels were the colour of beryl-stone and had faces and eyes'. Daniel 7:9 states 'his throne was like the fiery flame and his wheels as burning fire'. We can also add a line from Shakespeare's King Lear, 'but I am bound upon a wheel of fire'. Was the Motorcycle accident caused by a judgement from God, they will meet again, this time he lived. The accident was after all a problem with the 'wheel' locking; just moving so fast that the wheels catch fire. A runaway cartwheel was sketched by Bob for this track.

'Quinn the Eskimo': Although a man representing 'Quinn' appears on the sleeve the track was not included on the album. Manfred Mann had a massive hit with this quite excellent pop song. 'Manfred' of course took his name from the title of a book by Lord Byron, or is that just co-incidence. The song is subtitled 'The Mighty Quinn'. There are a few characters named 'Quint' in books but I couldn't find a 'Quinn'. Quintilian the Orator said 'Ambition may be a vice, but it is often the root of virtues'. Quinn the Eskimo himself is a character that people and animals will want to see, the song is the call by the town orator to gather around to see this man. Bob released his version on Biograph. There is so much reverb in the 'basement' that it doesn't sound like Bob. **'Minstrel Boy'**: A sketch by Bob shows a troubadour standing on a hill holding a badly shaped guitar and busking his music for coins. The idea presented by some that this is a song for a singer searching for religion seems crazy. The boy's name in the song is Lucky, and Bob would use that pseudonym as his Wilbury alterego. **'I Shall Be Released'**: This is one of Bob's great memorable songs. The Band included it on their 'Big Pink' album. Bob should have added this to his next album rather than just have live versions available. The song of a prisoner who watched the sun travel across the sky signalling the beginning and end of every boring day. Another prisoner says that he was framed, but the narrator has accepted his guilt and his serving his time. A man coming to terms with his own faults and recognising that he is the only person that can change. **'Get Your Rocks Off!'** : The title means 'to let your hair down'. The lyric style is the same that was used by the original version of 'Mona' played by The Jack Jackson Band. There is another song called 'Roll Over' with almost identical words. In fact that song also used the lines 'two old ladies sitting in the sand, each one wishing the other was a man'. That line was seized upon by Lonnie Donegan for his song 'Cumberland Gap'. In Bob's song the old ladies say 'Get your rocks off'. It must have been a strange neighbourhood where children shout out 'Get your rocks off' at a passing bus. There is a drawing in 'Writings and Drawings' showing a man standing on top of a van throwing 'rocks off'. An ideal song for audience participation but I don't think Bob ever bothered.

'Sign on the Cross': A lyric that is set out in four styles, two at eight lines, two at four, one at eleven and one at twelve lines. Bob is saying that religion has become a 'goldmine' for those involved. He continues by saying that from a young age he has been bothered by the sign of the cross. Not as bothered as I am. Ask the most religious person you know to show you where it states in The Bible that Jesus died on a 'cross' at Calvary. The 'Sign of the Cross' is everywhere, but why? If they couldn't get that right in the first place what about the rest of the christian imagery. It seems more likely that Jesus was nailed to a vertical stake his hands above his head. The 'keys to the kingdom of Heaven' appear in Matthew 16:19. Daniel 5:26 (NEB) stated that 'God has numbered the days', although the King James Bible substitutes 'kingdom' for 'days', which makes no sense. The 'cross' means so much and the narrator is advising us that it is important, the sculptor's chisel is always preparing crosses, one assumes for gravestones. Bob's Biblical thoughts were emerging here on this the most powerful of his compositions at the time. Included in 'Writings' not included in the songbooks and still it awaits an official release. 'Bessie Smith' and 'Katie's Been Gone' were also released on The Band's 'Across the Great Divide' boxed set where Bob was credited with being a backing singer. Other tracks such as 'Orange Juice Blues', 'Yazoo Street Scandal', 'Ruben Remus' may have included Bob in some capacity, they seem to be The Band tracks without Bob. We continue to wait for, 'Don't Try Me Now', 'Young But Daily Growing', 'The Hills of Mexico', 'Bonnie Ship The Diamond', 'One Single River', 'I'm Not Here' and Hank Williams' 'The Stones That You Throw'.

'Santa Fe' was a surprise release on The Bootleg Series, it had not officially appeared anywhere previously. A song recorded for fun which sounds fresh as a daisy. There are a few songs with the same title Van Morrison and Jackie DeShannon wrote another one together for Van's 'Wavelength' album in 1978. 'Watching the River Flow' was registered in 1971. The song is for a writer coping with writer's block. He sits on the river bank and watches the river and recalls what he sees in his lyrics. He is a rural surrounding wishes he was back in the city. He is oblivious to the disagreeable people around, it is all water under the bridge. 'George Jackson': Jackson was another of the many black men that the aesthetes considered to be incarcerated wrongly. Bob says that he got imprisoned for a $70 robbery, what he doesn't state was just how violent was that robbery. It also appears (confirmed by Bob's lyrics) that Jackson was an arrogant man who couldn't behave in prison. I am not excusing the fact that Jackson was killed in prison but if he continually harangues the warders and makes their life difficult they are certain to retaliate in some form. There was claim and counter-claim that Jackson had a gun concealed in his afro-hair, but we will only be told half-truths by each side, we are left to decide for ourselves. The Jackson facts are that he was imprisoned for one year to life for a gas (petrol) station robbery. He spent 10 years in jail almost 8 in solitary for bad behaviour. In 1970 he was charged with the murder of a prison guard in Soledad Prison. He was involved in committing many assaults whilst in prison. The parole board who released his partner in the robbery after three years, continually refused to release Jackson. On August 7th, 1970, Jonathan Jackson (George's brother) aged 17, entered a San Rafael courthouse alone. He had a bag of handguns, an assault rifle and a shot gun hidden under his coat. He gave three black men who were in the dock weapons and together with five hostages they left the courthouse shouting 'Free the Soledad Brothers'. Jonathan was shot dead. In August 1971 George Jackson was involved in a prison riot, he too was shot dead. The book of George Jackson's Prison letters was published by Penguin Books in 1970.

'Wallflower' this waltz was re-recorded and released on an album with Doug Sahm in 1973. A wallflower awaiting to be asked to dance. 'I'd Have You Anytime': This slow song was composed with George Harrison and was included on his 'All Things Must Pass' boxed set. It is an ordinary lyric with the title saying everything. The song's publishing was shared between Harrisongs and Big Sky Music.

The whole Basement Tapes album was just a group of musicians enjoying themselves. At the time the psychedelic rock music revolution was underway, The Doors and 'The End'. There were more tracks circulating on bootleg, Bob said that they had at least 50 on tape, enough for another double album. The truth was that it would be eight years before the selected tracks were released, Bob thought that everyone already had them so he was genuinely surprised by the sales of the double set. The collection would be released after 'Blood on the Tracks' so Bob was back at the top, but a lot of water had to pass under the bridge before then.

Bob had completed his first draft of 'Tarantula', MacMillan Publishers had advance orders for 100,000 copies. Bob in the quietness of Woodstock with his drug free brain, re-read the draft and thought it was terrible, he decided, to MacMillan's chagrin, to re-write it. What Bob never realised at the time was that the accident had changed his personality, what was a natural prose and poetry style now required extra time and labour. I stated earlier that many stars have problems sustaining the creation of great work, now it was Bob's turn on the treadmill. What came naturally from his spiritual muse now came from a realists brain who had been lucky enough to cheat an early death. Bob also realised that he had serious responsibilities to his wife and child, the mature man had emerged from the youth at the age of 25. The original draft of 'Tarantula' was a book which Bob could not now understand, I don't mean his comprehension had disappeared it just seemed to have been written by someone that Bob did not recognise. Bob re-wrote 'Tarantula'.

It was rumoured that Bob went back into the studio to start recording in September 1967. This may have been to register some songs on tape but no recording log book was completed. Bob started recording his new album in Nashville on October 17th 1967, three tracks were recorded with Charlie McCoy on bass and Kenny Buttrey on drums, Pete Drake was added on steel guitar for the last session at the end of November for two tracks.

Bob was also spending some time with Howard Alk searching through hours of film clips in the hope of making an half-decent film out of the Pennebaker residue called 'Eat The Document'. Bob had some contracts to fulfil, he owed Columbia an album, MacMillan a book and ABC television a Dylan-documentary which would ultimately be 'Eat The Document' but not until 1971. The documentary and many other versions are available on the bootleg market, one wonders how they escaped so easily. ABC TV returned the first edit of 'Eat the Document' as unusable.

Like the lyrics of 'The Man in Me' Bob was living in his personal Utopia (Utah) in the song, a love-in domesticity, it was time to perpetuate the myth and get another album out onto the market.

The 'JOHN WESLEY HARDING' album was released in March 1968. One track 'I'll Be Your Baby Tonight' the most easily accessible and memorable track had been included on Columbia's 'The Rock Machine Turns You On' sampler. It was arguably the greatest sampler ever compiled, every track is a winner from an equally brilliant album. In the USA the 'John Wesley Harding' album reached No 2 in the USA and No 1 in the UK for ten weeks. Bob never thought it was a very good album , 'just a bunch of songs', he didn't want the album hyped and it emerged quietly and took the charts by storm. It proved just how good Albert Grossman and his team were at maintaining the interest and impetus of Bob's career whilst he was injured. Albert may of course have learned a little from Colonel Tom Parker who kept Elvis in the public eye when he did his National Service. It has been a mystery to me over the years how some stars qualified for the USA Forces Draft and others didn't. Bob was rejected for service due to his poor eyesight, where are the photographs with Bob wearing spectacles? Some celebrities rushed abroad and remained deserter-exiles until there was an amnesty, others pretended to be homosexual or have religious pacifist beliefs, but what about the many others. A large number were singing songs against the Vietnam War but surely that was no reason for them not to be 'called-up' when they reached the correct age. In the UK no male at the age of 18 was exempt from the Armed Forces, all able bodied men born before the end of July 1940 were enlisted in July 1958, (the last batch before the end of National Service), in the USA the date was much later.

CBS never bothered to release a single from the 'Harding' album but 'Drifter's Escape' was the b-side of 'I Threw It All Away' taken from the next album. Jimi Hendrix made 'All Along the Watchtower' his own, the single reaching No 5 in the UK and No 20 in the USA not only his highest charting single in the USA but his only charting single in the USA.

The cover had little relevance to the album, the assumption that these were the musicians assisting Bob was soon dispelled. Searching for some significance small Beatle faces were found at the top when the sleeve was turned upside down, Donovan and the hand of God was to be seen emerging from the bark at the top of the tree. Have you ever heard such nonsense, the Polaroid photograph by John Berg was one of a series taken in freezing conditions in Albert Grossman's garden, hence Bob's hunched appearance. Bob in his suede coat is flanked by Lakhsman and Purna Das Baul of the group The Bauls of Bengal who Albert Grossman had imported to play some 'World Music' shows. They were travelling minstrels and had met Allen Ginsberg when he was in India searching for enlightenment. The big man with the spectacles was Charles Joy a carpenter working at Bob's house at the time who just joined the group for the photograph and of course everlasting fame. There is a fourth figure crouching at the front his cowboy hat just visible. The Bauls of Bengal released their own 'Bengali Bauls at Big Pink' album on the Buddha Label. There was also the thought that the initials of Bob's album 'JWH' were an abbreviated form of Jehovah. The jews didn't write out the full 'Jehovah' because of the 'fear' of God. The Tetragrammaton is JHWH short for Jahweh, but I don't think Bob even thought about it, until it was suggested later.

Bob had admitted to reading most of the time that he was injured, the album inferred that he had returned to the family Bible for some of the ideas. If you see a large Bible on a lectern it is usually opened halfway so that it looks equal on the lectern, in most cases the chapter on which it will be open is Isaiah, ideal for any passing browser. The other books near central are Jeremiah, Ezekiel, Solomon's Song, Ecclesiastes, Proverbs and Psalms. Bob admitted that the record was 'a fearful album, just dealing with fear of Satan the devil'. Bob was also known to have read Kafka, Brecht, Eliot, Byron, Kerouac, Sartre, Lorca, Thomas, Rimbaud, Blake, Whitman and many more. Bob was aware that people were reading into his lyrics influences of which he was not cognisant, he would now add some snippets knowing that the critics would be attempting to solve each track as a puzzle. Although Bob (and Van Morrison) would maintain the myth by stating that they songs were 'just songs with no message', it was a new method of selling albums to academics.

'John Wesley Harding'(1853/95): El Paso is a mexican town known to have a pioneering wild west past. The subject of Marty Robbins' song was not John Wesley Harding it was many years later that Bob Dylan decided to bring this particular gunfighter to our attention, and also to the notice of the people of El Paso who had all but forgotten him. The El Paso Council quickly found the grave at The Concordia Cemetery which and subsequently added a small marble headstone and plaque. This was to enable the occasional pop music enthusiast and tourist that might be drawn to the town to observe where the gunfighter was laid to rest, John Wesley Hardin lived in El Paso, (Bob added the 'g' to his surname, he thought that was the way it was spelled), Wyatt Earp, Billy the Kid and Pat Garrett (the latter two also subjects for a Bob Dylan song) also lived there during the lawless days. The original John Hardin is assumed to have been a distant relative to Louis Moondog Hardin the blind avant garde jazz musician, and the singer songwriter the late Tim Hardin, at least the surname was similar.

John Wesley Hardin was born in Texas in a small township called Bonham, his father was a methodist minister and gave his son the full name of the founder of that doctrine John Wesley. However methodism was far from the career that John Wesley Hardin would map for himself. At the age of fifteen John Wesley Hardin killed his first man. Hardin's arrogance and egotism had grown to such an extent that he expected everyone to be in awe of his charisma. A black man who would not move out of his way on the side walk was shot three times, sadly the majority white population congratulated him on the deed and they considered (along with the Judge) that he had killed the man in self defence. No weapon was actually found on the dead black man but there was an inference that Harding would not be aware of that fact. In the next thirteen years Hardin killed 39 more people and it is alleged that one of these was murdered because his snoring disturbed Hardin's sleep. The statistic of just thirteen years of killings was due to the fact that Hardin also spent fourteen years in jail for murder of a sheriff. It was after this term in jail that Hardin settled in El Paso and became a lawyer and gambler, he thought that if he lost at cards then the other players must be cheating. Hardin had learnt the rudiments of law whilst in The State Prison but his law-work is not well documented. He was finally killed by John Selman who shot Hardin three times, once in the head. The people were so surprised that Hardin had been shot that they left him laying on the floor of the Acme Saloon for many hours probably expecting his to get up dust himself off and walk out. Hundreds filed passed the body which was prostrate on the floor, his brains oozing out of his cracked skull. The local newspaper with a sense of humour stated that 'Apart from being dead Hardin appeared to be in pretty good shape'. The legend of John Wesley Hardin that has arisen since is primarily due to Bob Dylan's song and album title. It also evident that most people feel that he was a hero who only killed people who deserved to be killed. Dylan's song seems to be a loggerheads with the true account from the El Paso Press Archives. Dylan presents the gunfighter as a Robin Hood character who was friend to the poor. He also was 'Never known to hurt an honest man', but that must be in the eyes of the bigoted whites who started it all by approving the first shooting of the black man on the sidewalk. I have also endeavoured unsuccessfully to locate the details from the so called 'Chaynee County' that Dylan refers, it seems that Hardin helped sort out some form of situation there. Finally as it is known that Hardin went to prison for fourteen years it seems so strange that Bob Dylan should say that 'No charge held against him could they prove', but of course it could be another John Wesley Hardin entirely couldn't it?

'As I Went Out One Morning': Tom Paine is mentioned, the civil rights movement of the sixties used Paine's philosophy, Bob accepted the Tom Paine award in 1963, it was reported that he was just a little inebriated at the time. Paine also impugned causes that he thought were ridiculous and thus was often requiring protection. The fair damsel of the story getting the narrator involved in her causes might just be Joan Baez again. Bob found all the causes were themselves political it wasn't until he met Emmett Grogan some years later that he learned what a selfless and wonderful organisation was The Diggers of San Francisco, but more of that later. The damsel in chains might possibly be a euphemism for the civil right movement as a whole, if Bob had become involved then, in the words of the song, 'she might do me harm'. Bob was being wary of his career moves, a necessity for a man under constant criticism and re-evaluation. 'She' even pleaded from the corner of her mouth, if he accepted they would then go South to the centre of the segregational problems of the USA, to the area of Neil Young's 'Southern Man' with his cracking bullwhip. But why does Tom Paine apologise for her, it is a mystery. Bob has made him similar to so many other politicians who had exhausted their ideas but not their ideals. Paine shared one with Bob when Thomas Paine wrote 'It is important to the happiness of any man that he be mentally faithful to himself'. Thomas Paine (1737-1809), spent time in France under Napoleon and was imprisoned and almost executed because he reneged against the execution of Louis XVI, Paine returned to America in 1802. His most renown books are 'The Rights of Men' and 'The Age of Reason'. Thomas Paine wrote of religion 'Any system of religion that has anything in it that shocks the mind of a child cannot be a true system. In 'The Rights of Man' he wrote 'My country is the world, and my religion is to do good, those who expect to reap the blessings of freedom must, like men, undergo the fatigue of supporting it'. Bob has drawn the woman in her chains and Tom Paine running across the field in his 'Writings' book. **'I Dreamed I Saw St Augustine'**: St Augustine converted to Christianity in 387 AD and became a philosopher for God. He had been brought up as a christian but espoused gnosticism until returning to christianity. In the dream that Bob presents in the 'Writings and Drawings' book, we have a man carrying a blanket, (as the line in the song indicates), one wonders if it might be St Francis who has some parallels with Bob views. Francis was the son of a merchant, he observed the vast gulf between the rich and the poor. At the age of 25, St Francis turned to religious mysticism, his Franciscan Order had as its rule, poverty, personal sacrifice and pure love. Like the Saint in the song he searched for lost souls to save, deciding in his 'Canticle of the Sun' that all things are brothers and sisters to each other. Whether Bob saw himself as Francis of Assisi is debatable but St Augustine's doctrine is light years from this song. St Augustine thought that God would make good come out of evil, alternatively evil would not be allowed to exist. He was another of the Saints that forgave God all the bad things and credited him with all the good. St Augustine's doctrine was that 'sex is a sin', it was only permissable within the confines of a christian marriage. Semen passed the sins from one generation to another, only Jesus who was born without sex in an immaculate conception could be without original sin. Bob painted a picture to depict this song of a man laying on a bed smoking, he is looking up at the vision, the dream. The song itself is probably influenced by 'I Dreamed I Saw Joe Hill'.

    'All Along the Watchtower': Who is the joker and who is the thief, that is the question? They are most likely to be the music industry itself. Isaiah 21.6-9 mentions watchmen and the watchtower. Bob's emerging religious beliefs encompass all The Bible as does The Watchtower Society, The Jehovah's Witnesses. But what is Bob's reason behind writing 'along' when 'up and down, in or out' would have been simpler, knowing Bob's style of writing I think he just wanted to create a diversion. So the joker is advising the narrator with a smile and the advice is agreed by the thief and the narrator loses out. The Jehovah's Witnesses feel that the only way to live and to die is through the teachings of the Bible and they will lay dead and buried until God decides to resurrect them into his new Paradise after the apocalypse, which is foretold in The Bible. So perhaps that is the 'way out of here' to which Bob alludes. Bob did say that he wrote the song during a massive thunderstorm wondering how he was going to get out of the house, alive. When Bob would later find that he was also a christian he also continued with his Judaism, although this was many years after this song, it is pertinent to mention that The Watchtower Society are one of the few religious sects that have a firm belief of The Bible in its entirety. There has been so much nonsense attributed to this song, just about every poet that has been connected with Bob, however tenuously, has been invoked within this song. The complete song is only a dozen lines so how can Yeats, Rimbaud, Lorca, Kerouac, Burroughs, Ginsberg and even T.S.Eliot get in? It is more appropriate to remain with Isaiah, the place where nearly all open lectern sited Bibles sit perfectly and equally divided.

'The Ballad of Frankie Lee and Judas Priest': This Judas offers money to Frankie. Sign quickly or we will withdraw the offer? The temptation as depicted Goethe's Faust. Frankie indulges in the debauchery for 16 nights and dies of thirst. Bob had been encouraged to indulge and almost lost his life. Here in this lyric he was facing up to reality. A Dylan 'parable', tempted by the money, a sort of Faust meets the Samaritan song, or **'Frank** James meets Stagger **Lee'**. Now if Bob had written Jehovah's Priest in lieu of Judas which was just for the sake of obfuscation then the former would be the character offering a 'way out', once more we are back along the watchtower, it follows with an offer of 'paradise'. Kahil Gibran (1883-1931) wrote 'No man can reveal to you aught but that which already lies half asleep in the dawning of your knowledge'. As many writers eventually read Gibran I surmised that perhaps this was the basis for Bob's 'Nothing is revealed' quote. **'Drifter's Escape'** is almost the escape detailed in the previous track. Suddenly seeing the light after all the criticism. Judge and jury probably God and the angels, although God sends the lightning to the courthouse. A Judge without prejudice is a marvel to behold. The song does have some connections with Franz Kafka's 'The Trial'. Both the song and Franz Kafka's work was symbolic of the frustration of modern man. Of course this song has the scenario of a trial. In 'The Trial' Kafka wrote 'it is often better to be in chains than to be free', and 'you may object that it is not a trial at all, you are quite right it is only a trial if I recognize it as such'. Kafka uses a Cathedral priest to relate a parable of the guard at the entrance of the law, the new-comer waits patiently for admittance until the last moment of his life, only to learn just as the door is shut forever that it is meant only for him. The moral of both the book and this song is that everything must be left to fate. There is no real escape even for the drifter. The song uses the tune of 'The Wreck of the Old 97'.

'Dear Landlord' is a pleading to the music industry to wait for him to improve physically after his accident rather than just race to the studio for the sake of earning money. A great deal of discussion has passed concerning who was the real 'Landlord' it could have been Albert Grossman, the publishers of 'Tarantula', MacMillan, or it could have been advance payments that Bob had received from Columbia Records. Bob was living in the Woodstock house owned by Albert Grossman, he was Bob's actual landlord. Bob realises that the landlord has also suffered financially, they were both searching for aspiration and ambition, abstract notions, things that can be seen but not touched. **'I Am a Lonesome Hobo'** is a straight-forward song at last. He has never been caught begging which doesn't mean that he doesn't beg. How a previously rich man is now forced to scrounge for a living. This is advice to not become jealous and judgemental, trust your brother or you will end up destitute. **'I Pity the Poor Immigrant'** uses the same 'Peter Amberley' (Emberley) tune as used for Bob's ballad of Donald White. Again we are wondering who is, or who are, these immigrants. All Americans except the Red Indian are immigrants. In the last half of this century the immigrants have been lured to the country where the streets are paved with gold. As with most modern immigration the groups find their own areas and huddle together and their individual cultures usually mean the 'outsiders' move away to join their own clique. Bob said in an interview that Leviticus was one of his favourite Bible books. On this lyric he uses 'heaven as iron and earth as brass' (Leviticus 26:19&20), in the song Bob writes 'heaven like ironsides'. He also takes 'ye shall eat and not be satisfied'(Le 26:26) and writes 'who eats is not satisfied'. It continues with 'And your strength shall be spent in vain' (Le 26:20), Bob writes 'whose strength is spent in vain'. This was a positive move by Bob towards more obvious Biblical references. To fall in love with wealth itself must be one of the hardest emotions of which to come to terms, especially when it all goes wrong.

'The Wicked Messenger': The Achilles heeled winged messenger dashed from one gig to another, from one recording session to another until the accident stopped everything, in an instant. Proverbs 13:17 states 'a wicked messenger falleth into mischief, but a faithful ambassador is health'. If you can't bring good news then don't bring any. The congregation will only want to hear good news. It sounds like an aphorism but it is contestable, people love to hear bad news as long as it does not apply to them personally. Eli was the priest of Jehovah, his two sons were scoundrels, they used their high office for immoral purposes. As Eli could not control them Jehovah sent divine messages against Eli's house. Samuel is the messenger, not wicked himself but the message is as terrible as it gets. Eli fell back and broke his neck and The Philistines rose up against Israel. Bob fell back and broke his neck and the world of music held its breath. **'Down Along The Cove'**: The little bundle of joy might be Bob's second child, and the narrator wants everyone to see just how much they are in love. **'I'll Be Your Baby Tonight'** is so simple that is it a brilliant pop song. Almost a moon in June love song for his wife. It is so infectious that one is singing along after just one play. We were unaware at the time but this track which ended this great album was the prototype for the next album. This return to folk country would now veer towards full-country music and catch us all by surprise.

'Three Kings': This was the jacket note for the album. Written probably for children this is Bob's version of the three christmas visitors. The first lines are similar to 'Old King Cole was a merry old soul'. This piece could have been inspired by Brecht's 'The Good Person of Szechwan' in which three

Gods come to Earth to a place called Szechwan, China, in search of good people, they chose Shen Te a prostitute. After many twists and turns the plot has a moral, what begins as a search for an ego-ideal becomes the Gods looking for an ideal-ego, someone who is just like them to justify their own existence. Bob's Kings ask for and receive nothing, forgiveness is not an emotion they possess. These Kings are the nucleus of a 'creeping-consumption' that is spreading. In Bob's piece Vera taps her toe three times, like a circus horse. Allen Ginsberg had given some Bertolt Brecht books to Bob as a present when he was recovering from his accident. The notes inform us that Bob Dylan has come out with a new record without any of his own songs, this could be deemed almost clairvoyance for 'Self Portrait'. The three Kings are visiting Terry Shute and they are miraculously cured, one of a broken arm, one of a broken nose and the third was just broke. Frank who had punched his fist through a plate glass window is also unhurt. The whole piece is written in the whimsical style of Gertrude Stein who had been named in Bob's earlier 'Some Other Kinds of Songs'. Stein wrote 'Three Lives' the story of three female domestic servants, it bears no relation to 'Three Kings'. As mentioned earlier Bob added harmonica to Victoria Spivey's album 'Three Kings'. T.S.Eliot's 'Journey of The Magi' would make a perfect prologue to Bob's piece.

Bob's ambivalence with the songs on the John Wesley Harding album was not sustained by the public, they loved it. The reason that it was released so quickly after the tracks were completed was so that it could be in the shops before Bob changed his mind about the songs. Bob was trying to achieve the Gordon Lightfoot sound but admitted later that they never got it.

Abraham, Bob's father, died in June 1968, Bob went home for the funeral. It was second sudden loss after losing Woody Guthrie nine months earlier. In the midst of this sadness Sara gave birth to another son, named Seth Abraham Isaac Dylan.

It was in February 1969 that Bob returned to Columbia's, Nashville studio to record his next album. Charlie McCoy, Pete Drake and Kenny Buttrey were again in the band this time augmented by Robert Wilson (piano), Norman Blake (guitar), Kelton Herston (guitar) and Wayne Moss (guitar). With so many guitarists present it would have been helpful if the studio documents had been more accurate. On February 17th and 18th Johnny Cash joined Bob on vocals and additional piano was played by Hargus Robbins. Although just one Dylan/Cash duet was included on the next album they recorded together for two days, only the one track 'Girl of The North Country' was considered good enough to release.

'NASHVILLE SKYLINE' was released in May 1969, it climbed to No 3 in the USA and No 1 in the UK, it remained at No 1 for four weeks. During the same month Johnny Cash and Bob Dylan appeared together at a Grand

114

Old Opry Television Special. The earlier mentioned 'I Threw It All Away' single was more successful in the UK getting to No 30 but only No 85 in the USA. The album was met with critical antagonism, when he went electric they went crazy now he was returning to country-folk the went equally crazy. The album was short on time and the critics savaged it. At the time the USA was full of grievances, marches assassinations, violent demonstrations, the country had never been so politically desolate, the real desolation row had arrived. When everyone was expecting Bob to emerge with guidance for the youth he just stepped sideways and gave us a song album. Bob maintained that he was a song and dance man now he proved it. I personally have always considered this album a masterstroke, not for the songs but from Bob's resistance to being seen as a saviour or advisor. He was now a family man, a father with three children to support, why should he push his head above the parapet, he didn't owe anybody anything. Bob the political activist would have been harassed by the C.I.A. on one side and the lefty's on the other, he just couldn't win whatever he did, except of course by releasing a song and dance album without messages. That of course didn't stop people (yours truly included) searching for inner meanings when they were few and far between.

Bob made the statement that the songs on Nashville Skyline 'are the types of songs that I always felt like writing, they reflect more the inner me than the songs of the past'. The cover is Bob's interpretation of Eric Von Schmidt's cover which was carefully placed on the table on the 'Bringing It All Back Home' cover, the guitar is George Harrison's, Bob's suede jacket continues to be worn from album to album, the hat is from John Wesley Harding.

'Girl From the North Country', remembering Echo Helstrom and her family collection of country and western records, especially those of Hank Williams. The song was included on 'Freewheelin'' and now returns on a second album only this time it is a duet with Johnny Cash. They are out of time and in the wrong key. On the Johnny Carson Show where they sang the song they still sounded unrehearsed and neither knew how to end the song. The predominant reason for Johnny's appearance on the album was because Bob and his family were staying at his house in Nashville, Bob had some spare studio time so they decided to use it up together, just play and see what happens; the result was, not much. 'To Be Alone With You' might be known better as 'Is it Rolling Bob?'. The Bob Dylan country vocal sound for the first time on record, he had sung like this on his early un-official recordings. This was Bob's voice untainted by cigarette smoking. Bob said that he wrote this song for Jerry Lee Lewis, if he ever recorded it then I haven't located it. The 'night time is the right time to be with the one you love' was a line previously used by Ray Charles and Bobby Darin on the L.Herman composed 'The Right Time'. This is the song of the home-loving man that needs somewhere to relax and be comforted by the one he loves. **'I Threw it All Away'**: George Harrison had heard this song some time earlier, it was the first song that Bob wrote for this album. A superb song where the narrator realises that the problems with the relationship were in fact his and no-one else's. Sequenced after the 'To Be Alone' track makes this feel much sadder. Previously Bob had been ambivalent in his questioning love songs, here he acknowledges that it is his fault. But what or who did the narrator throw away, this must have had Sara wondering what and who he was singing about. If this was a belated song for Joan Baez then her version of Anne Bredon's, 'Babe, I'm Gonna Leave You', is a perfect riposte. The organist is not credited on the recording sheets, perhaps it was some over dubbed Hargus Robbins, but it certainly sounds like Garth Hudson. **'Peggy Day'** is awful, by natural association who is Peggy Night? This must have been codged together in the studio, surely there were tracks more pertinent to the album than this. There seems to be some confusion over the way Peggy Night (night) is written in the lyrics, it should be Night, surely. Bob said that this was written with The Mills Brothers in mind, they understandably never bothered to record it. The Tab Hunter version of 'Young Love' influenced the musical introduction, they are one and the same. **'Lay, Lady, Lay'**: Bob wrote this song for the film Midnight Cowboy but it was not completed in time. There is some confusion because some of the music encyclopedias state that Bob's song was actually heard and rejected. The film used Fred Neil's 'Everybody's Talkin'' sung by Harry Nilsson. Harry was one of the great songwriter's yet his two greatest hits were composed by others. Overtly sexual 'Lay Lady' was released as a single and went into the Top Ten in the UK and the USA. Kenny Buttrey was assisted by studio assistant Kris Kristofferson who held the cowbells and bongos drums for Kenny to strike. If you have Melanie's version of this song then you will know how good Bob's version is. The 'Writings' book shows a scene taken from a Van Gogh, a chair a bed and a mattress, a naked woman stands awkwardly in the centre of the room whilst the head of a bald and bearded man looks away in the foreground. It is perplexing because it is a little wooden bed and he is not smiling.

'One More Night': He is lonesome, he can't be what she wants him to be, so he loses her. The lyrics are designed to confuse. The woman is in love, is it with the narrator or another? The mind boggles, what did she want him to be, and what does he mean when he says 'he didn't mean to see her go'. Nice song, deliberately confusing. **'Tell Me That It Isn't True'**: This is almost a continuation of the previous track's theme. A man pleading for reassurance and a second chance. Apparently this song was originally intended to be a polka. In many of the 'wronged partner' scenarios the innocent victim is the last to know, and when they find out they want convincing that the information that they have just received is untrue. The song has been recorded

116

by many others but one of the most startling is by steel guitarist Pete Drake. His version is beautiful and although it is for the most part instrumental some of the lyrics are added using a mouthpiece as a speaker, in my opinion the best version of the song. The first line is taken from Hank William's 'You Win Again', the sentiments are the same, she has been running around with another. The trouble for any one sided love affair is that the one that loves most will forgive the errant partner. In Bob's song the narrator just wants her word that all the tales are false. In Hank Williams' song the narrator just caves in to love, she wins again.

'**Country Pie**': A song in which Bob is stating that he loves the Country and his wife and family. By this track in the album we were realising that something was amiss in Bob's ability to rhyme as he did on the previous albums. Bob finishes the song naming various pie fillings. '**Tonight I'll Be Staying Here With You**': So much for the itinerancy of Bob's songs, now he is so much in love he ain't going nowhere. Just like the last track on the previous album, he is staying and he'll be her baby tonight. As if answering the question as to the reason why Bob didn't want to be spokesman for anyone except himself, it is here in the lyric. Any poor boy can have his ticket to ride, he is staying at home. Tom Paxton settled into the same domestic bliss as Bob, John Denver did likewise and made himself into a comedian on British television. John Lennon, Tim Hardin and Phil Ochs all tried then died, Country Joe, John Prine, Tom Rush and so many others just lost their muse along the way, Bruce Springsteen never really had it, at least not for long. The 'Tonight' track was released as a follow-up single to 'Lay Lady' in November 1969 and only reached No 50 in the USA, possibly because everybody already had the album. The album was the last album of Bob's to be released in both stereo and mono.

Johnny Cash wrote the album cover notes for 'Nashville Skyline' and must have been astonished when he learned that he had won the Grammy Award in March 1970 for The Best Album Notes. He beat John Hartford, Rex Reed, Johnny Dodds II and Joan Baez. This was the year that Blood Sweat and Tears had ten nominations. The Johnny Cash prose was excellent, it covered imitation and emulation, the ability to rhyme the tick of time, the end of a friend, the end of end by 'math of trend', here-in, he writes, is a hell of a poet. The prose really needed to be transformed by Johnny into a song, it is a gushing outpouring on behalf of his friend Bob Dylan, but in a song it could be any friend.'**Nashville Skyline Rag**': Bob's first instrumental track, just like a track off the any Area 615 album, no more no less. The surprise again was that this track was nominated for a Grammy Award for The Best Country Instrumental Performance, but was beaten by Danny Davis and the Nashville Brass for their RCA album 'Play More Nashville Sounds'; Davis' band was the country equivalent of Herb Alpert's 'Mexican' Tijuana Brass.

There were just two remaindered tracks from the 'Nashville Skyline' sessions. **'Living The Blues'** which is a self-pity blues for the injured partner. It is a natural continuation of 'One More Night'. **'Wanted Man'** was written for and recorded by Johnny Cash, is not as good as the brilliant song of the same title sung by Frankie Laine. Bob's song is for a scoundrel on the road. He is wanted everywhere, and this song is a travelogue of place names. Bob does use one very interesting phrase in 'on the lam'. It gives the impression of being slang but really means 'making and escape', perhaps Bob hadn't lost the art of subconscious rhyming after-all.

Other tracks were recorded with Johnny Cash, it seems that they were just having fun in the studio. Tracks such as Jimmie Rodgers 'Blue Yodel No 5' and 'Blue Yodel No 1', Carl Perkins' 'Matchbox', Johnny Cash songs such as 'Big River', 'I Still Miss Someone' and 'Ring of Fire' written by Scott Wiseman. 'Mystery Train', 'Careless Love', Jack Clement's 'Guess Things Happen That Way', Jimmy Davis' 'You Are My Sunshine' and Arthur Big Boy Crudup's 'That's All Right Mama' and more are all wasting away somewhere in the CBS vaults. The album was so short at under 30 minutes that a couple of these songs could have been added as filler, at least to give the customer 'their money's worth'. If the Cash/Dylan duet was the best that they achieved then the decision to remainder the rest was a stroke of genius.

What people seemed to overlook was that the album could stand side-by-side with the new country direction taken by The Byrds with 'Sweet Hearts of the Rodeo' which was released nine months before Bob's album. Bob wrote 'Ballad of Easy Rider' (for the film in 1969) with Roger McGuinn but never took a writer's credit for the song.

During April and May 1969 Bob returned to the studio to record a series of songs that were his favourites written by other artists. Many of these tracks would come back and haunt Bob in 1973. Some of the tracks were also added to his next album.

We were now entering the time of the great Festivals. Newport Pop (August 1968), Miami Pop (Dec 1968), Newport 69 (June 1969), Newport Jazz (July 1969), Atlanta Pop (July 1969), Atlanta City Pop (August 1969) had all passed by. Woodstock was coming in mid August 1969 so Bob and his family intended to get out of town by sailing with The Band on the QE2 to England for The Isle of Wight Pop Festival. Before they embarked Jesse Dylan struck his head against a door and was knocked unconscious, to be safe in this situation Bob and family left the ship and flew on later meeting up with The Band in time for a days rehearsal in England.

Bob's performance in the I.O.W. was recorded and some of the songs were to be included on Bob's next album. At the festival Bob sang 'Desolation Row' and in the film of the festival (the studio version) plays over scenes of the perimeter shanty town set up by ticket-less fans so they could hear but not see. The double CD 'Message To Love' was released in 1995 including Bob who of course appeared in 1969, the track on the CD is the studio version from 'Highway 61 Revisited' with the first few seconds clipped off. The set also includes 'Amazing Grace' by 'The Great Awakening' which was played over the sound system at the beginning of each day. Some of the other artists on the Castle Records release were Free, Joni Mitchell, Leonard Cohen, Joan Baez, The Who, Donovan, Jimi Hendrix, Jethro Tull, The Doors and more.

Bob had also been back in the studio between March 3rd and 17th 1970 recording tracks for the new album. On June 9th 1970 Bob was awarded and Honorary Doctorate in Music from The Princeton University.

'SELF PORTRAIT' was released as a double album in July 1970. The cover was Bob's self portrait painting, it was his second cover art-work the first was The Band's 'Music From Big Pink'. The album was a mixture of old and new, songs by Bob and songs by others. The critics hated it and gave it a good trashing in the newspapers. The public were not so easily influenced and the album became Bob's third successive No 1 album in the UK and it reached No 4 in the USA. I have found over the years that it is the die-hard Dylan fans that disliked the album, as it continues to sell it must have a genuine popular appeal; I liked it mostly for its variety rather than its content.

A single was released from the album, the instrumental 'Wigwam' sounding more like The Ted Heath or Count Basie Big Band than a Bob Dylan track it reached No 41 in the USA as a novelty record.

When asked about the album Bob said that he was tired of the bootleg records that were available so he decided to put out his own. He thought the album was an answer to the treatment he was getting from 'people'. He didn't want attention, especially for things that he had never done. The album was released to get people off his back, they would not like him any more and would stop buying his records. He added that he was 'fed up with people that thought he was nonsense'.

It is difficult to know Bob's frame of mind at the time but the words attributed to him in interviews concerning the album were not made until 1981 and 1985, it is easy to be wise after the event, but one wonders why he would need to say it at all, he certainly didn't say it at the time. Can you imagine a man that has striven to be a success releasing an album in the hope of spoiling everything, a family man with three young children, of course not. I would suspect that Bob was again expanding the myth, but it shows a distinct cavalier attitude to his fans. If in his words 'the self portrait album was a joke to him' then it was no joke to the people that paid good money to hear his work. The whole routine of distancing himself from work that he considered substandard is understandable but to make out that the work was intended to ruin his fan-base is ludicrous. If he had been as outspoken at the time then one suspects that Columbia might have decided that he was a financial liability and litigation might have followed. It is obvious that Bob's opinion of the album changed because he defended it against Greil Marcus' ridiculous opening review gambit 'What is this shit?' by saying that Marcus' review was shit.

Van Morrison was more up-front with his remarks after he recorded his 'Bang Masters' as an obligation album for Bang Records. He recorded nonsense, stated that he had no interest in the album and left Eileen Berns the widow of Bert Berns to pick up the pieces of his now completed contract. As Berns was only the 'B' of Bang, 'A'hmet and 'N'ehusi Ertegun and 'G'erry Wexler being the other three partners it was most fortunate for Van that they decided against any litigation. I have always wondered just what direction Van Morrison might have taken with his career if his mentor Bert Berns hadn't suddenly died of a heart attack, but that as they say is fate.

The inference that Bob was suffering from writer's block and subsequently had decided to record other composer's songs was unfounded, here he was taking a break but still composing. Some of the reviewers heard lines in the songs that didn't exist, in real terms their summations only added to the myth, it didn't harm sales at all. A.J.Weberman was also making a nuisance of himself, Weberman formed his 'Dylan Liberation Front' to free Bob Dylan from himself. He also spent time searching through Bob's garbage in the hope of finding incriminating drug paraphernalia, he called this science of searching through rubbish as 'garbology', and eventually wrote a book titled 'My Life in Garbology'. By the time of his publication he was searching the rubbish bins of other famous people. Bob and Sara realised that Weberman had been taking their rubbish so the amounts of excrement deposited in the bin increased. Weberman arranged some unsociable behaviour outside Bob's house and upset Sara and the children. In fact Weberman is alleged to have entered Bob's home without permission shouting "I'm the landlord' because he thought that the 'Dear Landlord' song was about him. It was after he had upset Sara that Bob went out, found Weberman and gave him a slap or two, later mentioned in song. If this is true was Bob mob handed, he could hardly fight at Weberman's weight?

The site of Bob's Woodstock home was now common knowledge, the quiet village community was the subject of inquisitive tourists searching out the site of the Woodstock Festival which was held miles away in Bethel.

The opening track on the 'Self Portrait' album was **'All The Tired Horses'**. This could have been influenced by 'Odetta's' 'All The Pretty Little Horses' but they are different songs. Bob's song is just a couple of lines with 'Hmm' added as a harmony. Discarded as superfluous by journalists yet I would wager that anyone who heard the song once would remember it forever, it is extremely infectious. One wonders what input there was from Bob on this track we certainly can't hear him. **'Alberta No 1'** and **'Alberta No 2'** these versions of the traditional song are played at different tempos. Is this a person or place, the lyrics keep the secret. Doc Watson, Maxwell Street Jimmy, Big Bill Broonzy and Leadbelly all recorded their own versions. **'I Forgot More Than You'll Ever Know'**: Written By Cecil Null and recorded by Slim Whitman, Sonny James, The Davis Sisters in 1954 and re-recorded by Skeeter Davis. Bob sings the song very well in the style of Slim Whitman as a lovely country waltz; Pete Drake's steel guitar is superb. **'Days of 49'** was originally a traditional song but was registered by the Lomax Brothers and F.Warner. The band has that buzzing harmonica or is it a jaws harp playing. The session sheets state that Emanuel Green played violin and 'contractor', which makes me none the wiser, unless it makes that buzzing sound. The song was titled 'Tom Moore' at the recording session. Song about the American gold rush of 1849. I wonder what Bob had seen in the studio that makes him say 'Oh my goodness' in amazement halfway through.

'Early Morning Rain' is the beautiful composition from Canadian singer-songwriter Gordon Lightfoot. It is introduced by Bob's harmonica and sung in his best balladeer voice. The guitar sound is hispanic and William Pursell's excellent piano was added as an over-dub. **'In Search of Little Sadie'** & **'Little Sadie'** two versions of the same song one faster than the other. It includes some superb guitar picking by David Bromberg. It is the tale of Lee Brown who was sentenced to 41 years imprisonment for murder. It was also recorded by Jack Scott, Hedy West and the British group Trees for their 'On the Shore' album. The Folkways version by Clarence Ashley probably influenced Bob's version. In the song Lee Brown has already murdered Sadie in the first verse with a .44 pistol. He first went home before deciding to go on the run, he got as far as a town named Jericho before he was captured by The Sheriff. The key changes catch Bob out a few times as his vocal sounds distinctly out of tune. **'Let It Be Me'** was written by Mac Curtis from Gilbert Becaud's French version. A hit for the Everly Brothers and recorded by the world and its wife. There are versions by Elvis Presley, The Shadows, Willie Nelson, Peter and Gordon, Betty Everett, Jerry Butler, Glen Campbell and Mantovani and his Orchestra. Bob is singing in his 'Nashville Skyline' voice, the cymbal track should have been remixed on Bob's version when it was transferred to compact disc.

'Woogie Boogie' was recorded by Bob, Kenny Buttery and Charlie McCoy. Their track had Bongo and conga drums plus bass and harmonica. Four days later Bob Johnston added a 21 piece orchestra and three female vocalists in an over-dubbing session. The superb wailing saxophone was played by Karl Himmel, the arrangements were created by the almost unknown Bill Walker. At this session they also over dubbed, 'Early Morning Rain', 'Copper Kettle', 'Belle Isle' and 'All the Tired Horses'. **'Belle Isle'** includes a line perfect for this disjointed album, 'we come to you in disguise'. If Bob had already recorded the track prior to the orchestral arrangement being over-dubbed why was it allowed to display Bob as being out-of-tune? The orchestra is in a different key signature to that of Bob's guitar. **'Living The Blues'**: This was an out-take from 'Nashville Skyline', this could be a hybrid re-titled 'Singing Knee Deep in the Blues' with apologies to composer Melvin Endsley. This is a step back to the late 1950s, especially the great female backing singers with their 'ah-ahs'. **'Like A Rolling Stone'**: This is from Bob's first festival performance for years. Three years out of the spotlight then straight into the deep-end in front of Isle Of Wight's 200,000 fans, no wonder this is not the definitive performance.

'Copper Kettle': A song of moonshiners and bootleggers that don't pay their taxes. This was a massive problem at the time, although Bob was thinking more of paying their royalties to him than to the Inland Revenue. The song was written by Albert Frank Beddoe and was also recorded by Joan Baez. Beddoe recorded his version in Bexar County Texas but it was not registered until 1960. The song details how to distillate corn-mash whiskey, even the correct wood in the stove is necessary. The bootlegger just has to lay under a juniper tree (or bush) and relax whilst the whiskey makes his fortune. The song's narrator hadn't paid any tax since 1792. **'Gotta Travel On'**: It took seven composers to create this song. Paul Clayton and Pete Seeger (both are named in the composers list) recorded their versions. I have always preferred the version released in 1958 by Billy Grammer. Bob's backing singers really get out of control on this song. The song was recorded with the trio as for 'Woogie Boogie' and the session sheets for this track were lost. However Venetta Fields, Clydie King, Richard Darice, Billy Barnum, Ginger Blake and Gerry Engerman were the guilty singers, in my humble opinion they spoiled a good track. **'Blue Moon'**: This came as a shock to the fans, Bob Dylan sings 'Rodgers and Hart'. It does contain a super electric violin solo and coda from Doug Kershaw. This may have been a favourite song of Bob's mother. Bob sings it at the pace sung by The Colpix Records group The Marcels, who of course took the song to No 1 in the charts in 1961. **'The Boxer'**: This song was chosen for the album when Bob decided not to include his version of The Fairport Convention's 'Farewell Farewell'. As the Fairports had added at least one of Bob's songs on each of their early albums it would have been seen as a kind reciprocation. The song was a Dylan favourite it told the story of a man arriving in New York and suffering in a manner that Bob fantasized that he too had suffered, but Bob had it easy, only his memory of those events seems to have suffered. Bob sings a duet with himself which was a first for him on record, it doesn't work it sounds terrible.

'**The Mighty Quinn**' is a poor version live from the Isle Of Wight Festival. Bob sounds as though he is trying to sing like Buddy Holly. The first note sounds as though someone has just poked Bob with a sharp stick. The 'wow' shrieks are another continuing nuisance.

'Take Me As I Am' was originally subtitled 'Or Let Me Go'. A lesser known country song from Boudleaux Bryant which was recorded by such luminaries as George Jones, Bobby Bare, Don Gibson and John Lee Hooker. 'Take A Message to Mary' is another Boudleaux Bryant song this time co-composed with Felice Bryant. A massive hit for The Everly Brothers, tell her anything that you like but don't tell her I'm jail, or what I had done. 'It Hurts Me Too' is extremely similar to 'Dogs Run Free' included on the next album, on this version there is no female scat singing. It was originally composed by Tampa Red and the arrangement attributed to Elmore James, as 'It Hurts Me Too Blues', but registered to Bob Dylan on the album notes. 'Minstrel Boy' and 'She Belongs to Me' are average live versions taken from the Isle Of Wight. 'Wigwam' is Bob singing la-la-la to solo piano then the big band was overdubbed. It might sound like a throw-away track but I will bet that you can sing along to it before it is finished and can still remember how the tune goes.

Whatever the listener felt about this album when it was completed the tracks 'All the Wild Horses' and 'Wigwam' so invaded the psyche that they couldn't be purged, I found myself whistling both constantly. There were many out-takes some that Columbia would use for the infamous 'Fool Such As I' album.

Tarantula was finally published on November 11th 1970. The publishers found few modifications to the original text, many copies of the first draft were available as a bookleg. Tarantula received as much coverage in the newspapers as any new Dylan album. The copyright was registered at the time of the first draft as 1966. It was published in the UK in 1971 by MacGibbon and Key Ltd. Bob said that the book concerned a lawyer that leads his pig around on a leash and takes his paranoia seriously. Not sure whose paranoia, is it the lawyer, the pig or the writer? Bob also said it was about...a police chief that had his name engraved on his personal bazooka, Jesus as just another meat-head and other curious things. The New York Times wrote 'poet laureate of young America says it all once and for all.

Reading it again 25 years since I purchased my first copy it all seems so bland and conventional when once it seemed just like the hyperbole that greeted the publication. The critics said 'Surrealism on speed a fantastical journey through out life and times, a beautiful flowing stormy prose poem, a carnival of vitality and vision', I agreed with them all, but I was much older then I'm younger than that now, I think. Bob had re-written the book because he couldn't associated himself after the accident with what he had written before.

There are many good ideas but none are carried through with any conviction, it has always seemed to be a collection of characters with most chapters ending with a signed letter. We learn that 'he' likes his women 'raw' but with 'syrup'. There is a probable allusion to A.J.Weberman as the 'garbage clown' and the lawyer with the pig arrives early in the text. The whole book is written in what Jack Kerouac called 'spontaneous prose', which was originally James Joyce's 'streams of consciousness', that is not to say that Bob's writing bears more than a passing resemblance to either. Kaye Dunham's 'Black Betty Blam a Lam' becomes an essay, as does Crow Jane. The good Samaritan, Toby Celery, Lazy Henry, Homer the Slut, Julius La Rosa (he had song hits with 'Torero' & 'Domani'), Benjamin Turtle, The Dada Weatherman, Arnold Stang (he had a hit with 'Ivy Will Cling'), Angelina the Whore, James Arness (Matt Dillon in Gunsmoke), Bat Masterson, Fernando Lamas, Edgar Allan Poe, Great Glaspy (Gatsby?) are in different tales. One of the better essays is 'Sand in the Mouth of The Movie Star' as is 'A Blast of Loser Takes Nothing'. The best is 'I Found the Piano Player' because this is Bob telling it like it was, this is for Woody Guthrie and his Unionism. 'The Vandals Took the Handles' incorporates the death of Bob Dylan, in fact he was murdered, the tale is attributed to Julius the Honk. Bob has used many pseudonyms in the style of Jack Kerouac. I would suspect that the paragraphs concerning the Peter Pan of the throttle bums, the crash and the technicolour passion of berserk suicide, which are wonderfully surrealistic were added at the final editing.

Bob also takes the opportunity to write of raconteur Lord Buckley, E.E.Cummings and Arthur Conan Doyle, writers that Bob was reading at the time. Bob has a strange writing style, it contrives to make it difficult for the reader to maintain any comprehension. Bob may have been trying to emulate William Burroughs and Brion Gysin and their cut-up method but it is only Bob's trains of thought that are jumbled not the text themselves. Charles Bukowski's style runs through this reader's mind but again the similarities are tenuous. Bob does drop one name that possibly gave him the ideas to use as many strange names as he could conjure, that is E.E.Cummings.

Edward Estlin Cummings wrote 'The Enormous Room' which although presented as a novel is undeniably more fact than fiction. Cummings was an ambulance driver in France during World War I, he and his friend 'B' were accused by the French government of treason. They were sent to La Ferte Mace concentration camp, in Orne France. The book's title refers to the huge barracks where they were confined. Cummings created characters such as Mexique, Gypsy Wanderer, The Zulu, Surplice, Jean Le Negre (a gentle giant) and others, they were subjected to many traumas by their jailers but here individuality shone through. Tarantula (the copy I have) is also typed in lower case without capitals, the 'I' is 'i' throughout, and like Cummings it has unusual punctuation, odd juxtapositions of words and typographical eccentricities to provoke the reader into a deep intellectual study of the author's inner meaning; this could all be true of Bob Dylan. Read E.E.Cummings 'Collected Poems', 'Him' , 'Eimi' and 'The Enormous Room'

124

and I am sure that you will agree that there are some similarities with Bob's technique. In Tarantula Bob doesn't achieve the quality of his album cover writing, '11 Outlined Epitaphs', 'My Life in a Stolen Moment' and 'Advice for Geraldine' are all superior to anything within 'Tarantula'.

Leonard Cohen was a brilliant writer and poet who then got his work read by singing it, his crossover from writer to singer songwriter was more artistically successful than Bob's move from singer songwriter to writer.

Bob was at yet another crossroads. He had altered the text of tarantula because he was in mental conflict with what he had written before the accident. It was all happening for Bob, we had the situation of before and after the accident, before marriage and after marriage, before children and after children, before and after the flood. I have always contended that a man becomes a man when he takes responsibility for others, never mind the bar-mitzvah, the age of consent or reaching 21 years, it is the outlook that others need you to care for them that makes the man, the man is accountable for his actions, not in law but by self realisation. Bob was there now, he couldn't revert to the freewheeling lifestyle and he didn't want that either. His music and lyrics would never be the same again until anguish and torment and deprivation could awaken the innermost psyche. No person would wish another to return to difficult times for the sake of music, but one never knows what is awaiting us around the corner. Bob was in love and deservedly so, he was so happy it would be reflected in his work.

NEW MORNING NEW START

Be true to thy self as thou be not false to others.
Francis Bacon 1561-1626

Francis Bacon also wrote that 'young men are fitter to invent than to judge, fitter for execution than for counsel, and fitter for new projects than for settled business'. Bob was 29 years of age when he went in to the studio to record tracks for **'NEW MORNING'**. Bob was tired of the unwelcome attention he and his family were receiving in Woodstock so they all moved to New York. Beatle, George Harrison was again permitted to travel to the USA, he had been banned due to admitting smoking marijuana, he introduced Bob to smoking 'grass'. Bob Johnston was again to be the producer but this time Bob decided to record in New York. George Harrison was present for the first sessions in May 1970 but he was not detailed on the work sheets, Bob Johnston played piano with Charlie Daniels on bass and Russ Kunkel on drums. For other recordings Al Kooper, Ron Cornelius and David Bromberg were present, many of the tracks would be released on 'Dylan, Fool Such as I' after Bob had moved away from Columbia. The sessions continued through June, July and were completed in August.

'New Morning' was Bob's first album made and presented in his life of contented domesticity. It was released in November 1970 and gave Bob his fourth consecutive No 1 album in the UK, No 7 in the USA. Bob had recorded some of these songs at the time of the Self Portrait sessions. Bob wrote some of the songs for a Broadway Stage Show titled 'The Devil and Daniel Webster'. This was a Faustian play moved to 19th Century, New Hampshire, it was made into a film in 1941 with three titles other than the Broadway Show version. It was also 'All That Money Can Buy', Daniel and The Devil' and 'Here is A Man', and starred Walter Houston in his greatest performance as Mr Scratch with Edward Arnold as Daniel Webster. Bob wrote 'New Morning', 'Father of Night' and 'Time Passes Slowly' and took them to Archie Macleish the playwright and the Producer in Connecticut. The playwright must have written his own stage play for the original book which was written by Stephen Vincent Benet, the screenplay was by Don Totheroh. They liked two of the songs but not 'Father of Night' so Bob backed out of the show. It seems that Bob thought that should like all three or none. The story of Faust seems to be better served by 'If Dogs Run Free', time undoubtedly would run 'fast' if one was leading the Devil's debauched hedonistic lifestyle for 25 years. The cover picture has Bob in a mirrored pose to that of young Bob with Victoria Spivey on the back. The guitar that Bob is balancing belonged to Big Joe Williams, it has nine strings. On the album Bob's bad cold can be heard on some tracks.

'If Not For You': A song for depending on your lover and gaining strength from them. This was a massive hit for Olivia Newton John, it kick-started her solo career. George Harrison must have enjoyed recording with Bob because he included this on his 'All Things Must Pass' album. Bob said that he wrote the song thinking about Sara. A man proclaiming his love. 'Day of the Locusts': The first and last verse recalls Bob receipt of the Honorary Doctorate of Music from Princeton University back in June 1970. This could be a Randy Newman or Jim Webb song. The title is taken from the 1945 book by Nathaniel West. I could not learn if Bob had read the book but there are certain similarities. The book presents a diverse set of Hollywood personalities as seen from the eyes of Tod Hackett a young aspiring artist. There is a dwarf that believes himself to be Casanova, how tidy it would have been if his name was Tiny Montgomery. The novel is an indictment of a society that neglects spiritual values in exchange for self-gratification, as in Faust. The Locusts in the song will be critics. In Bob's song the middle section is a surrealistic dream in high temperatures. A man's head explodes, the apocalypse maybe, the temperature might be 90 degrees centigrade. The scientists maintain that after the apocalypse the insects shall inherit the Earth, so what will the locusts eat? The sound engineer has added the sound of insects, it is in fact the sound of early morning in a tropical country, not really the sound of locust's singing or eating.

'Time Passes Slowly': This is another song for the love of the quiet rural life where time passes so slowly. I always thought that time raced by when you were enjoying yourself. This rural idyll sounds extremely boring to these ears. This song could have been influenced by the Henry Treece poem 'Who Murdered the Minutes' a poem known to be a favourite of Joan Baez. Al Kooper and Harvey Brooks of 'Supersession' played on this track, it was a long time since Bob had been in the studio with these musicians on 'Highway 61 Revisited'. Apparently Al Kooper was exasperated over Bob's changeable behaviour, he said that Bob was becoming increasingly moody. Al said in an interview that many of the remaindered recorded versions were a marked improvement on the selections used. Bob is playing piano on this song. Later on the 'Time Out of Mind' album Bob remembered he once thought time passed slowly. 'Went to See the Gypsy' recounts Bob visit to meet Elvis Presley in Las Vegas. It was recorded at the time of 'Self Portrait'. I wondered if this song was another that was influenced by an E.E. Cummings novel 'The Enormous Room' which included Mexique the Gypsy Wanderer. There are characters in that book that would not be out of place on the Basement Tapes album cover. E.E.Cummings had been mentioned by Bob, but many people said that the song was another dig in the ribs for Albert Grossman, after all the gypsy in the song is a man. The song is set back in Minnesota and the gypsy seems to be able to perform magic. A lyric where

Bob is toying with us and laughing himself senseless at our conclusions. Al Kooper said that he had created what he thought was a superb arrangement for this song but Bob just discarded it as inadequate. **'Winterlude'**: This is a almost a skating waltz in the style of the Mexican Hat Dance. Winterlude in the song is a pet name for someone dear to the narrator.

'If Dogs Run Free': Piano from Al Kooper and scat singing from Maeretha Stewart, she assisted Al on vocals on a couple of his solo albums and his 'The Landlord' soundtrack. Bob sketched a dog with a man's head for this song in the 'Writings' book. An unusual lyric to say the least, dogs don't usually run free. In Federico Lorca's 'Casida of Lament' which was included on Joan Baez' album 'Baptism' released in 1968, Lorca states that 'weeping is an immense dog', could this lyric allude to the subject of constant sorrow, and weeping? There are a few song titles appearing within the lyric such as 'Mule Train', 'I Hear a Symphony', 'Tapestry', 'True Love', 'Que Sera Sera' (what must be must be), 'To Each His own', 'The Best is Yet to Come' and 'Stand Tall' but these maybe just coincidence, if not then this is a very clever song. **'New Morning'**: A new beginning to the day and maybe the career. A song for being happy to be alive, and now time passes quickly when only a few songs ago it passed slowly. We are constantly reminded that we are 'Underneath the sky of blue' but it would turn 'red' for Bob in 1990. There is a very short guitar break from David Bromberg where he puts so much into just a few seconds. **'Sign on the Window'**: Bob realising that parenthood is what life is all about. In the typed pages at the rear of the 'Writings' book Bob has typed 'But I was blind to the sign that says you're mine'. In the song the lyric says that Brighton girls are like the moon, they are I married one. If Bob is suggesting that these girls are round, yellow, covered in craters and very distant then I can tell him from experience he is wrong. **'One More Weekend'**: An up-tempo country-rocker, with David Bromberg playing dobro guitar. Al Kooper again on organ with Charlie Daniels on bass and Russ Kunkel on drums; Ron Cornelius plays second guitar. This is a song where the narrator needs just one more chance. Bob wants time with Sara alone without the children, he says come down to my 'ship' which sounds so much more expensive than a boat.

'The Man in Me': Is an important song comprising just four short verses. This is a song where the narrator realises that he is not in control of his destiny. He has become the partner in the relationship that loves the most. She has got through his defense mechanism and is now ruling the roost. He is trying to stand his ground, he doesn't wish to become a slave to her requests. He will do almost any task, it must be noted that he writes 'nearly any task'. If there are storm clouds perhaps the couple were starting to have strong differences of opinion. In the third verse he crumples completely, he is just happy if she is near, her out-look is not detailed. Bob takes the 'wonderful feeling' lines from 'On The Street Where You Live' from 'My Fair Lady', both songs are songs of anticipation, appeasement and hope. The lyrics of the song cease early and the backing singers, probably over-dubbed later, increase the length of the song. It is such an admission of devotion it would have been more powerful if it was included in a shortened version. I considered this song so important in the canon of Bob Dylan that the title of the book had to paraphrase it. Here we learn that the man in him is not the man he once thought he was.

'Three Angels': A gentle proselytizing song, possible based on Ruby Wright's 'Three Stars'. One of the angels was 'the wildest cat' which should be Gene Vincent but he was born in Norfolk, Virginia, not Montana. There have been a couple of important 'threes' in literature. Gertrude Stein wrote 'Three Lives' which was mentioned earlier in this book. Erich Maria Remarque wrote 'Three Comrades' in 1937; Remarque wrote 'All Quiet on the Western Front'. I think that Bob's lyric is much simpler. Somewhere in America there may be a statue high above the street of three angles each playing a horn, it is also a motif seen on many christmas cards, or just angels put on a pole as part of the christmas decorations. Although the intentions are for love and peace at christmas nobody pays the slightest notice to the angels or their significance. 'Father of Night': Is this gospel, is this a joke? There are many fathers, Bob is one, there is his own father, there is God Our Father who art in Heaven. This song is based on the Kolnidre Prayer of Yon Kippur, so it is The Lord God Our Father. The melody has a superb piano riff played by Bob, it similar to the long coda of Jimmy Webb's 'Laspitch' on his 1972 'And So On' album.

In December 1970 Bob learned that his investment in The Home-Stake Oil Production Company, a tax-sheltering company, proved to be fraudulent. Bob lost more than $120,000 to the Tulsa based group. Meanwhile Bob continued to work on 'Eat The Document' which still had not been seen anywhere. It would also be three years before the next album and that would be a soundtrack release. 'Eat The Document' finally got its premiere in February 1971 at The New York Academy of Music.

During March 1971 Bob, Bob Johnston and Leon Russell recorded two tracks. 'Watching the River Flow': A song for expressing how enjoyable country life can be. 'When I Paint My Masterpiece' is surely not for Bob the painter, his portraits may have been different but nothing exceptional, The Big Pink cover was in what must have been known as his adolescent period. Bob mentions The Big Police, they also came knocking at Minnie Wallace's door in her song 'Dirty Butter'. This 'Masterpiece' song was also recorded by The Band for inclusion on their 'Cahoots' album released in 1971. The song is a diary of a visit to Italy and Belgium. Bob mentions a gondola which means Venice, and then Rome, which he infers is not too tidy. He realises that Italy has plenty of history, the Coliseum, Botticelli, the Spanish Stairs or should that be 'The Spanish Steps' in Rome. A bumpy flight to Belgium and a Press Conference, all items for Bob's memory when he finally paints his masterpiece, so it is a painting!

Bob had written **'Bowling Alley Blues'** and **'I Love a Switchboard Operator'**(a.k.a 'On the Wire'), which he never recorded, he may never have devised a tune for them. In the latter lyric Bob professes his love for her, she gives him money, he is anticipating when they will be able to dance together on the wire.

Bob and his family spent his 30th birthday at The Wailing Wall in Israel. Bob also showed interest in a few weeks at a kibbutz where he could use the time to write some lyrics. As he didn't intend to work for the kibbutz his request was declined. The reason for Bob's trip to Israel was to enable him to travel to the roots of Judaism, the religion of his forefathers. He was becoming more ambivalent about theosophy in general, just like Bob's British equivalent, Van Morrison, they were both avidly searching for the truth.

In July Bob appeared in George Harrison's **'Concert for Bangla Desh'** at New York's Madison Square Garden. There was a triple album released of the concert with Bob appearing on one side of the six; the album went to No 2 in the USA. George said that until he saw Bob walk out on stage he had no idea if he was intending to play. He sang, George's favourite, 'If Not For You', 'Hard Rain' and 'Blowin' in the Wind'. The concert raised $243,418.50, the cheque was shown in The Rolling Stone Magazine.

'Watching the River Flow' was released as a single and went to No 24 in the UK and 41 in the USA. 'Watching' and 'Masterpiece' were added to the January 1972 release of **Bob Dylan's Greatest Hits Volume II**, which was titled **More of Bob Dylan's Greatest Hits** in the UK; it achieved No 12 in the UK and No 41 in the USA. Leon Russell claims that he wrote the music for both songs, he gave the musicians the chord changes and Bob walked around with his note book creating the lyrics. The b-side of the 'Watching' single was 'Spanish is The Loving Tongue' composed by Charles Badger Clark which would be included on 'Dylan' in 1973. Bob also recorded 'You Ain't Going Nowhere', 'Down in the Flood' and 'I Shall Be Released' with Happy Traum the last three were also included on 'Greatest Hits Volume 2'. Bob also played harmonica as a guest on 'Sammy's Song' which was included on Dave Bromberg's eponymously titled album.

Whilst I was awaiting for my own first son to be born in March 1972 I was at the hospital reading 'Soledad Brother' the story of George Jackson. It was the time of the activist, Angela Davis was extremely vociferous at the time. Bob recorded a song for, and titled, 'George Jackson', detailed earlier. Bob recorded the song with Dan Shugufale on steel guitar, Kenny Buttrey on drums and Russell Bridges on bass, it was over-dubbed into a big band number. Bob wanted the record played and stipulated that the same song should be on both sides of the single so that the radio stations couldn't just play the b-side; one side was acoustic the other the big band version.

Bob made a recording with Allen Ginsberg who had decided with Peter Orlofsky (his partner) to book some studio time. It is alleged that Allen and Bob created ten poems, three of which were recorded for the album to be titled **'First Blues'**. The album is very collectable and because it is so awful the copies that I have seen have been almost new. It is an album that one plays for curiosity purposes and then files away, it is so embarrassing that one needs to listen alone. I hope that I am not being too unfair with this criticism, you can make up your own mind. Bob can be heard singing on the passable 'Going to San Diego Blues'. 'Vomit Express' includes some Bob Dylan recitation, it concerns travelling on the midnight train with the junkies and the drunks is where the vomit in the title is manufactured. Allen Ginsberg plays the harmonium, apparently it helped him with his Zen meditation. 'Om My Song' with its Zen connotation is bad, William Blake's 'Tyger Tyger Burning Bright' is badly mauled and 'The Nurse's Song' may have been listenable in the days of psychedelia, now life is far too short. The backing vocals deserve a mention because they are perfect farmyard noises, they sound like bleating sheep, I say that with a full apology to sheep. Other tracks are 'September on Jessore Road'(apparently written By Ginsberg to make Bob cry) and 'The Jimmy Berman Rag', I suggest that you approach the album with great trepidation, and remember listen to it alone first.

Bob went to Wally Heider Studio, Los Angeles and played harmonica on Roger McGuinn and Jacques Levy's 'I'm So Restless' which was included on 'Roger McGuinn's eponymously titled album.

The Earl Scruggs album, 'His family and Friends' included Bob playing on his own track 'Nashville Skyline Rag'. Bob also helped Steve Goodman on a couple of tracks by playing piano, the two tracks involving Bob as Robert Milkwood Thomas, were 'Somebody Else's Troubles' and 'Election Year Rag' both included on 'The Essential Steve Goodman'. After playing harmonica for Roger McGuinn on 'I'm So Restless', Bob was soon back in the studio with friend Doug Sahm, sometimes known as Doug Saldana or even Sir Douglas. The album 'Doug Sahm and Band' was not released by Atlantic until 1973. Bob appeared on **'Wallflower'** a song that he had written and recorded himself earlier. An enjoyable country waltz with Bob singing back-up vocal, the engineer has turned up Bob's microphone and created a Dylan solo vocal. As mentioned the song was also recorded by Bob in New York with Kenny Buttrey, Dan Keith and Leon Russell, that version was released on the Bootleg Series in 1991. The song is for the person that is always left out especially at dances. Bob also appeared on vocals on 'San Antone', added harmonica to Willie Dixon's, 'Me and Paul', and guitar on 'Blues Stay Away From Me' which included David Bromberg on dobro guitar. Sahm and Dylan recorded a version of 'Just Like Tom Thumb's Blues' which so far has remained in the vaults. Arif Mardin played keyboards on the album but Bob was also mooted to be playing organ, it was not confirmed. Bob looks to be enjoying himself thoroughly on the cover, laughing on the cartoon cover and laughing with the band on the rear. Bob was not finished helping out others he played harmonica for Booker T and Priscilla Jones on their 'Chronicles' album on the track 'Crippled Crow'.

The book mentioned throughout this book, titled 'The Writings and Drawings by Bob Dylan' was published. Now we had all the lyrics of the songs, some were different to the recordings. The book also included a couple of pages of Bob's own typing complete with errors spelling mistakes, changes and cup stain. It was a welcome addition to the Bob Dylan canon, the problem is that any original hard-back copy when opened fully nowadays is that it just falls to pieces leaving a pile of loose pages.

Sam Peckinpah was preparing to film a Rudy Wurlitzer script for a western. Bob was requested to write a couple of songs for the movie. Bob wrote 'Holly's Lament' and 'Billy' and Peckinpah wanted Bob to travel to Mexico to be on the set. It is alleged that Peckinpah actually thought that Bob was Roger Miller, however Bob travelled, taking Sara along, to Durango to meet Sam. Sam found the songs emotional and was so impressed that he asked Bob to appear in the film, one assumes that he had already realised that it wasn't in fact Roger Miller. Bob thought that his part was in fact just added to an already completed script. Rudy Wurlitzer attempted to convince Bob that 'Alias' was well documented in the diaries of Pat Garrett. It had been rumoured but not confirmed that Bob was also offered the part of Holden Caulfield in the film version of J.D.Salinger's 'The Catcher in the Rye', the film is still to be made.

Sara a city girl was not happy in Durango, it was reported that Bob and Sara spent long periods of time in a sulk and not speaking to each other. During a break in filming for Christmas 1972, Bob and Sara travelled to England and stayed with George Harrison and his family. Back in Durango the film was running close to the budget and Producer Gordon Carroll had no intention of allowing for extra costs. Sam Peckinpah was forced to accept ordinary filming and performances to remain within the financial guidelines.

Kris Kristofferson had moved upward from his days as janitor for Columbia Studios Nashville. His gruff talking style and superb early songs had rocketed him skyward in the music business. He wrote 'Me and Bobby McGee', 'Help Me Make it Through the Night', 'Loving Her Was Easier' and 'Sunday Morning Coming Down'. Like so many composers he couldn't maintain the level of his early work, it was created when he was barely making a living. He was surprised to get star billing in the movie as Billy the

Kid with James Coburn as Pat Garrett, Jason Robards (Governor Wallace) and Richard Jaeckel as Sheriff Kip McKinney. Slim Pickens Jack Elam and Harry Dean Stanton were also present as was Rita Coolidge soon to be Mrs Kristofferson.

Kris and Bob went into the studio with Kris' band, they never saw eye-to-eye, and Bob accused Kris of interfering, Bob was unhappy with the recordings and would later re-record them in Burbank, California. As one of Bob's children was ill he took the child to Burbank to see a doctor and remained there to record. The soundtrack recording was to be over-seen by Jerry Fielding a composer famous for his soundtrack recordings. Fielding told Bob that the songs he had written were poor, he seemed to talk down to Bob, anyway Fielding walked out.

Bob had been given some guidelines for the scenes but according to Bob the film just uses the songs and instrumentals seemingly out of place. Whatever the truth Bruce Langhorne, Jim Keltner and Billy Paul acquitted themselves adequately and the result was a soundtrack equalling in my opinion any of Jerry Fielding's. The film itself was considered to be too long and many scenes were deleted. Later a 'Directors' cut was made with many of the scenes re-inserted. The directors cut version has Pat Garrett shot in the first scene allowing the film to be observed in flash-back. The film was not as good as Peckinpah's 'The Wild Bunch' but it certainly is better than many other westerns. Bob Dylan holds the attention of the audience whenever he is on screen as 'Alias anything you want'. He later said that he didn't do it for the money, he can't really remember why he did it. He found it was hours of boredom followed by a few minutes of hectic action. He decided to base his performance on how he thought Dustin Hoffman might perform it. Bob used the spectacles in the reading scene because Hoffman had done the same in 'Papillon'.

'PAT GARRETT AND BILLY THE KID' was released in October 1973 when Bob was not contracted to Columbia, but they purchased the rights to the soundtrack. The album cover was expected to have a painting (or paintings) by Bob, but apparently they were destroyed by mistake. The rear of the cover has a still (by Manuel Palomino) from the film showing R.G.Armstrong (Ollinger) pointing a rifle at Kris Kristofferson's (Billy the Kid) chest. A poster of other photographs was to be given as a free insert and the early album's credited Sara Dylan and Bob Jenkins with the photographs. The cover finally had just lettering with the credit for art direction and design going to John Van Hamersveld.

'Main Title' (Billy): A quiet shuffling introduction with Russ Kunkel's tambourine creating the rhythm for Bob and Bruce Langhorne's guitars. Booker T. Jones is playing bass. 'Cantina Theme' is slower with Russ Kunkel moving to bongo drums and Roger McGuinn joining Bob and Bruce on guitars. I doubt if this was written down, it is just a repeated riff. There are three versions of 'Billy', numbered 1, 4 and 7. The first is harmonica led and floats along until Bob sings. 'Billy 4' is more meditative and was recorded in Mexico City by just Terry Paul and Bob, they get a speaker each in the stereo, it has alternative lyrics and a different sequence of verses. The gist remains the same, but Bob does sound just a little inebriated. 'Billy 7': This version has Bob sounding like Merle Haggard, this is the only time that his vocal sounded as deep as this. 'Billy 1' sounds like the traditional folk song 'Red River Valley' which was written in 1896, but it is not so perceptible in the other two versions. The three versions are separated in the film without motive or feel for any continuity. Bob has written a superb lyric to suit the character. The song takes the relationship step-by-step. Billy realises his situation, it is one that he can't escape. The women and the other gunfighters wish to fight a duel with him. Of course he wasn't on the run for long. In the other films featuring Billy the Kid he is always presented as a loveable rogue, a characteristic that is far from the truth. An unintelligent oaf is closer to his personality. The version of 'Billy the Kid' (MGM/1930) with Johnny Mack Brown as Billy and Wallace Beery as Garrett was romanticised. The re-make in 1941 with Robert Taylor and Brian Donlevy was superbly photographed but the acting was wooden. Two others were even worse 'Billy the Kid vs The Green Baize Vampire' moved the romanticised story to a 'Kid' snooker player. 'Billy the Kid vs Dracula' had Billy as a hero rescuing his girl friend from Count Dracula, enough said.

'Bunkhouse Theme' is a guitar duet between Bob and Carol Hunter. 'River Theme' has filler 'la la la' vocals from Donna Weiss, Priscilla Jones and Byron Berline. 'Turkey Chase' has Byron Berline on fiddle and the infamous Jolly Roger on banjo, probably McGuinn. This up-tempo hop is excellent. It is reminiscent of Charlie McCoy's, 'Stone Fox Chase'. 'Knockin' On Heavens Door': The song is for a scene where the sheriff is shot. He wants his badge taken off and his guns laid on the ground before he dies. Bob has decided that death approaches like a long black cloud rather than the usual opinion that we slide along a tunnel towards a bright light. Eric Clapton had a big hit with the song. It was also recorded by Sandy Denny, Booker T., Guns and Roses, Jerry Garcia, Kevin Coyne and many more. It remains one of Bob's best and most memorable songs. 'Final Theme' is haunting, it has Gary Foster's flute as the lead instrument and Carl Fortina's harmonium fills the backing. It is the first track with drums, played by Jim Keltner, he sounds as though he is running in a new set of cymbals.

The album reached No 16 in the USA and No 29 in the UK. The album only included four tracks with Bob's vocals, which really was just two songs, but it was deemed as the album that completed the Columbia contract. 'Knocking on Heaven's Door' was released as a single and became Bob's biggest single since 'Lay Lady Lay', No 12 USA, and 14 UK. Bob had made his decision not to re-sign with Columbia. He was approached by David Geffen owner of Asylum Records and agreed a one album deal to make an album with The Band. Clive Davis had been the head man at Columbia for many years and had attracted some of the greatest American acts to the label. Davis had been suddenly dismissed by the Board of Directors for alleged fraudulent behaviour. Davis formed Arista records and started again. Harold Lieberson the new Columbia man couldn't agree a new contract with Bob's lawyer, David Braun, so Bob just had to move on.

Bob had been working on an album for 'Barry Goldberg' (Bob shared Production duties), Barry had been a member of Nick Gravenites and Michael Bloomfield's 'Electric Flag'. Bob assisted Jerry Wexler in the production of Barry's eponymously titled album and added background vocals. Although this was for Atlantic Records, Columbia (or Asylum) gave permission for Bob's name to be added to the credits. Bob's home in Malibu was being renovated so he rented an apartment close by and renewed his friendship with Roger McGuinn.

Understandably Columbia were not too pleased with Bob's departure so they quickly assembled an album of tracks that Bob had recorded for fun and released them as **'DYLAN'** in January 1974. It was deemed below standard, Bob had realised this fact, it was his reason for leaving the tracks in the vaults. With hindsight it is alleged that it was a deliberate act by Columbia, especially when one bears in mind the superb out-takes that were released on 'Biograph' and 'The Bootleg Series'. CBS then released a single, the album had reached No 17 in the USA, the single 'Fool Such as I' only reached No 55. The album cover was a serigraph made from a silhouette photograph of Bob. A serigraph is a colour print made using the silk screen process, which overlays the colours. If the serigraph was created by Richard Kenerson, different overlays are used for the front and rear, then what did John Berg who was detailed on the cover provide, apparently the original photograph was by Alan Clayton. We can only guess if it made any inroads into the sale of Bob's new Island album. Many of the tracks included on the 'Dylan' album were recorded at the 'New Morning' sessions, so at least Columbia who have been severely maligned for this release were in fact releasing Bob's most recent Columbia recordings. The 'Dylan' album has been suffixed with 'Fool Such As I' on the CBS compact disc release to make it easier for the public to recognise. I suspect that Bob was not too pleased with the 'fool' reference. The songs were an excellent selection, all tuneful and pleasant, if Bob had written any then they would have been claimed as masterpieces.

'Lily of the West': The title should also have (Flora) after it as written on the recording session details. Arranged by Davis and Peterson from the traditional song. The song is of a woman named Flora, she is a damsel from

Lexington. He courted her but she went with another man, a man of high degree. His mind distorted by desire caused him to stab her man. When he was in the dock she swore his life away but it didn't dilute his love. Dave Bromberg is on Dobro/guitar, Al Kooper on organ, Russ Kunkel Drums and Charlie Daniels on bass, and Ron Cornelius on guitar made a great recording. Bob's harmonica (if it is Bob) is playing as he sings which means that he liked the track enough to add an over-dub. There are backing singers which seem to have evaded the recording and over-dubbing sheets, it may be Carol Montgomery, Dolores Edgin and June Page who were used for the 'Self Portrait' extra sessions but of course it may be Maeretha Stewart and her singers. Joan Baez included this song on her 'Ballad Book' album. **'Can't Help Falling In Love'** used the same musicians as for 'Lily'. A song arranged by George Weiss with Hugo Peretti and Luigi Creatore. These last two producers also gave us the Stylistics and in the 1950s gave themselves top billing on singles that they produced; their 'Rockabilly Party' from 1957 sounds more like the Ray Conniff Singers. Al Kooper assisted Bob Johnston with the production on a few tracks, this being one of them, one just has to listen for Al's B3-organ. Elvis Presley's version was included in the film 'Blue Hawaii'. **'Sara Jane'** same musicians yet again on this traditional song. The title has been modified from 'Saro Jane' to make it more personal. Bob makes his version sound like a British sixties song. I can still remember the version on Folkways by Hermes Nye. The song must be for a very phlegmatic character. He takes his Saro Jane on a boat trip and he sings and rocks his Saro. The ship's boiler bursts, the captain falls overboard, the engine cracks and the engineer is killed, but all he does is sing and rock his Saro without a care in the world.

'The Ballad of Ira Hayes' was written by Peter La Farge (it is on his 'On the Warpath' album) and was released as the b-side of Bob's 'Watching The River Flow. Ira Hayes was one of the soldiers holding up the Stars and Stripes flag on Iwo Jima in the war photograph. Hayes was a Red Indian from Arizona who signed up to fight. The celebrity he received did him little good and he became a drunk finally dying alone in a ditch. **'Mr Bojangles'** was composed by Jerry Jeff Walker. To these ears Bob has created the definitive version of the song alongside that of The Nitty Gritty Dirt Band, they included it on no less than ten albums. **'Mary Ann'** is a traditional song and for once the backing singers are excellent on this track. Sailing away from Mary Ann and he may never return. If he had a flask of gin he would pour her a glass he sings, which is strange when he has sailed away. The song is faded just as it is getting under way.

'Big Yellow Taxi' there was some over dubbing on this Joni Mitchell song and there is an imperceptible splice of two takes. Bob adds his own verse adding a Big Yellow Bulldozer in lieu of a taxi. **'A Fool Such as I'** was written by Bill Trader and a became hit for Elvis Presley, it was the penultimate song from Elvis' pre-draft recordings. There is also an excellent version by the late Tommy Edwards. Bob's version was recorded over a year earlier than the previous tracks on this album. Charlie McCoy bass, Norman Blake guitar, Fred Carter Jr guitar, Pete Drake steel guitar, Robert Wilson piano, Kenny Buttrey drums and Charlie Daniels guitar are the musicians on this track. **'Spanish is The Loving Tongue'** is another earlier recording with the same band. Bob is singing with a chest cold, plenty of Spanish acoustic guitar in the background. The song was written by Charles Badger Clark, a song for a man breaking his own heart at the same time as that of his lover.

The critical abuse levelled at CBS and the album was strange indeed. The music industry is a business like any other. Bob Dylan was the 'flag-ship' star on the label, he was their Beatles, their 'Rolling Stones' and now they were losing him. The claims that CBS intended to ruin Bob's commerciality is absolute nonsense they owned the back catalogue and plenty of out-takes which would make them money. Why would they want to spoil that, they just wanted Bob back and the album was intended to prick the bubble of his ego, it would eventually work, but the bubble deflated very slowly.

Bob started touring with The Band on a 39 date tour to promote the new album. As it was Bob's first tour for almost 8 years the ticket applications were a staggering 5 million. Some of the shows were recorded for a later live album.

In February 1974 **'PLANET WAVES'** was released, it became Bob's first chart No 1 in the USA, in the UK it was released on the Island Label it only reached No 7. The single fared worse not charting in the UK but 'On A Night Like This' reached No 44. The album was originally titled 'Ceremonies of the Horsemen' (a line from 'Love Minus Zero') with the cover a gypsy painting by Bob. The final cover was another of Bob's paintings, possibly Bob in the centre with an anchor on his head, surrounded by two other figures. The figure on Bob's right could be Dylan Thomas and on Bob's left William Shakespeare. Bob has added a withered arm to 'Shakespeare' which gives the impression that he is blessing Bob. This is not a painting it appears to be a felt-tip and ball point pen drawing. Bob has a heart on his jacket and a CND sign in his left hand. What does Moonglow mean? A song of course, used as the title song of the film 'Picnic' and a hit for Morris Stoloff in 1956. Bob designed (if that is the word) the mess on the back cover. Some prose and a track list and band names with Richard Manuel spelled incorrectly as Manual, perhaps he changed his name once per-year. The UK copy had an insert which was the rear cover repeated without the prose notes at one side, one wonders why Island bothered. One idea was that the inner was intended to be stuck onto the rear because a couple of words were deemed offensive. If you have cover and insert then you can check this out yourself. The lyrics were the best since the accident the tunes were only average. **'On A Night Like This'** is another song in the style of 'Lay Lady Lay'. Put your body next to mine, the night must have been cold as there was frost on the windows, another good reason for getting close together. There is no ambiguity here, light the fire and I'll be your baby tonight. It seems that they have only done it once before. An up-tempo good-time song with Bob playing up and down the harmonica with great abandon on the fade-out. **'Going Going Gone'**: The previous track was for closeness and compatibility this song is for a relationship showing cracks. He is doing just like his Grandma once advised him, things will be alright at 'the end of the line', a lyric that would be used again later by a Wilbury. If he is thinking that he might go to the ledge, then he is near suicidal. There is some superb Robbie Robertson guitar picking between the verses. **'Tough Mama'**: The love of a dark beauty , Sara, or is he still talking to Joan Baez in his lyrics? This song has an excellent lyric too, clever imagery. Jack the Cowboy could be friend Ramblin' Jack Elliott, who has gone up North. The Lone Wolf was just a passing fad. Bob is her 'perfect stranger' and if Joan had recorded a song with that title all would be clear, she only recorded 'Wayfaring Stranger'. The object of his affection is a dark beauty, strange that he should think it was time that they met again to carve another notch. As he is offering a golden ring then Sara is an obvious correlation. She was his sweet goddess at the time, she will probably now have changed into the silver (haired) angel who also appears in the lyric. **'Hazel'** is a blonde. The songbook lists ten chords for this simple song. One critic wrote a long article on how many times Bob uses 'hill' in his lyrics, almost as often as Scott Walker and Van Morrison use 'rain'. Again Bob is on the hill waiting for Hazel. Bob writes 'a touch of your love' when so many other writers would have said 'hands or lips'. I tried to locate other songs with that line in their title but I could only find one by a group called 'Starpoint'; I suspect there are more. Bob is out of tune on some of this song when his volume rises, the track sounds like in-studio filler.

'Something There is About You': As song concerning the situation when somebody reminds you of sometime or place from your past. Danny Lopez and another (or the same) Ruth is mentioned, and the forgotten truth. This is just nostalgia for the days of the narrator's youth back in Duluth, which is mentioned. Of course a Ruth would emerge much later in Bob's story claiming that she had been close by Bob all the time. **'Forever Young'**: The song 'May You Always' obviously influenced the opening lines, it was originally recorded by The McGuire Sisters and Andy Williams sang it regularly on his television show. Bob expands the idea and creates his own great lyric which deserved an improved melody. This is Bob's desiderata, his rules for anticipation and happiness. This may be a father explaining how wonderful it is to be young to his youngest child. This idea was confirmed by

Bob in his Biograph album notes, he said "It was written for one of his boys, although much of the song wrote itself". **'Forever Young'**: A faster version opens side two of the album but the idea is lost in the CD format. The Biograph set released a third version of the song. This may have been Bob's registration disc and it is only when listening to this version that one realises that Bob has used the traditional melody used by Woody Guthrie for 'Grand Coulee Dam', with a touch of 'Wabash Cannonball'. **'Dirge'**: A dirge is a lamentation for the dead. The studio session sheet stated that this was titled 'Dirge for Martha', if that is a clue then I am unable to solve the mystery. This is another good song for an unnamed protest singer. As the narrator hates himself for loving her it can't be Bob considering his matrimonial position. Fibreglass is mentioned, is this a first time in any song? This is a remarkable lyric which Bob may have written from the female point of view. The two protagonists are extremely strong willed neither are able to apologise. Bob also changes tenses from 'I' and 'You' in the first verse to 'his' in the third. Why is the naked truth taboo and how near was Suicide Road? As this song is for a relationship that is over it seems as though this is on the album as a purgative explanation making the way clear for 'Wedding Song'. The staring into each others eyes until one would break may be an allusion to those terrible non talking, sulking sessions, that so many couples indulge. They may also be Bob staring into a mirror at himself, realising his own short-comings, or even staring out the critics until they blink and break!

'You Angel You': This has some superb playing from The Band, they are always excellent but sometimes they are just sublime. This track was almost a hit for The New Riders of the Purple Sage and was included on their 'Brujo' album. They also recorded an excellent version of 'Farewell Angelina'. The 'angel' has infatuated him so much that he can't sleep, he just can't stop thinking about her. No ambiguities here a nice unrequited love song, no more no less. **'Never Say Goodbye'**: A return to the scene set by 'Winterlude'. The frozen lake and the snow. Is this song for the blondes that went brunette and died, Edie Sedgwick, Nico or even Marilyn Monroe; she wasn't in either of the films made with the same title as the song. Is it the infamous Baby Blue who returns in this song. It is probably for Sara and for Bob's wish that they will be together forever. **'Wedding Song'**: A song that was added to the album at the last minute. It was recorded at the same time as 'Adalita' (un-released) and another attempt at 'Forever Young' in mid-November 1973. Was Bob's marriage back on firm foundations after Durango? The doubts the apologies, the changes since the cycle accident. So many people say 'since the War' for Bob everything was 'since the accident'. The engineer on this track, Bob Fabroni, offered to expunge the sound of Bob's jacket sleeve buttons which can be heard tapping on his guitar, but Bob said that he needn't bother. Bob's Blonde on Blonde songs had been introverted, in some songs he was heavily chauvinistic, here it is Bob the lover, professing his undying devotion, but does he sound just a little embarrassed to have fallen head line and sinker under the power of a woman. The first verse is a list of things of which he loves her even more. She gave him three babies, his happiness is her, and he will love her in eternity. Bob has never written a more profound love song ever. It is so beautifully written that I suspect that after the divorce the words would not be an embarrassment. Deeply in love but never effusive, this is Bob finding his redemption through finding true love. He is taking the stand-point of the lover trying to express just how strong his love is. It is only after the fire has dwindled a little that one learns that it is not as important as life itself, although some people do commit murder and suicide for the potency of their love. The melody line is so short the overall effect is diminished, just nine bars of 4/4, for eight verses.

'Back to the Starting Point' was written as the jacket notes for this album. Bob mentions Hebrew Letters on The Wall, Victor Hugo and Autumn Leaves. Bob refers to garter girls that stank sweating pussy. The piece continues listing things such as Jacob's Ladder, Bismarck, Duluth, Buddha and Eisenhower. There are also places and faces but it really is just a list, if it has any meaning then it is obfuscated so deeply that it becomes meaningless.

'Nobody 'Cept You': This song was played live at the concerts and was removed from the album to be replaced by 'The Wedding Song'. Bob played it in all the live shows until the 'Planet Waves' album was released then deleted it from the play-list. It finally was released on The Bootleg Series in 1991. It is bizarre that the album should include two versions of 'Forever Young' at the expense of this track. Here he openly states that the only person that really knows him is Sara. The reason why this was remaindered was due to this track also being a song of redemption through love. This and the 'Wedding Song' would have over burdened the album with near gushing love songs, in my opinion it was a good decision.

Bob was troubled by his difficulty in writing his lyrics in the same manner as before the accident. It was all natural before, the words just flowed now he had to work at them. The critics agreed that something had changed, and for once Bob agreed with them, perhaps they were not all imbeciles. The typewritten pages at the front and rear of Bob's 'Writings and Drawings' book presented the early method, he was Bob now resorting to rhyming dictionaries for help. All writers, not just songwriters, go through periods where their ideas seize up solid, the problem has to be worked through. One only has to look through songwriter's lists to see the few that maintained any longevity with quality. I mentioned earlier how many singer songwriters came up with three great albums and then struggled, Bob was already a long way from that category, he was now in the realms of writing genius.

I make no apologies for making the 'genius' statement, it is confirmed by so many. Bob added quantity to his quality, Leonard Cohen's out-put is slight in comparison, though equally strong. Bob Dylan was joining The Gershwins, The Beatles, Cole Porter, Irving Berlin, Lamont Dozier (with Brian and Edward Holland), Jerome Kern, Johnny Mercer, Duke Ellington, Gerry Goffin, Carole King, Oscar Hammerstein, Richard Rodgers, Jule Styne, Lorenz Hart, Sammy Cahn and James Van Heusen, Harry Warren, Harold Arlen, Burt Bacharach, Hal David and Hank Williams just a few composers with large portfolios of songs which are nearly all excellent. If we take composers that worked alone then the above list can be halved, but Bob eventually would be writing songs with a co-composer.

It was to be just one album away from Columbia as a new deal was agreed and Bob was back and presumably in charge of all his old remaindered recordings. In his opinion he didn't need another album of sub-standard material on the racks. Although in an interview in Montreal in 1974 Bob said of the 'Dylan' album " I didn't think it was that bad really".

The 'Planet Waves' tour with Bob and The Band had become the highest $ grossing tour in the history of rock and folk music. Forty shows in three weeks with almost $110 million in takings. The many millions that never managed to see the shows were partially rewarded with a live double album when **'BEFORE THE FLOOD'** was released in June 1974. The tour was produced by Phil Ramone and the album went to No 3 in the USA and No 8 in the UK; the UK issue was on the Asylum Label. As the re-release CDs were back on CBS perhaps the agreement was not finalised until after the album was released. The premise that the album title was based on Arthur Rimbaud's 'Apres le Deluge' is odd as that translates to 'After the Flood'.

The album was a mixture of the old and new with the predominant complaint that most of it seemed to be at the same tempo. There were a few acoustic songs but most was with The Band in which Garth Hudson created their recognisable sound. It was also a surprise the hear Bob sing 'All Along the Watchtower' in the style of Jimi Hendrix, an acknowledgement to the definitive version. The Beatles were gone, the Rolling Stones, Frank Sinatra and Elvis Presley were in decline, although not for live appearances, leaving Bob Dylan as the World's major attraction live and on record. The cover depicts the finale of most shows with the boxes of matches on fire and the gas and zippo lighters waving from side to side, nostalgic isn't it.

The live version of 'Knockin' On Heaven's Door' is filled with artificial emotion, far too melodramatic. 'It Ain't Me Babe' was played as a country march and 'Rolling Stone' played as a two-step. The acoustic songs were good, though 'It's Alright Ma' was played as though Bob might miss his train home. The Band versions were fussy with 'Endless Highway' a great bonus track.

A single was released to promote the live album 'Mostly You Go Your Way' which sounds in a word 'awkward', it reached No 66 in the USA. Bob was aware that he had to create a good album. Although his recent albums were continuing to sell well, they were just a shadow of his earlier material. He was still convinced that the accident had something to do with his inability to create lyrics as easily as before. He hadn't realised that his new found affluence and a new lifestyle might had influenced his ability to write. His contented family life was gradually entering a stage of turmoil, not good for Bob but good for his writing ability. Contentment seems to breed blandness in the work of all kinds of aesthetes. The problems of a now ten year old marriage and the response Bob had seen for himself from his audiences seemed to instill the importance of creating good work. He had a new set of songs and went into the studio with Eric Weissberg's band Deliverance. It included Weissberg on guitar, Tony Brown (bass), Richard Crooks (drums), Barry Kornfield (guitar), Tom McFaul (keyboards) and Charles Brown on guitar. They recorded 30 takes and had 12 completed songs by the end of the first day, after four more sessions including overdubbing the album was complete, the promotional copies were sent out. It was at this time that Bob decided that he would like to re-record five of the tracks. The musicians for this new session were Greg Inhofer (keyboards), Bill Berg (drums), Bill Peterson (bass) and Chris Weber (guitar). The final session added Peter Ostroushko (keyboards) and Kevin Odegard on guitar. The album had originally been completed by early October was now ready on the last day of December. There has been confusion who played on the album, there were few credits given, Buddy Cage (steel guitar), Paul Griffin (organ) and Tony Brown (bass) were also thought to be on some tracks. The confusion was compounded when the Telegraph Fanzine printed the musicians sheets in their issue 55. It became apparent that Tony Brown added bass to 35 takes, Paul Griffin organ to 'Idiot Wind', Buddy Cage over-dubbed steel guitar to 'Buckets of Rain', 'Meet Me in the Morning' and 'You're A Big Girl Now', the last two not detailed on the recording sheet.

The **'BLOOD ON THE TRACKS'** album was officially, released by Columbia in February 1975. It reached No 1 in the USA and No 4 in the UK. The single 'Tangled Up in Blue' only reached No 31 in the USA. Bob has said that when he writes songs they are not autobiographical, he actually wrote that in '11 Epitaphs' some years earlier. He had kept quiet for some time allowing reviewers critics and fans to make up their own minds on the subject matter of the songs. For 'Blood on the Tracks' Bob said that he was fighting sentimentality all down the line on this album. He tried to make the album like a painting, he succeeded because the tracks were more cinematic than most of his previous work. He then said later in New York in 1985 "A lot of people thought that the album pertained to me". That is alright as a statement but why didn't Bob add 'But it didn't'. He had to write the songs, in his word, 'consciously', where previously it had been 'unconsciously', he had to work at it. He decided that to write 'consciously' was a trick, a method of focusing one's mind to a specific point, like the sun through a magnifying glass. He also told us that he had to learn the technique from a teacher. One thing that Bob said that was extremely pertinent was "The album has no sense of time, there is no respect for it, you have yesterday today and tomorrow all in the same room, and there is very little you can't imagine not happening", a perfect description of an album which contains so much torment.

The teacher mentioned was Norman Raeben, Bob attended his classes in New York. Raeben's father was Sholem Aleichem who was characterised as Tvye and whose life was the essence of the plot of the show 'Fiddler on the Roof'. Raeben offered denigration and recovery courses, but of course Bob must have been a rarity as a singer that thought he had lost his muse. It must have taken extreme courage for Bob to enter psycho-analysis, it would be as difficult as an alcoholic admitting his problem. The remarks that Bob made concerning the 'time in the same room' must be attributed to Raeben, he would have taught realism and the art of painting pictures with words, painting Bob's 'masterpiece'. Raeben tried to teach Bob to paint, Bob attended the classes with rich old women, five days each week for two months. One can imagine Bob attending the classes and being informed that he was an artistic ignoramus and then asked to accept that fact before they could continue. Bob agrees that Norman Raeben changed Bob's personality, he was a changed man, this of course would have contributed to the gradual breakdown in the relationship with Sara, the album would depict that pain.

Bob had been friends with Ellen Bernstein for some time, she worked at Columbia Records and she has been credited with the healing of some of the scars inflicted on Bob by CBS. The 'Blood on the Tracks' cover used a Paul Till photograph modified to provide a dotted pseudo-pointillistic image. Paul Till also provided a similarly modified picture for the cover of Cherry Lane's publication of 'The Songs of Bob Dylan from 1966-through-1975' in 1976. The cover in dried blood colour included its own review on the rear surrounding a David Oppenheim painting; it was replaced with an alternative Oppenheim painting on later issues deleting the credits.

The lyrics on the lyric sheet were different to the lyrics in the songs because of the re-recording of the five tracks and the cover remaining the same as for the originals. The sleeve notes were written by Peter Hammill the husband of Shirley Maclaine. These notes won the Grammy Award for Best Album Notes at the ceremony in 1975. Other beaten nominees were Ralph J.Gleason, Benny Green and Tom T.Hall. Ralph J.Gleason conducted one of the most inane interviews with Bob ever, it is embarrassing to read. Bob found Gleason's questions so tiresome and weird that his exasperation is evident.

Bob answered some questions with "What do you want me to say?". It reads like an interview with someone being purposely derisory with the questions, Bob does his best before giving up. As it appears so poor on paper one wonders how the tape recording sounds. It was my contention at the time that Gleason just gave the typist the tape and then un-edited it appeared in print, surely he would have censored it if he had read it earlier. I would think that Bob gained some considerable satisfaction when Gleason's sleeve notes were beaten by the notes on his 'Blood on the Tracks' album. Bob continued to maintain that the songs for the new album were totally abstract, he had been taught to write differently. This added fuel to the fire and only made the critics and fans more determined to investigate every word for hidden truths.

'Tangled Up In Blue' looks back at Greenwich Village and the past, Bob never worked as a lumberjack or on a fishing boat. The tune is similar to that of 'Lay Lady Lay'. Bob altered the tenses between the first recording with Deliverance, what was originally 'he' and 'they', became 'I' and 'we', it seems that the songs might have been re-recorded only to make them more biographical. The Deliverance versions are as good (if not better) as the released recordings. If Eric Weissberg thought that because Bob wouldn't explain his open guitar tunings his band sounded out of tune then he was mistaken, they sound excellent. The tapping jacket sleeve buttons can be heard again on this track. I have always doubted the writer that considered this song autobiographical, it reads more like Bob's version of 'On the Road'. It is a life in a song but not Bob's. A woman whose flame has burned within him since his first meeting, when she was going through her divorce. They constantly meet and separate, the narrator reminisces, his friends are all settled but he is still a wanderer. Sir Thomas Wyatt (1503-1542) wrote 'Farewell love and thy laws forever, their baited hooks shall tangle me no more'.

'Simple Twist of Fate' is similar to 'Visions of Johanna'. The narrator sits reflecting on his life and fate. This is a song for the desire for a younger woman, he was born too late, he is in competition for her personal time with sailors. Similar in construction to the work of Jacques Brel and Kurt Weill. Joan Baez version on her 'Diamonds and Rust' album comes complete with her quite excellent Bob Dylan impersonation. A simple infectious and effective song. Bob uses his title as destiny and fate just like Henry Miller when he wrote 'Destiny is what you are supposed to do in life, fate is what kicks you in the ass to make you do it'. 'You're A Big Girl Now': She has grown up and thrown him out. He is full of self pity. He will try to change his ways but she will not even consider him any more. Time is used in this song as the enemy of love. This is just a song, there is nothing personal that I can understand. Bob became very angry that a lyric interpreter said that this concerned Sara, she was already a big girl when Bob met her. A lethargic slow song, Chris Weber's acoustic guitar and Greg Inhofer's piano is perfect, as is Bill Petersons bass and Bill Berg's under-stated drumming. A second version was released on Biograph, on this version verse 3 and 4 are reversed in sequence. The Biograph version includes an over-dubbed electric organ and steel guitar, the track builds as it progresses. Both versions are exquisite.

'**Idiot Wind**' blowing from the mouths of Capital Hill politicians, journalists and a lover. Christ the soldier on the cross, Roger McGuinn' and Jacques Levy's 'Chestnut Mare', blood on the saddle, 'Woody Guthrie and 'The Grand Coulee Dam', the disgraced President and Vice President. All these personalities are relevant. 'Yiddiot Wind' are the words Bob sings, however on the outtake with just Tony Brown on bass he sings 'idiot' precisely, it may be a yiddish play on words. This is clever because some of the lyric takes the female stance; as the song fades suddenly at the end we are left musing that there may have been some more verses. Bob actually sings 'We're idiots baby' and thus he shares the blame. The released version is packed with pain and sorrow, she is an idiot every time she speaks. The pain is truly felt because the solo version, probably recorded to register the song, has a verse which mentions imitators stealing his act and his money, and also very pertinently, others that have robbed him blind, his estranged wife will want some too. The album release of the de-personalised lyrics would be upstaged when the original was included on 'The Bootleg Series'. This track proved that Norman Raeben's critical analysis had worked and worked well. John Bauldie mentioned Shakespeare as one influence on this song, despair and sorrow are represented by Macbeth during his meditation where he states "A tale told by an idiot, full of sound and fury, signifying nothing". When Bob said to Mary Travers of Peter Paul and Mary, "A lot of people tell me they enjoyed the album-it is hard for me to relate to that-I mean people enjoying all that pain". I would add another piece from Macbeth 'Foul whisperings are abroad- unnatural deeds do breed unnatural troubles-infected minds to their deaf pillows will discharge their secrets'. Of course after a murder Macbeth adds 'Who would have thought the old man to have so much blood in him?' Bob's life was really becoming the living hell that he presents within this lyric. Sadly his answer was not blowing in the 'idiot' wind, he convinces himself that he is finally 'Free!'. Absolutely sublime Bob Dylan, a breathtaking song from the heart mind and guts of the man.

'**You're Gonna Make Me Lonesome When You Go**': The title could be a Hank Williams song, it would make a good hoe-down. The title says it all. This is the only time that Rimbaud was mentioned in a Dylan song when the narrator considers that all his relationships have been bad, just like that of Verlaine and Rimbaud. That relationship was bad for Verlaine because he was so much in love and so possessive. It became worse for Rimbaud when he was shot in the hand by Verlaine. The enforced separation of Verlaine's imprisonment coupled with Rimbaud's itinerancy meant that absence made the heart grow fonder. Of course Verlaine thought that Rimbaud was dead when he published Rimbaud's poems. Rimbaud described his relationship with Verlaine as a foolish bridegroom and a hellish bridesmaid, it can be found in 'Seasons of Hell'. Bob mentions shooting in the dark, a metaphor for taking a chance, not connected to Verlaine shooting Rimbaud. I love the lines where Bob explains that love has always hit him from below, and flowers are 'blooming crazy'. This infectious song is reminiscent of 'I Don't Care if the Sun Don't Shine', a hit for Patti Page and Elvis Presley. **'Meet Me in the Morning'** was considered a filler track by some lauded by others. Self pity, with a beautiful arrangement, Deliverance improve this track considerably with their musicianship. The song is of an eloping, they are up early in the morning and they are meeting at the station. Bob adds a line concerning the narrator out-running the dogs, what we never learn is if she actually arrived to go with him or did she leave him in his darkness of loss? Bob uses darkness in both the literal and metaphorical sense for loss of love. A blues with many different scenes passing across his mind. They have to escape through barbed wire and the listener has to delve through a series of metaphors but there is not enough information to solve the puzzle.

'Lily, Rosemary and the Jack of Hearts' is packed full of wild west cliches. Based on John Ford's 'Stagecoach' movie which was one of the most ridiculous tales of the wild west. The whole film is based on a stagecoach and its long trip across America chased by Red Indians. It presented Red Indians as brainless and inhuman but kind to animals. All the Red Indians had to do was shoot one of the stagecoach horses and the film and the lives of the travellers would be over. The Indians even jumped onto the horses, the travellers shot their guns at the Indians and the horses, Indians died, horses never acquired a scratch. The plot used for the film was Maupassant's 'Boule de Suif'. The gambler, the prostitute with the heart of gold, the outlaw, the corrupt business man, all seemingly intelligent, none realising that a dead horse would mean certain death to them all. The John Ford 1939 film with John Wayne was re-made in 1966 by Gordon Douglas with Ann Margret and Alex Cord, but it was a pale imitation of the original. The fast country style arrangement on this song should have been perfect for Bob's epic lyric. If the blues arrangement on the previous track was exemplary then this is the opposite, are the musicians (except for the drummer, Bill Berg) really as bored as they sound? It was recorded in one take and it is considered to have included some over-dubbing. Big Jim and the drunken Judge return. As I am a long time Robert W. Service reader, I have often wondered if Bob may have read 'The Shooting of Dan McGrew', there is an underlying sympathy in the two tales. Country Joe MacDonald made a complete album where he put his own music to Robert Service's verse, it was titled 'War War War, but Bob may have heard Lord Buckley recite his version of the Robert Service classic.

The gunfighter, Jack, arrives at the saloon bar swing doors, the bar goes quiet. He walks in and the babble of noise re-commences. Jack the stranger is waiting for the girlie show to start. Jim the diamond mine owner arrives with his bodyguards. Rosemary arrives apologises to Jim for being late and then sees Jack. Jim and Rosemary can't remember from where they know Jack. Lily and the dancing girls start their show and the Judge arrives at the bar. Lily and Jim were lovers. Jack and Lily are in the room together when Rosemary and Jim burst in. Jim intends to shoot Jack but Rosemary stabs Jim in the back with a penknife. Throughout the lyric there is a sub-plot of a wall being drilled. In verse 14 they finally get into the safe. Of course we then learn ....! An epic poem although Robert Service would call it verse, an ideal song for a video.

'If You See Her, Say Hello' is full of vulnerability, the usual situation where one lover has gone. The song may have been influenced by Gordon Lightfoot's song 'Sundown', it is mentioned in the lyric. Bob's song has a similar tune to 'Simple Twist of Fate'. The feelings are of hopelessness and rejection. It has again been depersonalised on the album issue from the original; 'kiss her for the kids' instead of 'kiss her once for me'. He is the hurt person, she is still in his heart. This is an imploring song, a realisation that he was wrong. One wonders what Sara felt when she heard songs like this. The situation must have been really bad for some time, very few men could be so desperate in public. The Deliverance original is again an improvement. It was inevitable 'in the cards', he can't stop thinking about her, although he says 'that he has learned to turn it off'. Elvis sang 'Just Tell Her, Jim Said Hello' a different song of course (written by Lieber and Stoller) but it must have influenced Bob's title. 'Shelter From the Storm' includes doom, toothless men, a crown of thorns, riding a mount, flower ladies, a one eyed undertaker, a hill top village. A scenario similar to 'Raider Stole a Morgen Mare' the traditional song of Black Jack. A woman is offering shelter, a self denigrating soul scourging song. There is a powerful dichotomy between on the one hand a protecting woman and on the other a religious fear of death or persecution. Bob has always presented to his public that he has a reasonably thick skin when under written attack, it has been an armour that was a necessity, a characteristic that many creative aesthetes lacked. Bob offered his innocence and got repaid with scorn, well that may be in love matters, not in lyric analysis. The problem has always been that he has attempted to achieve the impossible, the aspirations that others hoped he would continually create, in fact the impracticable. If ever a man needed shelter from the storm then it would be Bob Dylan, an armour plated mackintosh and umbrella perhaps. The line 'nothing really matters much, it's doom alone that counts' should be read in reverse 'everything matters' or there is no reason to bargain for one's salvation. One of Bob's best ever lyrics, the best 'since the accident' if I may use that phrase. It is a lyric that one can never tire of hearing or reading. Isaac Watts wrote using Psalm 90, as inspiration, 'Our God, our help in ages past, our hope for years to come, our shelter from the stormy blast, and our eternal home'. Isaiah, one of Bob's favourite Bible prophets wrote in Chapter 28 of the flash flood that would wash away Ephraim's drunkards. It also mentions Jehovah's 'crown of decoration', although Bob reverts to 'thorns' in his lyric.

'Buckets of Rain' is possibly a minor song pretending to be something bigger. The 'In the Summertime' tune from Mungo Jerry, a song where sun was more important than the rain. Both songs owe a more than a little to Mississippi John Hurt and James Wayne and their 'Travellin' Mood', which was also recorded by The Nitty Gritty Dirt Band. We have more self pity, an 'I am available whenever you need me' song. Like The Big Bopper the narrator 'knows what he likes'. During the album we had the wind followed by the warning to shelter from the storm, and then the rain arrives by the bucketful. Some composers use 'rain' as tears, a purgative that washes away problems, Bob uses is most often as an euphemism for 'memory'.

'Call Letter Blues' was remaindered and released on The Bootleg Series. When it was stated that it was withdrawn from the album because lyrics were personal Bob became incensed, one wonders why if it was untrue. No one would really expect Bob to be telling his children that their mother took a trip, with drug connotations. Also did he think we thought he was now making liaisons with call girls. This is just a blues no more no less. I mentioned earlier Bob's ability to ignore criticism but that does not apply to situations where his family is threatened by the remarks. 'Up to Me' has the same tune as 'Tangled Up in Blue'. The lyric presents the situation where the one that loves least has the upper hand and the other appeases every wish of their loved-one, every step in the relationship is 'up to him'. Twelve verses many that seem unconnected. He was working as a postal clerk, she disappeared into the officers club. Crystal, Dupree and Estelle make an entrance then leave the stage. It is the last verse that betrays any personalisation. This song was later released on 'Biograph'. It was also recorded by Roger McGuinn and included on his 'Cardiff Rose' album. The lyrics of the long gone lone guitarist playing for free reminds me of the song 'Superstar' which was so beautifully sung by the late Karen Carpenter.

John Landau thought that the album would be good for a while, he went on to state that Bob's work was impermanent, surely he never really thought that. He compared Bob with Charlie Chaplin and Elvis Presley. The album is an immense achievement, Landau was never more wrong. In his review Jonathan Cott compared Bob with Arthur Rimbaud and King Lear. Bob has regularly transcended his limitations, his albums become indispensable. He has always wanted to be perceived by his public as an 'outlaw' rather than a loving family man. In this respect his image has always been close to that of

Harry Dean Stanton, Marlon Brando, James Dean, Lenny Bruce and in the pop world Tom Waits. In July 1975, the 'Basement Tapes' which were recorded earlier (and detailed earlier) were finally approved for release by Bob, he was aware that the bootlegs were already available so there seemed little point in delaying the release any longer. Bob was also preparing 'The Rolling Thunder Revue' the name for his next tour. In late October they played an early morning set at Greenwich City's 'Folk City', it was a surprise performance to celebrate the birthday of the club's owner Mike Porco. The surprise was made even better by the arrival of Joan Baez, Phil Ochs, Allen Ginsberg, Ronee Blakely, Ramblin Jack Elliott, Mick Ronson and Bob's side-kick Bob Neuwirth. The 'Rolling Thunder Revue' played their first low-key date on 30th October, in Plymouth M.A. As the tour continued Roger McGuinn, Joni Mitchell, Patti Smith, T-Bone Burnett, came and went, violinist Scarlet Rivera came and stayed. On December 8th the tour finished with the 'Night of the Hurricane' at Madison Square Garden. Roberta Flack was added to the bill, and Muhammad Ali acted as master of ceremonies. This show was a benefit show for the appeal against sentence of Rubin 'Hurricane' Carter a boxer that had been convicted of murder. David Blue's album 'Coming Back For More' was released on Asylum Records and Bob added harmonica on the track 'Who Love'.

DESIRE AND COLLABORATION

The man's desire is for the woman;
but the woman's desire is rarely
other than for the desire of the man.
Samuel Taylor Coleridge (1772-1834)

The Rolling Thunder Revue was rolling to a standstill, Bob had been singing duet vocals with Emmylou Harris with Scarlet Rivera's violin supplying the new sound. Seven of the nine tracks on the new album would be collaborations with Jacques Levy, who had written songs with Roger McGuinn. 'I'm So Restless' had been recorded by Bob and Roger earlier for Roger's album. Roger and Jacques had been working on their version of 'Peer Gynt' (Gene Tryp) and Roger had a hit with their 'Chestnut Mare' with The Byrds. Jacques Levy had achieved a considerable amount of notoriety when his explicitly sexual show 'Oh Calcutta' opened in London; Jacques Levy was also a practising psychologist.

The **'DESIRE'** album (subtitled 'Songs of Redemption') had an excellent cover picture of Bob in cowboy hat and scarf and a coat with a fur collar, Jacques Levy is the bearded man leaning over Bob in one the pictures on the back of the sleeve. The sleeve is very similar to ex-Mama and Papa, John Phillips' 'Wolfking of L.A.' cover. Bob wrote notes for the 'Desire' album which commenced **'Where do I begin,** on the heels of Rimbaud moving like a dancing bullet'. Tracks on the album are welded together to form the notes which if it is to be believed were written in a bathtub in Maine under ideal conditions. Rimbaud's 'Deluge' is mentioned as is the old remark that Tolstoy was right. The album has more word pictures, a Tarot card mystery and more.

The sleeve notes of the previous album had won an award, for this album Allen Ginsberg would write his own review with Bob's blessing under the title **Songs of Redemption.** He writes that W.C.Williams said that Hurricane Carter could have been champion of the World, well there are plenty of 'could be champion boxers' in the World. Ginsberg was at a stage in his career when he decided that it was little point using one word when he could use five. Describing David Mansfield as 'Botticelli faced Little David Mansfield' must have worried Mansfield a little. Just before he died Ginsberg appeared on BBC-2 programme Face-to-Face and offered his body to anyone interested in using it. Needlessly to say this remark was deleted from the re-run; one wonders if it was because the BBC is not allowed to advertise! Ginsberg does write an excellent phrase when he writes 'To live outside the law you must be honest'. The way that Ginsberg wrote this article is as near as anyone has ever got to a Lord Buckley script with hints of Dylan Thomas, especially in his review of the track 'Isis'. Ginsberg signed off his sleeve notes as the 'Co-Director of The Jack Kerouac School of Disembodied Poetics, Naropa Institute, York Harbour, Maine. The collage of photographs and images on the cover rear included a portrait of Joseph Conrad, Bob had read his novel 'Victory' and based one of the tracks on it. The Empress Tarot card is prominent. The card for Le Bateleur in my pack resembles a young Bob Dylan, Le Bateleur is called the magician or minstrel but the correct translation is 'street performer' at least it is in my dictionary.

Since Bob had rejoined Columbia he was now recording only the necessary number of tracks. This may have been a decision made in management, if Bob moved to another label then there would be less songs available to cause distress and embarrassment. There is some controversy over the musicians detailed on the album cover with Eric Clapton's session believed to be the take used for the 'Durango' track. The first three sessions were packed with musicians and only the 'Durango' track was used. Present were, Dave Mason, Vincent Bell, Gerald Johnson, Eric Clapton, James Whiting, Mark Jordan, Scarlet Rivera, Emmylou Harris, Erik Frandsen, and members of the group Kokomo in Mel Collins, Paddy McHugh, Dyan Birch, Francis Collins and Alan Spenner. The actual musicians details omitted Rob Rothstein on bass (unless he used the name 'Rob Stoner') and Sheena Seidenberg on tambourine and congas; congas and bells by Sheena are mentioned.

'Hurricane' (BD/JL) : Is Bob taking up a cause, he had appeared with Phil Ochs on behalf of Chile, sung of Donald White, Medgar Evers, George Jackson and Hattie Carroll now it was Rubin Hurricane Carter's turn. Bob had read Carter's book 'The Sixteenth Round'. The track was re-recorded in late October 1975, three months after the first recording. The first version was wiped off the tape due to some factual errors in the text which the Columbia litigation team thought may be actionable. The indication that two of the persons involved in the case 'robbed money from dead bodies' was expunged. The original lyric also placed Alfred Bradley in the bar when it should have been Albert Bello. Carter had written his own story whilst incarcerated. In it he stated that he had been harassed by the police and ultimately framed for a murder he didn't commit. The Columbia litigation team missed the mention of Patty Valentine and were sued; Columbia won the case. At the next parole meeting Carter was released. Carter was not free for very long he committed another offence and was sent back to jail, not the best way to thank Bob for all the efforts on his behalf. The musicians for the re-recordings were the same team although the congas were played by Leon Luther, and the accompanying vocal was by Ronee Blakley and not Emmylou Harris. Steve Soles mentioned on the album sleeve as a backing vocalist was omitted from the recording details, he played guitar. So that the song could get radio-play a single was manufactured with the word 'shit' bleeped-out this has become very collectable over the years. What was immediately noticeable was the force of Bob's vocal, a power that had been missing for a few albums. Scarlet Rivera's brilliant violin accompaniment on this track has always reminded me of David LaFlamme's style especially his playing on the first eponymously titled 'It's A Beautiful Day' album and the follow-up album 'Marrying Maiden'.

'Isis' (BD/JL) : This includes Bob playing piano, it starts like 'Winterlude', is this lyric cut-up, is this just obfuscation, if there is a mystery can we solve it? This was the first song from the Dylan/Levy collaboration. The message is that relationships mend and break, it is the making up that is supposed to be such fun. The Goddess Isis will send you mad, she resurrected Osiris from the dead after her tears had created the river Nile. Robert Graves wrote his 'White Goddess' with Isis in his mind. Graves advocated the fact that every poet should die for his Goddess, one wonders why he never bothered to do it. With Bob mentioning Gold, a pony and riding, it brings to mind 'The Golden Ass' written by Apuleius before the year 124. Lucius is a curious young man. He asks a maid to steal a magic salve that would allow his to change into an owl and observe the World. She steals the wrong salve and he changes into an ass. He wanders through many adventures before the Goddess Isis changes him back into a man. The Empress is a symbol of action, Bob's tarot card on the cover has the modern circle and cross signifying woman, the card would usually have an eagle emblazoned on it. Isis is the universal mother Goddess and is depicted with a child in her arms, so Bob is referring to a mother, which is Sara yet again, but the wedding date in the song is May? The narrator can remember all the best things concerning their relationship, this so often happens as the brain dispenses with the adverse incidents. The two travellers go north, one offers his comfort the other his word, words? Jacques Levy was offering his word. The wordsmith dies he is entombed and our narrator continues alone. When he finally returns after his quest he is met by his Isis who welcomes him back. A nice story, a change is as good as a rest, variety is the spice of life, but will it last? Jacques said in an interview that the song had nothing whatsoever to do with the Egyptian Goddess, they just substituted The Pyramids for The Grand Teton Mountains. Bob would later sing of The Pyramids on a film soundtrack. The music is a strut-cum-waltz held together by Howie Wyeth's superb drumming, the violin becomes an intrusion as it never pauses during the song, Bob blows some intense mouth harp. Bob uses the same riff throughout, in all his career his songs have for the most part repeated riffs rather than built up to a climax.

'Mozambique'(BD/JL): A lyric for a man and a woman in seclusion away from others. Emmylou Harris sounds as though she is a little under rehearsed, which ultimately proved to be a correct assumption. She had the written lyrics and then followed Bob hoping for a nod and a wink as a cue, a 'billy' as it is called in the trade. Van Morrison had not heard the term and when Paddy Maloney of The Chieftains asked Van for a 'billy' as a cue, Van shouted out "Billy, billy!" and the band collapsed in helpless laughter, except for Van who stood perplexed at the microphone wondering what he had done. Mozambique sounds an idyllic place, I was there in 1977 take it from me it wasn't at that time. One wonders if Bob had ever been there or was imagining it as a paradise. Living on the beach in Mozambique in 1975 would not have been as wonderful as Bob makes out, I wonder if any one went there after Bob's advertisement in song to find out for themselves?

'**One More Cup of Coffee**'(Valley Below): This has a gypsy mood, coupled with the menace of a trip to 'the valley below'. A song of Platonic love, or should that be sex without love; apparently the opposite of Platonic is physical. She is illiterate, her father an outlaw landowner who teaches knife throwing, she and her sister and mother can see the future. But who is the narrator? It was reported later that Bob created this song from a story that Ramblin' Jack Elliott often told. As the father does allow for any strangers to intrude he must be a close friend, confused, good, have one more cup of coffee! '**Oh Sister**'(BD/JL): It could be for an imaginary 'big caring sister'. Joan Baez' wrote 'Oh Brother' in response to this song. She powerfully asks "How in the name of the Father did I become your sister!" Joan once on her soap-box really goes for Bob. She accuses him of disloyalty to his lifelong friends, she says that he is surrounded by sycophants and parasites, it makes her blood clot, although 'boil' is the more usual expression. She also informs her 'brother' that her love continues and makes him an offer. Bob's song uses Father in the Godly sense otherwise the song would become incestuous, Bob is also making an offer. The mournful violin is excellent when accompanied by Bob's harmonica.

'**Joey**' (BD/JL): A song for Joey Gallo a New York City mobster who was shot down in Little Italy. The lyric is questioning the reason for his death. A modern day John Wesley Hardin or Jesse James, criminals whose Robin Hood characteristics seem more important to Bob than their vicious murdering ways. They had a gunfight took five hostages and considered blowing them up, but gentle Joey said no. When he was finally convicted of conspiracy, one assumes to pervert the course of Justice, he was sentenced to ten years in Attica State Prison. When he was released he had read philosophy but wanted to return to the life as a mobster. It was a mistake to rob the club of another leading mobster, no wonder Joey was murdered, although the song asks the question at the end of every verse. The story was related to Bob and Jacques by Marty Orbach, perhaps she thought that Joey was a sympathetic villain. Allen Ginsberg thought that Joey was Villonesque and sympathetic, the concept of a romantic or a dreamer. At the later verses there is extra emotion in Emmylou's voice, but is she laughing? One would suspect that this song was more Levy than Dylan. The accordion creating the ambience of Little

153

Italy is by Dom Cortese but is this tune again not dissimilar to 'Shelter From the Storm'. The song was criticised for its content due to the success of the film The Godfather which proved that mobsters were wicked not just misunderstood. **'Romance in Durango'** (BD/JL): Written whilst in Mexico filming Pat Garrett. An escapist song, probably written because Sara was so bored down in Mexico. Magdalena and her lover on the run, it is only when they get to Durango that the romance and dancing can begin. This is another song ideal for a video, voicing descriptive pictures of the desert. Why would anyone want to eat hot chilli peppers in the heat of the Mexican day? The answer was that the whole song was based on a postcard that Jacques Levy had received from a friend. The picture on it was of a Mexican shack with chilli peppers on the roof, hence the first line of the song. Don DeVito the engineer for reasons of his own has moved the instruments around during the mixing, perhaps he wanted to create the situations where they are all moving about in a cantina band. We also have a version of the tijuana brass incorporating the accordion and harmonica.

　　'Black Diamond Bay' (BD/JL): Based on Joseph Conrad's novel 'Victory'. Lurking under the volcano which erupts in the song but not in the book where it threatens to erupt incessantly. The bay mentioned is the site of the bungalow on the island overlooking the bay. When I first read the book many years ago I was astonished that Joseph Conrad would use homosexuality so blatantly. Ricardo (described as short) and gambler-cum-mercenary Mr Jones are attracted to each other from their first meetings. Bob was known to dislike homosexuality. The eternal triangle of the book is clever because Conrad introduces a woman, Lena, who entices (if that it the correct word) Ricardo into heterosexuality until Mr Jones kills him in an act of selfish passion. Axel Heyst is a fourth (but leading) character in the book, he is also in love with Lena who he had once saved from the drowning; he eventually takes his own life. In the song The Greek commits suicide by hanging. Bob mentions that forbidden love was being contemplated in the song, this of course could be adultery rather than homosexuality. Bob does describe one of the protagonists as a 'tiny man', and when the volcano erupts he bites a soldiers ear, we are not told the reason for the bite. After plenty of descriptive action it is revealed that it was all on Television with Walter Cronkite. Very clever lyric formation, an outlaw on the run but still in love. Bob read the book and was inspired to a write the song, the variations make both book and song ideal companions for a night when one is home alone. This is an up-tempo song with Howie Wyeth's drumming again catching the ear. Bob uses a rat-a-tat-tat line in each verse which Wyeth apes on drums. I must admit to loving this track, Bob's enjoyment can be heard, it might have been improved without Scarlet's violin, but that would just leave Bob's rhythm guitar and Robert Stoner's bass. Bob sings this with his old attack, never letting up from start to finish. As I have said earlier Bob doesn't build songs to a climax he maintains the power of the riff. If there is a slight problem it is that the are playing faster at the end than at the beginning, but of course that may have been intentional.

'Sara': On this song Bob confirms that 'The Sad Eyed Lady' was indeed Sara. The chorus is one of the most easy to remember in the Bob Dylan canon. The song is packed full of questions awaiting an answer. Bob uses a scene on a beach where the children are playing happily as his fondest memory. This was the time when everything was perfect, two parents in love. Bob mentions that he had 'taken the cure', only just in time. Bob uses a sublime line to describe Sara as a 'Scorpio Sphinx in a calico dress'. At the end the beach is deserted only the flotsam and jetsam of their love remains, but not quite. The ending has Bob needing her help and asking for the key of the door so that he can return to his glamorous nymph with her arrow and bow. Sung happily this is as sad as it gets, and ingeniously the lyric does not blame either party. Bob singing a song so personal and so full of pain one wonders if we should be listening. There is no doubt in my mind that this is a beautiful song with no ambivalences for us to explore. As Ginsberg so rightly said "There is enough person revealed in this song to make Walt Whitman's whole nation weep".

'Golden Loom': This song of Islamic magic was remaindered. The washing of feet, the lifting of veils. The golden loom may just be an euphemism for the female delta. Medusa the Gorgon turned men to stone. Red haired women do not have red public hair it is blonde, golden, it is all there in the lyric. John Bauldie thought that this was alchemical symbolism and Jungian archetypes, although he did qualify his remark by adding obscure allusions to both. Bob could be playing tricks with us again, there is a weaving apparatus loom and there is also 'rising appearance as something far away', to loom up out of the darkness. A golden loom a golden apparition, it is all fantasy. 'Abandoned Love' was released on 'Biograph'. The narrator is tied by his love and devotion. The door key that was wanted at the end of 'Sara' is now turning, he is locked out of the bedroom. He will follow his children wherever they go. This is so sad, he is not free until his love subsides and is pleading for another chance. What we don't know was how many chances had gone begging previously. The song progresses as if it is therapy, the undying love in the early verses gradually changes verse by verse. By the last two verses he has decided that she is strange and that he will abandon love. He still hasn't quite convinced himself as he asks for just one more try at love before he goes. Howie Wyeth leads the track on drums, Scarlet Rivera saws away and adds little, Rob Rothstein plays bass. A great bouncy beat and Bob sings out at full volume. He loves her but she's strange, cross him off her list.

155

'Money Blues'(BD/JL): Is really the opposite, a blues for having no money. The divorce settlement couldn't be that bad. Anticipation of being left with no money at all. In fact it can happen especially if the bank account is frozen during settlement discussions. The woman can make life simple or difficult for the man in a divorce, hell hath no fury like a woman deciding how much she wants. **'Catfish'**(BD/JL): A song for Catfish Hunter a baseball pitcher worth $millions. Reggie Jackson and Billy Martin are name-checked. Hunter started life on a farm, played for The Yankees and helped them win 20 games each season. The harmonica is played by James Sugarblue Whiting, and the slide guitar is by Erik Frandsen. Eric Clapton was on this recording session and said that it was all totally disorganized madness. A version of the song was included on Kinky Friedman's 'Lasso From El Paso' album, detailed elsewhere. **'Rita May'** (BD/JL): This may be based on 'Maggie May', which originally meant 'Maggie will'. Is this the love for an intelligent or loose woman, or both. It was alleged to be for Rita Brown a lesbian writer. If he hangs around her he will go blind. If she is a lesbian then we know what it is that makes a young frustrated man go blind. The 'Desire' album was a revelation for the violin of Scarlet Rivera, apparently Bob wanted to record some harmonica and violin duets but they ran out of time.

Bob and Sara were already on their Minnesota farm when the album was released. It Made No 1 in the USA and No 3 in the UK, Bob's first platinum record. 'Hurricane' the single reached No 33 in the USA and No 43 in the UK. The follow-up single was 'Mozambique' it reached No 54 in the USA in April 1976. Sadly Bob's friend and mentor John Hammond died and Bob appeared at his tribute show where he used the Jacques Levy modified lyrics to 'Simple Twist of Fate'. Bob also assisted on one track of Leonard Cohen's latest album 'Death of a Ladies Man' which was produced by Phil Spector. The album was excellent and different but Leonard Cohen did not like the Spector frills that were added subsequently. Phil Spector expressed an interest in producing an album for Bob which was not carried through. The Leonard Cohen track incorporating Bob was the risque titled 'Don't Go Home with Your Hard On' with Bob and Allen Ginsberg on backing vocals.

Bob and the Rolling Thunder team went into the studio to assist Kinky Friedman with his album 'Lasso From El Paso', an album which is originally to be titled 'Asshole From El Passo' until management intervened. The musicians included The Band, Roger McGuinn, Ringo Starr, T-Bone Burnett, Steve Soles, Rob Stoner, Howie Wyeth, David Mansfield, Dr John, Bob Neuwirth, Ronnie Hawkins and one Little Jewford Shelby playing 'Camel' on 'Ahab the Arab'. Bob's 'Catfish' is included as is 'Banana's and Cream' written by Kinky and Jeff Shelby. The sleeve notes explain that 'Sold American' was recorded live with Bob Dylan and the Rolling Thunder Revue, but Little Jewford Jeff Shelby, now I wonder who he is?

The Rolling Thunder Revue was soon back on the road again. The show at Clearwater, Florida was taped for an NBCTV special but was later rejected, reason unknown. However shows recorded at Fort Worth, Texas and Fort Collins C.O. were spliced to create a new live album titled 'HARD RAIN' which was released in late September 1976. The album did very well reaching No 3 in the UK and No 17 in the USA. A film of the shows was accepted by NBC and it fulfilled the contract.

The new Rolling Thunder tour was stage managed by Jacques Levy who of course had prior experience with 'Oh Calcutta'. Bob was becoming tired of singing the same songs ad infinitum and Jacques attempted to freshen up the approach and the performance. Howard Alk was filming the shows he and Bob were to make a film of the events titled 'Renaldo and Clara', an unscripted 'fly on the wall' documentary of the revue both on stage and behind the scenes. Sara was in the film, she was not happy in being away from the children, she appeared in long scenes with Joan Baez. Both Sara and Joan played 'Clara' to Bob's 'Renaldo'. It wasn't totally unscripted as Sam Shepard was asked to write some dialogue but due to a confliction of ideas with Bob most of Shepard's lines were discounted in lieu of improvisation. The whole film is of a man alienated from himself it was supposed to be Renaldo's Dream, which may have been a better title.

Bob appeared on Bette Midler's album 'Songs For the New Depression', it was a duet of Bob's 'Buckets of Rain'. He did another duet with Eric Clapton on Eric's 'No Reason No Cry' album where they sang 'Sign Language'.

Bob was going through more personal changes. He was drinking heavily and becoming difficult, especially with Sara, the sulks were now more on than off. Sara had cut-off her relations with Bob. Joan Baez was in the 'Renaldo' film, prior to her joining the tour she hadn't spoken to Bob for eight years. Their first meeting for years was filmed with Joan in a wedding dress and Bob as a masked man. Filmed by Jack Baran a 'film-maker' he had the extra problem of attempting to get all the different personalties onto the same wavelength. The egotists, the drunks the drug takers, the bad time keepers, the insomniacs and the ever changing schedules must have created nightmare. Jack Baran actually appears in the film as a truck driver giving Sara and friend Helena a lift. The primary problem with the film is that everyone is always either looking at or waiting for Bob. All the anticipated silences are quickly filled by someone desperate to fill the void. It was alleged that many scenes where Bob's relationship with Sara evolved were edited out, to that I say, understandably so. If a divorce was on the horizon Bob would hardly want his innermost thoughts presented to the Law Court on film as evidence.

Whilst the tour and filming was in progress Elvis Presley died and Phil Ochs committed suicide. Eric Clapton was recording his 'No Reason No Cry' album and Bob had written 'Sign Language' for Eric to include, Bob also gave his **'Seven Days'** to Ronnie Wood it was included on his album 'Gimme Some Neck'. Bob's live version of that song from Tampa, Florida, was released on The Bootleg Series in 1991. It includes T-Bone Burnett, Steven Soles, Mick Ronson, Bob Neuwirth, Scarlet Rivera, David Mansfield, Rob Stoner, Howie Wyeth and Gary Burke, five guitarists, a violin, a bass and a mandolin. The words 'seven days' are prevalent in The Bible as is the number seven. It is a sacred number within Judaism. As one will realise it is mentioned throughout Genesis, Exodus, Leviticus, Numbers and Revelations all books read by Bob. Is it solely by chance that 'seven' appears 'seven' times in the song 'seven days'?

On November 25th 1976 Bob joined The Band on stage for their farewell concert **'The Last Waltz'**. Held at The Winterland, San Francisco. Bob sang 'Baby Let Me Follow You Down', 'I Don't Believe You', 'Forever Young', and joined the all star finale of 'I Shall Be Released'. At the concert Bob met Emmett Grogan and they liked each other immediately. Grogan was the inspiration behind The Diggers of San Francisco, providing free help, accommodation and food for the needy. Although Bob seemed in good spirits at the show his marriage was about to fall apart. Sara went to Hawaii with the children for a break and Bob started an affair with their house-sitter Farida McFree. On March 1st 1977 Sara Dylan filed for divorce, if she hoped for a quick result then they forgot the acrimony and the growing animosity that is caused by the agreement of terms. I have watched so many amicable breaks suddenly turn sour once the solicitors get involved. I am not saying that's what happened here but two people who were once madly in love now found each other unbearable, but time heals. Bob had the added advantage of being able to announce and share problems to the World through his music and touring, Sara sat back quietly with Jesse (11), Anna (9), Samuel (8), Jakob (6) and Sara's daughter Maria Lowndes (15). I agree with one writer when he wrote that both Bob and Sara's facial characteristics are similar, they could in fact be brother and sister. If one looks at married friends, if they look the same then there is every chance that they like the look of their own face, narcissism, we all know opposites attract. It is likely that Sara and Bob were not opposites they were so similar in character that neither would give an inch and thus the protracted outcome of their divorce deliberations, it is all very sad. The divorce became final on June 28th, 1977.

Bob continued with his work with Howard Alk on the 'Renaldo' film project. When they started they had more than 400 hours of film, this was eventually condensed to ten. The film and the divorce meant that the year was dead as far as Bob's career was concerned, he was a hermit. It was February 1978 before the film was premiered in Los Angeles. If Bob was reticent in giving out any information concerning his lyrics this was not the situation with the film. He gave out a vocal digest of the story...Man sell house and horse-goes out on tour-sings-has a fight-meets a woman....and that is it.

The film has a narrator in old friend David Blue, he mentions the early days at Gerdes Night Club. To make it confusing or should that be interesting Bob is Renaldo and Ronnie Hawkins plays Bob Dylan. A carnation is passed around representing a vagina, both Joan and Sara are Clara. However Sara, alias the real Mrs Dylan is portrayed by Ronee Blakley. Confused, good, in addition to this Ramblin Jack Elliott plays Lougheno de Castro.

An art house movie is the result, possibly loved by Bob's fans but I would guess that he hoped for a much wider appeal. In a word it is 'inadequate', hardly worth the time and effort except for the live show scenes. They are excellent, 47 songs, Bob in hat and painted white-face at the peak of his stage performances. The distributors Circuit Films was set up by Bob and run by his brother David Zimmerman. Another record rarity evolved with a four track EP being released with 'Isis' and 'It Ain't Me Babe' plus Bob's versions of Curtis Mayfield's 'People Get Ready' and the late Johnny Ace's 'Never let Me Go', the latter a duet with Joan Baez.

Bob had a new manager in Jerry Weintraub surely he, Howard Alk, or someone would have told Bob that the film was poor, seems not. Perhaps the scene in the 'Eat the Document' movie where Phil Ochs was thrown out of the car for daring to criticise meant that Bob was now surrounded by sycophants just like Elvis Presley had been.

Bob was now seen about town with singer Helena Springs, he also entertained Emmett Grogan at his home where he gave Emmett some acetate recordings from his early days. (Grogan died soon after but his story is so powerful I have included it at the end of this book with that of Edie Sedgwick). The acetate recording which later emerged on bootleg discs were taken from 'Another Side of Bob Dylan' sessions 1964, Newport Festival Rhode Island 1964, Highway 61 Revisited sessions 1965, and four 10" acetates of 'Tombstone Blues', 'From A Buick 6' (titled 'Lunatic Princess'), 'Queen Jane Approximately' and 'Positively Fourth Street' (titled 'Black Dalli Rue'). The collectors market value of this hoard would have been massive. There were some long awaited gems. 'Mr Tambourine Man' with Ramblin' Jack Elliott, the Newport Festival version of 'All I Really Want to Do' with the last verse spliced onto the 1965 workshop performance. 'I Shall Be Released' was an un-released version with the last verse containing parts later edited out.

During the 1978 tour with the 'Street Legal' band, a performance (1st March) at Japan's Budokan Concert Hall was recorded for a later release. Bob was kept in the public eye by the release of Martin Scorsese's film 'The Last Waltz' featuring Bob and The Band, Van Morrison and more. A triple album was also released to coincide with the premiere. Strangely Emmett Grogan was not in the film, or was he, there are only a few photographs in existence of this enigmatic character. Bob's tour reached Earls Court Exhibition Hall in London during June 1978, in March 90,000 seats are sold out in just eight hours. In July Bob joined Eric Clapton at a Festival held at Blackbushe Airport in Surrey, England, the audience was estimated to be 250,000. The special security arrangements were later published in the British Rail News. Bob was taken to and from Waterloo Station to Fleet station in his own special train. Bob had visited New Zealand where he met Ra Aranga on the beach whilst they were both jogging. The meeting with this Maori Princess meant that Bob returned to New Zealand for a few days after he finished recording the Street Legal album.

Between April 25th and May 3rd Bob recorded the tracks for his 'STREET LEGAL' album, the title named after jargon for a customised car that was permissable for use on the roads. This album took just five days to record the previous three studio albums had taken six days each. The 'Street Legal' album was released to coincide with his European tour and the album reached No 2 in the UK in July and No 11 in the USA in August.

The Howard Alk cover photograph showed Bob peering out from a stairway as if to see if it was 'all clear' to emerge. There was also a Joel Bernstein picture of Bob having a meal with George Benson and another by Alk of Renaldo in white face singing. The album was dedicated by Bob in memoriam to the late Emmett Grogan. The Marty Feldman credited on the album was not the British comedian with the big eyes, he was Bob's accountant.

'Changing of the Guards' is this Alice in Wonderland, Lewis Carroll wrote 'meaning what you say is not quite the same as saying what you mean', almost a perfect description of Bob's lyrics over the years. To that I must add another line from 'Alice in Wonderland'...'everything's got a moral, if you can only find it'. Sixteen years in the song means 1978 back to 1962, Bob's career to date. There are Tarot references here as on the previous album. Is it for peace in love, inner peace or world peace? Writer Bill Butler published books on the Tarot, it was created in the 13th Century as a game and subsequently used for fortune telling. The Tarot pack of cards comprises of 78 cards, 56 of which are Arcana-Lesser, 22 are Greater-Arcana. The King and Queen of Swords are from the Lesser, Death, Tower, Sun, Moon are greater. As this album was coinciding with Bob's 16 years in the music industry, Bob sings of 16 banners, Psalm 20:5 states 'in the name of God we will set up our banners: The Lord will fulfil all thy petitions'. Stepping from the shadows of the marketplace, merchants and thieves hungry for power add to these folk archivists and managers. The 16th tarot card is The Tower usually with a grassy bank on the card, Bob sings of the tower and meadows where the lady of fortune was born. The Tower card, according to S.MacGregor Mathers a writer on the subject of The Tarot, signifies the destruction of an out dated idea or philosophy. Did Bob just spread out a Tarot and write the song, is this his own fortune that is told here? Jeremiah, Chapter 6 and Acts Chapter 12 have guards soldiers and chains, and the latter (verse 13-16) has Peter 'Knock Knock knocking' on the door. The lyric is impenetrable and the usual remark made in this situation is that it conveys a new spiritual awareness, which of course is absolute nonsense. There is another connection with T.S.Eliot who used Tarot references such as the man with three staves and the hanged man in his 'The Burial of the Dead' (from The Waste Land, 1922) which Bob would have read at the time he wrote 'Desolation Row'. Only Bob really knows, he has created an enigma and his isn't telling but I bet he's laughing at our flailing in the darkness. The song fades-in as though we have already missed a couple of verses, it opens as powerfully as it ever gets musically, but there is a gentle band fade-out at the end; this ending is extended on the 1999 re-mix by 30 seconds.

'New Pony' sounds like the re-use of Jacques Levy's 'Chestnut Mare', is the pony a young filly, a woman, or is pony a metaphor for horse which is slang for heroin, amphetamine, speed. The pony is named Lucifer a strange name for a female. The lyrics are deliberately difficult with voodoo, Miss X, Lucifer and a magical horse and feet that walk by themselves. The blues riff is excellent the backing singers are an awful intrusion, the singers responsible were Carolyn Dennis, Jo Ann Harris, Steve Soles and Helena Springs. They are singing 'how much longer' which is from Jeremiah 13:17 (NEB), the preceding verses may be pleading for adultery and lewdness to be cleaned up, Bob may have read of Miss X and her brothel, of course Miss X is a name used for an unnamed woman in a divorce. The musical highlight is Steve Douglas 'dirty' saxophone sound. The inclusion of Douglas had some critics stating that Bob was copying Bruce Springsteen. This obviously touched a nerve in Bob because he responded by saying that Clarence Clemmons couldn't be spoken in the same breath as Steve Douglas, no offence but Douglas was much better. I wonder if Clarence Clemmons did take offence or did he agree? I read that one critic thought that this song was influenced by Charley Patton's, 'Pony Blues', apart from a blues beat and the word 'pony' they are totally different. The only 'Pony Blues' which has any influence on Bob's song is the version by Son House. Both Bob's pony and Son's know how to 'foxtrot lope and pace'. The rather pedestrian guitar solo may be by Billy Cross but is more likely to be Bob. The 1999 re-mix of the album includes 10 seconds extra at the end of this song.

'No Time to Think' traditional folk tune which sounds like campanology without the bells, Alan Pasqua's keyboard is switched to 'chime-piano' for some of the later verses. The song sounds like a track by The Strawbs, Bob sounding like their vocalist Dave Cousins. The references that Bob sounded like Stevie Wonder are balderdash. The thesaurus was out for this composition, there can be few sets of lyrics with so many words ending in 'y'. The rhymes are exceptionally ordinary and rather than spontaneous they have the feeling of a rhyming dictionary. Bob makes Tarot references with Death, The Magician and The Empress, there is no time think at the time of death. Although the lyric looks impressive and clever it is nonsense. Words with no connection are run together to appear intellectual. We are presented with verse after verse of unconnected gibberish, Bob should have used the first and last verse and improvised the remainder. The minstrel is playing, it is time for us all to dance around the maypole. **'Baby Stop Crying'** has the band taking some faltering notes early on wondering if Bob is going to call a halt, he doesn't so off they all go regardless. The narrator is attempting to console a woman who has been hurt by love. The woman is known to the narrator because her sadness is affecting him. Sounds like a father giving advice to a daughter. He trying to be tender but he does advise her in the very first line that he was a bad man. The ability to advise can only be achieved through experience. **'Is Your Love in Vain?** : Alan Pasqua plays organ just like Al Kooper. Bob seems to want to alienate himself from all women with this condescending and patronising lyric. Bob would realise that the words would be attributed to him, whatever he said to the contrary, this is as chauvinistic as he has ever achieved. He is asking her if she loves him, because he has been hurt before. He needs reassurance but it is so arrogant to ask her, if her love is in vain, only he knows the answer. He then condescends to give her a chance in such a manner that would have most women reaching for their coat and leaving, and of course slamming the door. She will be permitted to do his sewing and gardening, is this man serious? The tune is similar to Elvis Presley's 'Can't Help Falling In Love', Hugo (Peretti) and Luigi (Creatore) registered it as their's in 1961. Bob has changed the melody to create one of his most melodious songs.

    'Senor (Tales of Yankee Power)' has menace in Mexico, this sounds like man at the end of his tether with American foreign policy. This has always reminded me of Joseph Conrad's 'Nostromo' itself a tale of a South American revolution. They may be no connection but the two protagonists are preparing for some fight as they overturn the tables and are ready to make their exit. Nostromo (like America and Bob's Yankees) becomes gradually richer as time progresses but he professes love to both Linda and Giselle and the love tryst causes his death. The wicked wind still blows and she is wearing an iron cross, the symbol of Nazism and fascism. I wonder if Bob is pointing his finger at the foreign policy that loves and protects its neighbours as long as they have something that they need. **'True Love Tends to Forget'** is repetitive and weak, Bob sings that he is weary. The backing singers need re-mixing, maybe even erasing. A song for remembering the good times and forgetting the bad. Do not forsake me oh my darling the lines from 'High

Noon' return but there is no ultimatum in Bob's lyric. The wilderness and the reeds could refer to Moses who spent time in both. **'We Better Talk This Over'**: A stormy relationship, a song for swinging divorcees. As the marriage vows are mentioned this is a song for a man feeling distanced from his family, the distance is presented by the use of the telescope. The tangled situation, the inability to face each other, the awareness that she may wish to hurt him all pass by in the lyric. He is hoping for a chance meeting when they might rekindle the friendship they once had, he also infers that he would like to turn back the clock. Two people who were once so much in love are now just one person in love, the other will not risk another reconciliation.

'Where Are You Tonight? (Journey Through Dark Heat)': The organ makes this sound similar to 'Like a Rolling Stone'? Lost dreams, misguided loyalty, and misguided faith, the narrator can not believe that he has survived. Bob might just be wondering how he survived and Elvis, Janis, Jimi, Jim, Phil Ochs and so many others didn't, in these situations many people turn to religion. The forgiveness to any God for all the bad things that happen and the thanks for all the good things continues unabated. Marcel and St John the narrator's travelling companions are described as strong men belittled by doubt. The doubt over St John was not in his letters, if he really wrote them, that is if Bob is referring to John the Apostle the author of three chapters in the New Testament. Marcel in Proust's 'Remembrance of Things Past' was full of ambivalences. In the first part 'Swann's Way', Marcel is full of doubt and emotional weakness, the most important thing in his life was a kiss goodnight from his mother. The 'stream of pure heat' is taken from Daniel 7:10 and of course the previous verse mentions the 'wheels of fire', so Bob would be aware of both. 'Valley of stones' is taken from the Book of Micah so the Biblical references continue unabated. Robert Johnson emerges when Bob uses his line of 'the juice running down my leg'. With so much temptation being realised and resisted in the lyric it is apt that Bob mentions 'Ain't Too Proud to Beg' a hit in 1966 for The Temptations. The listener wants to sing 'how does it feel' each time the last line of the verse sung, this is a great lyric with so much to investigate, it seems that Bob wrote it exactly with that in mind. A.J.Weberman was convinced (as are most others) that his fight with Bob Dylan was the inspiration for Bob writing the line 'On Elizabeth Street' and 'it felt out of place, my foot in his face', a happening seven years earlier. A.J.Weberman has a strange egotism, he finds references to himself in songs, he even considers that Paul Simon wrote 'You Can Call Me Al' for him, there is an analysis of that song by Weberman on his own website.

The album was savaged by the critics and deemed 'anti-music' whatever that is. Greil Marcus said that it was 'sexist mannered crap-Bob ain't what he used to be'. He continued by adding that the album contained 'wretched performances' and that Bob sounded 'utterly fake'. He thought that 'Is your Love in Vain' sounded like 'Cant Help falling in Love' before becoming 'Here Comes the Bride'. He, like everyone else, is entitled to his opinions but did he really listen to the album; it is much better than Marcus' snap decision. I also agree with the critics who said that although Bob was again working alone he was struggling with his ability to write 'unconscious' poetic lyrics. The rhymes and couplets are available in most rhyming dictionaries, there is little lyrical spontaneity. The songs were registered to 'Special Rider Music' yet another publishing company controlled by Bob and his management, 'Big Sky' was still in business, it may have been for tax advantages or better deals could be struck with BMI, BIEM, ASCAP and other major music controllers. 'Street-Legal' (hyphen added) was finally re-mixed in 1999 and re-released. Don DeVito moved Bob's voice forward and the backing singers backwards, the improvement is immense, it is essential to hear the modified album.

Dave Marsh writing for Rolling Stone thought the album was a joke. He thought that Bob's idea of 'Alright, I'll fall in love with you', was the strangest idea of how love works, of that no one can disagree. He continued by writing that 'Senor' was a pastiche using the best moments of 'Hotel California'. The Rolling Stone Magazine printed two reviews of the album side by side, the Editor Jan Wenner then responded in the following issue to both reviews with his own, more level headed approach. He compared 'Senor' to 'Desolation Row' and continued to give the album his approval.

The single 'Baby Stop Crying' reached No 13 in the UK Bob's highest single placing for five years, thanks to the tour. A second single 'Is Your Love in Vain' was not so popular and only reached No 56 in November 1978. Bob continued with his touring completing the American section after 3 months and 62 shows on December 16th 1978. With the divorce problems now history, Sara was alleged to have received $13 million, it seemed that Bob was doing everything possible to fill his time and as he was on tour with so many people around it was impossible to be lonely. On this tour Bob was unusually polite to his audiences, he was known for saying absolutely nothing from start to finish, now he was saying "thank you" and announcing the last song and the next. Perhaps he wanted to appear polite and well-bred, especially as the divorce proceedings made his behaviour appear unreasonable. To be fair we all knew Bob was polite, his parental upbringing in Hibbing ensured that, it was the myth, the other Bob Dylan that was difficult, confrontational and inflexible.

Another live album was released. Bob had formed his own label Accomplice Records, but the double album still came out on Columbia during May 1979. **'BOB DYLAN AT BUDOKAN'** was only intended for Japanese issue but the bootlegs were available and so it was released in UK where it reached No 4 and in the USA No 13. Bob toured Japan to promote the sales of the album which was recorded back in March 1978. It was the Bob Marley influence that made Bob include the three backing singers just like Marley's 'I Three', they were carried over onto the 'Street Legal' album. This Budokan album also took some ideas from Elvis Presley's Vegas shows, the razzmatazz and the glitz. The album was a reminder of shows where the artist was at last considering the audience rather than pretentiously playing for himself. Bob had also had many of the songs re-arranged so that they would not sound stale, not just for his own repetition night after night but to make the songs sound new for the audience. This live album was a superb reminder of those performances, but now Bob was searching for his own truth, just like Van Morrison they both decided there must be an answer somewhere so it was time to check out as many religious avenues as possible. Both these aesthetically charged individuals would investigate and eventually emerge with their own hybrid religions. The 'Budokan' album liner notes were as reported at the time 'wise-guy' stuff. The cover photograph was by Joel Bernstein, the album had an insert with poster and the lyrics. Songs like 'Oh Sister', 'Cup of Coffee' and 'Shelter from the Storm' were as good if not better than the originals. 'Like A Rolling Stone' was just like the previous live album but 'Times They Are A-Changin'' needed changing.

MINE EYES HAVE SEEN THE GLORY

Art and religion are means to similar states of mind.
Clive Bell 1881-1964)

Euripides wrote 'money is the wise man's religion', Harry Emerson Fosdick added 'nothing in human life, least of all in religion, is ever right until it is beautiful'. To my mind Michel de Montaigne (1533-1592) was closer when writing 'our religion is made so as to wipe out vices; it covers them up, nourishes them, incites them, fame and tranquillity can never be bedfellows'. If the religion selected is christianity then so many born again christians are extremely selective, adultery, avarice and fornication can be conveniently deleted and forgotten. In San Diego Bob stooped to pick up an object thrown onto the stage, it was a small silver crucifix which Bob was observed to be wearing on the following day. It was in a hotel in Tucson, Arizona that Bob got his message.

"Jesus tapped me on the shoulder",
"Bob why are you resisting me?" he said
I said "I'm not resisting you!"
"You Gonna Follow Me?" Jesus said
Bob replied "Well I Never Thought about that before..."

Bob had experienced some form of religious experience, he never tried to hide it. He said "Jesus put a hand on me, it was a physical thing, I felt it all over me, I felt my whole body tremble, the glory of The Lord knocked me down and picked me up". He continued by saying "There was a presence in the room that couldn't be anyone else but Jesus, I truly had a born again experience, if you want to call it that". Some years later he would say that he had never been 'a fundamentalist or born again', in his opinion those were "Just labels that people hang on you".

Whatever the real truth Bob certainly changed direction towards religion. It seems unlikely that Bob would 'play' with religion to create the myth, it is a subject far too serious with which to meddle without true feelings. Christianity inspired him, Bob was now encompassing the whole King James version of the Bible, both Testaments. Bob didn't think that he was preaching but with the punk music movement at its peak Bob was almost his own Deity, especially for those people who think that all religion is within the inner man.

Bob then attended the Bible classes of Hal Lindsey and was trained how to go out and preach the word of God. In Bob's musicians there were already born again and practising christians in David Mansfield, Steve Soles and T-Bone Burnett. Bob wrote new songs and asked Jerry Wexler and Barry

Beckett to produce his new album at Muscle Shoals Studio, Sheffield, Alabama. This would be an evangelistic album. Cliff Richard was still the leading singer-christian in the UK (he still is) and Van Morrison had gone through his 'period of transition' and was searching for his God in the pastoral beauty of the English and Irish countryside. Bob was saying the same when in an interview in New York he said "Beauty can be very deceiving and it is not always of God. Beauty appeals to our eyes, the beauty of the sunset, that's God given, I spend a lot of time dealing with man made beauty, so sometimes the beauty of God's world has evaded me". This would parallel the thoughts of Van Morrison and of course the earlier mentioned Harry Emerson Fosdick.

The message would not get across if the songs were poor, obviously Bob's audience would be confused, but for many years Cliff Richard had undertaken pop tours and then separate evangelistic tours with no detrimental effect to his popularity whatsoever. The new Dylan album required a contemporary sound and Mark Knopfler and drummer Pick Withers from the group Dire Straits were employed to augment the band of Barry Beckett (keyboards) and Tim Drummond on bass. Helena Springs, Carolyn Dennis and Regina Havis added background vocals and The Muscle Shoals Horns of Harrison Calloway (trumpet), Ronnie Eades (baritone saxophone), Harvey Thompson (saxophone) and Charlie Rose on trombone.

'SLOW TRAIN COMING' was released on an unsuspecting public in August 1979, and achieved No 2 in the UK and No 3 in the USA, another platinum album, Bob certainly had God on his side. The album was a fire and brimstone-watch out for the apocalypse album, where was Bob's free and wide instinct of the earlier albums. Just like Alice Bailey's dweller on the threshold we had to agree with the belief and the proselytizing or be deemed prejudiced and intolerant. Bob went into conversation saying that these religious songs seemed to write themselves and that they frightened him. He also considered giving the songs to backing singer Carolyn Dennis for a solo album.

The 'Slow Train Coming' album cover depicted a train almost going off the rails, they were being replaced by new or repaired rails. One worker's axe is symbolically changed to appear to be a cross. I have always thought it bizarre how the cross and crucifix have become symbolical of christianity when neither appear anywhere in New English Bible, if you want to prove me wrong then find the reference. Cross over, crossbars (Kings), crossed over, crossing, crossness and crossways but no suggestion that Jesus carried a cross to Calvary. Crucify and Crucifix are two other words that do not appear anywhere in the NEB, 'Hell' from The King James' Bible is now 'Hades' (NEB). Calvary and the crosses first appeared in the work of Psalter in 855 AD and of course by natural association the scene on the hill with the three crosses at its crest became symbolic. John Bunyan mentioned the cross in Pilgrim's Progress (1678), and William Blake sketched crosses. Rembrandt painted his version of Christ's entombment in 1639 and Mantegna's painting in the Louvre, Paris, also continues the 'cross' theme. In fact one can walk most art galleries with religious works of art and see crosses as the most significant sign of christianity.

There was more symbolism on the rear of the cover where a thin figure (possibly Bob) is looking up at a cross which is supported by four stay cables. In the statements that Bob made at the time he was talking of The Bible being the only word, Jesus Christ explaining (not preaching) he was The Truth, The Way and The Life. He also insisted that some special preparations were necessary for everlasting life after the apocalypse that would be by fire this time, not water. His whole conversation was that of a Jehovah's Witness. There are only two kinds of people the saved and the lost after Armageddon. All his ideology at the time was taken direct from the scriptures of both Testaments. The Jehovah's Witnesses extract their doctrine from the complete Bible and that allowed Bob to be close to Christianity and Judaism.

'Gotta Serve Somebody' was released as a single and reached No 24 in the USA. The song also won The Grammy Award for Best Rock Performance by a Male. Bob beat Joe Jackson, Robert Palmer, Rod Stewart and Frank Zappa. On receiving the award Bob said "I didn't expect this and I want to thank The Lord". Bob was understandably surprised when Jerry Wexler's anticipated sequence of the album did not include this track. Bob had to exert some pressure to get it included. Later Bob said that he preferred Shirley Caesar's version of the song. The 'Slow Train Coming' album was also awarded The Dove Award for 1979, an award reserved for religious or gospel inspirational albums. In the L.A.Times Bob said in response to a request concerning Bob's christian messages "I know what some people have been saying, but this is no fad, it's the future we are just laying the foundation". 'Gotta Serve Somebody' is similar lyrically to the Memphis Slims' song 'Mother Earth'. Devil or The Lord the choice is yours, don't get it wrong. I have never agreed with Bob's philosophy within this lyric. Why do we have to serve somebody? Why do we need to select Devil or The Lord? Does that mean that providing that I am honest and live in accord with the Ten Commandments I am serving The Lord? If the last theory is true then I must be serving The Lord although I am an atheist. Of course, I repeat, adultery and illicit fornication does not apply, it is a conveniently over-looked commandment by all the characters that Bob brings to his song and of course many born again christians. But it is all alright one can be a re-born-again and again christian and start all over again at will. I wonder how many of Bob's flock rushed to those self-serving mercenary television evangelists, they add an alternative connotation to 'serving someone else in the hope of serving The Lord'. In the lyric Bob infers that he was once nicknamed 'Zimmy'.

'Precious Angel': The truth is in our heart, Bob's vision. Sister Mary Alice Artes, Bob's advisor, was explaining Buddha and Mohammed but not Jesus. To understand and be sure then the seeker must learn of other religions. I have learned that is not the case desired by each religion. Each religion puts the 'fear of God' into their 'flock' and many restrict the study of alternatives. What God gave, no one can take away, sings Bob, had he over-looked the rock-suicides, had he forgotten murders? Believe me, man can take away anything, he can destroy everything. Does Bob sing 'you either got faith' or 'Jah either got faith', the songbook states 'Ya'. The last verse indicates that we should not be enticed on the way out of Egypt (Islamic), Ethiopia (Rastafarianism) to Christ, what does that mean? It is my opinion that one has to be absolute in one's certainty before inflicting beliefs on another. Spreading the 'word' does so much more for the 'teacher' than it does for the convert.

'I Believe in You': The opening lines are an adjustment of the opening lines of 'Smoke Gets in Your Eyes'; Bob's title fits nicely into the other song too, try it. This is one of those songs that can mean devotion to so many, 'you' can represent, a child, God, a wife, a friend. Frank Loesser's song with the same title has the lines 'a seeker of wisdom and truth' and refers to 'faith in my fellow man', just like Bob's song it can suitably apply to religion or a person.

'Slow Train': This a slow blues. Bob mentions the holy slow train on the sleeve notes of 'Highway 61 Revisited'. One wonders what Bob's close friends thought of his inferences of being disgusted with their principles. The travelling journeyman evangelist within Bob exudes here as he picks on others such as sheiks walking around like Kings. If Bob is inferring that sheiks wear nose rings then I have never seen one. If it is a metaphor for them being led like cattle or being treated like puppets by women and politicians then again Bob is wrong. The EEC and American grain surplus mountain comes in for criticism showing an adolescent lack of knowledge of how world finances operate; plenty of grain is eventually distributed. Why would Thomas Jefferson turn over in his grave? Jefferson drafted The Declaration of Independence, became the third President of the USA and petitioned for religious freedom, perhaps it is because Bob considers The Laws to be outdated. The backing singers are under better control on this album. This song is almost Jehovah's Witness in style as we are reminded what awaits the unbeliever. The believer will be resurrected for an everlasting life of love and happiness in paradise. Bob has a go at sheiks for wearing their 'fancy jewels and nose rings' yet on the sleeve inner Bob is wearing diamond rings on four fingers. One thing that I found reassuring about this song is that at least the train is coming at us around the bend, 'slowly'.

'Gonna Change My Way of Thinking' could be Blood Sweat & Tears, great band sound which has one thinking back to the slow rock beat songs of 'Blonde on Blonde'. It was recorded by just Bob with a quartet of Barry

Beckett (keyboard), Tim Drummond (bass), Mark Knopfler (guitar) and Pick Withers on drums. The over-dubbing was performed by Mark Knopfler alone so the brass might be keyboard created. The sentiments are 'Whosoever is not for me is against me'. In Mark 9:40 what is actually written is "For he that is not against us is on our part"; and Luke 9:50 'Forbid him not, for he that is not against us is for us'. Bob sings 'she can do the Georgia Crawl' which he extracted from Blind Willie McTell's 'Broke Down Engine' a song he would record himself for a later album. Bob uses the line of 'Sons becoming husbands to their mothers' as a euphemism for those 'motherf*****s'. We are being led astray, change before it is too late, the 'day and hour no man knoweth' (Mark 13:32). Bob in his last line displays his Watchtower Society affinity with the explaining that he believes God created the world rather than the big bang, one wonders what his opinion was on Darwinism. **'Do Right To Me Baby (Do Unto Others)'**: This preaches that we don't do anything to anyone that you wouldn't have done to yourself. The remark that the narrator doesn't want to be buried does not coincide with his earlier song's beliefs. This is Bob's twenty personal commandments. It is pleasing to note that he doesn't want to commit bigamy or wink at anybody. He may be against belief in Darwinism as he doesn't put any faith in scientists. It is sad that he doesn't want to amuse or play with anybody, all he really wants to do is baby be friends with you, perhaps. The song has a moderate beat jazz combo backing. **'When You Gonna Wake Up'**: God doesn't make promises he doesn't keep; an aphorism. Bob names Karl Marx and Henry Kissinger in this song as philosophers that have polluted our thoughts. This song isn't religious it is political. Bob lists sinners that are destroying the fabric of society, he calls for us to wake up to the reality. Bob one assumes has woken to that fact, we should do what he is doing, is that singing about religion for money? What does he think the poor and weak will be able to do. He provides his cure-all panacea, believe in Jesus that is all we have to do, so what was Jesus doing when we got in the mess in the first place. I will add my own atheist view, God doesn't care! Good kind and honest people care but they are by virtue of their situation too weak to fight the charlatans. I repeat, 'they' need the help and he doesn't care! **'Man Gave Names to All The Animals'** is 'all things bright and beautiful' revisited, a song for the children in us all. **'When He Returns'**: This is as written in the Book of Revelations. It is all coming, retribution, apocalypse by fire (last time it was water), repent and become a christian before it is too late. The end is inevitable but prepare yourself for the resurrected life, it is written. As the last apocalypse by water was a purging of sins didn't God return at that time and re-create his paradise free from strife and fear? Does this mean that infallible God has got it wrong twice? If we are waiting for God to return, where has he gone? So when humans finally press that destruct button, I say humans because it is just as likely to be a woman war-monger as it is for a man, will it be God's apocalypse or man's armageddon? There are more questions than answers, cue Johnny Nash.

Some tracks were remaindered. **'Ye Shall Be Changed'** has more apocalyptic warnings. If you have all the sins and your wife and kids have left you then you will be changed. The title is sung as an aphorism, you will be changed like it or not, or when you've had enough. The song is only average and for once deserved to be remaindered. The song was included on the Bootleg Series. **'Trouble in Mind'** was the first song recorded for the album and was released as a single as the b-side of 'Precious Angel'. 'Trouble in Mind Blues' was written by Richard Jones in 1926. In the blues he says that he is intending to lay his head on the railroad line and let the train pacify my mind, well that is one way to do it. **'Ain't No Man Righteous, No Not One'** has been difficult to locate. According to John Bauldie, it was later recorded by the reggae band 'Jah Mallah'.

The songs on this album had found yet another publisher in Warner Brothers Music. Bob's 'Slow Train Coming' tour across the States wasn't well received. He ended the tour with a 14 night residency at The Fox-Warfield Theatre in San Francisco which was completed on 16th November. Many of the dates had Bob's songs greeted by bad mannered booing, almost back to the days of The Newport Festival. This audience unhappiness was not due to the religious songs but the lack of any of the earlier work. Being denigrated for righteousness sake is all part of the religious dogma, but one suspects that Bob anticipated some of the aggressive antipathy. The album sold well, if he lost any fans then they would soon return, Bob did not intend to be dissuaded from his new found course. If anything Bob was buoyed up by his christianity, it made him perform better and seem almost fire-proof in his bewilderment of the audience dissention.

If Columbia had trepidations concerning the album one can wonder why. Bob's fans would have purchased the album regardless, but now Bob was appealing to the massive gospel religious market in the USA. The Patty Valentine versus Columbia case was in court concerning the use of her name in 'Hurricane'. Bob was a jew that had become a christian. There were reports that Bob suddenly found himself more accepted in Hollywood because of his new beliefs. I consider that statement bizarre as nearly all the management and musicians in the music industry are jewish.

In February 1980 Bob was back in the Alabama recording studio with Jerry Wexler and Barry Beckett. There were some changes in musicians, Tim Drummond on bass and Barry Beckett on keyboards remained as did Regina Havis on backing vocals. Clydie King and Mona Lisa Young came in as singers with Terry Young and Spooner Oldham on keyboards, Fred Tackett was on guitar and Jim Keltner on drums.

The new album **'SAVED'** was released in June 1980 to apathetic fans in the USA where is only reached No 24, but in the UK it rose to No 3, which was astounding considering the content. It was later acknowledged to be Bob's lowest selling album ever. Now the publishing company was The Fort Knox Music Company. The album cover was in the style of William Blake with the hand of God reaching down and an electro-religious charge being given to five hands reaching up to be blessed.

This cover painting was by Tony Wright, but there was an alternative painting showing Bob playing harmonica in concert, but this was not acknowledged, The Guinness Book of Rock Stars infers that Bob Dylan painted this picture, if it was true, (it wasn't), then his work had moved on a great deal since Self Portrait. There was much discussion at Columbia concerning the new album it was reported that for once even Bob was unsure if it should be released. Columbia hated the album and didn't want another Dylan-Gospel album. They also disliked the cover so much they changed it to the painting of Bob standing playing the harmonica as soon as possible. A live album was recorded but it was shelved, 'Saved' went into the shops. Bob never considered that the critics views were part of being persecuted for righteousness sake, he reneged against the reviewers. Bob said that he was fortunate to be in a position to release an album like 'Saved', especially as it didn't have the kind of songs that were on the previous album. So Bob truly realised the album was sub-standard but times had changed, years ago he would have returned to the studio and started again. The musicians used on the album performed excellently it was just the quality of the compositions.

'A Satisfied Mind'(Hayes/Rhodes): This was a country hit for Slim Whitman and Porter Wagoner; Joan Baez sang it on her 'Farewell Angelina' album. Bob sings it almost a-cappella, like a rap-song. **'Saved'** (Dylan/Drummond): This is a hellfire preaching song, sung to a gospel rhythm. These songs by virtue of their proselytizing theme have to be personal. I wonder how Bob's mother felt when she heard the opening lines. Without an explanation it expresses that he was born ruined. Christians are born with the sins of their parents and that is why they are baptised, it a purging of those sins. I just think that Beatty would have preferred hearing it in less powerful rhetoric. Bob has been saved by the blood of the lamb. In Biblical terms lambs are the un-luckiest of beasts. I have always thought that the Book of Numbers was an animal balance sheet. The early chapters call for five lambs to be sacrificed, this goes up to seven and fourteen as the book progresses till more than 300 get their death sentence before the book ends. By the end of Bob's song I think we are convinced that he has been saved.

'Covenant Woman' is a song written for Mary Alice Artes, she was Bob's religious mentor. She was named as Queen Bee on the cover of Street Legal. Artes a black actress who had found God helped Bob with his searching. I never believed the rumour that Bob gave her an 'engagement' ring in 1980. One writer thought that this song should have been titled 'Sunny Day Woman No 1 and 2' and I whole-heartedly agree, a superb idea. It is evident that Bob considers that the Lord had sent Mary Artes to him, so he must care, the Lord that is. A song of trust and gratefulness that deserved a full orchestral arrangement. A 'covenanter' is a person who upholds and protects the two 17th century Presbyterian covenants. Presbyterianism is a protestant form of Calvinism. Calvinism emphasises predestination and justification by faith. The Covenant was God's promise to the Israelites and their promise to worship him alone. It is now recognised as a binding contractual agreement. I make these observations because it creates ambivalences with the song's title. The covenant is part of The Book of Jeremiah which Bob features on the album sleeve as it goes from Genesis to Revelation. Bob has a covenant he says so in the lyric, the song reinforces his promise. William Blake wrote a poem titled 'Mary' who was born with a 'different face' and was denigrated by others more fortunate. Both Blake's and Bob's 'Mary' gave them, inspiration, truth and beauty in a form that neither thought existed. **'What Can I Do For You?'** has some of Bob's new harmonica style, Larry Adler influenced rather than blues harp. What can you give the Lord who allowed his son to die for you? The answer supplication in thanks for the renewal that he now feels. **'Solid Rock'**: Has a Steve Miller band style riff, like 'Living in the USA'. Bob said that Jesus is the 'solid rock', the foundation to which we should be subordinate; tenacity perseverance and endurance are the watchwords. **'Pressing On'**: There can be no turning back. Bob answers the age old request in this song. Everyone wants proof, a sign. Bob says that it all comes from within, the problems stemmed with Adam not doing as he was told. Resist temptation, fight Satan, Bob is also saying that he is pressing on to the higher calling of his Lord. Leonard Cohen gave up everything to find his God, he lives in frugal surroundings isolated with his Zen Master. I don't suppose that Bob was considering taking his devotion that far.

　　'In The Garden': Nicodemus was a pharisee the ruler of the Jews, he asked questions of Jesus. After Jesus had been crucified Nicodemus secretly brought myrrh and aloes and assisted in dressing the body for a jewish burial. I have always thought it unusual that such a well known man as Nicodemus was only mentioned in the Book of John. Of course Bob is referring to the non-converts when he sings 'Did they see', but it was quixotic to use the line 'when he healed the blind, did they see?' They didn't know he was the Son of God in the garden of Gethsemane. In The Bible both Matthew and Mark agree that it was 'a' garden in Gethsemane not 'the garden'. The answer to all Bob's questions within the song is 'No!' and I suspect that a gospel service somewhere will make it into a call and response song. The song title was also used by Van Morrison on his 'No Guru No Teacher' Album in 1986. **'Saving**

Grace': The title was also used by Steve Miller for a song and album. The expression 'saving grace' sounds Biblical but is not. The realisation that he is a survivor when so many others have been incarcerated in their pine-box for eternity. The Jehovah's Witnesses are in their box awaiting their resurrection which Bob mentions in the lyric. Bob's road leads to Calvary whilst William Blake's and John Milton's lead to their personal Jerusalem. The wicked will know no peace. Bob feels comfortable protected by his 'saving grace'. I would like to know what sort of kind and loving God would inflict so much pain and hardship on poor patient Job, he even had his whole body covered in botches, (Boils in NEB). 'Are You Ready': A song with a rhetorical question. He is ready for judgement day but are you? The apocalypse will be swift, as you don't know when it will happen use your time now to prepare for it. At least these religious fanatics will know at that time if they have been wasting their time, I just hope they all get the opportunity to say "I told you so!" If Bob was into Jesus and the New Testament he had not forgotten Judaism and he includes a tract in the cover from Jeremiah, Chapter 31. The inference being that the houses of Israel and Judah will conjoin eventually and a 'new' covenant will be instituted. In Bob Dylan's psyche they already had done so, his belief encompassed the complete Holy Bible. Bob was also spending some time re-studying Judaism with The Lubavitch Sect, hence the tract on the latest album cover.

Every track recorded for 'Saved' was included on the album. The gospel shows continued with Bob polishing up his Elmer Gantry lectures. Although many of show reviews were biased against Bob it became obvious that Bob didn't know one Jerusalem from another. One is in Israel the other is William Blake's Jerusalem that we were building amongst those dark satanic mills. In the November 1980 shows Bob was actually singing his rendition of Peggy Lee's (and Elvis Presley) 'Fever', and 'Abraham (Lincoln) Martin (Luther King) and John (Kennedy)' a song written by Dick Holler which had been recorded by Marvin Gaye, Dion and Smokey Robinson. Although Bob was still into his religion he reverted to playing more of his 'oldies' during the 1981 tour.

'SHOT OF LOVE' was released in August 1981, still a big hit in the UK it climbed to No 6, but missed the top 30 in the USA stalling at No 33. The cover design could have been from the Roy Lichtenstein school of art, he painted pictures that were very similar. Painted by Pearl Beach it shows the big-bang that started it all for the non-religious. The rear was to have a collage showing the rear of a Cadillac with the registration No 666 a symbol for the beast, the devil from Revelations. The cover rear actually had a photograph of Bob with a rose, except for Brazil which used the Cadillac collage. If it was a wild flower then we could assume that Bob was thinking of William Blake and thus searching for his 'heaven in a wild flower'.

Bob thought that the album was something that could have been made in the forties or fifties, a cross element (section) of songs on it, the critics all they talked about was Jesus this and Jesus that, like it was some kind of Methodist record. Bob was correct of course but who can blame the critics when all Bob seemed to be doing was proselytizing with religious fervour. This was to be part three of the born again era albums, the last part of the jigsaw. Bob had written many of the songs whilst out on a holiday on a schooner in the Caribbean. Bob retained most of the musicians from the previous album, adding Danny Kortchmar and Steve Ripley on guitars, Benmont Tench on organ and Willie Smith on keyboards. Clydie King was still leading the backing vocals, Bob and Clydie were 'a unit' at the time.

'Shot of Love' was produced by Bumps Blackwell, one of the last songs he ever produced before he died. Bob said that although he only did this one song for Bob he considered Blackwell to be the best. Bumps was the producer of Little Richard the rocker that Bob so admired in his youth, so one can understand his remarks, but possibly it was a little inconsiderate towards his other producers; Bob had used some pretty good producers over his career. Bob lists some of the things that are bad that can be replaced by a shot of love. Bob really loved this song and urged people to listen to it to gain inspiration and to know just where his feelings were in 1981, he said it was his most perfect song. In fact this is extremely powerful in the images it presents. The 'shot' is helping to ease the pain, helping him to understand. In verse four the scene becomes different, who has done these things? They murdered his father, is that the Jews or the Romans? They raped his wife, who raped Mary? Whose life is he considering taking? His babies would be born with the sins of their parents so the 'poison pen' is sexually relevant. If this verse is meant to be The Lord speaking then only the wife raping is a misinterpretation. Is this the view of some downtrodden man not connected with God? Verse four is almost Jesus waiting in Gethsemane for the inevitable, the last verse is the religious fanatic finding that he is alone realising people don't want to be preached at all the time. The song requires a really deep investigation especially as Bob considers it so important

'Heart of Mine' is a very good song. It doesn't have to be seen as religious. The lyric is for self-realisation once more. When any person understand's their own imperfections and wishes to contain and control them, then a personal achievement is the result. It may just be the ability to give up smoking or drinking, two things that people give up so easily when they are faced with the choice of life or death. In his song Bob is controlling his heart, his desire. He realises that he is full of guile but surely he is not malicious. 'Property of Jesus' has a great horn arrangement in the Blood Sweat & Tears style. This is a song for those people who move away from the religious amongst us. In Matthew Chapter 5 there are the lines 'Blessed are they which are persecuted for righteousness sake for their's is the kingdom of heaven'. They need to be impugned, criticism is a drug, they just need a shot of it.

'Lenny Bruce': Is a welcome relief from all this evangelism. This harks back to the Greenwich Village days. Bruce died in 1966 of a drug overdose. Lenny was hardly a comedian, he was a raconteur the objects of his barbed wit were made amusing by ridicule. Bob infers that Bruce was killed rather than suicide. Bob once rode with Bruce in a taxi for a mile and a half Bob stated that it seemed like a couple of months. Lenny Bruce thrived on criticism, it gave him the publicity his career required. Bob's song is good but it is Tim Hardin's song that has the deeply felt feeling that Bob's performance lacks. Verve Records released a CD with Tim's complete Verve recordings but never bothered to include 'I Remember Lenny Bruce' from 'Tim Hardin 3'. Bob says that Bruce fought a fight where every victory hurts, Bruce only fought battles he knew he couldn't win. Few people fight The Establishment and win, in fact I can't think of any. **'Watered Down Love'**: Is a love song, it isn't a religious song. Bob does slip in the word 'transgression' but the narrator is talking to a woman that is either wary of getting involved or just wants a relationship. Bob doesn't use the old expression of 'true love' it has mutated to be 'pure love'. **'Dead Man Dead Man'**: This may allude to Lenny Bruce again, the establishment can't see the sins and responsibilities of their actions. It is the narrator sermonising, a man (or all men) who is (are) in Satan's clutches. Here the christian is angry because of the hedonistic attitude of others. The doctrine of atheism is that there is no doctrine, life is life and death is death, simple. The narrator 'can't stand it'. Why is it that the religious feel threatened by the realists, providing they live by the laws of the land they are no threat to anyone. It is a weak faith that can't withstand criticism. Bob's frustration with 'man' is evident in this lyric, just because he has seen the light he thinks everyone else should do the same.

'In the Summertime' is another good song, although he sounds weary, although that may be meant to portray his inner well-being and calm, it was lacking in the lyrics of the previous track. This is another love song either for a woman or Jesus, it can be read either way. Bob continues with his resurrection thoughts as he will keep the 'God' given gift unto the grave and then unto eternity. The track includes some superb harmonica. **'Trouble'** the apocalypse is coming. Bob again makes a list of poor management by the politicians, what he over-looks is that the vast majority of them are practising christians. We must remember that according to The Book it is inevitable, the apocalypse is coming, we can only delay it as long as possible. Once more we can hear the button on Bob's jacket sleeve tapping on his guitar. **'Every Grain of Sand'** was written for Nana Mouskouri, she was a ballad singer and now is a Member of The European Parliament representing Greece. This uses William Blake's 'Auguries of Innocence' according to John Bauldie. Blake's poem opens with 'To see the World in a grain of sand, and Heaven in a wild flower'. Although Bob's lyric is written in the same meter and style there is no overlap in ideas. One has to remember that Blake rarely if ever went to church once he was out of his father's control, Blake said that man lives within. God manifests himself in man, and becomes **the man in him**. Blake was a free thinker, that is why others such as Van Morrison have been drawn to his work. Bob has composed a superb lyric for coming to terms with reality. Bob writes of 'the hour of my deepest need'. The Bootleg Series released an earlier recording that has Jennifer Warnes on backing vocal and an extraneous barking dog; Fred Tackett plays guitar with Bob on piano. To these ears the quiet version is an improvement over the full production released on the album. The penultimate line was different 'a perfect finished plan' sings Bob. Bob has rarely written such a beautifully emotive Blakean line such as 'I can see the Master's hand in every leaf that trembles', it also a statement that our local Jehovah's Witnesses use when explaining the wonder of God. Did they get it from Bob Dylan or did he get it from them? I have been lost in admiration for this lyric, this poem, since I first read it. It really needs reading rather than hearing, 'the broken mirror of innocence', 'the bitter dance of loneliness', I could go on forever. When Allen Ginsberg said that he considered Bob Dylan the greatest poet of the 20th century he meant what he said. This lyric is as good as William Blake and he didn't have the additional problem of putting 'Auguries of Innocence' to music. This 'Every Grain' track was also included on the soundtrack CD for the Melanie Griffiths, James Woods film, 'Another Day In Paradise'.

'**Groom's Still Waiting at the Altar**' was the b-side of the single 'Heart of Mine' but was added to the CD release and later vinyl album issues. A bounce beat rocker. Who is Claudette? There are more apocalyptic thoughts for the break down of society. If Bob has ever written a song ideal for Mick Jagger to sing and prance around the stage, then this is it. '**You Changed My Life**' was released on The Bootleg Series. Bob thanks to the Lord for turning his life around, people had invaded his privacy and were making his decisions for him, does that mean the God was going to make those decisions in future? At first the band sound a little ragged but Bob persists and a decent version gradually evolves. '**Need A Woman**' this was recorded in re-written form by Ry Cooder on his 'Slide Area' album as 'I Need A Woman'; Ry didn't take any composer registration. Ry changed the lyrics to avoid the ambivalence of Bob's words; Ry Cooder made it into a story. Bob wasn't happy with the song it was remaindered and never performed live. Doesn't seem to be a religious song and reading Ry Cooder's lyrics is a puzzle, the similarities with Bob's are few and far between. Bob's version is really good, one wonders why he disliked it. '**Angelina**': According to John Bauldie this song's lyrics are so intense that perhaps Bob didn't know much about it, perhaps his sub-conscious spontaneity kicked in once again. A long song at almost seven minutes it is deep dark and superb. Released on the Bootleg Series. Surrealistic lyrics of singing to a dream woman finding God in the body of a woman? A very unusual lyric, she has seen him before, his eyes were like slits. He is worshipping a woman with the head of a hyena. He asks the question why does he need to ask God questions if he (she) can read his mind. She is his friend and his enemy, she has servants a black Mercedes Benz and has to decide if she wants Jerusalem or Argentina. Who is trying to take heaven by force, is it the grim reaper who is the unknown rider on the white horse? The ambiguities just increase the more one investigates, we are in the valley of giants full of sweet peaches, milk and honey, but it necessary to beat a path of retreat past an angel with the four faces. I repeat my opening remarks, deep dark and superb. **'Caribbean Wind'** was another out-take from these sessions and was released on Biograph, an up-tempo rocker. Bob said that he never understood what the song was about after he finished it, which was probably true of 'Angelina'. He was in St Vincent on his Caribbean holiday, he looked out of the window and saw some women working on a tobacco field on a high rolling hill. A lot of the women were smoking pipes, it set Bob thinking about living with somebody for all the wrong reasons. **'Heart of Mind'** which had been the B-side of a single was also included on Biograph. Bob said that it was written for someone that just liked having Bob around.

I could never understand the ambivalence towards this album by the critics, but there again I liked the variety of 'Self Portrait' so what do I know? Bob Dylan thinks that this is one of his best albums, it certainly is in the top five as far as I am concerned. The Shot of Love Tour began in October 1981 in Milwaukee. If Bob was a born again christian he still gave his son Jesse a Bar-mitzvah into Judaism, perhaps Jesse had found his own way religiously. It is one of the great dilemmas for parents, do they force their child along the lines of their own personal belief, or do they allow them to find their own truth? I belong to the second school of thought. As an atheist, I do not feel antagonism for religions, I even thirst and yearn for their belief, their assuredness, but they often attack my atheism as if it is a threat to their beliefs.

JEHOVAH TO PAGAN AT A STROKE

My atheism is true piety towards the universe
and denies only Gods fashioned by men in their
own image, to be servants of their human interest.

George Santayana (1863-1952)

March 1982 saw Bob elected to The Songwriter's Hall of Fame, in June he joined Joan Baez at The Peace Sunday concert in California. They sang 'Blowin' In the Wind' and 'God on Our Side'. Bob was at last moving away from his religious crusade and was back in the studio with Mark Knopfler making a new album. Since Mark worked with Bob on 'Slow Train Coming' he had now become a major force in the music industry with Dire Straits a major group. Mark's vocals very often could be confused with Bob in his mumbling style which was gradually percolating through his live shows. Bob had recorded tracks ready for release when he decided to change some tracks. The bootleggers had a field day with the out-takes which created a much better album. 'Blind Willie McTell', 'Foot of Pride' and 'Julius and Ethel' were discarded for lesser material. Bob could still write a good song only now he couldn't tell good from mediocre.

Recorded in April 1983, **'INFIDELS'** was released in the following November. This time Bob selected Power station Studios, New York. The album title said so much, after all the religious dogma now Bob titles an album infidels which means agnostics, atheists, heathens, heretics, pagans, unbelievers, one wonder why Bob had to go from one extreme to the other, it was just his little joke. Apparently when Bob decided on the title he didn't know the meaning of the word infidel. He wanted the album titled 'Surviving in A Ruthless World' but when he realised that the previous albums had all started with the letter 'S' he decided that it should be changed. Bob admitted to Kurt Loader at Rolling Stone Magazine that he had never been an agnostic, always believed in a Superior Being, in the World to come after armageddon every soul will be alive either in holiness or in flames. To coin a phrase he had suddenly moved from 'almighty to alrighty'. In the same interview Bob expounded his views concerning the prophecies in The Book of Revelation. The leaders of the world powers are already playing God, politics are corrupt, they are the instrument of The Devil, both Testaments are equally valid. Bob was confirming what the fans and critics had been saying for many years.

'Infidels' had the rhythm section of Sly Dunbar (drums) and Robbie Shakespeare (bass) which was an inspired choice, to my ears they have always been one of the best ever. Mick Taylor who had served some time with John Mayall's Bluesbreakers and The Rolling Stones came in on guitar. Mark Knopfler on guitar and Alan Clark on keyboards completed the recording

179

group but there are definitely other musicians on the out-takes. Once the recording details are published I would expect to find Kenny Buttrey, Rob Stoner, Howard Wyeth and Charlie McCoy on some recordings.

The cover of the album was just a bearded Bob wearing sunglasses which reflected the cameraman, the drawing of a man kissing a woman on the cheek on the rear reminded me of a Frank Sinatra record, no one was more surprised to learn that at these sessions Bob had recorded a Sinatra song. Bob also repaid Sly and Robbie for their efforts by appearing on their 'Language Barrier' album, Bob sang on the track 'No Name on the Bullet'. The 'Infidels' album should have been a double including all the out-takes it would then have become almost as good as 'Blonde on Blonde', the album itself was good but it could have been brilliant.

'Jokerman': Soddom and Gommorah, Daniel's fiery furnaces, the break down of society. There is some great over dubbed harmonica, and under-stated guitaring. The lyrics were changed and the verse order altered during the recordings. Bob not only mentioned the Books of Leviticus and Deuteronomy in the song he continued the reference in interviews. Leviticus is a Book of legislative writing. It includes regulations for sacrifices, the installation of the priesthood, laws of hygiene, Israel's day of Atonement and the consequences of obedience and disobedience. Deuteronomy like Leviticus was written by Moses. It includes Moses' four discourses and his song and final blessing. It is the fourth discourse that includes the conclusion of the covenant with Israel. Bob refers to the 'law of the jungle' which can't refer to Moses. The Jokerman will have to be Satan or any false God. As an aside you may not realise that Satan appears in the Old Testament and The Devil in the New Testament. The song was also subjected to the promotional video format. Images are presented for each verse of the song, with Bob on camera for the chorus. We are endowed with the idea that Ronald Reagan might be the jokerman in question. The predominant problem with Bob's videos (any videos) is that it destroys the imagination which they lyrics create. Where once we remembered songs for the content or with whom or where we were at the time we liked them , now the visual images come to mind, but as they say, that is progress. In this particular video works of art from 1400 to the modern day were used. The Aztec 'Goddess of Earth' dated 1400, Turner's 'Slave Ship', 'Man in Bondage' by William Blake and the original Joker from the Batman DC comics are featured. Other paintings by Goya, Munch (The Scream, of course), Picasso, Durer, Michelangelo (David), The Musicians' Hell by Hieronymous Bosch and more, at least 26 in total pass before our eyes, locating their titles is a great puzzle to help pass many hours.

'Sweetheart Like You' was the obvious single from the album yet it only reached No 55 in the USA in January 1984, it deserved better. This is advice to the wayward but affluent woman, she should find a partner and salvation. Here was a man that hadn't sustained his own relationships, went from woman to woman advising the best course of action for others. Don't do as I do, do as I say, one of the predominant themes of all religious dogma. Not every one has the confidence to meet a partner so simply. It is fine for a celebrity where advances are made towards them on a regular basis, perhaps Bob was now too far removed from real society. The song is superb even if the advice is a little adolescent. In the video that Bob made for MTV to promote the album the song is sung to a woman sweeping up the floor of a night club after it has closed, the band are continuing to play. The story unfolds within the mind of the cleaner. Bob uses writer's-license with a line from 'Boswell-Life' by Samuel Johnson (1709-1784) who wrote 'Patriotism is the last refuge of the scoundrel'. **'Neighbourhood Bully'**: This could be for Israel and their relationship with the Arabs. A riff song packed with ambiguity, apparently Bob has been taught that Jesus could stop things from going wrong, so why doesn't he and our Father bother any more? Sickness to health, bombs, lynchings, but do the jews or the arabs have God on their side, of course the winners have God on their side, only the winners. Through history the 'bully' nations have eventually crumbled. This bully must now be The United States of America. Randy Newman sang of America's position in the World when he wrote that no one liked the Americans so 'let's drop the big one (Bomb) and see what happens'. In my travels through the third world I have noticed that the people like the last person that helped them out forgetting all the previous aid. As The USA is now the World's Policemen it is relevant to note that the only time their country has been attacked on their own soil was at Pearl Harbour and that was in the Pacific. The 'scars' that Bob alludes are all mental, the American Bully has many more years before it goes the way of The Roman Empire. This an excellent song even though the backing is extremely simple.

'License to Kill': This track was the first take, Bob never thought they ever played it better subsequently. This isn't James Bond licensed to kill, this is the nations with the power to kill and maim. A song of disarmament for the world, because man has manufactured enough bombs to complete his own destruction. In this disarmament struggle what I want to know is, if one country manufactures arms secretly when the rest have none will they not then be able to exert their authority over the rest? It will be the creation of another neighbourhood bully, which was mentioned in the previous song. It is human nature to be aggressive, disarmament is the ideology of appeasement and supplication. I suspect that this song is meant to be understood in transposition, he says what he doesn't think, it is all meant to be reversed. The views of the simple folk are presented as the chorus, a woman on his block asks the question. This version and the out-take both stop suddenly at the end. Richie Havens sang a super acoustic version of this song on his 'Sings Beatles and Dylan' album. Although the title of the album states 'Beatles' Richie also sings songs from their solo years by John Lennon and George Harrison.

'Man of Peace': A cautionary song concerning Satan, who comes as a man of peace and convinces you of his 'good' intentions. It is your achilles heel that Satan is after so watch out he is just waiting to tempt you. Satan comes in many disguises of course and most of the wares on offer are man-made anyway. Satan has all the best music and the most attractive women so why doesn't God get a few glamorous women and create some music that is not considered to be The Devil's? Bob might be advocating that God needs a better public relations team. 'Union Sundown': This song includes Clydie King on vocals on what is an 'I've Been Everywhere' song, nothing is made in the USA any more. It is alleged that Running shoe giant 'Nike' has never made a trainer in America, surely that can't be true. The song infers that American business prefers to use foreign, almost slave labour, it is cheaper. Bob told Kurt Loader that he had read that 'the Chevrolet was assembled in Argentina by a guy earning 30 cents a day, Bob thought that the guy would be better off without the 30 cents. 'I and I': This is the 'I Three' and Bob Marley revisited. The narrator says it is a long time since a strange woman slept in his bed. A 'slovenly woman blues'. The King that wrote the Psalms was David and his Queen consort was Abishag. Aristotle (384-322 BC) wrote 'Dignity does not consist of possessing honours, but in deserving them'. The last verse reads as though Bob is continuing to struggle with his religious leanings. In the last line the inference is clear, everyone has made money from him but he learns that he has very little of his own. The Bible has many strange women, they come and go with great regularity. King Solomon who followed David to the throne loved many strange women, some are listed in 1-Kings 11:1. At a time when men have such a problem keeping one woman happy, Solomon had 700 wives and 300 concubines, one wonders what he did on his day off. 'Don't Fall Apart on Me Tonight': Bob sounds vulnerable on this lovely song. This is evidently personal but the name means little to me. She blew the mind of 'Jackie P.' in St James Street which is in London. A baffled millionaire drummer, a painting in the louvre? Bob has realised he can't give the real names and is creating an impenetrable 'stainless steel house' for protection. The song ends with the narrator continuing to plead for her not to fall apart.

The 'Infidels' out-takes were on the streets on a bootleg cassette before the official album was released, surely another first. 'Dark Groove' and 'Don't Fly Unless it's Safe' were both (one assumes) warm up instrumentals, perhaps Bob intended to add a lyric later. 'Lord Protect My Child' shows concern for a child by the parent as the child sets out into a wicked world. Bob's worst fear in the song 'Hard Rain' was to bring children into this world, but all will be well seems to be the answer to the anxiety. Improve the environment for our children, yet it is the young children that are creating this awful increase in crime in the more affluent countries. If the parents are not concerned what their children are doing, why should others care about the environment. How many times do we hear a mother on Television answering child crime by saying "there is nothing for them to do around here no facilities". After both World Wars there was nothing for children to do or have but they didn't go around mugging old ladies, robbing houses or stealing cars for a joy ride. We are in a no win situation, until parents are made to pay for their children's criminal activities nothing will improve. Bob realises this in this song, and as Bob had the same trepidation years before he was a father it doesn't bode well for the future. In the song the father is separated from his children and prays for the Lord to oversee and protect them. Bob had also stated that he was on the side of choice when it came to abortion. He told Kurt Loader "Anti abortionists never volunteer to look after the child they try to save. That problem is left to the woman who can't afford to support the child and could be prevented from the problem by the termination of the unborn child".

'Angel Flying Too Close to the Ground': This was a hit for Willie Nelson and was used as the B-side of Bob's single 'Death is Not the End'. It is superb, Bob has made the definitive recording of the song, try to hear it. In retrospect most of the women in Bob's songs are 'angels', why doesn't he sing about the type of woman that he is really attracted to, beautiful women, mostly with ample breasts? When he is not singing of angels he uses 'Angelina' as a name and of course 'evangelist' has an angel lurking within; even the infamous 'Geraldine' is an 'angel-ride' anagram, I could go on but I won't. Johnny Depp writing in The Rolling Stone Magazine of his love of the Beat Generation writers, especially Kerouac and Ginsberg, concluded his quite articulate and eloquent article by referring to the Beats interestingly as follows..'so in the end, what can anyone, scholar, professor, student or biographer really say about these angels and devils who once walked among us, though maybe just a bit higher off the ground?' In the article Depp also feels that without Kerouac, Ginsberg and Burroughs we would never have got Hunter S.Thompson or Bob Dylan. An interesting yet debateable premise. 'Foot of Pride' has great vocal, there is a difficulty to locate just what is going on in this song, a 'you get what you deserve' song? Biblical allusions, perils of vanity, false prophets who extract money from the weak and gullible. Money from sin without any of the consequences. Watch out when the foot of pride comes down just like the opening credits of Monty Python's Flying Circus. A play on the joke where God stamps down his foot. Babylon, the apocalypse will sort them all out. Satan is present in so many people, it has to be recognised, but how? 'Julius and Ethel' concerns the Rosenberg's who were executed for selling secrets to the USSR. They were accused of selling the details of how to create the atomic bomb. Whether this is true or not the Rosenbergs were executed at the time when the USA was searching out communists and making their lives intolerable, political cleansing as it would be called now. I would like to hear a Red Indian's opinion on ethnic cleansing too. The song feels out of place on this collection which was probably the reason for not including it on 'Infidels', but it would have complemented Bob's early albums as this is a veiled protest song. One wonders what made Bob return to the theme of The Rosenbergs. They were also mentioned in 'Gold Turkey' the album by National Lampoon in 1975. **'Blind Willie McTell'** this was remaindered in favour of 'Union Sundown' which beggars belief. This is a masterpiece that Bob didn't think he recorded properly. It continues the theme of 'Foot of Pride' the state of the corruption. It is so good that any bluesman would be astounded, but it was remaindered. The tune is 'St James Infirmary Blues' and St James Hotel is mentioned within the lyric. There were two versions one acoustic one with a band, both are wonderful, if Bob thought that it never achieved the ambition that he had for the song, then someone should have told him, did Mark Knopfler not think this to be a great track? **'This Is (was) My Love'** (Jim Harbert) is better known for the version by Frank Sinatra in 1967 taken from his 'The World We Knew' album, that album included his duet with daughter Nancy on 'Something Stupid'. It was unusual to hear Bob singing a Sinatra song, apparently there are versions by Bob of the Porter Wagoner and Tom Jones hit 'Green Green Grass of Home' and Mark Knopfler's 'Sultans of Swing' in the vaults at Columbia.

'Tell Me' is the way to start a conversation at the commencement of a relationship with a new person. confess one's feelings, superb rhythm from Sly and Robbie, one out-take has arguably Bob's best ever vocal performance, his voice sounding similar to that of David Bowie. In the song she is looking at him and thinking of someone else, how to achieve this extra sensory perception is not explained. Some gentle Knopfler dobro supported by Mick Taylor and of course the sublime Sly and Robbie.

'Someone's Gotta Hold of My Heart' from the 'Infidels' sessions was later re-written and re-recorded as 'Tight Connection To My Heart' and used to open the 'Empire Burlesque' album. The original version is almost as good as the later song, Sly and Robbie are as flawlessly synchronised as ever, and it contains some of the best controlled drumming Sly Dunbar has ever put on record. 'Death is Not The End' is very similar to Leonard Cohen's 'Suzanne' and would later appeared on 'Down in the Groove'

'Infidels' was another popular album, it reached No 9 in the UK but only No 20 in the USA but went Gold in the USA anyway. It is an album that has improved with age. In an interview Mark Knopfler was asked the question concerning track selection. He may have got Bob off the hook by his response when he said that he felt throughout the recording that Bob was under some form of pressure. Mark thought that Bob had a deadline to meet with the album and the track selection suffered accordingly. It must be said that Bob presented enough tracks for two albums, including the instrumentals, so possibly the album might have been completed sooner. Bob might have been suffering from the separation from his children, the problems coupled with the melancholy had heralded the return of his spontaneous lyricism. He was artistically enhanced at the time but personally intensely desolate.

Bob was now a divorced father of five, he had houses in California, a farm in Minnesota, a house in the Caribbean and a yacht estimated at the time to be valued at $250,000. It was also reported that he had lost (or sold) the publishing rights of all his pre-1974 recordings. Bob agreed to appear on The David Letterman Show on 22nd March 1984. He was accompanied by Tito Larriva (guitar), Barry McBride (bass) and Charlie Quintana (drums) the members of the group 'Plugz', some reports stated that the band was in fact The Cruzados, they had just changed their name. Bob played harmonica on a track called 'Rising Son' on The Cruzados first album, on Arista Records. The David Letterman performance was one of the most appealing for many years. Bob had rehearsed two songs with Plugz but decided to play three, putting them on the spot in more ways than one. 'Licensed to Kill', 'Jokerman' and Sonny Boy Williamson's 'Don't Start Me Talking' were the tracks played. If Bob put Plugz in an unenviable situation The Lord was watching to redress the balance. During 'Jokerman' Bob suddenly found that he had the wrong harmonica. He started searching around for the correct one whilst the amused band members kept playing the same section over and over until he was ready, they arrived at the second chorus before Bob was ready. The audience was in hysterics and Bob enjoyed it too, David Letterman was so pleased he asked if they could play again the following week, they didn't. It is bizarre how The Letterman Show creates these little gems of performances. I remember Van Morrison and Sinead O'Connor singing a duet, they danced away from each other and when they came back to the microphone they bumped into each other. On the Letterman Show various artists album the collision can be clearly heard.

Another live album was released in December 1984, titled 'REAL LIVE' taken from European tour shows in London, Dublin and Newcastle. It wasn't well received by the public and only reached No 54 in the UK and as low as No 115 in the USA. Bob was continuing to play his old songs but it was obvious that he was becoming tired of the continuous repetition night after night of the same songs. Even though he juggled the sequence and changed the songs from show to show it was becoming ever tiresome.

The band on 'Real Live' included Mick Taylor and Ian McLagen from The Faces, Greg Sutton and Colin Allen providing the Sly and Robbie rhythm. Both Greg Sutton and Ian McLagan had their names spelled wrongly on the cover. If Mick Taylor was subdued on 'Infidels' then he made up for it on 'Real Live' with plenty of solos, as did Carlos Santana. Bob had to take more control to stop the excessive soloing. When the European tour had reached Ireland, Bono and Van Morrison were two of the artists to appear on stage with Bob. The 'Real Live' album was a reasonable album and was worth owning for the rare performance on disc of 'Tombstone Blues' and probably the definitive Dylan performance of 'Tangled Up in Blue'. For the incidentalists 'Real Live' was the first Bob Dylan album to carry a computer bar code.

In January 1985 Bob joined other top stars to record in Los Angeles. The charity album **'We Are the World'** (USA for Africa) was recorded. The single which included (amongst others), Michael Jackson and Lionel Richie (they wrote the song), plus Ray Charles, Bruce Springsteen, Paul Simon, Hall and Oates, Stevie Wonder, Billy Joel, Bette Midler, Dionne Warwick, Kim Carnes, Harry Belafonte and of course Bob. The stars had just a few seconds at the microphone in which they had to make their instantly recognised vocal sound. The single sold 7 million world-wide and the album did excellent business. Tracks on the album came from Steve Perry, Pointer Sisters, Bruce Springsteen, Prince, Chicago, Tina Turner and Huey Lewis. 'Tears are Not Enough' was another track on the album created by The Canadian Allstars which included amongst others, Neil Young, Sylvia Tyson, Oscar Peterson, Joni Mitchell, Gordon Lightfoot, Dan Hill, Ronnie Hawkins, Burton Cummings and Bruce Cockburn.

'EMPIRE BURLESQUE' was released in June 1985. The musicians Benmont Tench and Mike Campbell came from Tom Petty's band, The Heartbreakers. Bob didn't use the same musicians for each song but Sly and Robbie remained on a couple of songs. George Baker was employed to re-mix the album and seemed to have purchased a new reverb machine as the album was full of it. The album was the first by Bob to include the lyrics printed on the sleeve. I was reliably informed that Bob had inserted into the lyrics at least eight lines from Humphrey Bogart films. Key Largo, The Maltese Falcon, The Big Sleep were all used, but surely lines from Bob's songs could be extracted from many films. On the other hand Bob might just be playing another of his games with us. If the latter is true then it really must have been a person with a brilliant film brain that located them. All you have to do dear reader is find them, here is one, "I'll have some rotten nights, but that will pass", The Maltese Falcon, now its your turn.

'Tight Connection To My Heart' is an infectious call and response song subtitled 'Has Anyone Seen My Love? The song name checks the film (and Gene Pitney song) 'Town Without Pity', 'Madame Butterfly' and Hoagy Carmichael's 'Memphis in June'. Mick Taylor, Sly Dunbar and Robbie Shakespeare, Ted Perlman on guitar and Richard Scher on synthesizer formed the group for this track. The video was extraordinary, in one scene Bob is arrested by police and his baggage is searched, then we are in a Japanese red-light district with a couple of ladies of the night entering a club. Bob is then singing at the club as the ladies synchronise their miming to Bob's vocal. A policeman is stabbed by a woman and Bob finds himself in jail, he is bailed out and Bob secures both girls as his own, they then join in with the song. **'Seeing The Real You At last'** is full of indecision. Bob sings of The Storm rather than a storm. The lyric is written like a letter sent to the woman that has caused him all his troubles. All separations are demanding especially divorces. Stubbornness and a demanding woman, the self-pity, the why me attitude is still there just below the surface. If he is offered an olive branch it would be accepted by him. Quite moralising and at times self-congratulatory, but it is a powerful song. When one is in love the faults in the other partner are transparent it is only when love dies that they appear like heated invisible ink. The lyric deserved a better melody.

'I'll Remember You' is a duet between Bob and Madelyn Quebec, she might know the words but not when to sing them, she is probably watching Bob's lips and adding her lines as close to his as possible. It might be Benmont Tench (Tom Petty Band) or Al Kooper on the organ but they are not named on the album notes. There is too much reverb on the drums of Jim Keltner, it makes them sound synthesized, which of course they may well be. Bob's song has the same sentiments as the other song with the same title. That song by Johnny Mercer was taken from the film 'The Fleet's In' and was a hit of Jimmy Dorsey in 1942 and again for Frank Ifield in 1962. **'Clean Cut Kid'**: Remaindered from the Infidels album. Some rock 'n' roll for the sentiments of a nice child going astray. An anti-war song, only the people with the strictest moral standards are allowed to go to war. I believe Keith Moon of The Who drove a Rolls Royce into a swimming pool, but never went to war. I originally thought that much of this song could be attributed to the late Emmett Grogan. In his autobiography he admitted to murder, he went to adult prison when only a youth, a clean cut kid that couldn't adjust to the rat race, perfect description of Grogan. One day someone will explain to me how so many of the American protests singers, clean cut kids, avoided the draft and thus avoided the Vietnam War that they were so aggressively against, surely they can't all have police records making them unsuitable for the military. Elvis Presley did his national service, a list of the stars of stage screen and music that didn't would make interesting reading.

'Never Gonna Be The Same Again' is ruined by excessive technical gimmicks, tubular bells, a celeste probably synthesizer created, it seems to be the rule of 'if we have it in the studio let's use it'. The song simmers from cool to hot then fades out, 'fades to black' as Don Fagen sang in 'Haitian Divorce'. There are similarities to Dusty Springfield's 'You Don't Have to

Say You Love Me', from 1966. 'Trust Yourself' is repetitive, is it parental advice or interference, if you have a gift or a talent then someone is waiting to exploit it, against your own interests. Alternatively this might be political advice, on copper coinage it states in God we trust, this is a call to look after oneself, then you can't blame anybody else if it goes wrong. The song can scarcely include heretic advice especially from the evangelistic mind of Bob Dylan. Samuel Butler wrote 'To put one's trust in God is only a longer way of saying that one will chance it'. 'Emotionally Yours' was written for Elizabeth Taylor. Bob and Michael Jackson sang a duet at her 55th birthday party. The song is excellent, the synthesized strings are a nuisance but one can forget them when watching the video. In the film Bob is playing acoustic guitar whilst a shop-window model spins slowly on a turntable. She comes to life but eventually returns to the turntable making it all a dream. Hardly revolutionary (pun intended) but very enjoyable. You only receive love and understanding if first you give it, 'what you sow so shall ye reap'. A simple melody and Bob stretches the title over six notes, and sounds particularly uncomfortable so doing. 'When the Night Comes Falling From the Sky': A searing epic of a song, the Bootleg Series version includes Little Steven Van Zandt and Roy Bittan from Springsteen's E-Street Band. The out-take is full of enthusiasm, which is lost on the officially released version. Arthur Baker had remixed the track and modernised it, one wonders why? The video seems to be a continuation from the previous track. The video was titled 'When the Night 'is' falling from the Sky'. Pay your dues, face up to reality before it is all too late, fire and brimstone, armageddon, apocalypse, watch out! Five well constructed verses, she will find him the wastelands of her mind, he sent her his feelings, it all sounds like unrequited love so it comes as a surprise to learn that he is seeking his freedom, from the world which 'you' deny.

'Something's Burning, Baby' this is Bob's 'smoke gets in your hair'. Once more Bob has hidden other song titles within the text. 'Somethings Burning'(Kenny Rogers), 'What in the Worlds Come Over You'(Jack Scott), 'Answer Me'(Nat Cole), 'Midnight Train'(Gladys Knight), 'What's Going On'(Marvin Gaye), 'Roll Away the Stone'(Mott The Hoople), 'Don't (Not) Fade Away'(The Crickets), perhaps the bloodhounds of London are a modifications of Warren Zevon's classic 'Werewolves of London'. In Bob's lyric something may be burning but it all seems like the relationship is cooling down. Bob mentions Jack Kerouac's 'Mexico City Blues' and possibly alludes to Neal Cassady's crazy driving. Two synthesizers are chiming in the back ground, Don Heffington's drums sound like tin boxes, Robbie is hard to hear over the bass drum. There was a much better out-take remaindered. 'Dark Eyes' is played as a solo acoustic song. Bob now has compositions titled 'Dark Heat', 'Dark Groove' and now 'Dark Eyes'. There are a pair of dark eyes on the rear of the sleeve, taken at the time of one of the party pictures in the 'Biograph booklet. However these eyes in the song could be the prying eyes of the paparazzi and critics. Bob is composing to the best of his abilities but he cannot hope to achieve the aspirations of the listeners. The tune is hymnal with suggestions from Isaac Watts', 'When I Survey the Wondrous Cross' and William Whiting's 'Eternal Father, Strong to Save'.

There were some remaindered tracks. **'Go Away Little Boy'** is an up-tempo rocker with Benmont Tench in good form. You'll never miss what you never had are the sentiments of the song. The song created from the female point of view, we hope. Bob returns to his early vocal style where he sings the last word sharp. The song is incomplete and stops dead. **'Who Loves You More?'** is probably a homage to the style of Fats Domino. She is the answer to his prayer in this slow rock song of unrequited love. It builds from a quiet start to a loud climax. **'Waiting to Get Beat'** the moral is that it is better left on the shelf. The title infers that a man is waiting to be assaulted on the corner of the street. A reggae song which sounds as though it had been given the George Baker treatment, but without any good points. Phasing and mixed staccato electronics intrude, it is mercifully short. **'The Very Thought Of You'** was a surprise I was expecting Bob's version of Ray Noble's classic British song, but it another reggae song. An infectious but lightweight song, possibly could have been put to good use as a single's b-side. The song is so simple that the listener can hum along before it is finished. **'Straight 'As' in Love'** a studio warm-up, sounds like a created in the studio filler song. The band tune up before Bob sings a sexist song of a girl who has very little brain but never mind she can make crazy love, which is enough. To be fair the band creating a wall-of-sound riff play very well and are together and tight when Bob suddenly changes the pace. **'Drifting Too Far From Shore'** was recorded originally without Bob's vocal which was added for the next album and of course, the superb **'Danville Dame'** (or 'New Danville Girl' on the out-takes cassette) of which more of later.

'Empire Burlesque' did better in the market place than 'Real Live' in the UK it reached No 11 in the USA No 33. Bob did the rounds of interviews and MTV shows in an effort to promote the album. As usual the critics expected more than they actually got, the fans were reasonably happy with the new album. It did seem to these ears that the best tracks were included on the album with the exception of the E-Street version of 'Night Comes Falling Down'. A Bob Dylan painting is included in the CD booklet, he doesn't credit it as by himself. There is a dark eyed woman on the rear of the cover. She is a mystery, apparently Bob can't remember who she is. What we do know is that the photograph was taken at a party that seems to be on a yacht or on a balcony. A photograph which shows Bob with three men and three women was included in the Biograph booklet. The dark eyed girl on the rear of the cover is actually sitting on Bob's knee in that picture.

Bob then went on television in front of the largest Worldwide audience ever at Live Aid. He was accompanied by Ron Wood and Keith Richards from the Rolling Stones. It was alleged that Keith and Bob had 'words' before they went on and were both in an adolescent sulk. Bob was introduced by Jack Nicholson another of America's great short actors, (why are they all so tiny), as America's great voice of freedom. What resulted was one of the most embarrassing performances in rock. The trio didn't have time for a sound check, they started playing 'When The Ship Comes In' and Bob couldn't hear himself through the monitors. What he could hear was the USA for Africa brigade rehearsing 'We Are the World' and thus he went out of tune, if he was ever in tune in the first place. It would have been more professional to have stopped and asked for the monitors to be turned on. Bob carried on regardless in good music hall trouper style, whilst the world watched and cringed in acute mortification. Bob must have been aware that he was singing for Africa yet he mumbled on about the problems of the American farmers, Farm Aid was to come later. Although Bob Geldorf agreed that Bob was terrible in Live Aid it really was only Freddie Mercury and Queen that gave a great performance.

For Farm Aid, Bob was concerned that he would make an idiot of himself again so this time and after a call from Tom Petty he agreed to sing with them. Willie Nelson inaugurated Farm Aid which was held at The University of Illinois, Champaign, Illinois. Bob was not finished assisting charitable causes when he joined 49 other artists for Artists Against Apartheid, they sang 'Sun City' which reached No 38 in the USA and No 21 in the UK.

In January 1986 Columbia Records released **'BIOGRAPH'**, a five album boxed set which included 53 songs compiled by Jeff Rosen (Special Rider Music) from Bob's out-put between 1962 and 1981 but only 18 un-released tracks, which seemed a very low percentage. Although it was a high priced collection it still made No 33 in the charts in the USA. In this book I have discussed those 'out-takes' in the time period that they were recorded. The accompanying booklet included a photograph of Bob's parents taken in 1939, Abraham looks just like Bob.

In the sleeve notes written by Cameron Crowe, Bob told him that at the time of 'Infidels' he was writing a book titled 'Ho Chi Minh in Harlem' and wanted to write a book of people he knew, in the way Jack Kerouac had done; Kerouac gave them all new names that the readers had to work out for themselves. Bob also wanted to record a concept album in the manner of Willie Nelson's 'Red Headed Stranger', or even a children's album and an album of standard songs. In fact the discussion with Biograph was one of Bob's most revealing interviews; all that was needed was better information concerning the many photographs. The box cover and design was by Nick Eagan, it uses a Daniel Kramer photograph overlaid over two others of Bob.

On January 20th Bob was back in charitable action when he appeared at the concert to celebrate the first Martin Luther King Day; it was organized by Stevie Wonder. In February, Bob was back on tour in Japan and Australia this time backed by Tom Petty and The Heartbreakers. Bob continued to sing other composer's songs, he was always trying to liven things up on stage by catching the Heartbreakers off guard, however they proved they could match him through any key, rhythm or song change. It was Bob's method of avoiding the boredom of repetition, it worked he appeared to be enjoying himself immensely. He also started introducing the songs, before 'In The Garden' he would say "This is about my hero Jesus, why not make him yours too". He also regularly said "I don't ask for your pity, I ask for your understanding". A strange remark, I doubt if anyone in the audience ever pitied him, as for understanding, he says the songs are not biographic so what would we have to understand? Bob was now unconsciously creating more ambivalence, it is almost an admittance that the songs he wrote were intimate tales from his life, a belated confirmation in a few words.

Bob and Sam Shepard wrote a lyric and song together and titled it 'Danville Girl'. The poem was another painting with words scenario suitable for a short film or promotional video. It was shelved at the time and changed to 'Brownsville Girl' for inclusion in the next album, which was to be called **'KNOCKED OUT LOADED'**. The album was produced (except for one track) by Sundog Productions. It was released in August 1986. Tom Petty and The Heartbreakers, Al Kooper, Ronnie Wood, Dave Stewart and T-Bone Burnett appeared on the album. Al Kooper never a shrinking violet said that there were superb versions of these songs just remaindered, some were not even given the benefit of consideration for the album. The words 'knocked out loaded' were taken from Dr John's version of 'Junko Partner'.

The sleeve was a segment from a Charles Sappington painting. A girl is ready to smash a terra-cotta pot on the head of a Mexican bandit who is strangling her man, a duel in the sun. The Mexican is turning his head in awareness so the next scene should show the pot missing him. The sleeve also listed thanks to a hundred or more people, restaurants, musicians, and of course females.

'You Wanna Ramble'(H.Parker Jr): A blues by Little Junior Parker with additional Bob Dylan lyrics. Bob's version has the early archive rock recording sound. I have always thought that 'Raunchy' the Ernie Freeman 1950s hit was based on Parker's riff. The line for $1500 you can have anybody killed is enough to put the fear into anyone that wants to ramble all the time. **'They Killed Him'**(Kristofferson): Bob added a children's choir to this gospel song and one wonders why? Mahatma Ghandi, Martin Luther King and of course Jesus, all martyrs to the cause. Sundog Productions are the guilty producers, the drums are too loud the children's choir superfluous. Kris

Kristofferson had 'Abraham, Martin and John' in his mind when he composed the song, that is according to the Columbia promotional sheets at the time. The word 'they' is the important word, who is 'they', they were all killed by different sects for different reasons, they can't be encompassed in one 'they'. The song originally came from Kristofferson's album 'Repossessed'. **'Driftin' Too Far From The Shore'**: Don't dispense with your basic principles? The riff seems to be a close relative to 'When Doves Cry' by Prince. Ron Wood guitar, Benmont Tench piano, John Paris bass and Anton Fig drums on this track; is the money 'sent' in the song the alimony payment? The mention of making love to a servant has a particular relevance to Bob Dylan, but his father's house would be a church. The estranged woman is seen as lucky by the narrator. **'Precious Memories'**: This track was arranged and registered by Bob but there are earlier recordings by Willie Nelson, Roy Acuff, James Cleveland, Jim Reeves and more. A country goes reggae song, the tune is almost a slowed down version of Paul Anka's 'It Doesn't Matter Any More'. Memories of happy occurrences and good people is a precious memory for us all. Bob remembers his parents and his contented childhood. **'Maybe Someday'**: This may have been spliced from a longer recording the voice starts immediately and there is no introduction. It sounds like Al Kooper on organ but no keyboard player is credited. The narrator has been hurt by love, he is trying to tell her what she has given up by leaving him for another man. There were obviously rows, he feels that he should have broken down the bedroom door. The narrator was a gambler who never came home until he had lost all of his money. He sounds like a whining unsentimental moron, he was fortunate that she stayed with him as long as she did.

'Brownsville Girl'(Dylan/Shepard): Sam Shepard won the Pulitzer Prize in 1979 but came to the attention of the music public when he was the partner of Patti Smith. His earlier claim to fame had been as drummer with The Holy Modal Rounders. His relationship with Bob was cultivated when he worked cataloguing the happenings of The Rolling Thunder Revue. His next move was to become a film star. So the original 'New Danville Girl' from 1984 became an eleven minute song. The original out-take from 'Empire Burlesque' is as good if not better that the new recording. Bob has changed a few lines for the new recording and there are differences concerning a car that broke down in verse 15 of the original and the new version has 17 verses against 16. The song was another of Bob's pleasure in the scenes of the wild west and was inspired by Gregory Peck's 1950 film 'The Gunfighter'. There is another consensus of opinion which thinks the film was 'Duel in the Sun' another Gregory Peck classic, this time from 1946. The story is of a half-breed girl that causes trouble between two brothers. The film was Directed by King Vidor, but four other Directors went un-credited, one was David O.Selznick the screen writer of the film. Bob has used the song as an analogy of a man who wanted to give up the profession he was in and settle down to a quiet life. This of course would be easy for Bob in a few years he would be out of the public eye, a gunfighter would be dead if he didn't give up in time. An outstanding track with a melody not dissimilar to Randy Newman's song 'Sail Away'. The first two verses are the film memories the remaining four are the nostalgia of a trip with a special woman to Mexico. As he drives the same journey with another woman his thoughts keep returning to the first trip and the first woman. They call in at a place he had visited before to see Henry Porter and Ruby, she calls her home the land of the living dead. Suddenly he is being shot at. Bob uses a superb line which indicates the state of his poetic mind when he writes 'If there is an original thought out there I sure could use it right now'. Bob's line is similar to that of Ralph Waldo Emerson (1803-1882) who wrote 'It has become practically a sort of rule in literature that a man, having once shown himself capable of original writing is entitled thenceforth to steal from the writings of others at discretion'. To this I would add Robertson Davies' (1913-1995) remark 'The most original thing a writer can do is write like himself, it is also the most difficult task'. In the song we are suddenly brought back to reality as it is all a daydream and the narrator is waiting in the queue to see a Gregory Peck film. Gregory Peck was shot in the back. The song is of epic proportions even if the rhyming verse is a little laboured.

'Got My Mind Made Up'(Dylan/Petty): A hybrid Bo Diddley cum Willie and The Hand Jive riff to create an excellent rhythm. The Tom Petty Band are the accompaniment. Going to see a friend that has been living in Libya for three years. The narrator has made his mind-up that he is going abroad and nothing can dissuade him. 'Under Your Spell'(Dylan/Sager): Written with Carole Bayer Sager, this song also mentions the album title, nice love song with a tune from another song. In fact the song line is 'Knocked out and loaded'. Recorded with Dave Stewart at the Eurythmics' 'The Church' studio in London, ex-Blondie band member Clem Burke is on drums. The song of an errant woman although the lyric is so sparse and ordinary that it just seems to be a man and his thoughts of the woman. He was under her spell at the start. She will never get rid of him, he is out of his head, a lyric so thin and tiresome it should have been remaindered.

A disappointing album, hardly a song to remember. So with the embarrassment of the Live Aid performance, this album only managed to get to No 35 in the UK, it died a death completely in the USA. The album had shunned the technical gimmicks that had spoiled 'Empire Burlesque' and listener was left wishing for some technology to lift the album. Bob must have sunk to an all time professional low when the reviews and fan response to the album was recognised, now he decided to return to films.

'Hearts Of Fire' was a film co-starring Rupert Everett, Fiona Flanagan and Bob Dylan. It was Directed by Richard Marquand who had achieved some success with 'Jagged Edge' and 'Return of The Jedi'. Bob's part was to be a singer songwriter who had lost his charisma and the ability to write good songs as he slides down the celebrity list towards ignominy. The film was made in London at the end of 1986 but was not premiered until October 1987. The album of songs from the film preceded being available in September 1987. During the period that the film was in the editing stage Bob toured the USA with The Grateful Dead, they accompanied Bob and then played a set twice as long on their own. In October 1987 Bob commenced his European Tour in Israel (not part of Europe) accompanied by Tom Petty and The Heartbreakers. At the final show in Wembley old friends Roger McGuinn and George Harrison joined Bob on stage. The 'Hearts of Fire' film was premiered in London some months after the original USA showing. The reviews had been terrible, the fans anticipated the worst which probably made them feel the film was a little better than expected. How many times do we see films that are lauded throughout the newspapers and we when we get to see them we sit wondering what all the fuss was about. The album cover had Fiona in the spotlight and the faces of Bob and Rupert at the bottom just above their name credits. Richie Havens who also appeared in the film was not given much credit for his performance.

Bob played the part of Billy Parker, a rock musician, his music had inspired more than one generation, but now he was on the downward spiral. He was still popular but only on the strength of his previous material, ironically Bob arrives in the first scene on a motor-cycle. There was sadness as Director Richard Marquand died of an heart attack, at the age of 50, before the film was premiered. The soundtrack recording was released and sounded like a 'quick-fix' recording, very poor. The album included Rupert Everett's version of 'Tainted Love' and Fiona's 'Let The Good Times Roll'. She makes a decent effort at the Shirley & Lee classic, but of course the album was purchased for Bob's songs. One song 'Had A Dream About You Baby' was also to be included on Bob's forthcoming solo album. 'Night After Night' by Bob was quite ordinary, but his version of John Hiatt's 'The Usual' is the best thing in the film. Bob also sang 'Couple More Years' which was a Dr Hook song composed by the late Shel Silverstein and Dennis Locorriere.

The film was awful, available on official video in a matter of months. The screen play was written by one of the greatest ever screen-writers in Joe Eszterhas and the incidental music (there isn't much) was by John Barry. Even Joe and John had an off day, one review stated 'a tedious expose of the world of rock music-lacking in excitement, a sad end to the career of Richard Marquand who died soon after finishing it'. The synopsis in Halliwell's guide states 'A female rock star succeeds with the aid of a reclusive star and a weary British rocker'. The film was different to the novel by Larry Milne, and perhaps it was Eszterhas that changed the character of Billy Parker. He was supposed to be the Nickel and Dime bandit in disguise, the Billy Joe Shaver song 'Five and Dimer' was considered for the film but it wasn't used. The bandit was a robber on a motor cycle in disguise and the clues in the film were supposed to lead us to Parker. At some time this was all changed, or perhaps that sub plot was left on the cutting room floor, if that is the truth then we should see the director's cut, it can't make the film any worse

Bob said that he did the film because of the large fee he was offered. He may have read the script as a continuation to one of his favourite films, Elia Kazan's, 'A Face in The Crowd'. Bob told Robert Shelton how much he enjoyed that film, originally shown in 1957 based on the book 'Your Arkansas Traveller' by Budd Schulberg. This film was of a small town yokel that becomes a fast talking philosopher through a show business television appearance. Billy Parker in 'Hearts of Fire' was a has been with a considerable loyal fan base, Bob may have considered this film to be his notion of appearing in that similar film. Both films had little sophistication in their style, there is no implication it is all spelled out elaborately for the viewer. Bob did learn one thing from the film when Producer Iain Smith introduced him to Springbank Scotch Whisky. Bob enjoyed the drink so much he imported it to the USA and he eventually became an Honorary Member of The Scotch Malt Whisky Society.

So Bob had now released a poor album followed by a much worse film and soundtrack, yet his fans were as loyal as ever. We were already aware that Bob could not tell good songs from bad, what was it that made him think that this film was anything but appalling, doesn't he trust anybody's advice any more, or are they too sycophantic to dare to go against his opinion. At the time of 'Hearts of Fire' Bob was also in a BBC documentary titled 'Getting to Dylan', it was shown in the 'Omnibus' programme. In that programme Bob was interviewed as he sketched with his felt tip pen, a portrait of the interviewer. It was in this programme that I noticed something that I had never realised, Bob draws with his right hand but signs his 'Bob Dylan' autographs left-handed. As he continues to sketch the limitations of the interviewer are exposed, weak and uninspired questions which Bob handles very easily. On the trailer wall behind Bob is a picture of Elizabeth Taylor torn out of a daily paper. To one question asking him why he stopped to sign autographs at a particular session Bob answered "Sometimes it is easier to be polite than it is to be rude". He says you have to trust yourself, that song is then added over the interview. Bob also said of the fans, and presumably the critics, "They don't know me and I don't know them".

Bob joined U2 on 'Rattle and Hum' and his live performances with Tom Petty were continuing to sell out everywhere. It must be said that I have met some Dylan fans who saw every show in Britain and then travelled to Europe so Bob might have been singing to almost the same audience every night.

'DOWN IN THE GROOVE' which was released in June 1988 was simultaneous with Bob suffering from writer's block. The album was intended to be nearly all cover versions, another 'Self Portrait', this album lasted just 30 minutes. The cover photograph by Peter J.Carni is quite beautiful, Bob in the spotlight alone and acoustic. The delay of the album's release was again blamed on the cover art (it always is blamed, and not only for Bob's albums), there exists a discarded cover with a desert road leading through some palm trees, a wit noted that the album title might have been 'Down in the Grove'. As it was the 'groove' it has sexual connotations in which we will not delve too deeply; the delve pun is intended.

'Lets Stick Together' (Harrison): A Wilbert Harrison song although it has often been attributed to Memphis Slim. Harrison had an International No 1 hit with his 'Kansas City' in 1959, his 'Let's Work Together' only reached No 32 in 1970 in the USA with Canned Heat reaching No 2 with the song the same year in the UK. Harrison was originally a one man band in the style of Jesse Fuller, he first recorded in 1952. Bob probably chose the song because of the lyrics. They are asking for a married couple to stay together and consider the children, the marriage vows are sacred. A reasonable vocal performance but it does have a very poor harmonica solo. 'When Did You Leave Heaven?'(Bullock/Whiting): The song was written in 1936 for the Daryl F.Zanuck film 'Sing Baby Sing' which starred Alice Faye. A hit for Tony Martin in the USA and for Caroll Gibbons in the UK. The song is for a patronising man to sing to a naive lady. She is an angel how long has she been living outside of heaven. The synthesizer introduction and solo was played by Madelyn Quebec. The singing is so bad that if it was sung as a local saloon bar then the patrons would ask the singer to stop. 'Sally Sue Brown' (Alexander/ Stafford/ Montgomery): Great under-rated Arthur Alexander song taken from his 'Shot of Rhythm and Blues' album. Alexander also wrote 'Anna' which was on the Beatles' first album, and 'You Better Move On' which was recorded by The Rolling Stones. He was best known for his cult single 'Black Night'. 'Sally Sue Brown' is registered to June Alexander who may have been his wife. An unrequited love song, which Bob sings reasonably but what does that backing singer think she is doing, name withheld as protection.

'Death is Not the End' is a track remaindered from Infidels, Sly and Robbie rhythm section once again, the first track on the album written by Bob. The title is the religious slogan that they hope ensures that their converts remain attached. The song starts with lyrics which must have been inspired by first lines of Paul Simon's, 'Bridge Over Troubled Water'. The song also includes 'comfort' and 'a helping hand' which were also part of Simon's song.

It was claimed that this was also influenced by William Blake, Dante and John Bunyan. Dante would assure us that the pain continues unabated after death, Bob is saying that the pain only occurs in this life. Bob's vocal is so lethargic and quiet perhaps he attempting to give the impression that he is close to the 'end'. **'Had a Dream About You Baby'** is like 'I don't care if the sun don't -shine'. This is Bob's 'Lady in Red' she appears in the last verse. Eric Clapton and Ronnie Wood are playing but they really could be anyone on this recording. Beau Hill produced this track and played the keyboards, he was also a guitarist and a member of the group 'Airborne'.

'Ugliest Girl in The World'(Dylan/Hunter): A collaboration with Robert Hunter of The Grateful Dead. One moment Bob is professing love and christian values that next we get this assault on women that suffer ugliness through no fault of their own. They are born with it Bob, only inner ugliness is cultivated. I don't think he made many new female friends with this track. Of course the two composers are a couple of the most attractive men in the world, aren't they? Bob is suddenly mocking the afflicted. On careful listening it sounds as though the backing singers are singing 'He's so ugly' for most of the time, perhaps to redress the balance a little. **'Silvio'** (Dylan/Hunter): Garcia, Mydland and Bob Weir of The Grateful Dead are adding backing vocals, this is Dylan and the Dead. I have never thought that Bob had much influence on these awful lyrics. Some are so excruciatingly poor that one wonders why Bob bothered to play this live. Surely Bob didn't write 'click my finger and require the rain' and 'honest as the next jade rolling that stone'. The tune is the same as (or similar to) Fats Waller's 'Your Feet's Too Big'. **'Ninety Miles and Hour'**(Down a Dead End Street) (Robertson/Blair): This was a Hank Snow song. The composer Don Robertson himself had a hit with 'The Happy Whistler' in 1956. He also wrote more songs for Hank Snow and some for Elvis Presley. This is a song of brake failure on a motor-cycle, which may be Bob's reason for recording the song. The love of travelling at speed it is part of the relationship of the songs protagonists. Willie Green and Bobby King add the backing vocals. Bob dispenses with the tune and sings it as a slow talking song. **'Shenandoah'** (trad arr. Dylan): Bob has created this to be similar to Odetta's version, the backing singers close the song. This pales into insignificance when compared to Van Morrison's orchestrated version. **'Rank Strangers To Me'** (Brumley): Larry Klein is on bass (Joni Mitchell's husband) for this Albert Brumley blues. Recorded by Doc Watson whose version Bob may have heard. When one spends time away from one's friends returning is difficult because they have little in common with you. The town however small will soon forget the itinerant. The song is of only strangers being at his home when the prodigal son returns, they are as much a stranger to him as he is to them. Bob added harmonica to another Albert Brumley song 'Come Back Baby' on Carolyn Hester's album which John Hammond produced in 1961. Once more we received a poor album, surely it could have been topped up with some out-takes. So an album which included such luminaries as Hip Hoppers-Full Force, Eric Clapton, Mark Knopfler, Ronnie Wood, Steve Jones (Sex Pistols), Paul Simonon (Clash), Jerry Garcia, Bob Weir, Brent Mydland, and more culminates in a album that would have been rejected by every label if it had been recorded by a new group. When I listened to the album again for this book it has the charm of 'Self Portrait', I realise now that we were expecting too much from a man in the depths of writer's block. Bob promoted the album with another tour, he performed shows in Birmingham and London in June 1988.

THE ONLY WAY IS UP

I am better than my reputation.
Friedrich von Schiller (1759-1805)

The Grateful Dead shows had been recorded for a live album release scheduled for early 1989. Bob recorded **'Pretty Boy Floyd'** which was added to the various artists tribute album for Leadbelly and Woody Guthrie; titled 'Folkways, A Vision Shared'. Bob decided that it would be an enjoyable interlude to record with some old friends. George 'Nelson' Harrison, Jeff 'Otis' Lynne, Roy 'Lefty' Orbison (named after Lefty Frizzell), Tom 'Charlie T.Jr' Petty and Bob 'Lucky' Dylan formed **The Travelling Wilbury's**. It was alleged that this started when Jeff and George were deciding who they would include in their fantasy groups, they selected one each in turn like selecting two soccer teams. The first group name was 'The Trembling Wilbury's', I am reliably informed that there was steam train called the 'Flying Wilbury', possibly the one shown on the album leaflet of the second album. All of their career's needed some impetus and this was a perfect vehicle for their songs. Back in 1963 Roy Orbison had been offered Bob's song 'Don't Think Twice' which he refused as he had just written 'In Dreams', perhaps he should have recorded both. With Bob's career at its nadir the phrase written by Thomas Lewis (referring to health) 'most things get better by themselves-most things are better by morning', could well apply. Lucky Wilbury didn't look very lucky he wasn't able to raise a smile on either of the albums. This first album was a real back to basics effort, as they were working at Bob's home studio without an engineer, it meant doing their own electrical connections and microphone settings. They had such 'schoolboy' fun they managed to record a tune a day. The enjoyment of the quintet shines though the songs. It went double platinum, only George had done that previously with the Beatles. The cover has potted histories of the protagonists with creased and aged photographs used. They were written by E. Norti-Bitz and Hugh Jampton, two names that have to be spoken out loud for effect, one wonders why Jeff Lynne (the culprit) didn't add Hugh Jarse to the credits. If you don't know what a 'hampton' is then go and ask your grandfather.

    'Handle With Care' was released as a single. They were trying to think of a title for inspiration when George saw this written on the side of a cardboard box in Bob's garage. Nelson actually sings 'Handle me with care', the bridge of the song is sung by Lefty. **'Dirty World'** was intended to sound like a formerly known as Prince song, the consensus of opinion was that it didn't. It is slightly similar to Cliff Richard's, 'Please Don't Tease', and finished with 'Buttons and Bows', remember east is east and west is west. On **'Rattled'** the drumming is a drum stick tapping on the kitchen fridge. This is superb rocker in a pastiche of the old styles, Jerry Lee Lewis might have sung it as his follow-up to 'Breathless'. It is probably Nelson playing in the guitar style that James Burton used on Elvis' records. **'Last Night'** is an innocuous riff pop song concerning what went on last night. Jim Horn has over-dubbed saxophones to the track. **'Not Alone Any More'** is this a confirmation of Bob's feelings in 'To Be Alone With You'? This (and the former song) were written for Roy Orbison's voice. Lefty is not on top form here although he does sound effortless. Rain, heartache and pain, are all constituents of the song, as one would expect from Roy. **'Congratulations'**: 90% composed by Bob, it has some comical things in the song. She has left him so he gives his congratulations, in a hope you are satisfied manner. Lucky is after one more chance. **'Heading for The Light'**: Sounds like an E.L.O. song. Otis sings of 'the light' but is nothing to do with religion. He is in a hole with his problems and trying to get out, his dreams are coming true, and there is nothing in his way. Jim Horn plays the track out on saxophone. **'Margarita'**: A synthesized sound which is not credited on the sleeve opens the track. Lucky sings what sounds like in studio filler as they move from one riff to another, arriving at the Willie and the Hand Jive beat. **'Tweeter and The Monkey Man'**: The highlight of the album with a lyric that mentions Bruce Springsteen song titles, Thunder Road and Mansion on the Hill which is also by Hank Williams. The others were in awe of Bob as they observed how he wrote this from start to finish in double quick time. The two protagonists in the song were drug dealers. A great song from Lucky (remember that was The Minstrel Boy's name) which should have been retained for a Bob Dylan album. The scene gradually unfolds and would be ideal for a video. There is also an excellent arrangement incorporating a twangy guitar. Tweeter and the Monkey Man are not loveable rogues in the normal Bob Dylan style. **'End of the Line'**, they recorded the video for this the day after Roy Orbison's funeral, they were buoyant by the fact that the day before died they were able to tell Roy the album had gone platinum. A perfect album closer with all the quintet taking their verse.

Although few people were aware of it at the time, Bob had purchased The Orpheum Theatre in Minneapolis, Bob and his brother David sold it in November 1988 for $1.4 million. In December Bob joined Crosby Stills and Nash, Tracy Chapman and The Grateful Dead in an SRO concert at The Oakland Music Festival. In January 1989 more honours were bestowed on Bob when Bruce Springsteen inducted Bob into the Rock 'n' Roll Hall of Fame. Bob joined in the all star finale.

Bob's career needed a lift and **'DYLAN AND THE DEAD'** was released in February 1989 in a superb Rick Griffin designed cover. Rick was famous for his Grateful Dead posters and for The Fillmore Auditorium posters. He was recognised as a good surfer but his art was the recognisable blueprint for the psychedelic era, totally original and beautiful. Sadly Rick Griffin died in 1991, at the age of 47 in a motor cycle accident. Although both sets of fans would want the album it didn't do very well in the charts, No 38 in the UK and No 37 in the USA. The problem was that it was again another very poor album. The critics and fans alike were dismayed that the tracks released were considered to be the best from their double-headline tour. The cover promised so much with its old steam engine thrusting out between a skeleton playing harmonica and a painting of Bob Dylan.

Seven tracks are average but two are dreadful as were the reviews, understandably. In fact Bob Weir was making puzzling statements before the album was released making sure that the punters realised that it was a Bob Dylan album not a Grateful Dead record. Weir said "I would be loathe to figure what is going on in Bob's head, the guy is a mystery to me from top to bottom, I would have used some better cuts for that album, but nope'. Mickey Hart added that they were backing Bob but none of them knew the songs. Can that be true, apart from 'Joey' most people could have sung along, perhaps The Dead never listened to Bob's records. As the picture with the CD booklet shows The Dead sitting enjoying a joke with Bob one wonders why Bob Weir never asked the question he posed later. Surely Bob would have listened to them if they had suggested changes, it would have been 6-onto-1, but it seems that they never asked. The album was later designated as 'released for historic value'. The Grateful Dead recorded most of their shows anyway, so recording Bob's shows with them was instinctive. When the tapes were mixed it was always intended to be a Bob Dylan album, although it was mooted that perhaps it should be released on The Dead's Relix Records Label. A bootleg titled 'Dead's Choice' was available which most people agree is a great improvement on the album that was ultimately released.

'Slow Train': is the best on show, they sound well rehearsed and Bob is on top form, he does forget some of the words and does his usual mumble at times. **'I Want You'**: Jerry Garcia plays a decent guitar solo as Bob decides to dispense with the later vocals and concentrate on onomatopoeia until the chorus arrives and we get, 'I one chew'. **'Gotta Serve Somebody'**: Must be chronicled as containing one of the worst backing vocals in the whole Dylan canon, were they expecting a different tune. Take the lyric sheet from the original album and follow Bob's vocal here, a good game I assure you. **'Queen Jane Approximately'**: This was to be the first live version of this song on an official release. The audience surprise can be heard. It really is quite a competent performance. Bob dispenses with verse two, changes 'repetition' to a mumble and 'conclusions' in verse four become 'situations'. He also mumbles words in the last verse making the meaning almost totally incomprehensible, then sings it again differently, still a mumble, a sad mess. **'Joey'**: The Dead play excellently on this track. Mickey Hart's drumming and his aptitude for maintaining a constant beat-tempo and Phil Lesh superb bass are highlights on this track, equal to Sly and Robbie at their best. Bob had a long lyric to remember and apart for changing the odd word here and there he performed adequately. I disagree with the critics who thought that this was as low as Bob could get. **'All Along The Watchtower'** is sadly rendered impotent. Not a good choice for The Grateful Dead and their laid back sound. Jerry Garcia does get to play some reasonable solo breaks. Bob sounds so fed up with singing it one wonders why it was chosen. There are long breaks in the track where nothing is happening and we are listening to the rhythm section. **'Knockin' On Heaven's Door'**: Bob insists that we know the title by repeating it ad infinitum, meandering on and on well after our patience has been exhausted, it is really awful.

Bob really needed to make a good album, although his shows were still selling-out his albums were not selling. Daniel Lanois who had produced U2 and Robbie Robertson was a called in to produce the next album, in fact Bono recommended him to Bob. Lanois said that "If Bob was feeling the pressure then he certainly didn't show it, he was oblivious to it, he arrives at the studio works for eight hours and then goes home". He continued by saying "Bob is one of the most concentrated lyricists I have ever seen, and he wrote some great songs this time around". Daniel Lanois played on all but one of the ten tracks on the album recorded in New Orleans.

'OH MERCY' was released in September 1989 to good reviews, it was destined to become his most popular album of the 1980s. It made No 30 in the USA and No 6 in the UK, no mean achievement bearing in mind the lack of success of the previous albums. The cover was graffiti on a brick wall of a couple dancing separately, painted by Romero Trotsky Williams, the cover was designed by Christopher Austopchuk. The painting was a mural on the wall of a chinese restaurant in New York. Williams was paid for his work and it ignited his career as an artist. Bob claimed that these songs were written his old 'stream of consciousness' style, the kind of song one writes in the middle of the night. He was considering another album of cover versions but couldn't find any suitable songs, at least that is what the promotional blurb stated.

'Political World': A video made directed by John Cougar Mellencamp introduces a beautiful woman in a restaurant which is decorated with military uniforms. No one is listening to Bob the vocalist, a few people dance as he plays on regardless. So its a political world, the problem is that Bob just states the obvious in this lyric. He does write that in this world everything is 'hers' and then immediately adds or 'his' to be 'politically correct'. I don't agree that when we are born we are trained to take the easy way out, nor do I agree that peace is unwelcome. The truth is that the listener wonders why Bob has become so ordinary in his lyrics especially after a few albums ago it all looked so promising again. It is my opinion is that when he de-personalises the lyrics they loose their power. When Frank Sinatra was at his peak people listened to him because he was saying to your partner in love the things that you would like to have said. I realise that would be true of anyone singing the songs but with Sinatra it was different we knew he had been there, loved and lost, known poverty, had a career that needed revitalising, he had been to the top and back to the bottom. Bob's didn't sing other writer's ballads very often so his songs needed to come from the heart or they sounded totally emasculated like 'Political World'. An incessant driving beat in 4, not a tune a rap, one wonders if Bob really believes that 'peace is not welcome at all', it is just so difficult to achieve. **'Where Teardrops Fall'**: Bob might have been suffering from a sore throat as he sings like Tom Waits. He adds a sarcastic Country and Western sound to his voice which is in mock sympathy with the music genre. The song is for the healing of the wounds of the heart. The teardrops have been falling and he is going to meet her. Those lonely teardrops, his pillow was never dry, that's what Jackie Wilson said. Daniel Lanois' lap-steel guitar introduces the song and adds a country feel throughout. David Rubin plays 'scrub board', a return to skiffle and the 'washboard' as it is called in the UK. A song titled 'Teardrops Fall' was a minor hit for The Crickets.

'Everything Is Broken': This is a blues containing a list of broken items, promises, rules, words, an adult cautionary nursery rhyme. Another video was created this time by Jesse Dylan now aged 23, my time how time flies. The remarks I made for the first track on the album are as relevant for this track. This was assumed by the critics to be Bob's view of his world at the time, an assumption of which I doubt. **'Ring Them Bells'**: Moderately slow, in 2, in quasi gospel style, that is the advice on the sheet music. This is a return to Bob the evangelist. Ring out the bells, help people that need help, suffer little children come to me. This is Alfred Lord Tennyson revisited. He wrote 'Ring Out, Wild Bells' in the same style as Bob using the title phrase to present different actions and people. Tennyson celebrates the end of a year and rings the bells for mankind, grief, false pride, lust and an Christ. Bob's subjects are different in flowers, innocence, the chosen few and God. Why does Bob select Peter? The Lord said to St Peter 'Get behind me Satan', Peter also cut off a man's ear and Jesus healed it back on, hardly a subject for rejoicing. Can Bob mean anything when he writes that the Bride is running backwards, people often run backwards to escape in dreams. The sacred cow is sacrificed and burnt and appears in The Book of Numbers, Chapter 19, but apart from waiting for the sun to go down before one dips one's finger into the cold ashes, there seems little relevance for Bob to mention it in the lyric. Jesus loved Martha and her sister and her sick brother Lazarus. Jesus went to Lazarus risking being killed by those that wished to stone him, he arrived too late, Lazarus was dead. Jesus brought him back to life, but did he, earlier in John, Chapter 11, Lazarus was only sleeping. Bob returns to his chosen few, his lost sheep, the time when innocence dies. This is a song for the investigators, I hope I have given you food for thought, but who is Saint Catherine? **'Man in The Long Black Coat'**: This is a jazz waltz. The man in the long black coat is the grim reaper. The Bible has no black coats, it is full of sleeveless coats and coats of mail. However in Isaiah the Israelites were putting on their coat of vengeance and their cloaks of zeal. A trip with the Grim Reaper will eventually happen to us all, according to Bob it is what happens next that is important. What we need to bear in mind is that this song might be totally innocuous and the girl has just left Bob and gone off with a man wearing a long black coat, as simple as that. There is a threatening tone which can be heard in Bob's vocal. The guitar which is phased from speaker to speaker only helps check out the stereo system it adds nothing to the song. Written in the studio, there was just one take and this is it, a superb spontaneous song. The extra insect noises were, we assume, not Bob's idea, the first time we have heard the insects since 'Day of the Locusts'.

'Most of the Time': Cyril Neville (from The Neville Brothers) who augments on percussion and Willie Green on drums are exceptional, but they are set a long way back in the mix. The sentiments are that time heals, albeit slowly. Looking on the bright side when things are bad. The song is for a man trying to convince himself that she is forgotten. In the last verse he has come to terms with the situation but loses it again with the last line, most of the time. The video for this song had eight cameras running simultaneously so they could be spliced together. The video is a lip reader's delight as Bob is just about incoherent on the vocal. The track used for the video recording is an alternative take, so completists will need both recordings.

'What Good Am I?': Some heavy soul searching by the narrator in this song, possibly Bob's slowest rhythm. We are all flawed in the eyes of God. This is a catalogue of emotions which opens with gentle thoughts and ends with serious overtones. A christian message for the listener to do the opposite to the narrator. The sentiments are similar to Anthony Newley's 'What Kind of Fool Am I' which is another questioning song of missed chances and delayed realisations. **'Disease of Conceit'**: A song with no melody, that is a contradiction in descriptive terms. One would assume that Bob just went to the studio with the lyrics and hoped that the musicians might find a melody. It opens like 'Lucky Old Sun'. The pretence that conceit is a disease is nonsense, it is a state of mind, an over-rated opinion of oneself. In Bob's case the word 'conceit' might describe our views of his work, he has always maintained they are just songs. It is also the high often exaggerated opinion of one's accomplishments. The narrator has recognised how awful this trait is but does it have such a powerful effect on others as Bob maintains? The persons who come into contact with conceited people either discard the friendship of constantly ridicule the person. Only when the conceited person has power over them, as for example an employer, can the characteristic be deemed hurtful. The sycophantic acolytes that are attracted to pop stars such as Bob will give him illusions of grandeur but apparently he has recognised the problem. **'What is it You Wanted'**: The songbook words include the question mark in the text but not in the title, so it must be a rhetorical question or a statement. A demanding woman or a demanding God? One feels as though Bob is deliberately obfuscating the lyrics so that we would have the job of solving the puzzle. The last line 'are you talking to me' comes straight from the film 'Taxi Driver', the line 'do I have it here in my hand' must have raised a few smiles in the studio. The narrator is very wary of the approach from the woman, does she have an ulterior motive for her kiss in the shadows? I suspect that the people in power who have considerable affluence always ask themselves if new persons joining the clique are honest and sincere. The problem for Bob is that all of the clique that are not family are employees, none would wish to lose their jobs by being too ethical. One wonders why Daniel Lanois mixed the guitars so far back. A lovely song with a catchy repetitive tune, sounds like a relaxed song that J.J.Cale might compose. **'Shooting Star'**: One wonders who it is from the past that the narrator thinks of when he sees his shooting star. I thought the wish never came true if you explained the secret wish. He thinks of her, then wonders if he has become what she wanted. The song segues into an apocalyptic warning but by the end we are reassured that tomorrow will be another day. Sung to an old Scottish folk song melody, on what is a very nice slow song.

The sessions in March and April 1989 produced some quality out-takes. **'Series of Dreams'** appeared with a late over-dubbing session in New York, on The Bootleg Series. The overdubs were preformed by Peter Wood on keyboards and Rick DiFonzo on guitar. A video was created probably to sell the 'Bootleg Series' collection. The video splices together 'a series of pictures' with splashes of colour, it would have suited any selected track, it has no bearing on this particular song, except perhaps the title. There is also a short insert from Bob's first ever promotional film for 'Subterranean Homesick Blues'. The song thinks in a series of dreams. Once again a remaindered track that would have improved an already good album, but was shelved. It was revealed later that Daniel Lanois wanted to include this on the album but Bob refused his request. The song builds in intensity, the images are fleeting and symbolic. A great shuffling beat with Bob in his deeper voice. The four guitars, Dylan, Lanois (12 string), Rick DiFonzo and Mason Ruffner give this song the sound of The Byrds. The synthesized strings are perfect as are Cyril Neville's 'talking' drums. A magical track used to close the wonderful Bootleg Series, I expected the wall-of-sound orchestration to ruin everything and I was never more wrong. Absolutely sublime Bob Dylan.

Once again the studio sessions from March and April 1989 were available on bootleg cassette ages before the album was released. 'God Knows' and 'Born in Time' were remaindered but appeared later on the 'Under The Red Sky' album. 'Dignity' mentions Prince Philip, perhaps Bob realises that 'dignity' can not be photographed, it is abstract. The song was used later on the 'Unplugged' album and in the television show of the same name.

The 'Oh Mercy' album was a welcome improvement on the other albums of the 1980's, the songs were for the most part slow and relaxed. Bob appeared at the 'L'Chai to Life' telethon with Harry Dean Stanton and Bob's son-in-law Peter Himmelman, he was married to Bob's step-daughter Maria. Bob appeared with Peter Himmelman at Chadbad TV in 1989. In 1983 Bob had studied at The Brooklyn Chadbad Lubavitch Centre where they taught Hasidic culture. Hasidim is sect formed by jewish mystics in Poland in 1750. It was a continuation of an anti-Hellenistic movement dating back to the year 2 B.C. In January 1990 Bob was back on tour and in Mid-January opened The St Paulo, Brazil, Rock Festival, with Tears For Fears, Marillion, The Eurythmics and Bon Jovi. Another award was bestowed on Bob in France, 'Commandeur dans l'Orde des Arts et Lettres'. The award was presented by Minister for Culture Jack Lang at a ceremony held at The Palais Royal, Paris. In June 1990 Bob was again on tour in Europe. In Dublin, Bono joined Bob on stage, in Athens, Van Morrison, in Amsterdam, Nina Simone.

Bob's childhood home, 2425 West 7th Street, Hibbing, Minnesota was purchased by Greg and Donna French during August 1990 for $57,000. Bob's problems grew when Ruth Tyrangiel claimed to have lived with Bob Dylan for 20 years and also had contributed to his business decisions and his songwriting. She was asking for damages (or palimony) of $5 million.

As Daniel Lanois had produced the previous album expertly he was asked to do the follow-up. In the interim something happened and the album was eventually produced by Jack Frost (whoever he is) with Don and David Was. 'UNDER THE RED SKY' was released in September 1990 reaching No 38 in the USA and No 13 in the UK. With the expectations high after the improvement of 'Oh Mercy' the disappointment was immense. What we got were haphazard ideas, poor singing and even worse, predictable songs. Sweet Pea Atkinson singer with the 'Was not Was' band assisted on vocals and a host of guest stars were included. George Harrison, David Lindley, Elton John, David Crosby, Al Kooper, Bruce Hornsby, Robben Ford, Stevie Ray Vaughan, Jimmy Vaughan, Paulinho Da Costa, Waddy Wachtel were also playing but they couldn't save the album from ignominy, in fact none of them sounded any different to a group of unknown studio musicians.

The cover of Bob crouching is very similar to the inner photograph on 'Infidels' taken with Jerusalem in the background. This is not the same place nor are the clothes the same. The rear cover has Bob sitting on the stone steps in front of someone's house No 323, Bob is wearing his Nike training boots.

'**Wiggle Wiggle**' the nadir of all titles, and maybe even of all compositions, wiggle like a bowl of soup...what! This song sounds as though it was remaindered from The Wilburys' sessions. It should have been on their album where it would have been received as an amusing interlude. It is a bright shuffle and I thought after the first hearing that it was a new dance, but it isn't. What Bob writes are the most ordinary rhymes of his career and it becomes a collection of unconnected nonsense. The problem for old rockers like me (and Bob) is that I raved about songs like 'Buzz Buzz Buzz' by The Hollywood Flames in my youth, it is that we just didn't expect it of Bob. One of Bob's first ever recordings was of 'Buzz Buzz Buzz', which has lines like 'twiddle-ee-diddle-ee-dee'. '**Under The Red Sky**': The lyric begins as if it was inspired by Tommy Edwards' version of 'The Morning Side of the Mountain'. Bob also uses 'wind blowing high and low' from the Scottish folk song of 'Marie's Wedding'. The 'key to the kingdom' is a Biblical expression from Matthew 16:19 and of course it has been used in music many times, The Moody Blues used it as the title of their last album and both B.B. King and Chris Farlowe have used it as a song title. Bob's song (like the first track) sounds like a song for children, he does collect nursery rhymes within the song. Who is the un-credited accordionist, is it Bob, he does play on another track later in the album? '**Unbelievable**' starts like The Bell Note's 'I've Had It' from 1959. This has a 1940s boogie shuffle beat, great rhythm but little or no perceptible melody. A video was made of this song, Bob is a chauffeur his passenger is a live pig. Then another chauffeur is driving along with Bob as the passenger. Bob's driver chats to a woman at a bar and three men pick a fight with him, he and the woman fight them off, the man and woman drive away. She then leaves the car and entices the man into the long grass for seduction. They are then off to a Motel where he is signed in by a beautiful receptionist. I hope you are you with me so far. The first woman leaves in her convertible with the man's wallet. The receptionist forces her charms on the poor man, he escapes and is given a lift by Bob the chauffeur, who now has the man's wallet and his car keys on his front seat. We then notice the car registration is LSD...all unbelievable isn't it. The women were played by Sally Kirkland and Molly Ringwald, well I did tell you they were lovely. The lyric is an improvement even though the rhyming dictionary has been out again. The bridge of the song concerning the blind man being deceived is excellent, although Bob loses his way in his search for words beginning with 'in' or 'un'. If there is a moral a message then it is lost in Bob's effort to appear eloquent with his long words. It is unbelievable that such a seemingly clever lyric should sound to un-improvised.

'**Born in Time**': Where is David Crosby on this, he is credited as taking part. The lyric is quite clever at the start noting that we dream in black and white. Bob resists the obvious when he writes 'you came, you saw' but he doesn't let her conquer. Bob does insert a Little Richard line with 'reelin' with the feelin'. He is running short of time but she can have what remains. The out-take of this track sounds very similar to Bonnie Tyler's 'It's A Heartache', but that was lost on the official release. '**TV Talkin' Song**': Bob has walked around London and visited speaker's corner in Hyde Park. Bob mentions that people talk there, well almost. There are people standing on soap boxes ranting on and on about politics and religion. The crowd usually just heckle, there is very little intellectual discourse between speaker and audience. Many of the religious fanatics that speak there are just hoping to be heckled so that they can claim that they are attempting to spread the word of God and being denigrated for doing it. Bob heard a man comparing God with the antichrist namely television. The television is the most powerful media, it has its own religious programmes and complete channels. Occasionally small chaotic scenes emanate from disagreements but whenever I have been to speaker's corner there is always a policemen standing nearby. The scene of a 'riot' as described by Bob was probably only created for and on behalf of the television crew who just happened to be there at the time, what a coincidence. The scenario that people will be (or are) controlled by the media is becoming more certain as time progresses. Bob may have seen David Cronenberg's film 'Videodrome', where media controls the psyche. In Bob's song the fights and the people arguing for and against the media are later shown on the media, it all comes full circle. Although the lyric is a description of a real scene Bob has created an excellent ambivalence in the manner of his early recordings.

'**10,000 Men**': Bob's favourite Books from the Bible, he said so in an interview, were Leviticus and Deuteronomy both have 10,000 men put to flight in battle, the Book of Judges Chapter 4 has many groups of ten thousand men. Bob's lyric means nothing, but the 10,000 men do have seven wives each, just when (he) I thought one was enough, these 70,000 wives are all just out of jail. Bob tries to be 'Captain-Howlin-Beefheart-Wolf' at times. The Was Brothers have left the tuning up on the record, perhaps they wanted us to be aware that they had bothered to tune up. The guitar of David Lindley is playing that Elmore James riff in the background the other guitars are by The Vaughan Brothers, Jimmie and Stevie-Ray, it could be anyone as they play so anonymously. '**2 x 2**': More numbers, one would be excused for thinking that this was the story of Noah and his Ark. What Bob has done is taken the tale of the Ten Little Indians and fashioned a collection of unrelated ideas. This could be the mass exodus towards California and the flower power children. At least Bob thinks that many made the journey to heaven's gate rather than hell. They are turning the key in the gate as the song ends. Bob does mention the Ark in one line. The piano is by Elton John, David Crosby is just audible in backing vocals. **'God Knows'**: Bob again mentions that the apocalypse will be by fire next time rather than Noah's flood. Of course if there is a God then he would know and control everything, the million mile walk by candlelight that Bob mentions sounds tiring, the longest distance in miles in the Bible is just seven. The expression 'God Knows' is also natural parlance for 'I don't know' which if used in this song turns all the logic on its head, try it and see what I mean. We need to rise above the darkest hour. According to Horace Greeley (1811-1872) the darkest hour is when 'a man sits down to plan how to get money without earning it'. This is one of the few Bob Dylan tracks where the sound volume actually grows as the song progresses.

'Handy Dandy': Al Kooper plays very well here but it is not 'Like a Rolling Stone'. I was informed that this song was written about Frank Sinatra, I doubt very much if Bob Dylan would write a song like this about Frank, I think the name Nancy would be a coincidence. This is for a man that has everything also has an abundance of girls, if you have wealth then you have to secure it. It is a song for all the super-affluent people who become targets once they are rich and famous. This man also has a fear of criticism even when asked "What are you made of?" If a mobster or playboy wishes to own up to being a 'handy dandy' with an access to guns then sobeit, as it is the lyric could be for any evil rich person, well almost. **'Cat's in the Well'**: Bob wins the band loses, awful apocalyptic children's song. The cat is a metaphor for the World, the Wolf is God. The horse goes bumpety-bump does it Bob, and does he sing "the silence is sticking her deep?" The song re-uses Little Richard's 'Lucille' riff to reasonable effect.

'Shirley Temple' was the remaindered track which we were told to expect on a future album. The track was originally written by Don Was and his wife for Paula Abdul, but she didn't record it. Was (not Was) recorded a demonstration disc which Don played for Bob. Bob changed the lyrics and Was (not Was) recorded it as 'Mr Alice Doesn't Live Here Any More', for their fifth album in 1992; the whole album was shelved. On Bob's album credits Carole Childs is mentioned, she was Bob's lady of the moment. Echo Helstrom, Joan Baez, Sara Lowndes, Clydie King, Carole Childs, Helena Springs, Dana Gillespie, Sally Kirkland are just a few ladies that we knew about, one wonders what songs each lady thinks were written to (or concerning) each of them.

Bob also recorded his version of Elvis Presley and Little Richard's, **'Money Honey'** and Elvis Presley's, **'Anyway You Want Me'**, which Don Was thought were excellent. Carole Childs was producing an Elvis Tribute album, Bob did the tracks as a favour to her. Bob didn't feel the band had really got into the 'groove' for inclusion on the album. That can't be true when one evaluates just what was included on the album. It was true that Bob has his work compared to what he had achieved many years earlier. As most singer songwriters aged they became more intellectual, Van Morrison is a bench mark for that. He was ever searching for his religious truth, he added a couple of tracks to every album to get the critics searching out their inner relevance, it is a game to him. Morrison is one composer who has matched Bob album-for-album and still churns out good stuff, but would anyone expect 'Wiggle Wiggle' from a Doctor of Letters, hardly. Bob has little to prove to his audience (nor has Van Morrison), they want him to succeed, but at this moment of time in 1990 Bob seems to have given up. Perhaps he reached his pinnacle of education years ago, perhaps he spends too much of his time touring so that he won't be lonely. He just wants to be master of his own destiny, but someone has to tell him without the fear of retribution that his work was now at its lowest point ever. Bob (and Van) consider critics fair game for denigration, they don't understand, they try to make themselves appear intellectual, are two remarks often aimed at us. The critics can't always be wrong, many artists pretend they pay no attention to what is said, but they do. They are quite happy to accept the accolades bestowed on them in the name of their industry, they also have to suffer the outrageous slings and arrows. If a graph had been drawn after 'Dylan and The Dead' the downward line would have been at the lowest part, after 'Oh Mercy' it would have moved up but now the red line is drawn down the wall heading towards the skirting board.

After the promotion of the album had subsided Don Was said that it was difficult to create great tracks when the lyrics were only written a couple of minutes before they were sung. At the mixing stage Bob re-wrote many of the lyrics and re-recorded them, Don thought that many were better in the original form.

We did get another Wilburys album cleverly titled **'Travelling Wilburys Volume 3'**, my how we searched for volume 2, no we didn't. The group was now a quartet but all their names had changed. Of course Roy 'Lefty' Orbison had died after making his first ever decent album. He was always a great singles artist but his albums were just the singles and filler tracks until he released the 'Mystery Girl' album. We now had, Muddy (Tom), Boo (Bob), Clayton (Jeff) and Spike (George) Wilbury, ably assisted by Jim Keltner, Ray Cooper, Jim Horn and Gary Moore. The comical sleeve notes were written by Professor Tiny Hampton which again refers to the size of his most important member, and continues from his big brother on the previous album; it is taken from cockney rhyming slang for 'Hampton Wick'. The CD booklet also gave dance instructions concerning the Wilbury Twist, which of course we all tried, perhaps we didn't. In one picture the quartet are playing guitar in the kitchen, on the front cover Boo has his baseball cap turned around, a fashion statement?

'She's My Baby': This includes Gary Moore on the guitar solo. This sounds like The E.L.O. Put it in the oven and it will be good. A good pop rock opener, in the Chuck Berry style. 'Inside Out' has Boo and Muddy on vocals but again sounds like The E.L.O. The grass isn't green the sky isn't blue, twist and shout upside down. The bouncy track has some excellent harmony vocals. 'If You Belong To Me' is a love song, she would be happier with him, just like running scared. Boo on harmonica and vocal. Boo almost starts laughing at the start of verse two, but recovers his composure. A jaunty pop song full of bonhomie. 'The Devil's Been Busy' would have been an ideal moralising track for Bob's 'Shot of Love' period. Muddy sings, Spike is on Sitar. Apparently wicked isn't bad and not knowing is better. '7 Deadly Sins' uses Blue Moon as a basic chord sequence, as the quartet create their own doo wop song. Jim Horn is on dirty saxophone, sounding just like Earl Bostic. The sins are different they are new, such as, goodbye and told me a lie, looked my way and smiled. 'Poor House' is hillbilly-rockabilly. A happy shuffle beat for a sad tale of being put in the poor house. This is a pastiche of Byrds harmonies and any old style country singer. 'Where Were You Last Night?': The question gradually stretches to week and year. The tune of the mid-section break deserved a song of its own. 'Cool Dry Place' is a walking blues. Jeff Lynne sings that he joined The Idle Race in amongst what is an excellent lyric. Everything can go wrong with anything if you don't carefully read the instructions. 'New Blue Moon' is a play on the 'old blue moon', but it is almost unrecognisable. They create another good light pop song. Boo sounding like Dave Cousins of The Strawbs again. Some elegant slide guitar is played by Spike. 'You Took My Breath Away' is a Spike vocal, with Jeff Lynne accompanying in his best John Lennon voice it sounds just like a Beatle song. 'Wilbury Twist' is so catchy it will drive you mad. The dance instructions are available on the insert. The simple tune masks some excellent musicianship, listen to the guitars and the piano riffs. A song guaranteed to make you tap your feet. If it is similar to a previous song then try 'Resurrection Shuffle' from Ashton, Gardner and Dyke.

'Nobody's Child' was also recorded at the time but as the title track of a CD for Mrs Harrison's Romanian Angel Appeal. They all take a turn on the vocal as on all the other charity appeal records that were recorded.

BACK TO THE ROOTS

In my beginnings is my end.
T.S.Eliot (1888-1965)

Bob's 'Never Ending Tour' finished in 1991 when G.E.Smith left the band, Bob said it would end when he left. Bob appeared on Chadbad TV singing 'Sold American' with singer crime writer Kinky Friedman in April 1991. **'THE BOOTLEG SERIES'** was finally released, the fans and critics were amazed at the quality of the remaindered tracks. As detailed earlier some were so brilliant it beggared belief that Bob could have left them off the albums. The album 'Biograph' (it was stated at the time) was not endorsed by Bob, yet he assisted with the booklet details, so he must have taken considerable interest. The cover shows Bob's 1974 Passport, not only is his birthday incorrect he has grown to 5'-11". Jeff Rosen has retained many tracks for a second Bootleg Series, but of course he intended to release cleaned up versions of Bob Dylan Live at The Albert Hall as the second part of the series. The Bootleg Series was originally intended to be a much larger collection, we still await 'Wild Wolf', a definitive version of 'Dink's Song' and 'Bourbon Street' and others from the Infidels Sessions. The Bootleg Series is an essential purchase, Biograph fills gaps, the third Bootleg Series could be even better.

Bill Clinton was elected President of the United States and Bob sang at his inauguration celebration. Sung was hardly the word he had never mumbled so much in a performance in his whole career. I have played the video over so many times, my young children used the performance as a party game cruelly calling it 'spot the word'; of course this was in an effort to prove to me (unsuccessfully) that Bob Dylan was useless as a singer. I had to admit that Bob's hooded appearance at the inauguration is as near as embarrassed as I have ever been with a Bob Dylan performance, except for Live Aid. Michael Stipe read the lines from Woody Guthrie's 'This Land is Your Land' which would have been more pertinent if it had been read by Bob. Bob was also shown on the BBC-2 British television programme Arena. It showed a duet of Bob and Van Morrison sitting on a hill with The Acropolis in the background, Bob doesn't know the words of Van's songs but they managed to look quite professional if more than a little unrehearsed.

After the improvement of 'Oh Mercy', 'Under The Red Sky' had put him back down again. Bob was enjoying his music but not composing, he decided to revert to his early days and record an album of old folk and blues tracks. **'GOOD AS I BEEN TO YOU'** was released in November 1992. His lust for touring was unsatisfied and he just kept on going. The bewilderment of his die-hard fans meant for once the concerts were not full, he was mumbling the songs so the audience had to know the lyrics themselves, any new listener would wonder what on earth he was singing about.

'Good As I Been To You' was solo Bob, just guitar and harmonica. If you think that Bob had stopped playing his little games on us then forget it. The CD booklet had just clouds inside but if one holds the card vertically then in the clouds is the silhouette of Bob's head and harmonica frame. The cover uses a Jimmy Wachtel photograph which shows Bob with the shortest hair length for some considerable time. The album and the following 'World Gone Wrong' owe a considerable debt to the six album set 'Harry Smith's Anthology of American Folk Music' released in 1952 by Folkways Records, many of Bob's tracks are versions of the songs contained therein.

'Frankie and Albert': This was the correct title during the latter part of the 19th Century, it was much later that 'Johnny' interfered. Albert is caught in bed with Alice Bly and shot dead by Frankie who is sent to the gallows. There are literally hundreds of versions of the song nearly all titled Frankie and Johnny by artists such as Elvis Presley, T.Bone Walker, Furry Lewis, Memphis Slim, Louis Armstrong, Lonnie Donegan and Sam Cooke. There are so many songs that portray the betrayal by a woman who fosters a love affair with material gifts. Robert Johnson's 'Kindhearted Blues' is one such blues. For me the definitive version is from Mississippi John Hurt, he called his blues 'Frankie'. **'Jim Jones'** was better known as 'Jim Jones at Botany Bay'. Originating in London it concerned deporting criminals to Australia. Jim Jones was sent to New South Wales for poaching. The new melody was written by Mick Slocum of The Bushwackers for their 'Shearer's Dream' album. Bob thought that it was traditional as it had been recorded by John Kirkpatrick and Martyn Wyndham Read. On the Bushwackers' album it stated 'Traditional arranged by The Bushwackers', which was a mistake, so one can understand Columbia and Bob's bewilderment. Honest as ever Columbia Records paid Mick Slocum his correct royalties. However Bob's 'Chimes of Freedom' sounds very similar and was recorded before the 1977 registration of Mick Slocum's song, could this be argumentative, I doubt it. One thing that is certain, although Jim Jones was being deported he still hadn't learned his lesson he sets out his manifesto for murder in the last verse, the floggers that would flog him for poaching were in his eyes the criminals.

'Blackjack Davey': The 1624 execution of a criminal, another lovable rogue. The song uses the old 'Raggle Taggle Gypsy O' and 'Seven Drunken Night' tune popularised by The Dubliners. This 'Davey' song mentions shoes of spanish leather, now there is a coincidence. Davey elopes with an under aged young lady. The girl was married to another and the husband follows their trail. When he catches up with them he asks her to return but she just says goodbye. This female logic lives on, a woman in love will give up everything and live in a tent for the chance of true love. I have always thought that the lyrics in this song perfectly capture the 18th century romanticism of the books of American writer Eleanor Wylie. She probably influenced Donovan with her book 'Nets to Catch the Wind'. **'Canadee-I-O'**: A song for living in a remote uncompromising place. The definitive version appears on Nic Jones' 'Penguin Eggs' album. A sad song with a happy ending. She is a stowaway on a ship with the assistance of a sailor. She wants to see her true love in Canada. The sailors find the woman dressed as a sailor and threaten to throw her over board. The Captain intervenes and says she can stay in the sailor's clothes. Later she is married to the Captain and is wearing silks and satins and advising others to take a chance, like she did. The girl that disguises herself as a sailor in order to go to sea is an age old theme, Joan Baez sang 'Jackaroe' which is just one example. **'Sitting on Top Of The World'**: Howlin Wolf and Cream recorded songs with this title. The Mississippi Sheiks and The Chatman (aka Bo Carter and often spelled Chatmon) Brothers recorded the version that Bob heard. Bo Carter (real name Armenter Chatmon) wrote 'All Around Man' possibly the most sexually explicit blues ever written. Apparently 'Sitting on Top' was co-composed by Little Walter Jacobs, but Bob's album states 'Traditional'. The narrator seems to be a happy-go-lucky character and presents a phlegmatic attitude concerning the events that surround him. The backing guitar riff is the same as the Grinderswitch instrumental that disc jockey John Peel has used as his theme song for many years. **'Little Maggie'**: A Bill Monroe bluegrass song also recorded by The Watson Family. Bill Monroe had been a long time favourite of Bob but this (I believe) was the first time that he actually recorded a Monroe song. Maggie has a rifle and a pistol, drinks whiskey and wine, a tomboy in the Annie Oakley, Calamity Jane fashion. **'Hard Times'**: A Stephen Foster song, one of his darker ballads written just before he died. The hard times and strife are perfectly described in Charles Dickens' book of the same name, and of course 'Oliver Twist'. The song is actually written from the point of view of someone who is affluent thinking about the poor. The lyric is as pertinent now as when it was conceived.

'Step It Up and Go': This is the best advice possible to an errant lover, if her husband comes home early 'step it up and go'. The same tune was used by Bill Haley for his 'Rock A-Beatin' Boogie' and Bill Virtue for his 'Guitar Boogie Shuffle'. The song is packed with good advice for the man, only the girl named Ball in the song seemed to have any success, she gave a little but took it all. The Memphis Jug Band recorded it as 'Bottle It Up and Go' in 1932. **'Tomorrow Night'**: This melody was used by Tommy Edwards for his song 'Mr Music Man', it also similar to 'Don't Get Around Much Anymore'. Bob's song was written by Sam Coslow and Will Grosz, in it the narrator wonders if this is just a one night stand or if she really means what she said last night. The song was first recorded by Lonnie Johnson and popularised by

Horace Heidt. Elvis Presley sang his version on the 'Mess of the Blues' and 'Elvis for Everyone' albums. **'Arthur McBride'**: Paul Brady was mentioned in the Biograph notes as a singer that Bob listened to regularly he recorded a version of this song, but it was probably Martin Carthy and Dave Swarbrick's version that Bob had heard. This concerns the Irish sailor's press gang of the 19th Century. The song is superb, the two men are approached in friendly convivial conversation to enlist in the army. When they refuse and before they can draw their swords they are knocked unconscious by a shillelagh. **'You're Gonna Quit Me'** is the song that includes the album title in the lyric. Written by Arthur Blake in 1928, also known as Blind Blake. If you leave me then you are dead, what a nice thing to say to your lover. **'Diamond Joe'**: This must have influenced Bob's 'Rosemary and The Jack of Hearts'. Recorded by Tom Rush for his 'Blues Songs and Ballads' and by Jerry Garcia by his 'Almost Acoustic Band'. This is an old cowboy song, Joe is a gambler, I am sure that he was a bounder rather than a 'rounder' which is what Bob sings in verse six. Tom Rush included another gentle version on his 'Got a Mind to Ramble' album released on Folklore in 1963, he also sings 'rounder'. **'Froggie Went A-Courtin''**: The final line is if you want any more you can sing it yourself, which nicely rounds off the album. A Burl Ives hit Registered by George and Gerry Asby. A list of creatures, the mouse, the rat, the moth, the bug, the bee, the flea, the cow, the tic, the snake, the cat, and of course the lily white duck. Burl Ives also sang 'I know an old lady' that swallowed a spider, which also has a list of animals and insects that get eaten be each other.

As usual Bob came in for assorted criticism for the album, it was not as expected. Bob just could not win whatever he tried, it would never achieve the aspirations of others, perhaps the critics should record an album themselves and show Bob what they wanted. For any one that enjoys and excellent solo folk albums then this is as good as they come. A return to the roots of the first album, good lyrics, good tunes, excellent guitaring and singing, what more did they expect?

Bob attended his own **30th ANNIVERSARY CONCERT** with a host of stars with G.E.Smith back as director of music for the night. The album and subsequent video are excellent reminders of Bob as he was and is. Bob was introduced by his friend George Harrison, as Lucky, Zimmy and Bob. He opened his set with 'Song To Woody' which of course was where it all began for us. Bob thought that it was the songs that were important on the night, not the show, this was lucky because most of the performances were pathetic and under-rehearsed, even Roger McGuinn was average. Booker T, Johnny Cash, Eric Clapton, Tommy Makem, Carolyn Hester, George Harrison, Chrissie Hynde, Kris Kristofferson, Roger McGuinn, Pearl Jam, Tracy Chapman, Willie Nelson, Tom Petty, Ron Wood, Neil Young, Johnny Winter and many more played on the night. Eric Clapton made 'Don't Think Twice' into a superb blues. Although The Concert was made available on double CD, or treble album the best buy was the video. The video cruelly included Sinead O'Connor. For some reason known only to himself Kristofferson introduced her as 'brave'. The audience would not allow her to sing, they booed and howled until she petulantly threw off her ear phones and shouted human rights and anti-racists slogans, 'everywhere is war' she shouted. She finally left the stage falling tearfully into Kristofferson's arms as he helped her from the stage. She emerged for the finale. If anyone made any apologies or mentions of the fiasco, none were shown on the video of the event. The album sleeve notes were written by Rolling Stone writer David Wild. The design was created by making Bob's name in the photographs from the show by Chris Austopchuk.

Willie Nelson's taxation problems were well publicised. Stars such as Paul Simon, John Hiatt, Peter Gabriel, Lyle Lovett, Bonnie Raitt, Sinead O'Connor either sang on his record or gave songs to help him. Willie sang Bob's 'What Was it You Wanted' from 'Oh Mercy' and they were together on **'Heartland'**, but no not really. Don Was had the instrumental track which was remaindered from Bob's 'Under The Red Sky' album, it had Bob singing a few words and humming along. Don who was producing Willie Nelson's album 'Across The Borderline', asked Bob for his permission to finish the track with Willie. The extra lyrics were created and Willie sang over the demonstration tape and hey-presto a minor classic was born, as simple as that! To my ears Willie's album was his best since 'Red Headed Stranger' in 1975.

The partial success of the 'Good as I Been' acoustic set meant that Bob wanted to do another 'unplugged' album. **'WORLD GONE WRONG'** was released in November 1993. In the sleeve notes Bob confirmed that The Never Ending Tour had ended when G.E.Smith had left the band in 1991, but all Bob did was find alternative titles for the continuing tours. If the previous album was predominantly ancient folk this one was ancient blues. Bob had always liked the blues because of its simplicity, it enables the singer to say things in an immediate manner. Bob actually said of the blues, 'The construction is rather attractive because it is so simple'.

'World Gone Wrong': This could describe Bob's 1980s career. Based on a Mississippi Sheiks song titled 'The World is Going Wrong'. As a musical family they were important, they also recorded as The Chatman Family, Mr and Mrs Chatman had eleven sons. It is thought that the group photograph included on Taj Mahal's 'De Ole Folks At Home' album includes the Chatman Family. All the sons were multi-instrumental. Armenter 'Bo' Chatman also recorded as Bo Carter. The Mississippi Sheiks shows would include all types of music and impersonations of other stars of the day. **'Love Henry'**: A Cecil Sharp collected song originally by Tom Paley, he was a member of 'The New Lost City Ramblers'. In 1914 the song was titled 'Young Hunting'. There is also a Scottish text dated 1827 which titles the song 'Young Redin'. The lyrics Bob uses were registered in 1950 as sung by Lena Hill Lexington. This is recognised as a folk song not a blues and was regularly sung by Pete Seeger. A powerful song which opens so gently and lovingly. Suddenly she plunges a knife into his heart and throws him into the well for seeing another woman. The lyric then returns to her gentle loving nature as she calls for a parrot to land on her knee. The parrot has seen enough and is not taking any chances. The sentiments are parodied in Alfred Hitchcock's 'Psycho' where after the murders Norman Bates sits with a fly on his hand that he doesn't intend to hurt, just to show how kind he is really. Even that film wasn't what it seemed, the famous shower scene was directed by Saul Bass and not Alfred Hitchcock. **'Ragged and Dirty'**: It is included on Stefan Grossman's 'How to Play Guitar' album and in the accompanying book. A song of self pity. Bob's note states that 'one of the Willie Brown's did this' which is true, Willie Brown from Arkansas recorded it in 1942. Before that in November 1926 Blind Lemon Jefferson recorded his version. Sleepy John Estes recorded his version in 1927 as 'Broke Hungry, Ragged and Dirty Too' and then as 'Broke and Hungry' (it is the second line of the lyric) when he recorded his re-emergence album with Michael Bloomfield in 1964. It uses the 'That's Alright Mama' tune once again. **'Blood in My Eyes'**: A video was made for this track in Camden High Street, a photograph from the session was used for the cover. Bob wearing a black undertaker's top hat and long black coat was filmed walking around London's Camden Town. Bob juggles and the director cuts the film before he drops the balls, he then acts like The Pied Piper and leads a procession over the Camden Lock Bridge. He is then sitting looking like a redundant undertaker in Fluke's Cradle Cafe (name has now changed) on the opposite side of the road to The Compendium Bookshop, which is where the cover picture is taken. The painting on the wall behind Bob is by Peter Gallagher. It is a painting of 'Meursault the Murderer', he appeared in the Albert Camus novel 'L'Etranger'. The painting is not unlike Bob's own style of portraits. Bob never breaks into a grin during the video, he maintains his 'dead pan' Buster Keaton straight face, the Director insists on some very close, close-ups. The song in its original form is on an album by The Mississippi Sheiks, their version is blithe and optimistic Bob's is sombre.

'Broke Down Engine': The gambler that loses all his money and then prays to God to get it back, he has also gambled away his woman. Originally by Lonnie Clark in 1929 and Blind Willie McTell in 1931, who recorded it many times. He once recorded it under the name of Barrelhouse Sammy for Atlantic in the early 1950s. The songbook for the Bob's album has many superb photographs from The Library of Congress but none are credited. On the page opposite this song a middle aged white man with holes in his shoe soles is playing a fiddle. This is no ordinary fiddle it is made out of a solid block of wood, there is no sound box, one wonders just what sound it produced. This track is the best performance on the album, everything is perfect, and the object of his affections can even do the Georgia Crawl. **'Delia'**: Another Blind Willie McTell song (his version is 'Little Delia'), also recorded by Stefan Grossman as 'All My Friends Are Gone'. Little Delia was murdered by Curtis who got sentenced to 99 years. Delia of course was mentioned in Bob's book Tarantula, she was Delia who was called Debra when she walked around in her nurses uniform. On Bob's album notes for this album Delia is herself, not Queen Gertrude, Elizabeth I, or Evita Peron, so it has taken a few years for her to decide who she really is. Bob sings over and over 'all the friends I ever had are gone', which was a sentiment of Bob's some years earlier in 'Tangled Up in Blue'. Rounders are in evidence in the lyric again, it seems that this is an Americanism for 'bounders' as in cads and men of no fixed abode. Three are shown in the photograph on the opposite page to the lyrics in the song book. **'Stack A Lee'**: Stagger Lee was a hit by Lloyd Price in 1958. Bob created the title with the 'A' so the nearest in similarity was Furry Lewis and Frank Hutchison's, 'Stackalee' all one word. (In Bob's sleeve notes he names him incorrectly as Frank Hutchinson). The Stacker Lee was a steamship belonging to Mr Lee and his Lee Shipping Line. He named his ships after members of his family and workforce. The ship is also mentioned in Frank Hutchison's (or Robert Wilkins') 'Alabama Blues'; Woody Guthrie's version was titled 'Staggolee'. The story is of Lee and Billy Lyons squabbling in the dark over throwing a seven spot card or an eight, it has become one of the great recordings moving from folk through blues to rock. Bob explains this song as 'a monumental epic of blunder and misunderstanding'. In Bob's and Mississippi John Hurt's version Stagger Lee kills Billy de Lyon for stealing his $5 Stetson hat. When Stackalee is back in jail Billy Lyons haunts him wearing that Stetson hat. There seems to be no historical proof that 'Stagger Lee' really existed as a person.

'Two Soldiers': An American Civil war song. Bob refers to Hazel Dickens and Alice Foster who recorded the song for Folkways. Of course Tom Jones recorded 'Two Brothers' a similar song, Rolf Harris had a massive hit with 'Two Little Boys', all three songs concerned the American Civil War. The words are credited to Virginia Francis Townsend, and the poem which was also titled 'The Battle of Fredericksburg' was printed in the poetry sections of local newspapers. The version Bob sings was collected by Alan Lomax from Monroe, Cathlyn and Bert Gevedon of West Liberty, Kentucky in 1937. Bob's lyric is as sung by Mike Seeger who was a member of 'The New Lost City Ramblers', both Bob's and Mike's version also includes Alan Lomax' extra verse. This is another track where Bob sounds like a vocal imitation of David Cousins of The Strawbs. **'Jack-A-Roe'**: Another Tom Paley song written about either Jack Frasier or Jack Monroe or both. There is an inference that this concerns women working on a ship. Working their trip so that they could be with their husbands. Some women even disguised themselves as men to work on ships. This was mentioned in respect to Joan Baez earlier, she sang this song on her 'Joan Baez In Concert Part 2' album. Bob's version has two extra verses. Bob's version mentions 'Jackie Frazier', Joan's just Jack the sailor. As both the woman and the man are 'Jack', Joan's version doesn't make much sense without 'Jackaroe's' lover being mentioned. At least this song has a happy ending, she finds him dying, nurses him back to health and they both live happily ever after. Bob had included 'Canadee-I-O on the previous folk album which was also of a woman dressed in sailor's clothes. **'Lone Pilgrim'**: Bob had heard Doc and Merle Watson's version of this song. This was thought to be the only non-traditional song on the album registered to White and Pace but without any knowledge of their publisher or performance rights society. It was first located from an 1847 anthology of songs originally derived from 'White Pilgrim' from 1838 by Jack Ellis. It was the song of a travelling preacher named Joseph Thomas. Bob's song 'Death is not the End' could have been influenced by the sentiments of this song. In Bob's album notes he remarks that the lunacy of trying to fool the self is set aside at some given point. If I understand the song it is of a man that has a religious experience whilst standing by the Lone Pilgrim's tomb. He returns to the tomb and dies on it releasing his soul and thus joining the Pilgrim. I don't understand where Bob draws his 'hegemony' reference juxtaposed with the 'needs of mankind' in this song of dying happily.

The album notes indicate that Bob continues to have a mind that flits from one idea to another. Bob finds circumstances within these simple songs that to me bear little or no relationship with the songs' sentiments. What Bob does is write a sentence concerning the song and then fly off at tangent giving his views on a multitude of subjects. Commerce, politics, corporate man, psychosis, corrupt religions and exploitation all in the first few lines. Bob brings all the protagonists and their problems up to date. He mentions that Stack-A-Lee would not have a 'cell' phone in his cell, although Bob calls it a wall phone. Billy killed by Stackalee did not have insurance nor did he get airsick. The notes are more interesting than Bob had written for many years but the last few lines mentioning the 'Never Ending Tour' should have been separated.

In the Biograph notes Bob told Cameron Crowe how he disliked the singers that prostituted their art for commercials. He wouldn't allow his songs to be used to sell anything. It was in 1994 that Coopers and Lybrand the auditors and accountants used 'The Times They are A-Changin' for their advert, Bob wasn't the vocalist it was sung by Richie Havens, taken from his

'Beatles and Dylan' album. Woodstock celebrated with a concert titled 'Woodstock 94', 300,000 people paid to be there, one wonders what percentage were also at the original concert. The site of the 1994 concert was Woodstock not Bethel where the first one was performed. This time Bob was there and so was Joni Mitchell, most lay-people would guess that they were at the original, they weren't. Bob had seen Eric Clapton, Bruce Springsteen, Neil Young and others perform on MTV's 'Unplugged' of course Bob just had to do it too. Bob was reported in the tabloids as attempting to get Michael Barrymore out of the best suite at The Crown Paza Hotel in Manchester, and for accidentally knocking Carole King into the orchestra pit after hugging her on stage. Carole broke her arm, as a performer has to keep going Bob continued to play 'Real Real Gone' whilst Carole was helped away to hospital. The tabloids attempted to make Bob appear uncaring which was nonsense, if he had jumped into the pit to help her he could possibly have made her injuries worse.

'BOB DYLAN'S GREATEST HITS VOLUME 3' was released in November 1994. The cover was what Bob called a 'dignified' picture of himself taken by Ken Reagan during rehearsals for The Rolling Thunder Revue. Only one of the tracks could be classed as a hit, 'Knockin' On Heaven's Door'. To make the completists spend out money for one track **'Dignity'** was included from the 'Oh Mercy' sessions. I have always wondered why Bob never changed the word 'mirror' to a word he could pronounce easier and of course The Duke of Edinburgh, the Prince at last became famous in song.

The 1994 film 'Natural Born Killers' included Bob Dylan singing a song in its soundtrack. The CD leaflet was one of the most difficult to understand, the participants were not listed clearly, it seemed that Warner Brothers never wanted to publicise the many superb tracks that were included. Leonard Cohen's 'Waiting For The Miracle' and 'The Future', Patti Smiths 'Rock 'n' Roll Nigger', Duane Eddy's 'The Trembler' rubbed shoulders with Nine Inch Nails' 'Burn' and 'A Warm Place' and The Hollywood Persuaders' 'Drums-a-Go-Go'. Bob added **'You Belong To Me'** the Pee Wee King, Red Stewart and Chilton Price classic song known to everyone as 'See The Pyramids Along The Nile' and a gave good performance of the song. The song was a hit for Jo Stafford in 1952. One wonders if Bob understood the content of the film it was hardly in sympathy with his religious beliefs.

'UNPLUGGED' was released in 1995 in both video and CD format. MTV had started the series as an idea that the stars should revert to acoustic performances. Neil Young and Eric Clapton performed outstanding shows. When Robert Plant, Jimmy Page and Bruce Springsteen performed their show the format was modified accordingly but wasn't titled 'Plugged-in'. Bob's performance was top-notch, it is arguably his best live recording. In a polka dot shirt similar to his apparel at The infamous Newport Festival he played 'With God on Our Side'(without the World War II verse), 'Desolation Row' and of course 'The Times They Are A-Changin'. Bob wasn't even mumbling them, 'Like A Rolling Stone', 'Knockin' On Heaven's Door', 'Shooting Star' 'Dignity' all superb. It may be just me but 'Dignity' possibly due to the heavy drumming of Winston Watson reminds me of the group 'Sweet's' smash hit 'Blockbuster'. Bob looks diminutive standing between John Jackson (guitar) and Tony Garnier (Bass), both 6'-0" tall and wearing hats. Bucky Baxter remained seated playing steel and slide guitar and mandolin, whilst Brendan O'Brien added the Al Kooper flourishes on the electric organ. In his live performances Bob would often 'pretend' to be playing a screaming guitar solo, but on this show he really played one, no question. So he sang some of the songs in abbreviated form, and changed vocal key and octave halfway through a sentence, so what, for this show the versions were perfect. Most of us were watching anticipating another fiasco that the critics would make a serious meal of, they couldn't, even the mistakes were perfect. The whole series of 'Unplugged' needed Bob to do a show, he was the godfather of acoustic music. The cover had MTV Music Television prominently on the front with Bob's photograph 'touched-up' to look so young. There is a deep black line which changes the shape of his left cheek. The CD release had a dubbed-on audience reaction and the tape loop is so short on 'Knockin'' that the scream arrives so regularly in the backing that it distracts the concentration of the listener. Apparently this was re-mixed out, yet every disc I have heard includes this babel. A case of spoiling the ship for a ha'peth of tar.

Bob added the rockabilly track **'Boogie Woogie Country Girl'** to Doc Pomus Tribute Album titled 'Till The Night Is Gone'. Bob added **'My Blue Eyed Jane'** to 'The songs of Jimmie Rodgers - Tribute, released on Bob's own Egyptian Records Label. He also recorded Johnny Cash song **'Ring of Fire'**, written by Merle Kilgore and June Carter, for the film 'Feeling Minnesota'. As this track included Bernard Edwards and Nile Rodgers in the band it might have been one of the tracks recorded by Bob with Nile Rodgers production for an album that was never released. A 'Shelter From the Storm' out-take was also included on the soundtrack recording of the film 'Jerry Maguire', it has an alternative sixth verse, which I am yet to find.

Another release in 1995 was **'Bob Dylan, Highway 61 Interactive'**. This CD-Rom enabled the computer operator to access a multi-media trip through 30 years of Bob's songs, 40 song extracts, 10 full length songs, paintings, videos (4) and photographs. The viewer can click back into time to The Rolling Thunder Revue or a 3-D virtual reality Greenwich Village. The performance of 'Queen Jane Approximately' had never been seen before, at least that is what the blurb stated at the time. The disc also provided encyclopedic knowledge of Bob's career including a listing of cover versions, lyrics and album liner notes. Bob did attempt his own unplugged session in November 1993 when he recorded at The Supper Club, New York. As the CD-Rom shows the performances were excellent but the lighting was poor, the camera work average, apparently the latter was the reason that Bob shelved the project. There are many errors but as writer of Dylan books I am aware that Dylan fans like to delve as deep as they can into all Dylan product; I have already ordered my flak jacket. The CD-Rom is essential to all completists but far too expensive for most pockets. One important fact that came to light in an interview with Telegraph Magazine was that the 'House of the Rising Sun' electric version 'was' recorded in 1962 and not a 1964 over-dub. Graphix Zone the creators of the CD-Rom were adamant on that fact, they received the numerical mix numbers and said that they were accurate. As the 'House of the Rising Sun' tape was missing from the 1962 box, I would personally have thought that it had been taken to perform the over-dub, another mystery?

At the end of 1995 (12th December) Bob sang at Frank Sinatra's 80th Birthday celebration. The video of the show presents Bob singing 'Restless Farewell' to a bemused Frank and Barbara Sinatra. Bob was introduced as 'Not so old, young blues eyes'. Bob's performance prompted Don Rickles to suggest to Bob "You gotta stop mumbling when you sing, people don't know what you are singing about!" Bob's response was not noted but he did appear in a photograph with Frank and Bruce Springsteen taken after the show. Song writer Gerry Goffin released a solo album titled 'Backroom Blood' which includes two co-compositions with Bob Dylan. 'Time to End This Masquerade' (adequately describes the song apparently) and 'Tragedy of the Trade' which was reported to be an improvement when compared to the other song. Bob also had another book published titled **'Drawn Blank'**. We had seen his 'Writings and Drawings' back in 1973, this was the second portfolio of his art. My opinion is that his drawings are an art teacher's nightmare. If these scenes and portraits were not from a celebrity then no publishing house would give them a second glance. Bob does not name his portraits, this makes it difficult for the viewer to decide if they are a good likeness or not. Bob's perspectives are wayward, but of course this may be intentional. His stairway only takes the eye a short way up the stairs. Bob's work has been compared to Gauguin, Cezanne, De Kooning and Van Gogh which in each case must be the analysis of a diehard fan. What I would say is that he has improved immensely since 1973. A photograph of Bob in his studio is far more interesting with the paintings shown in their actual size. One which is similar to the famous Tretchikov painting is very good, as is another self portrait showing a bearded and hatted Bob. The woman female nude lying face down is awful as are the other unclothed ladies. These are drawings and sketches of a man who would like to be recognised for another style of art rather than film, poetry and music. They are only good and valuable by association with

Bob's name, not for their quality. We are still awaiting his 'Masterpiece'.

Bob's son Jakob now a member of the group Wallflowers had their album 'Bringing Down the Horse' achieve 3 million sales, Bob has never had a triple platinum album. Some interviewers asked some strange questions concerning Bob being envious. Bob soon put them straight, he was a grandfather and a proud father why should he envy his son his success? The only thing that Bob had trepidation for was that his son might be hurt by the 'sharks' that lurk within the music industry. Bob was reinvigorated by the response to 'Unplugged' and went on tour with a 'Greatest Hits Tour' with the songs changed each night. Suddenly the clock had been turned back 20 years, the song Dignity described his new performances. As if this wasn't enough Bob was back in the studio recording an album full of new material. If Bob had been upset by Daniel Lanois strictness at the time of 'Oh Mercy' it was all forgiven because Daniel was employed to produce the new album. They recorded in Miami, Florida.

In 1997 we had the release of **'TIME OUT OF MIND'** with Bob and Daniel present on all tracks playing a hoard of instruments. Apart from Jim Keltner who played on seven of the eleven tracks Daniel Lanois had arranged for a new team of musicians. The out of focus cover photograph shows Bob surrounded by all the technology, playing an acoustic guitar. The CD itself was printed in the old pale blue 'Columbia Viva-tonal recording' design, which was once used for negro-recordings. Removing the CD an empty studio is shown in the back of the box. The album has a theme of taking things easier, a possible a reference to Bob's hectic lifestyle up until God gave him the fright of his life, the sudden realisation that his time might be up. He was stricken with chest pains and then declared fit by his doctor after a medical examination. The pains persisted and were so debilitating that it affected his breathing; the final diagnosis was histoplasmosis. This is a swelling around the heart of the fatty tissue, although it was reported that the problem was toxoplasmosis which is a protozoal disease characterized by jaundice and convulsions. After he was discharged from hospital he was treated for pericarditis which is the inflammation of the membranous sac that encloses the heart, brought on by histoplasmosis. Bob was ill for six weeks, he had no energy and had difficulty getting out of bed. He was gradually weaned off the medication, he said that he had little time to do anything except concentrate on breathing. He made a full recovery and his meeting with Jimi Hendrix, Woody Guthrie, John Lennon and Elvis Presley was subsequently cancelled. In the new album the theme of walking is everywhere, Bob said that when he first got home he could hardly walk around his garden, he was that weak. In the interviews Bob repeated the line 'those old songs are my lexicon, my prayer book' which of course is taken from Wink Martindale's 'Deck of Cards'. Bob also said Hank Williams sang 'I Saw the Light', and that he had seen the light also, so had Todd Rundgren of course. Although the album was completed before he was taken ill the tracks are overtly concerned with life's reality, there is no popular idealism. There are some differences between the songs 'sung' and the original songbook lyrics. I have noted these at each track.

'Love Sick': This is the first of the songs on the album where he is walking. This is certainly a Lovesick Blues. At one point he wishes that he had never met her, later he would do anything to be with her. A video was made, recorded in The New Daisy Theatre, Memphis. Rachel Di Paolo a model dressed in black bra and panties dances as a silhouette, Bob who is wearing a white hat is in a window, other scenes are shot in the Memphis streets. Bob vocal sounds like a less coarse version of Tom Waits, there is some slight phasing on the voice. A slow plodding beat with waves washing on the shore cymbals, the backing is The Doors influenced, Jim Dickenson's light electric piano touch is just like that of Ray Manzarek. In the songbook Bob wants to take the road 'and' plunder, he sings 'to' plunder. 'Dirt Road Blues' mentions the narrator's eyes bleeding, blood in his eyes, nothing left to see, chains are shattered, was he 'bound in cold irons'. This is rockabilly, an attempt to recreate The Sun Records sound of 'That's Alright Mama', listen through the sound to the upright bass playing of Tony Garnier. It has been a long time since Bob sounded so at ease in a recording, it just floats along. In the lyric Bob is walking again, he once again Bob mentions a shadow and a cloud. Charley Patton wrote 'Down the Dirt Road Blues' where he was leaving and he too is waiting for a ride. Bob's trip is to see his lover, Mississippi John Hurt's ride was to see his Lord, we think. Enoch Brown also went 'Down the Road' in his blues but all he was seeking was a better place to live, a least they were all walkin'. The last verse is amended in words and meaning. He walks the road and is 'right beside the sun' and in the last line he 'puts up a barrier to keep himself away from everyone'. The verse sung on the CD is less powerful, all he wants is for her to 'holler out his name'.

'Standing in The Doorway': Bob wrote 'Standing on the Highway' in 1962, a blues with tune similar to 'Fixing To Die Blues'. That song was for a hitchhiker. Elmore James sang of 'Standing at The Crossroads' where he was waiting for his woman but she was out with another man. Woody Guthrie and Cisco Houston adapted 'Danville Girl' in 1963, it was written in 1927 and was known to be sung mostly by Doc Boggs. There is a similarity between Bob's song and 'Danville Girl' as he passes the cheap cigar to the singer on the platform. In the Book of Isaiah there are many references to the 'dark' and the 'sun' but these were chance similarities. The slow song opens like Elvis' 'Can't Help Falling in Love'. Is Bob becoming more aware of his age and how time races, 'got no place to turn nothing left to burn' also 'I know the mercy of God must be near, when I hear the church bells ringing I wonder who they're ringing for'. This could be a marriage or a funeral, as one gets older the latter becomes more central in one's thoughts. In Bob's song Paul Simon's line, 'slow down you move to fast', is recalled in the first verse. In verse two the narrator is deciding whether to kiss or kill her, in Bob's 'Standing on the Highway' he was swearing that he didn't want to kill nobody's kids. There are more ambivalences in the middle section. Who is it that might 'get him', he is on the train still thinking of her. The lovely tune is like a hybrid of 'Nevertheless' and 'Try a Little Tenderness', and some of the sentiments have also been incorporated. The narrator will eat when he is hungry drink when he's dry is a line straight from the late Jerry Lordan's 'I'll Stay Single' which I doubt if Bob has ever heard. When he says that he will live his life on the 'square' it may be Bob's first Masonic reference. Freemasons are known to be 'on the square'. I am not suggesting that Bob has become a Freemason but there is an important parallel in the remark. Freemasons believe that there is one God. That one God in which all religions believe, it could be the next step in Bob's search for awareness. His itinerant lifestyle would probably be set against his becoming a Freemason. Bob concludes the song in a matter-of-fact fashion when he concludes that she just left him crying. This isn't the only song with this title 'The Flock of Seagulls' and 'Soul Asylum' both recorded their own 'Standing in The Doorway'.

'Million Miles': Big Boy Crudup 'That's All Right Mama' makes another appearance, albeit slowly, this time she can do what you gotta do. The narrator thinks that maybe in the next life he will be able to hear himself think, just like in the previous song some days everything goes too fast. The opening line is archetypical Dylan 'You took a part of me I really miss', is that herself, his sex life, his peace of mind or his children? Still I maintain that couples that separate only remember the good times and Bob mentions that his 'memory is in a ditch'. The distance between their personal differences is a million miles, but that will close with time. A ragged opening as the musicians search for a rhythm, Jim Keltner is using plenty of cymbal early on but it seems that he got the message and played quieter. Ostensibly a riff song with little tune and the band just shuffle along till the fade out. It is the penultimate verse that Bob changes from the songbook to the CD. He wants to be rocked until there is nothing left to feel, and everything gets real, this is diluted on the sung version. **'Tryin' to Get to Heaven'**: This is a natural progression from the previous track as time is healing the wounds. The narrator is walking again, he is searching for the heaven of ecstasy rather than the Holy place in the sky. 'Mary Jane' the Scottish folk song includes the line 'I was riding in a buggy with Miss Mary Jane' which Bob uses in verse four, albeit totally out of context with the rest of the song. Does Bob sing 'midnight ramblers' in the last verse or is it 'midlife'? The tune is reminiscent of another but Bob has concealed it perfectly, this is a great song with a very catchy melody.

' **'Til I Fell in Love With You':** Another woman has stolen the narrator's heart. The expressions of love are excellent, only Bob Dylan would find all these metaphors so perfectly. He is under the power of a woman's love. The line where Bob is a-fire with love hoping for the rain, yet the clouds pass by, is as good as he has written in ten years. But what has God got to do with it? Bob feels that God is his shield and won't lead him astray, perhaps he considers God saved him from his recent illness. Surely Bob knows by now that when love arrives everything else goes straight out of the window. The third verse is where Bob inserts his conflicting testimony. This takes the song back to the days of girls and boys, here the narrator tells her that she will remember him when he finds fame and wealth. The last verses are desolate and despondent, he has achieved his ambition but he remains alone thinking of her. Another riff blues with an excellent understated guitar note catching the ear at the end of each couplet. Lenny Welch sang 'Since I Fell For You' in 1963, a song with a very similar sentiment. **'Not Dark Yet':** The video shows Bob dressed as a Mississippi riverboat gambler. When Bob sings 'I know it looks as though I am moving but I'm standing still' he probably means that he either is treading water professionally or the narrator is suffering from some debilitating 'nervous' illness. The nerves are naked and numb. There are similarities with the Everly's 'I Wonder if I Care as Much', in an interview Bob said that he borrowed a line from a jug band guitar figure. The most likely is The Memphis Jug Band's version of 'K.C.Moan'; this was confirmed by an interview with David Gates for Newsweek. With critics searching for every glint of truth in the lyric it was mooted that 'any one's eyes' might have been meant to be 'anyone's 'I's as in I and I. Does Bob sing a 'world full of lies' or is it 'whirlpool', the song book states the former.

'**Cold Irons Bound':** The narrator thought some of them were his friends, he was wrong about them all. Is he singing of the love of a woman child, Angel or God, he found his world in her but your love hasn't proved true. The tale could be that he is being taken to jail to serve hard labour with the cold irons on his ankles. She has invaded his psyche and just passes him by on the way to church. A foot-stomping rhythm created by many over-dubs, the musicians are absent from the playlist. This certainly is a great rockin' track with a superb mid-section break. In verse four does Bob sing 'The reality has too many heads?', it sounds like the R.T., radio transmitter? The production and mixing are perfect, Bob is always audible over the morass of sound. This track won Bob a Grammy Award for the Best Male Rock Vocal performance of the year. Bob makes the word 'torn' sound like 'turn' which reduces the impact from songbook to CD. He also sings of 'finding his own' rather than 'his world'. **'Make You Feel My Love':** This was recorded by Garth Brooks and included on his 'Limited Series' album that went platinum. Garth's version and Trisha Yearwood's are included in the soundtrack CD of the film 'Hope Floats'. These two recordings will earn Bob more royalties than he will get for his own album. When the Garth Brooks' single reached No 1 in the Billboard Country Charts it achieved another first for Bob Dylan. The song was nominated for a Grammy Award in the Best Country Song Category. Bob originally wanted Billy Joel to record the song. The answer's blowing in the wind are now blowing wild and free in the lyric. Verse five with its highway of regret and the winds of change is superb imagery harking back to Bob's earliest work. When we compare Bob's version with that of Garth Brooks the simple answer is that Garth makes the lyric sound innocuous, Bob sings as he goes 'crawling down the avenue, to make you feel my love'. We listen and believe what Bob sings, when Garth sings we sing-along with him without bothering much with the words. The song is a descending chord sequence used in thousands of songs, it is always easy to sing and memorable, this is the song that you find you are whistling after the album is finished. **'Can't Wait'**: This song is another of Bob's which contains so many other song titles, some slightly changed. 'It's Late', 'Walk The Line', 'After Midnight', 'I Can't Wait', 'Waiting For You', 'Wait For You', 'On the Way Up' 'I'm, Your Man' and we are only just out of the first verse, you can continue dear reader. If it was intentional then it is brilliant, it is probably subliminal. This song sounds as though the musicians are awaiting Bob's nod to stop playing, but they just meander on playing the blues riff that Bob has used so many times before. How many lyricists, apart from Bob Dylan, would rhyme 'wait' with 'disintegrate', very few is the answer. This is a superb love song with wonderful lyrics. I can't think of anyone who could write this lyric without it sounding twee and trite. It is neither and the last verse, again with its song titles, is the highlight of this album's writing. Bob is still wondering how much time he has left, it is becoming a constant theme after his rubbing-shoulders with death. As the song was written before the illness perhaps Bob is becoming clairvoyant. Bob sings 'might' in the verse three in lieu of 'would' in the songbook, giving the verse less impact. He also for no apparent reason changes 'fate' to 'day' in the penultimate line, which doesn't rhyme. **'Highlands'**: This is the closing epic, a magnum opus. A long song at 17 minutes the opposite of Blonde on Blonde's 'Lowlands', revisited. A troubadour walking the streets in an empty and bleak city and dreaming of The Highlands of Scotland. In the mid-section Bob re-creates scene of a man that walks into a restaurant which is empty except for the waitress, they flirt until the mood dies. The complete song is in two parts, of the 20 verses the middle seven are for the waitress and the customer. In the Scottish part the narrator is dreaming of living near Aberdeen. A mention of the swinging chariots of the negro spiritual are added because they are coming to take him home to the highlands. We must remember Robert Burns and his 'Farewell to the Highlands' which Bob paraphrases 'My heart is in the highlands, my heart is not here'. Bob substitutes horses and hounds a very English pastime for Burns' wild deer and the roe, (fish eggs or more deer?). The narrator's constant musing is stopped by people going about their everyday business or a mangy dog. The realisation that the years are passing and there is less to say could be Bob's opinion of the state of his life and mind. The nonsense of trading places with them if he could is just romanticism, of course he could secrete himself away in Scotland, the place is almost empty. Robert Burns was the Bob Dylan of his day, (reverse that phrase if you prefer), there are many correlations between the lives of the two men. Joan Baez could be Burns' Jean Armour, and Sara could be Highland Mary, Robert Burns' wife. Both Burns and Dylan had strong religious feelings, both had problems with excesses of their lifestyles, both loved the company of beautiful women. 'Highlands' ends with a mention of another folk song 'Over the Hills and Far Away' which was recorded by Shirley Collins, Tom Hart and The Yetties. That 'over the hill' line reminds me of C.S.Lewis (Anthony Hopkins) remark in the 1993 film 'Shadowlands' when he says "Happiness is not wanting to be anywhere else, not waiting for anything new to happen, not looking around the next corner or over the next hill'. A remark perfectly in line with Bob's feelings within 'Highlands'. Malvina Reynolds' prediction will eventually spoil the highland hills, remember she once wrote 'little boxes on the hillside and they're all made out of ticky tacky and they all look just the same'. The sung lyrics are as written except for the restaurant scenes. The 'hard' boiled eggs were originally 'soft'. There are other changes where in the book the waitress says "What'll it be", instead of Bob asking her 'Tell me what I want?". She also offers to bring his the eggs where in the song Bob says "That's right, bring me some".

According to Duke Robillard in an interview for Isis Magazine there appears to be four remaindered tracks namely **'The Girl From the Red Shore'**, **'Doin' Alright'**, **'No Turning Back'** and the Mark Twain influenced **'Mississippi'**. The latter might be the reason that Bob was dressed as a Mississippi gambler in his waistcoat and striped shirt on the CD cover, Daniel Lanois must have decided to remainder it, Duke Robillard thought it was the best track. Greil Marcus never a man to say something nice when he could say something controversial called the album (in Mojo Magazine) 'As bleak and blasted as any work a major artist in any field has offered in ages', which I construed as praise. He qualified his term of artist as 'a person with a reputation and an audience to lose'. For me the album has a confidence a self assuredness that has been lost by Bob for many years, there are many aphorisms. It is a singer coming to terms with inevitable death. For most of us we only become aware that life is finite when we lose one of out parents, Bob lost one some years ago perhaps it has taken these years to come to terms with the loss.

The New York Post revealed that during the time that Bob recorded this album he was alleged to be 'intimate' with Raquel Welch and that some of the songs might be for her. It is so reassuring when 'old people' prove what they can do without Viagra. Bob was also awarded an honour at The 20th Annual John F. Kennedy Centre Awards. Bob attended with his family, (except Jakob a member of the group The Wallflowers who was playing a gig elsewhere), and his mother Beatty. Opera singer, Jessye Norman, actor, Charlton Heston (why does his name always remind me of a London bus route), actress, Lauren Bacall and dancer, Edward Villella were the other award recipients. President Bill Clinton said "Bob's voice and lyrics haven't always been easy on our ears, but throughout his career Bob Dylan has never aimed to please". Well I suppose as he is The President he can say any old rubbish he likes, perhaps he needs to borrow Bob's thesaurus and be little more precise, we know what he meant but others might be a little perplexed. Bob could have made the same remark for Bill Clinton's saxophone playing and we would all know what he meant. Bob has nearly always aimed to please, his lyrics have been intimidatory at times and his voice is an acquired taste, perhaps that is what Bill intended us to hear. The Christmas TV show of The Gala Concert, which included G.E.Smith and Don Was in the band, had Walter Cronkite calling Bob "The rolling thunder of American music", he compared Bob to 'Mark Twain-a 19th century troubadour-a civil war type-Walt Whitman-Bob Dylan was standing in the fire and capturing the sound of the 60s society'; phew!!

The album went platinum selling one million copies in the USA. 'Blood on The Tracks' remains the only two million seller which I find extraordinary. The Greatest Hits sets must have sold more. Albums such as 'Blonde on Blonde', 'Bringing It All back Home' and 'John Wesley Harding' don't feature in the million seller list, how is that possible, when 'Before the Flood' is a million seller. I remember that Pink Floyd's album 'Dark Side of the Moon' had been in the Billboard Top 200 albums for ten years and yet was still indicated as only selling 500,000 copies, so I suppose anything is possible in the world of pop music. The album won two Grammy Awards at the 40th Annual Awards Ceremony. It won The Best Album of The Year and Best Contemporary Folk Album. The album shot back up the USA charts, as winners always do when people wonder how this missed such a gem. At the ceremony Bob sang 'Love Sick' whilst a group of people danced behind him on the stage. One dancer named Michael Portnoy became somewhat of a distraction to Bob and after a short pause Mr Portnoy was hustled from the stage, there was no complaint. A video of 'Not Dark Yet' was shown, slow motion street scenes, distorted camera lenses and some black and white shots are merged as Bob 'almost' lip-synchs the song.

A video and book appeared in the shops with the title 'The Music of Bob Dylan' in October 1998. On closer inspection it proved to be by Fred

Sokolow. Recorded for Stefan Grossman's Guitar Workshop, Sokolow teaches the chords and the finger picking of nine of Bob's greatest hits, including 'Lay Lady Lay', 'Mr Tambourine Man' and 'Blowing in the Wind'. Bob gave the song 'Mississippi' to Sheryl Crow to sing on her album 'The Globe Sessions'. Bob met up with Al Kooper again when he recorded a version of 'Chimes of Freedom' harmonizing with Joan Osborne, the song would be included in a Televised Mini Series titled 'The Sixties'.

If the problems with the Ruth Tyrangiel court case weren't enough Bob then had Susan Ross preparing to dish the dirt. She was preparing an expose book stating that Bob secretly had two wives, more children, and an extremely complicated love life. She also stated that she would set the record straight by countering and proving the errors in the misinformation spread to the public by Bob's publicity machine. One wonders if this misinformation might include the details that Bob didn't run away and join the circus at the age of 13, nor did he run away to Chicago at the age of 10. At least it would allow The Guinness Book of Rock Stars the opportunity to change the first lines of their Bob Dylan listing.

Bob continued to tour and appeared in a double bill show with Van Morrison which became a triple header when Joni Mitchell joined. This was then three singer songwriters that explained their life loves and religious feelings in songs. All three complain that is it just a job and that the songs are just songs, of course they are.

THE BOOTLEG SERIES VOL 4-5, BOB DYLAN LIVE 1966, The Royal Albert Hall Concert was Bob's longest album title so far, it was released in November 1998. The title was only used because that is what the album has been recognised as being since 1966. It was in fact the recording from The Free Trade Hall, Manchester, 17th May 1966. Beautifully cleaned up re-mixed to stereo sound as though it was recorded, thirty years ago; well what did you expect. The concert, and the 'Judas' call with Bob's reaction has been available on vinyl and CD for thirty years, but the re-working made the album an essential purchase for Dylanites. The re-mix was engineered from the original three-track by Michael Brauer and Steve Berkowitz, Brauer said that he tried for 'more of a centred image, although he didn't want to go mono. There are a couple of obvious tape splices, although the booklet suggestion that the listener might need head-phones to hear them makes me wonder if their ears need a good syringing. For me the beauty of the release is that Mickey Jones (Bob Dylan's favourite drummer at the time, probably still is) can be perceived for the brilliant musician he is, my vinyl bootleg never captured the drum sound properly.

THE MAN IN HIM

What a heavy burden is a name that has become too famous.
Voltaire 1694-1778

At the time of writing this book Bob is back on the road touring with Paul Simon. The duo met at Willie Nelson's 60th birthday party, six years ago and Bob renewed the acquaintance by calling in at Paul's New York apartment. The meeting was intended to be a one hour chat concerning their performances during the connected tour. They jammed until the early hours of the following morning. The pair alternate opening the show, with each set intended to last 75 minutes. The two men come together at the end of the show to perform at least three songs, but not the same three songs each night. Bob was singing 'Not Fade Away', duets with Paul Simon included 'The Sound of Silence', 'I Walk The Line', 'Blue Moon of Kentucky' and 'Knockin' on Heaven's Door'. Paul announces to the audience that he thought "Capeman' was good, very good", my opinion is that it would have been enhanced by the inclusion of a memorable tune. Bob's set which mixed old songs with the new had Charlie Sexton playing lead guitar. Bob must like 'Love Sick' from his last album as he used it as the encore. This of course brings us up to date, Paul Simon is still crazy after all these years and Bob is still love sick.

Bob did make a statement concerning his songs which was a revelation. He said "Travelling touring and recording is my life-sure my songs are about real people, you have probably recognised all the people in them one time or another". He also said in an interview in 1990 that **"People can learn everything about me through my songs**, if they know where to look-they can juxtapose them with certain other songs and draw a clearer picture". To that I say we are trying Bob, we really are!

All through his career Bob has maintained that his two main influences were Woody Guthrie and Jimmie Rodgers, to them I would add Blind Willie McTell, Odetta and Leadbelly. One wonders why Bob didn't record an album of their songs when he was suffering his writer's block, surely it would be a way of saying thank you. It is easy to be Bob Dylan, what is difficult is attempting to live up to the expectations of others. Bob agrees that his marriage was a failure but as a father and mother, Bob and Sara did just fine. Of the critics and writers Bob encompasses us all in the same category as 'stupid and misleading jerks'. He said "Critics are fools they limit their subjects to their own unimaginative mentality-they never stop to think that somebody has been exposed to experiences that they haven't been-it is not the experience that counts it is the attitude towards the experience".

Firstly Bob I assume that you don't like us. Secondly it seems a very strange statement. Does Bob assume that the experiences that he has are the only experiences? My response was the same when I wrote my responses to Van Morrison's remarks which were in the same vein. Both artists consider that we are locked up in our own little worlds, they don't realise that they are locked up in theirs. Critics are 'so called' experts, which seems to infer that it is Bob that is the expert. Although Van Morrison admits that he has been searching for the truth Bob denies the fact, he found his, or it found him. One suspects that he thought he found it with his Bible studies, after all his doctrine does seem to cover the full Bible rather than just one Testament. Writers are 'frustrated novelists' is another jibe levelled at us, but again Bob thinks that the only job on earth worth doing is a singer songwriter, but what else can he do? Bob has also said that he feels that the fans understand his songs, so why can't the critics? He certainly would be little help to me in my previous profession as a ballistics engineer, and I can assure that I have plenty of experiences doing that.

Bob says "Why should you want to know about me, I don't want to know about you". For a celebrated Doctor of Letters to make such a ridiculous statement beggars belief. Bob you are a celebrity, you have promoted yourself and your music as a celebrity, people want to know about you. As for the probing into his private life there are limits, A.J.Weberman over stepped them, any intrusion where the children might be physically or mentally hurt is totally out of order, there are few writers that would disagree. In fact apart from tabloid journalism it doesn't happen very often in the music industry.

Bob has used ideas from Villon and Rimbaud and many others, it is part of the art of writing. I repeat again T.S.Eliot's remark 'immature poets imitate; mature poets steal'. To use an idea and turn it on its head has been Bob's technique and by so doing he has created his own style. It is true that as he has aged it has become more laboured and difficult. Bob hasn't extracted much from the French Romantic poets, they were led by Victor Hugo and Charles Baudelaire, the latter was part of that movement and also the following one called The Parnassian Movement. This included Tristan Corbiere, Paul Verlaine and Arthur Rimbaud and we know Bob read and used some of their ideas. This movement was a backlash against romanticism a purging of emotionalism. There were other poetic movements in France such as Symbolist, Lyricism, Cubism and Negritude. What is obvious is that Bob would have been seen as part of the Surrealism Movement, in fact he is part of it. It started in 1916 with extra politicalisation arriving in the poems in 1925. Reading the poems of Andre Breton, Tristan Tzara, Jacques Prevert, Robert Desnos and Philippe Soupault the Dylanologist might wonder if they could be put to music. It is important to realise that if one doesn't read French then it is important to try more than one translation there is so much variation, we are trusting the emotions of the linguist.

It is so much easier to write poems and music in isolation when there is no one to intrude into your solitude. Exploitation is everywhere in the music industry people stand in line to be exploited. Bob doesn't want to be constantly reminded who he is, if he did he would start dissecting his own work. A person doesn't like to feel self conscious. Little Richard said "If you don't like your picture being taken then you got no business being a star". The consensus of opinion is that Bob is an absolute delight to be with, he is charming and friendly. When his bodyguards and sycophants arrive on the scene he immediately becomes the other Bob Dylan.

William Holden said to Gloria Swanson in Sunset Boulevard "There is nothing tragic about being fifty, unless you are trying to be twenty-five". Bob has always been unhappy when people ask him if his songs are personal. He would respond with "People don't ask Elvis Presley about you ain't nothing but a Hound Dog by saying is that the way you feel about a person or people". Of course they don't firstly Elvis didn't write the song, secondly his songs were selected by others and thirdly who cares? Bob has always taken risks in his career moves, why doesn't Paul Simon suffer the same treatment? Simon is rarely criticised, his music is not deeply investigated. Paul Simon is known to have a large ego, when Art Garfunkel was asked why he left the duo he was astonished to be ask the question. Paul Simon was not happy with Art getting all the attention, he broke up the duo. Art said that he sang the songs as well as he knew how, did Paul want him to sing them poorly? I saw the video of Paul Simon's 'Capeman' show in preparation, all the participant were gushing in their accolades of Paul's music. They were all nervous to criticise, it didn't take much of a musical brain listening to the songs to realise that they were extremely poor, but no one told him, perhaps he wouldn't have listened if they had told him. The show flopped so did the album.

Joan Baez has written so many songs for Bob obviously the love of her life, just listen to 'Diamonds and Rust' and 'Oh Brother'. Richard Farina called Bob the 'blue eyed minstrel' in his song 'Morgan the Pirate'. Jackson Browne called him a prophet in his 'Looking Into You'. Bob was a 'mystery man painted like a clown' in Roger McGuinn's 'Take Me Away' and George Harrison included a line for Bob in his 'Behind the Locked Door'. Eric Anderson presumably wrote 'The Hustler' for Bob and David Bowie was more obvious with his 'Song For Bob Dylan'.

Bob claims that his favourite female singer is Um Kalthoum, the Egyptian Diva who died in 1975. She lived in Cairo and was patronised by King Farouk and subsequently President Gamal Nasser. After the end of Nasser's rule her health deteriorated. She was immensely popular in Israel and all over the Middle East, her celebrity level has never been equalled subsequently.

What we have learned of Bob Dylan is that he hates to be alone, there seems to be no other explanation for his constant touring and recording. In the early years Bob Neuwirth was always around, in my investigations it is difficult to locate any statements from him concerning Bob. The musicians that give interviews where Bob is discussed rarely mention his private life. I suspect that Bob can't distinguish real friends from sycophants and until he is in dire need (which I hope is never) he will never know. Age creeps up on us all, Bob is a proud grandfather and loves his children. He seems to have only found real happiness with Joan Baez and for the first few years with Sara.

As in the song he will do nearly any task, it took a woman like her to get through to a man like him. Written in 1970 the 'Man in Me' was an anticipation, a realisation, the ecstasy and the fear of life all in four short verses. I just hope that in some of my ideas within this book I have managed to locate that man in him that we don't know and will never know. It is the not knowing that makes it all so interesting.

I will leave the last word and advice to Lewis Carroll (1832-1898) from Alice in Wonderland...

"You are old" the young man said
"And your hair has become very white; yet you incessantly stand on your head-do you think that at your age, it is right?"

EMMETT GROGAN

From Ringolevio to the Diggers to Dylan's acetates.
A strange and unusual story of an enigma.

Come and see me at Woodstock, was the invitation from Bob Dylan to Emmett Grogan. Bob has always presented to everyone his interest in Robin Hood characters. Jesse James, Lord Byron and John Wesley Harding to name just three. Emmett Grogan sits nicely in this company, but only for the middle years of his life. Emmett was born Kenny Wisdom, he only changed his name to coincide with his 'Digger' life style in the flower power days of the late sixties.

This enigmatic character that was to become Emmett Grogan born in 1944. He was Kenny Wisdom, he was also the 'Ringolevio' champion of Brooklyn, living a life of petty crime. Ringolevio is a game played all over the world in the days before computer games and television. Two teams, usually boys, catch and imprison members of the opposing team. They can be released by tagging (touching) and then they can return to the field of play to catch and imprison others. In the U.K. the game was called 'Releasio' or occasionally 'Tin Can Tommy', but the similarities of the tame British game are few and far between. In Brooklyn it was almost for real. An area of town was selected on the map, people captured would be beaten and bloodied, the game could continue for a week or more. A dangerous and terrifying pastime, Kenny was the champion. He could sit hidden for days at a time without food, only moving out of his hide for water. He would use his time carefully, conserve his energy and then make his attacks when the others were tired and injured.

The turning point was a particular game where two 'ringed-prisoners' had escaped, their vaulting a wall coincided by chance with the sounding of a burglar alarm. A police patrol saw two youths running, called for them to stop, when they did not, they shot and killed them both. These youths thought that the call to stop was from other members of the opposing gang, not from the police. Kenny was devastated, he hated the police with such a vengeance, it lasted for all his days. However his increased dislike for them in latter days was for something far less serious.

Kenny started a daily drug habit at the age of 15, he attempted an armed robbery, which failed, he and his accomplice were arrested. Kenny was and 14 years old. Kenny did not wish to be sent to a reformatory so he pretended he was 16, he gave his name was Kenny Mullane. He was sent to an adult prison where he went into drug-withdrawal and passed out. In the prison hospital Kenny managed to convince the staff that he was epileptic and not a junkie. Kenny had been beaten up by the police, prior to his remand and he claimed the blow to the face brought on the spasms, he also lied that it had only happened once previously, again caused by a punch. It was five months before his hearing, he had learned a great deal from the other convicts. At the hearing he proved he was only 15, the embarrassment of the police department, coupled with Kenny's threats of litigation, meant that he was immediately released without a stain on his character.

His parents had thought that Kenny had run away, they were so pleased to see him, the prodigal had returned. He commenced studies at a Jesuit School, his best friend Louis, taught him to speak properly and how to lose his Brooklyn accent. Kenny had many female admirers, his new voice meant that he also could attract upper class affluent women. He carefully checked out the premises of their parents and started a very lucrative career as a burglar. Success followed success, he purchased quality clothes from Brooks Brothers, and put all the remaining stolen money in safe deposit boxes. This was the precocious guile of a 16 year old, he continued to survive on the few dollars that his parents gave him as pocket money, no one suspected his wealth, except for his clothes.

After selling large numbers of stolen objects to corrupt brokers, the underworld learned of his crimes, in a couple of burglaries Kenny had inadvertently stolen from some mobster gang-leaders. Kenny took his money, and flew to Rotterdam and on to Paris, he had accumulated $40,000 dollars. He preferred Italy, it was the first time he had seen countryside and farm animals, previously he had only lived in towns. He met some friends who were mountaineers and with them climbed 'Il Cervino' and 'The Matterhorn'. He lived the high life, and purchased an apartment in Heidelberg.

He was arrested in Rome for possession of drugs, which was untrue, he had been framed. Kenny learned that it had been arranged by Squint Lazlo a wronged mobster in New York. Kenny was only 17, he was released suddenly without explanation and returned to USA, where according to his own biography, he then murdered Squint Lazlo. The coroner claimed that Lazlo suffered accidental death whilst cleaning his shot gun. The story was that Kenny had actually made him clean the gun, ensuring that Squint's fingerprints were all over it. Kenny returned to Italy, read extensively the work of The Beat Generation' writers. Kenny wrote and presented scripts to Italian film makers and was accepted into the Italian Cinematographer's Circle. He made two films, only average in quality and content and then decided to move for a change of scenery. He went to Dublin, and found himself in an area of the city habituated by artists and writers. These aesthetes were unhappy with President De Valera's surrender to Britain and their commitment convinced Kenny that De Valera had misrepresented the feelings of the people of Eire.

Kenny joined an Irish Republican Army command and assisted in blowing up a command post in Forkhill, Armagh, later he demolished a road bridge. As he was now running short on funds he worked in a brewery and robbed houses at night. Once his affluence returned, he went to London with a beautiful actress and set up home in Soho. Kenny started writing pornographic literature, a new friend, Matt, printed and sold the booklets around the seedy bookshops. The books were an instant success and sold 1500 copies in 3 weeks. It came to an end when the London-mob, who had not been receiving any commission, nailed Matt to his floorboards through his knees. Kenny tried to purchase a gun to kill the mobster that had inflicted the injury on Matt. Unluckily he attempted to purchase the weapon from an undercover policeman and was then arrested, he was sentenced to 10 years in Parkhurst maximum security prison on the Isle of Wight. By a strange quirk of fate the policeman was involved in creating evidence in other cases so all his arrests were considered null and void; Kenny was released. He returned to the USA, with what remained of his money from crime.

He returned to robbery, he was blowing a safe in a warehouse in London when Joan Baez and Donovan led a peace and love procession passed the door. The safe only contained $300, a passive alarm system had alerted the police. Kenny escaped through a window with his passport, the money, and flew to USA, arriving almost destitute and untidy. He was only 21 years old, it was 1965, he was back exactly where he started.

He was drafted into the US Army, and although he had an attitude problem was deemed the best recruit without really trying. The others soldiers resented that fact that he found it all so simple and increasingly made his term with them more difficult. During a patrol, Kenny jumped up with a loaded bazooka and aimed it at everyone until he was finally overpowered. The Army confined him to hospital where he was certified as a schizophrenic. It was in the hospital that Kenny decided to change his name. Thinking of William Bonney, John Wesley Harding and Robin Hood, he decided to modify his name to grandfather's gaelic name. Thus, O'Gruagain, became Grogan and Emmett Grogan was born, or rather created.

On his discharge Emmett went to San Francisco and met a war veteran named Bill Graham. Bill had just leased the Fillmore Auditorium, Emmett had joined a mime troupe. The Flower Power scene was in motion, Emmett wrote and printed a magazine titled 'The Digger Papers'. He formed The Diggers movement who were based on the original Diggers from 1649. These original Diggers were reformers and agrarians, Emmett wanted the same for his Diggers, albeit an alternative type of reform radicalism.

He set up a free soup kitchen where people would arrive and say "Oh no not Soup De Jour again". The public took notice when an article called 'Take a Cop to Dinner' was written, the politicians were concerned that something REALLY FREE was available. The concern spread to the local shops and businesses.

It was now 1966, 'Free Frame' was inaugurated, a free food and rest area. It was next door to a Krishna Temple and the monks complained to the police, the noise was too loud and interrupted their meditation. The subsequent police raid saw Emmett arrested yet again. The police made a mistake with his arraignment number, and Emmett walked free yet again. Emmett's life was now full of free giving, he would write and speak out against those who pretended that they were giving and were just soaking up publicity and making money out of

237

the teenagers. Free Frame had doctors providing free medical care under the Home Free slogan. Be-ins, Clean-ins, Love-ins were all the vogue at the time. The Diggers ideology was 'If you got nothing, then you have got nothing to lose'. In New York, Abbott (as Emmett always called him), Abbie Hoffman and his wife Anita met Emmett in the street. Emmett noticed how Hoffman was only interested in talking about himself, yet he agreed to work with him. The reason seems to be because Hoffman was eager to succeed, in anything. The friendship lasted only a short while, Emmett's writings were plagiarised by Hoffman's cronies, so that they could individually achieve self recognition, contrary to the ideals of The Diggers. An Anarchists Ball was arranged, all free, thousands of people arrived necessitating its moving to the massive Tompkins Square, which was ringed by police. Emmett never appeared, a police friend informed him that a 'Hit Man' had been employed in the crowd to kill him. However the Anarchists Ball surprised the police, there was no trouble of any kind and over 100,000 persons were present. Emmett dropped into the background of The Digger scene and became an elusive enigmatic character. Reporter John Gruen caused considerable problems, predominantly because Emmett would not agree to his wishes for a long interview. Newspaper headlines of 'Hero Hogan stirs up Lower East Side', were not helpful.

Emmett returned to California with Natural Suzanne, she had been his lady friend for some considerable time. The Grateful Dead, Janis Joplin, Country Joe and the Fish, all performed shows free to provide funds for Free Frame. Bill Graham continued to help, announcing at a show that Emmett's life was in danger, subsequently scores of weapons and boxes of ammunition arrived at Free Frame, from well wishers.

Emmett decided that the best decision now was to move to New Mexico for a while. The trucks continued to deliver free food and supplies to the needy around San Francisco. Emmett went back to nature with an Indian named Little Bird. They lived in to the wooded areas on El Rito, hunting gutting and cooking food, also surviving on wild life and vegetation. He had taken Natural Suzanne along, she returned by air and Emmett hitchhiked back to San Francisco.

Emmett's writings now were parables and filled with political polemic. He went to London to attend 'The Dialectics of Liberation Conference'. It was attended by Allen Ginsberg, R.D. Laing, William Burroughs Stokely Carmichael, and other anti-establishment activists. Emmett learned his speech by heart and practised arm gesticulations. After his turn to speak the audience gave him a ten minute standing ovation. Emmett waited for the audience to settle down, he then announced that he had no idea who wrote the speech, the last time it was delivered had been 1937, at The Reichstag by a Mr Adolf Hitler. The audience was silent in their embarrassment, Emmett vacated the stage in the same silence with a huge grin on his face. Emmett was totally against the Eldridge Cleaver, Stokely Carmichael, Huey P. Newton call to arms rhetoric and said so on many occasions. The Haight Ashbury was now in disarray, Chocolate George and Super

Spade were murdered, although both deaths had the appearance of accidents. Mutilations of many corpses seemed a growing concern, until the perpetrator was arrested, he was found with a severed arm from his latest victim, it was on the back seat of his car.

Although Emmett was not a hippie, he resented the term when applied to him, he certainly resembled one in appearance. He continued to drive the food delivery truck, delivering the free food, but few people knew him as Emmett Grogan. A meeting Emmett arranged with Governor George Romney of Michigan, could have gone disastrously wrong. In real terms Emmett kidnapped Romney and his wife, drove them around in his truck explaining the situation with the people of the area, those in most need. Emmett, who had evaded and lost the Governors security guards, then returned Romney safe and sound, and drove away. After taking a walk one evening, Emmett got badly beaten up in an mugging, yet managed to probably kill one of the attackers. Returning to his room to recover, a friend gave Emmett half an ounce of 90% pure Heroine, Emmett once more became a dependant junkie. A total change in outlook followed, he had always had an enormous ego which had caused many problems, suddenly he was introverted, and reclusive. He stopped delivering food, and attending Free Frame and vanished from the scene. He heard about the detoxifying drug methadone, and checked into Mendocino Hospital for help.

It was 1968, Emmett was clean and back on the road, now he was delivering methadone to junkies who requested help. Bob Dylan had heard of Emmett Grogan, and luckily Bob's friends managed to contact Emmett. Bob invited Emmett to Woodstock to his house for a few days. Emmett found Bob totally opposite to what he had anticipated. A friendly happy and gregarious man who could talk for hours on end. The persona of Bob at the time was of a recluse who was difficult and egotistical, all incorrect according to Emmett. Blonde on Blonde had been released to ecstatic reviews, Emmett loved everything about that double album set. Emmett was so thrilled to be sitting on the second step of a wooden flight of steps with the screened porch at the top, the house owned by Bob where film editor Al Gable once lived. Emmett was also taken by the slightness of Bob's body yet the strength that it contained. A man hailed as a genius for singing poetry and playing the guitar and harmonica. Emmett's sense of humour felt that the difference between genius and craziness is very close. If the same man had strapped a bass drum to his back, and a pair of cymbals between his knees, Bob might have been hailed as a crazy eccentric.

The discussions went on for hours, they found how they both had an affinity for wild west characters, not the heroes but the villains. They loved the writing on gravestones in Boot-Hill cemeteries. Whilst Emmett was at Woodstock, Gregory Corso the poet also stopped by for a day or two. Corso was driving a pink limousine at the time and insisted on calling Bob, 'Robere' for some reason known only to him. They discussed the anticipated epitaphs for their own gravestones, before Corso left as fast as he arrived. Al Grossman Bob's manager stated that few people have ever conversed with Bob on the close level of Emmett Grogan they had this, intimacy. Emmett was shown what he decided was a most amusing film, which was eventually to be released as 'Eat The Document'. Bob was extremely impressed by the selflessness of Grogan and they kept in touch.

It was not until 1975 that they met again, this time at Emmett's house. They continued where they had left off before, Bob gave to Emmett some acetate recordings from his early days. These included songs, all in mono, from Highway 61 Revisited, Another Side of Bob Dylan, Newport Folk Festival 1964, and two 10" 45s. One of 'Lunatic Princess' and 'Tombstone Blues', the other 'Black Dalli Rue' and 'Queen Jane Approximately'. Many of the recordings include Tom Wilson's (producer) voice and alternative verses, which were edited out before release of the final albums.

In 1969 Emmett was again arrested, yet as in all previous arrests he was released. Emmett sat and wrote the 'It is Not My Fault !' letters, which were given to Al Aronowitz, they were a succession of statements all prefixed with It's not my fault. For the first time Emmett was actually claiming some responsibility for many of the good things that had happened. Keeping his egotistical nature in control for all these years had been difficult, yet here was a man that few people knew, or would recognise. A man who had done so much selfless work, after such a life of crime, crime which had actually paid.

The new reason for which Emmett hated the police was the fact that one of his remand incarcerations had deprived him of his hard earned suntan. Emmett was fair skinned, red haired, and freckled, except for a few sunny months in Italy. The police coerced by Squint Lazlo had deprived him of his golden skin. Lazlo paid the price in full, the police never managed to pin anything substantial on Emmett. Even in the days of collecting money for Free Frame when businessmen had accused Emmett of threatening behaviour, nothing was ever proved. Emmett was one of the announcers on The Band's 'Last Waltz' film, but which one, can you tell, this enigma has no public face. So little has been written about Emmett Grogan, none of his ladies seem to clarify any of the ambivalences that surround his life. Bob Dylan dedicated his Street Legal album to Emmett. Emmett died on a subway train from what the coroner states were natural causes. Apparently Emmett was on the train dead for two days before anyone realised that he was not just a sleeping hippie. Even in death the persona of Emmett Grogan is with us, but predominantly due to his relationship with Bob Dylan. Surely if all the reports are true, then Emmett Grogan lived 100 years before he reached the age of 21, perhaps he too is destined to 'Stay Forever Young'. Perhaps he is still alive, was it Emmett in the train, or did he just want to fade away quietly ? The legend lives on. He could hide for extremely long periods of time. Remember he was after all the Ringolevio champion. He could still be hiding.

EDITH (EDIE) MINTURN SEDGWICK
(The girl in the leopardskin pillbox hat)

She enchanted people with her face and her energy, men fell in love with her at first sight, they say she had everything. Edie was born in Santa Barbara on 20th April 1943. Due to manic depression psychosis her father Francis, was advised by his doctor not to have any children, Edie was the seventh of his eight children. Her father also known as Duke or Fuzzy, was a larger than life narcissistic character. He would be similar to John Benedict, the Rock Hudson character in the film 'Giant'. Benedict, like Duke, owned an enormous ranch and had a strange attitude towards his offspring. Edie was Duke's favourite child, she always knew exactly when and how to approach him. As they lived on an enormous ranch, Edie would always get the best looking horse. All the children rode horses probably before they were walking. Edie was called 'weedles' by her father, and he brought up the entire family in almost complete isolation. The family photographs which depicted them all together, were photo-created, they rarely were all in the same room, except at christmas.

Oil was located on the vast ranch, and the money literally poured in. Edie's wonderful relationship with her father was to take a turn for the worse. Duke considered himself to be an adonis and his wife would always turn a blind eye to his philandering. Edie by chance walked into The Blue Room where Duke was making love to an unknown lady. Duke chased Edie, slapped her in his angered embarrassment and called for the doctor. Duke asked the doctor to provide tranquillises and to inform others that Edie was a dreamer and could not be trusted. This seemed a terrible way of claiming that he was not sleeping around, when it was common knowledge.

The medication made Edie extremely moody, but she was happy in her schooling. She was extremely manipulative, and created petty jealousies, but all for fun. She loved violent weather conditions and would often ride horseback through terrible thunderstorms, she was however frightened of the dark. She became acutely anorexic, but these were in the days before the self-activated vomiting was recognised as an illness. Duke decided to send her to Silver Hill mental hospital, where she associated with alcoholics, schizophrenics, and lunatics, yet the overall atmosphere was that of a very salubrious country club.

It was at Silver Hill in 1962, that the first alluring photograph was taken, Edie lying on a bed with her legs in the air. The picture was just an adolescent pose, Edie had no idea how photogenic she was. She would later be described as a camera object. She also attended Bloomingdale Mental hospital, never understanding the reason for it. Edie was 20 years old before she was discharged. She was desperate to make up for lost time and lost her virginity to a young Harvard student, who she taken to her grandmother's flat. She became pregnant, which was aborted immediately, due to her psychiatric condition.

Edie became an art student in Cambridge Massachusetts, her tutor Lily Saarinen considered her to be extremely talented, her paintings and sculptures of horses were extraordinarily excellent, she said. Edie had a mental blockage, unable to sketch men on horseback. This was almost certainly due to her dislike of Duke her father. She was photographed in a fox fur pillbox hat, at her 21st birthday party. Her escort at the time was Ed Hennessey, he reported that she changed her dress three times during the party, due to perspiration caused by her non-stop energetic dancing. Sadly, a few weeks later, her brother Minty Sedgwick hanged himself from the top of his bathroom door, he was one day short of 26 years old. Minty had found out that he was homosexual and explained it to Duke. He flew into a rage, and had Minty committed to Silver Hill hospital. Edie was inconsolable. A friend John Walker took Edie to the cinema in an attempt to cheer her up. The film was 'The Blue Angel', a film filled with brutal exploitation, authoritarianism, humiliation. The film also includes a straight-jacket scene, Edie cried out aloud in horror and fled.

Edie's sculptures were creating a fame for her in Cambridge, she decided to move and live in New York. She attended a salon every day where her shapeless legs were pummelled into shape. She created new fashions, she wore red fox fur waistcoats with pillbox matching hats and high heeled boots. She also perfected her entrances into parties and restaurants. She commenced taking LSD, and was stopped by the police for driving on the side-walk and for driving through red traffic lights, on acid. She was becoming notorious, her intention was to be noticed.

It was at The Kettle of Fish restaurant that Edie first met Bob Dylan. It was christmas and it was romantically snowing. Bob said after the meeting to Bob Neuwirth "You have to meet this terrific girl". Bob Neuwirth's recollection of Bob's relationship poor, but it seems that for some considerable time they went to clubs and restaurants as a threesome. Edie never paid any of her invoices and thus restaurants, limousine companies all gradually refused to serve her. Edie just found alternatives. Edie would always turn on her little girl lost routine whenever it suited her.

Edie's brother Bobby was killed in an accident, he was run down by a bus. Once more she was plummeted down to the depths of despair. Her life eventually took a turn for the better, she met Andy Warhol in January 1965 at Lester Persky's Club. She was wearing her leopardskin pillbox hat and a suit to match. Andy had also made friends with Lou Reed, John Cale and Nico, members of the pop group The Velvet Underground. The Factory Studio was the place of work for Warhol, he commenced making short films, Edie was exactly the face he wanted. In truth Edie legitimized Warhol, she brought him out from being an artistic interior decorator. Edie and Andy dressed alike, twins, both with silver hair, both appearing androgynous. Edie's co-star in the film 'Vinyl' was Gerald Malanga, a strange torture scene was included. The next film 'Kitchen' was difficult for Edie, the drugs seemed to stop her remembering her lines, and made the filming difficult and tiring for all the crew. 'Beauty Part II' was a film which depicted Edie in bed with Gino Piserchio for a full 60 minutes, but with both characters dressed in their undergarments for the complete film. Vogue Fashion Magazine showed interest in using Edie as a model, she was to be the American equivalent of the British model Twiggy. Edie became the 'Youthquaker', the most famous girl in New York. She met Mick Jagger in an arranged photo-shoot which almost got the two of them crushed in a stampede of journalists and photographers. Truman Capote the writer said that Andy Warhol really wanted to be Edie Sedgwick.

Edie met Dr Charles Roberts, the drug doctor, he was immortalised in the song Dr Robert by the Beatles. The doctor injected Edie with vitamins and drugs, Edie like a speed-ball, part cocaine-part speed, and pure sex. At least that was the advertised reaction of the drug. Bob Neuwirth, Bob Dylan's closest friend and Susie Burden took Edie to Joan Kennedy's party in Hyannis Port, after taking Dr Roberts' injections. Edie was asked to meet Bobby Kennedy at Max's Kansas City restaurant, but stayed just five minutes, Bobby's body guard had smelled marijuana. Edie performed at Delmonico's with The Velvet Underground, it was 1966. Bob Dylan and Edie decided that they would like to make a film together. A close friend Jonathan Taplin (road manager for Dylan and Judy Collins) states categorically that 'Just Like a Woman' by Bob Dylan was written for Edie and most definitely not for Joan Baez. The lyrics fit Edie better than any other lady friend at the time.

Edie's face remained childlike and her wasted figure exaggerated that fact. What Bob especially liked about Edie, apart from her looks, was that she always stood up to him, no sycophantic behaviour. Edie continued to make films for Andy Warhol, after the eleventh the relationship turned sour. During the making of 'Chelsea Girls' she stated that she would have to be replaced, as she had signed a contract with Albert Grossman, Bob Dylan's manager. Nico was also a friend and confidant of Bob Dylan, he had met her in Europe, and he watched her in the Velvet Underground on a few occasions. Bob Dylan was to eventually compose a song for her, she included it on one of her solo albums. Bob was regularly dating Edie, inviting her up to his home in Woodstock. As she had signed with the same manager, the efforts to find a decent script for a Bob & Edie film began in earnest. Bizarrely whilst Bob was dating Edie, he suddenly married Sara Lowndes, Edie once more went into a deep depression. She was consoled by Bob Neuwirth and they made a short film together. In the film Edie once more was wearing her trade mark leopardskin, riding a stuffed rhinoceros on casters up 5th Avenue. Andy was angry that Edie had dropped him, Andy was subsequently shot and injured by Valerie Solanis, because he had turned down her script. The Warhol injury received little press coverage, because Bobby Kennedy was assassinated at the same time.

Edie was becoming unstable due to upper and then downer drugs. She continue modelling, she burned down her flat in an accident with lighted candles too close to the drapes. Edie moved to The Chelsea Hotel which was already full of artists and singers. For the first time for years Edie went home for Christmas to her family, all her friends in New York had done the same and she did not want to be alone. Duke found out that she was a junkie and called the police, he had her incarcerated in a mental hospital. Strangely Edie's father could not show any love to anyone except himself. Edie escaped hospital and returned to the Chelsea Hotel on West 23rd Street, New York.

Edie continued her relationship with Bob Neuwirth, he was almost certainly the love of her life. When Neuwirth explained that he wished to end the relationship, Edie stubbed out a cigarette in his face. She felt that she was his sex slave, he was the only man who keep up with her insatiable appetite for sex and more sex. Leonard Cohen visited Edie at The Chelsea Hotel, he asked her to move the candles to a safer place. She paid no attention, subsequently The Chelsea Hotel caught fire, Edie escaped with minor burns, her cat died in the fire. After treatment and leaving hospital, none of her friends could trust her not to burn their houses down. Robert Margouleff, who didn't like Edie much was the only person to give her sanctuary.

Robert Margouleff was making a film titled 'Ciao Manhattan', he invited Edie to take part. This he later considered a mistake, she just could not learn her lines. Edie's hands had been badly burned, but luckily they were not deformed, her facial burns were easily covered by make-up. Edie once again met Bob Dylan, he was staying at The Castle Hotel, a beautiful old building designed by Frank Lloyd Wright. Bob's best friend at the time was Patrick Tilden, Edie fell in love with Patrick almost immediately. Bob wrote 'Leopardskin Pillbox Hat' for Edie, Nico agreed that it was Edie that was the subject. Nico stated that if you listen to the lyrics carefully, the listener will realise that it is a very sarcastic song. Bob also mentions 'the doctor' in the lyrics, it may be Doctor Roberts again. If Tilden was Edie's new love at the time, then Bob created the usual ambivalences in the song. He wrote 'well I see you got a new boyfriend, you know I never seen him before'. This would also be a red-herring if the new man at the time was Patrick Tilden or perhaps John Taplin, Dylan's road manager. The reference may even have been for Bob Neuwirth.

Nico had a crush on Jim Morrison and as he was known to love red haired women, she had her hair died. Afterwards she said that Jim made her feel like a silly teenager in love. Edie's father, Duke, was rushed to hospital, he was diagnosed as suffering from cancer of the pancreas. Edie was in Gracie Square Hospital with drug problems when Duke died on 24th October 1967. Edie's latest love was Kit Carson, as she was constantly on speed and Kit was straight, he had difficulty in keeping up with her sexual appetites. Kit could not take any more six-day-sex sessions and moved to Texas, to recuperate. It was four days later that the police located him to explain that his 'wife' Edie was in Warwick Hospital New York, severely ill. It was drug related once more, Edie was committed to the Manhattan State Asylum.

Edie was released into the care of her family. She returned to the ranch, it was August 1968. Edie was having difficulty walking without falling over and her speech was mumbled and garbled. However Edie said that these latest problems were not drug related. She said that she was riding on the pillion of Bob Dylan's motorcycle when they had a serious accident. No one believed her, or Bob when he stated that he had a motor-cycle accident, was it the same accident? Edie was soon back on the drugs, when she was stopped and searched by police for erratic driving she made things worse by kicking a policeman up the arse, she ended up with five months probation. Drugs again, and she was back in Santa Barbara Hospital. She was born there, and her father had died there, it was almost full circle.

Margouleff wanted to finish the 'Ciao Manhattan' film, Edie agreed, but had an operation to increase the size of her breasts. This made continuity difficult especially in the nude scenes of the film, they never bothered to try. Watching the film, it is simple to see the parts added later; pun intended. The soundtrack of 'Ciao Manhattan' includes John (Papa) Phillips, Richie Havens, Skip Battin, Kim Fowley, and Kim Milford. Margouleff would later form Tonto's Expanding Head Band, and record synthesizer albums. Edie fell in love once more, this time with Michael Post, they married. The happiness that ensued enabled her to finally become clean of the drug addiction. This was her first real happiness since the fateful day that she stepped into The Blue Room and caught her father in illicit sex. Fate once more took control, Edie got an ear infection and was allergic to the analgesics, she was diagnosed as suffering serum sickness and she was back on pills again. The couple lived an almost Dickensian lifestyle, he would go to art college, she would sit next to him an hold his pencils; Charles Dickens wife did exactly the same. Edie was suffering from paranoia and nightmares, but an old friend Tom Goodwin met her again by chance. He managed to get Edie in to a fashion show scene in the television show 'An American Family'. Edie can be seen in the audience, the viewer is naturally attracted to her, she stood out from the rest.

At last things were improving, Mike Post took her home from the party after the Television show, Edie had not been so happy for years. They had been together now for exactly twelve months. When they got to bed Mike thought that her breathing was noisy, a very chesty sound. He held her tight and they drifted off into sleep. The alarm clock sounded at 7.30am, Edie was cold and motionless, she was dead. The police and doctor arrived but she had been dead for some hours. Edie Sedgwick was 28 years old. The coroner's report stated that she had died of a barbiturate overdose, the death was undetermined, accident/suicide, 16th November 1971.Edie was beautiful, with an innocent child like appearance. She could turn situations to her advantage, by pretending to be vulnerable. Duke her father must bear the moral responsibility for this lovely girl's sad life, although in his life time he showed no remorse. Edie was for a time his favourite child, the gulf between them that he created could never be closed.

ACKNOWLEDGEMENTS

For their knowledge:-

Kurt Loader, Rolling Stone Magazine/...Allen Ginsberg, Sleeve Notes/...Roy Kelly, The Telegraph/...John Way, The Telegraph/....John Bauldie, The Telegraph/...Peter Viney, The Telegraph/...Greil Marcus, Mojo and Rolling Stone/...Georgen Antonsson, The Telegraph/...Matthew Zuckerman, Isis Magazine/...Steve Roeser, Goldmine Magazine/...Martin Carthy, Isis/...David Gates, Newsweek/...Derek Barker, Isis/...Don Was, The Record Collector Magazine/...Dave Marsh, Rolling Stone/...Jan Wenner, Rolling Stone/...Ben Cruikshank, Art Beat Reader Magazine/...Michael Krogsgaard, The Telegraph.

For their kindness and assistance:-

Nick Leese, Rob Nicholls, Dave and Dina Thomas, Donna Winterbone, Harry Allen, Mark Lynch, Tony Coleman and of course Zilliah.

For French translations:-

Roger Shoulders and Gloria Sleeman-Hiscock

The publishers of Bob's lyrics:-

Rams Horn Music, Special Rider Music, Dwarf Music, Rams Horn Music, Big Sky Music, M. Witmark & Sons, Music Corp of America, Warner Brothers Music, Fort Knox Music.

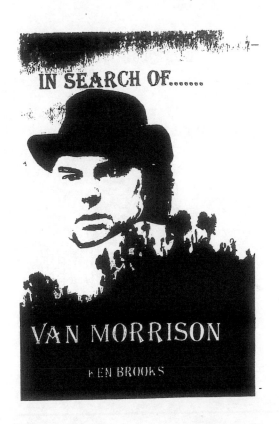

IN SEARCH OF.......

VAN MORRISON

FEN BROOKS

Van Morrison is totally dedicated to his art of creating music, his work is vast and uncompromising. This in depth investigation is an attempt to find through Van's influences and his lyrics, just what makes him tick. Van is a self taught intellectual, a Doctor of Letters and an O.B.E, which makes him a suitable target for tabloid journalism, his celebrity makes an anonymous life impossible. Van Morrison is a genius with almost 40 years in the music business, he is a teacher to his fans, a shy man who continues his life-long search for the ultimate truth. We can never be sure just how close this analysis gets to the inner man, the author's life has many correlations with that of Van, making this an book a most enjoyable journey.

IN SEARCH OF VAN MORRISON
ISBN 1 899882 95 2
Paperback 210 x 150mm £ 8.99

AGENDA LIMITED, UNITS 1 & 2, LUDGERSHALL BUSINESS PARK,
NEW DROVE, LUDGERSHALL, ANDOVER, HAMPSHIRE, SP11 9RN

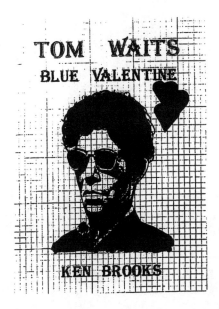

Revised Second Edition with new facts and information, also includes review and analysis of Tom's 'Mule Variations' album and details of his other recent projects. Not content being a brilliant singer-songwriter, Tom ventured into films working with Sylvester Stallone, Michael Wadleigh, Chris Cain, Francis Ford Coppola, Hector Babenco, Robert Altman and a starring role for Jim Jarmusch. Tom's songs have been influenced by Jack Kerouac, Neal Cassady, Nelson Algren and William Burroughs. Tom worked with William Burroughs creating a stage show. Tom has also created a show based on Alice Liddell, she was Alice in Wonderland. This is a track by track and film by film overview of Tom's career, the ghost of Jack Kerouac is everywhere.

TOM WAITS, BLUE VALENTINE
ISBN 1 899882 75 8
Paperback 210 x 150mm £ 6.99

AGENDA LIMITED, UNITS 1 & 2, LUDGERSHALLL BUSINESS PARK,
NEW DROVE, LUDGERSHALL, ANDOVER, HAMPSHIRE, SP11 9RN

JONI MITCHELL, PAVED PARADISE. Joni rose to fame in the sixties with beautiful albums such as 'Ladies of the Canyon and 'Clouds'. She is also an accomplished painter, and many of her album covers have displayed her artwork. She wrote the song for Woodstock but was not present at the festival of love. She uses her lyrics to speak to ex-lovers and new lovers making some of her songs heart-rending and personal. All Joni's officially released albums and compact discs are re-evaluated track-by-track, plus biographical details and relevant influences. Joni joins Leonard Cohen, Neil Young and Gordon Lightfoot as the greatest Canadian singer songwriters of the generation. Joni's love of folk music merged into jazz and then rock 'n' roll, her lyrics are always thought provoking, after all she has seen the World from both sides now.

JONI MITCHELL, PAVED PARADISE
ISBN 1 899882 85 5
Paperback 210mm x 150mm PRICE £ 6.99

AGENDA LIMITED, UNITS 1 & 2, LUDGERSHALL BUSINESS PARK,
NEW DROVE, LUDGERSHALL, ANDOVER, HAMPSHIRE, SP11 9RN

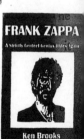